The Comprehensive Guide to
SUCCESSFUL CONFERENCES
AND MEETINGS

Leonard Nadler
Zeace Nadler

The Comprehensive Guide to
SUCCESSFUL CONFERENCES
AND MEETINGS

Detailed Instructions and
Step-by-Step Checklists

 Jossey-Bass Publishers

San Francisco • London • 1987

THE COMPREHENSIVE GUIDE TO SUCCESSFUL CONFERENCES AND MEETINGS
Detailed Instructions and Step-by-Step Checklists
  by Leonard Nadler and Zeace Nadler

Copyright © 1987 by: Jossey-Bass Inc., Publishers
                       433 California Street
                       San Francisco, California 94104
                       &
                       Jossey-Bass Limited
                       28 Banner Street
                       London EC1Y 8QE

Library of Congress Cataloging-in-Publication Data

Nadler, Leonard.
  The comprehensive guide to successful conferences
and meetings.

  (Jossey-Bass management series) (Jossey-Bass
higher education series)
  Includes index.
  1. Meetings—Handbooks, manuals, etc. 2. Congresses
and conventions—Handbooks, manuals, etc. I. Nadler,
Zeace. II. Title. III. Series. IV. Series: Jossey-
Bass higher education series.
AS6.N24   1987   658.4'563   87-45412
ISBN 1-55542-051-6 (alk. paper)

Manufactured in the United States of America

The paper in this book meets the guidelines for
permanence and durability of the Committee on
Production Guidelines for Book Longevity of the
Council on Library Resources.

JACKET DESIGN BY WILLI BAUM

FIRST EDITION

Code 8733

A joint publication in
The Jossey-Bass Management Series
and
The Jossey-Bass Higher Education Series

Contents

---

ix

Preface

An increasing number of people are participating in conferences and meetings, with a corresponding increase in the number of people who design and plan these events. There is every indication that this trend will continue. However, the people who are called on to organize conferences and meetings are frequently asked to do so with little or no background or training. Although some sources are available to assist these people, no one book describes the whole process and offers complete, specific advice and guidance.

The lack of such a resource is the main reason we decided to write this book. A book on a similar topic, which we wrote several years ago (Nadler and Nadler, 1977), was received well; many readers praised its helpfulness—but they also asked for a great deal of additional information. The evident need for a full-blown resource on designing conferences led us to write this book, which is a companion volume to our earlier work.

One special feature of *Successful Conferences and Meetings* is the many checklists that appear at the beginnings of most of the chapters and elsewhere in the book. We have developed these checklists over the years for our own use and for use by clients who have consulted us about conference planning. Since 1978 we have taught a course on conference design at George Washington University, and these checklists have been tested by students taking the class, many of whom are active in planning conferences and meetings. The checklists in this book are comprehensive, and each item on each checklist is thoroughly discussed—a feature that makes this book unique.

Please note that you do not need permission to reproduce the checklists! Indeed, they are designed to so that you can easily reproduce and use them each time you are involved in designing a conference or meeting. The bottom of each checklist mentions its source, and as long as this is left on the reproduced form, no permission from the publisher is needed. This is done purposely to make this book as useful for you as possible.

There is some repetition of content among chapters, which is unavoidable. Planning conferences and meetings involves activities that are not discrete but that interrelate. Consequently, each of these chapters, while integral to the whole, is also an independent unit. We believe that this structure will aid the reader who wants full information on one area to find it quickly and easily.

Who Should Read This Book

Successful Conferences and Meetings is written primarily for people who devote a major portion of their time to designing and planning conferences and meetings. Many of these people are professionals and so have encountered many of the problems and processes described in this book. Even experienced planners, however, will find the book helpful in reinforcing and reexamining their planning and organizing skills.

In addition to professional meeting planners, an increasingly large number of people are called on, usually with little or no notice, to design conferences. This book provides all the necessary details to help these designers meet such challenging assignments.

Conference sponsors will find this book invaluable as a description of what conference coordinators or designers need to do. And suppliers of conference services, who often do not know the design process, will be able to use this book to find out how their services fit in to the overall conference plan.

Site personnel, such as staff at hotels, motels, and conference sites, have generally not studied conference design. They may be familiar with some parts of it, but this book will enable them to comprehend the whole process and see how their facilities function within the larger plan.

Overview of the Contents

As with other activities, there is a constant search in conference work for models, critical paths, or helpful road maps. While it has not yet been possible to develop one model to satisfy all the variables to be considered in conference work, we have tried to reflect the general flow that occurs in most conference planning in the sequence of the chapters.

One of the first considerations is the design of the conference and the related events that make the conference more than just a series of meetings. The next steps are to find a site with appropriate function rooms, select the speakers or presenters, and evaluate audiovisual needs. When these basic considerations have been addressed, attention can be directed to such topics as food and beverage functions, exhibitions, companions, marketing, public relations, transportation, and entertainment.

Important factors that are integral to conference planning are the budget and the form of registration. After the groundwork has been laid, the remaining concerns are finalizing the program, providing for follow-up and evaluation of the conference, and—the payoff for all the planning—conducting the conference.

Chapter One provides readers with an overview of the field and definitions of terms commonly used in practice. As is true in many emerging fields, there is no general agreement on terms, but our definitions will assure the reader of consistent usage throughout the book. Chapter One also includes a discussion of a status chart, which will help facilitate the control of the various, often simultaneous, activities involved in conference design.

The relationship among the conference's purpose, participants, and design is discussed in Chapter Two. The formation and use of a design committee are explored, and guidelines for selecting committee members are provided. Every conference must have continuity, which should be reflected in the theme, logo, climate, setting, scheduling, and main event. Scheduled events form the core of the conference, and additional activities of general or special interest can also be included. A great variety of strategies can be used to design core and auxiliary conference sessions; more than thirty-five strategies are listed and briefly described in this chapter.

Chapter Three presents examples of four different conference designs, which show some of the possibilities available to designers. These examples are referred to in later chapters.

Chapter Four provides material on those activities and events related to the core of the conference that are available to assist participants.

Sites for various kinds of conferences are discussed in Chapter Five. There are many types of sites, and each has its advantages and limitations. The sites usually consist of function rooms, where the conference events take place; these are discussed in Chapter Six.

Presenters (speakers and resource people) are the topic of Chapter Seven. It is important that the presenters be carefully selected. In this chapter we describe a process developed expressly for this purpose, which will enable the presenters to meet the expectations of the participants and the coordinator. Many presenters use audiovisual equipment and materials; these aids are examined in Chapter Eight.

It is the rare conference that does not have at least one food or beverage function. Although participants generally do not attend for the food and beverages, they often expect that these will be provided. Such functions are discussed in Chapter Nine.

Exhibitions, as Chapter Ten demonstrates, can range from one small table to five hundred or more booths. There are many reasons to have exhibitions, and they should be related to the theme of the conference and the interest of the participants.

Some conference participants are likely to be accompanied by spouses, friends, or other interested parties. Conference designs sometimes provide very little for companions of participants, but their presence at conferences is significant and increasing—and thus must be considered by conference planners. This topic is discussed in Chapter Eleven.

Most conferences require some sort of marketing, as indicated in Chapter Twelve. Marketing has a close connection to public relations, which is explored in Chapter Thirteen, but these fields are different. Each makes a specific contribution to helping the designer plan an effective conference.

Transportation is considered in Chapter Fourteen, and this category includes travel to and from the conference as well as transportation at the conference site or city. Not all conferences provide entertainment, a topic treated in Chapter Fifteen. When entertainment is included in the design, however, the coordinator must devote special attention to it.

All conferences and meetings have budget constraints, and Chapter Sixteen presents a pro forma budget that outlines the items to be considered. The budget should not dictate the design, but neither can the design ignore budgetary limitations.

The registration process must be carefully planned before the conference begins, and Chapter Seventeen presents suggestions for organizing it. Registration is the first activity in which all participants make direct contact, so its importance goes beyond mere clerical chores. The participant book, as described in Chapter Eighteen, is usually provided at registration and contains all necessary information for conference participants.

As with registration, evaluation and follow-up must be planned before the conference starts. The success of every conference should be assessed in some way, and planning for this phase should start with consideration of what will be done with the evaluation results. Chapter Nineteen provides guidance on these matters.

Chapter Twenty describes the work that still must be done during the conference, but emphasizes that if planning has been carried out thoroughly, the major tasks will have been taken care of before the participants arrive.

At the end of the book, we provide listings of available resources. The items we have included are designed not only to be helpful to the reader in themselves but also to indicate directions for further research, since new resources are constantly being developed.

Two topics are covered only briefly in this book: models and professional preparation and growth. This brevity reflects the relatively recent emergence of the field; these areas are still in the developmental stages. Formal models for conferences may never be developed, but other fields, such as adult education and human resource development, have models that can be used for small conferences organized primarily for learning purposes. Mention is made of some of these models in the first three chapters and also in the bibliography.

As is true for many emerging fields, most of the people working in the area of conference design came to it by chance or were temporarily assigned to the job and opted to continue. Some of the organizations and publications in the field (see Resources section) offer short-term workshops and conferences that can help practitioners enhance their competence in planning and design. Academic study of this field is fairly recent and has not yet coalesced to form a curricula; consequently, no academics have emerged who could help guide those who are just entering the field or seeking to improve their competence. However, it is only a matter of time before this occurs.

Meanwhile, we are confident that all people involved in the field will benefit from the compilation and organization of the numerous elements required for successful conference planning offered in this book.

Washington, D.C.   Leonard Nadler
July 1987   Zeace Nadler

The Authors

———————•◦•◦•———————

Leonard Nadler is professor of human resource development in the School of Education and Human Development, George Washington University. He is also a partner in Nadler Associates. He received his B.B.A. degree (1948) in accounting from the City College of New York, his M.A. degree (1950) in business education from the City College of New York, and his Ed.D. degree (1962) in educational administration from Teachers College, Columbia University.

His major activities have been developing concepts and models in the field of human resource development. He has received numerous awards, including the Gordon Bliss Award (1978) from the American Society for Training and Development (ASTD) and was chosen as one of the ten outstanding trainers by the readers of *Training Magazine* in 1984. In 1987 he was the first recipient of what will be the annual Distinguished Contribution to Human Resource Development Award of ASTD. He is the author of over 150 articles in various professional publications, and his books include *Managing Human Resource Development* (1986, coauthor), *Clients and Consultants: Meeting and Exceeding Expectations* (2nd ed., 1985, coeditor), *Handbook of Human Resource Development* (1984, editor), *Personal Skills for the Manager* (1982), *Designing Training Programs* (1982), and *Corporate Human Resource Development* (1980).

Zeace Nadler is a partner in Nadler Associates. She received her B.A. degree from Brooklyn College in English literature. She has helped many authors get published and has edited all the published works listed above.

Together, Leonard and Zeace Nadler have written several articles and coauthored *The Conference Book* (Gulf, 1977). They have been involved in various phases of conference planning since the mid-1960s and have served as conference coordinators for international as well as national conferences. They teach a course in conference planning at the George Washington University.

The Comprehensive Guide to
SUCCESSFUL CONFERENCES
AND MEETINGS

Chapter 1

The Changing Conference and Meeting Scene

A great many people throughout the world are involved in conferences, conventions, meetings, symposia, workshops, seminars, and a variety of similar events. This book is about those activities. For purposes of simplifying terminology, all these activities will be called *conferences* in this book. When the text needs to differentiate, that point will be made.

What Is a Conference?

For the most part, a conference is a group of people who come together for a variety of purposes and vary in size and duration. Conferences range in size from ten to ten thousand people or more depending on a variety of factors that will be discussed in the remainder of this book.

Why Have a Conference?

An almost limitless number of purposes prompt people to sponsor or participate in a conference. Among the most common is the annual event—the conference that is conducted each year. Some membership organizations are required by law to have annual business meetings, and these are usually conducted during the annual membership conference. Small organizations, particularly those that are local, may have conferences more frequently than once a year. Large organizations usually have at least one annual national or international conference, supplemented by local or regional conferences during the year.

Some organizations sponsor conferences for the general public or for specific target groups. *Training: The Magazine of Human Resource Development* started conducting an annual conference several years ago. It became so popular that the magazine now conducts annual conferences on both coasts! The leading publications in the conference field (*Meetings News,*

Successful Meetings, Meetings and Conventions) also sponsor annual meetings.

Conferences are also held to make decisions. The most common of these is the political conference, generally called a convention, which is held to nominate people for public office and to make decisions about the party platform. Various government bodies also use conferences to make decisions, particularly when it is important to involve many different people from the community.

Disseminating information is another important reason for a conference. Various kinds of information can be shared with targeted groups or with the general public. Information dissemination is often a main purpose of conferences held by professional societies.

The inspirational conference, particularly well known in religious circles, can be used to make a community aware of a need, galvanize people into thinking about an issue or problem, or arouse them to take some specific action. Closely related is the conference intended to motivate or boost morale, such as a conference for salespeople.

A conference can also be used for problem solving, particularly when all those involved in the problem are participants. This type of conference can be difficult to design; a great deal of effort must be expended on logistics so problem solving is facilitated rather than impeded.

Many conferences are held for learning purposes. When the learning is specifically for a present or future job, the terms *human resource development, training, training and development, training and education,* or something similar are used, and much of the material in this book will be helpful to those planning this type of conference. For detailed information on specific elements of training, such as objectives and design, see the Bibliography in Chapter Twenty-One.

This book does not discuss incentive travel and trade shows, which generally involve different kinds of planning and implementation than the type of conferences covered in this book.

The Sponsor

Conferences are always offered by a sponsor—a generic term for the organization sponsoring the conference.

There are three types of sponsors. Membership sponsors, such as societies and associations, sponsor conferences for their members. Although attendance is generally not restricted to members, the major focus is on members and the goals and mission of the organization.

Employers sponsor conferences for their employees and for others related to the organization, such as customers, stockholders, agents, distributors, and franchisees.

A large group of sponsors provide conferences for the public, often called public seminars. These can be divided into those conferences held for profit and those that are not for profit. Government agencies and community groups tend to offer nonprofit public seminars. The for-profit public seminar is offered by many different types of sponsors, including magazines, professional societies, companies, and individuals who wish to sell a product in conjunction with a conference.

The Coordinator

A sponsor often designates a single individual to assume responsibility for the conference. The common title for this position is *coordinator*, but other titles are also used, such as planner, meeting planner, designer, consultant, conference director, and arranger. In this book, the term *coordinator* will be used to mean the person who has prime responsibility for a conference.

The coordinator can be either internal or external. An internal coordinator (that is, a member of the sponsoring organization) may have a different job title if called on to act as a coordinator only at special times. This situation has begun to change in some organizations, as evidenced by the formation of such groups as the Society of Company Meeting Planners and the Society of Government Meeting Planners, whose members' major responsibility is to serve as their organizations' coordinators.

The sixth annual Dollars and Census Survey, conducted in 1985 by *Meeting News*, reported data based on responses from 600 internal coordinators. A breakdown of the respondents by sex was 52.9 percent males and 47.1 percent females. Of the males, 84 percent had college degrees, whereas only 61.4 percent of the females held such degrees. The average salary of the males was $42,339, while that of the females was $27,049. For both groups, the top salaries went to those with more than ten years' experience. Regardless of sex, those with fewer than two years' experience were making $24,389. The respondents reported an 8.3 percent increase in salaries for 1985 over 1984, which is higher than the general increase of salaries in the United States for that period.

The data were obtained from two groups: those employed by corporations and those employed by associations. On the corporate side, 67.5 percent of the meetings involved fewer than 500 participants. On the association side, 68.7 percent of the meetings involved 1,000 or fewer participants.

An external coordinator is generally engaged in the conference business either full time or as part of other work in related fields. Increasingly, companies are being formed to provide external conference coordination services.

The job of coordinator is a fairly new occupation, and as with any new field, it has significant problems as it struggles for high standards of professionalism. One approach being considered to raise professional standards is a certification program, though there is little evidence in any professional area that certification results in improved performance. One group, the Convention Liaison Council, in order to "encourage and recognize professionalism in the industry" has implemented a testing program designed to produce Certified Meeting Professionals (CMPs). The council administers a written examination and evaluates the applicants' experience. (Information and applications are available from the Convention Liaison Council, P.O. Box 1738, Alexandria, VA 22320.)

As the field expands, academic preparation for the profession is also developing. Since 1978 the George Washington University has offered a course on "Designing and Implementing Conferences and Meetings." Other universities are beginning to offer similar courses, and some are contemplating degrees in the conference management field.

The Participants

The person who takes part in a conference is generally called a participant, attendee, registrant, or conferee. (Some conferences may use other designations for historical or practical reasons.) In this book, the term *participant* will be used.

In addition to general participants, some special types of participants deserve special mention. International participants (usually preferred to "foreign" participants) are generally those participants who come from a country other than the one in which the conference is being held. Some conferences prefer to use the term *off-shore,* but this is ethnocentric as well as inaccurate. Mexico, for example, is certainly not off-shore from the United States.

At one time, inviting international participants to a conference in the United States was unusual. This has changed: International travel, in some cases, is easier than domestic travel, and governments that formerly restricted international travel for their citizens have become more lenient. Particularly in the physical and social science fields, many more international participants attend conferences than in the past. Coordinators should not perceive international participants as an additional burden but as an additional resource, since they bring interesting and challenging opportunities to the conference. Efforts must be made to facilitate their participation. Suggestions about how to do this are made throughout this book.

Another special participant population are the handicapped. (The term *disabled* has been used, but *handicapped* is preferred.) Harold Snider, of the Society for the Advancement of Travel for the Handicapped, estimates that 36 million handicapped people live in the United States. It is estimated that 13.1 million were in the work force in 1982. The blind participant may need some assistance to maneuver in unfamiliar terrain. Some sites have elevators with braille numbers that are readily usable by blind people. Some blind people use guide dogs that are permitted in most hotels and other conference facilities. It is necessary, however, that conference staff know how to react to the dogs, and if blind participants are expected, special briefings should be held.

In recent years laws have encouraged or required facilities to provide ramps and similar facilities for wheelchair participants. Some elevators now have buttons lower to the ground so that a participant in a wheelchair can easily reach them. If participants using wheelchairs are expected to attend, this must be considered when setting up the meeting rooms.

Deaf people can communicate in a number of ways, but signing, using the hands to make letters, words, and phrases, is one of the most common methods in use today.

Some hotels make special provision for handicapped participants, such as special rooms for those in wheelchairs. For the deaf or partially deaf, they provide a system of lights to signal smoke alarms, telephone calls, or knocks on the door. These units are provided at no extra cost at most Holiday Inns, for example.

Figure 1 presents a checklist of items to be considered for handicapped participants, and these considerations are discussed throughout the book.

More older participants are attending conferences, and special plans for them are sometimes needed at conferences. In the future, conferences may place more emphasis on having medical attention readily available. The duration of sessions may have to be considered. Loss of acuity may mean using audiovisual materials in different ways than we have been accustomed to.

Others Involved in the Conference

Conferences require a great deal of administrative and clerical work, and to accomplish this the coordinator needs a *secretariat.* This term is common outside the United States and is now gaining acceptance in conferences inside the United States. The secretariat can be an individual or a group working under the coordinator's supervision. Before the conference, the secretariat typically handles such tasks as corresponding with presenters, working with suppliers, communicating with participants, and obtaining participant materials and preparing name badges. During the conference, the secretariat is responsible for registration, supplies, and crisis management. After the conference, it is responsible for follow-up activities. Specific secretariat duties are discussed throughout the book.

The coordinator usually works with a *design committee,* a group of people designated by the sponsor to have responsibility for all or part of a conference. The coordinator might be the chairperson of the design committee. The extensive work of the design committee is discussed in Chapter Two.

Coordinators often overlook *local convention and visitors bureaus* (LCVBs) as a special resource. There are over 400 LCVBs in the United States, and their range of activities includes assisting in site selection, handling hotel reservations, providing printed material about the city and its environs, arranging for volunteers and/or paid help for registration, and helping with other conference-related activities. They are frequently funded by a local tax on hotel rooms or by contributions from local suppliers and merchants. Many LCVBs are members of the International Association of Convention and Visitors Bureaus, which recently celebrated its seventy-second annniversary. The association includes over 241 bureaus in sixteen countries.

Coordinators need numerous *suppliers*—the wide variety of people and companies who support a conference. This category includes hotels and sites, travel agents, airline and bus companies, badgemakers (when made externally), public relations organizations, printers, drayage companies, projectionists, electricians, and so on.

Figure 1. Considerations for the Handicapped.

_____ Is at least one entrance ramped or at ground level with no steps?

_____ Are doors at least thirty-two inches wide?

_____ Can the doors be opened easily?

_____ Are the thresholds to the buildings and rooms no greater than one-half inch in height?

_____ Are sloping ramps provided where there are stairs?

_____ Do the ramps rise no more steeply than one inch for each twelve inches of length?

_____ Are there level or nearly level walks leading to the building?

_____ Do the sidewalks near the site have curb cuts (ramps) at crossways?

_____ Are there elevators connecting each level?

_____ If there is not an elevator operator, are all elevator buttons in easy reach of a person in a wheelchair?

_____ Are all elevators marked in braille or with raised notation?

_____ Are public restroom doors at least thirty-two inches wide?

_____ Are restroom stalls at least thirty-two inches wide and equipped with grab bars?

_____ Does the site provide lower hand-activated drinking fountains for wheelchair users?

_____ Are wheelchair-accessible public restrooms available on each floor?

_____ Does the site have lower public telephones for wheelchair users?

_____ Are any public telephones equipped with an amplifier for a hearing-impaired person?

_____ Is there a TTY (special telephone hookup) available for deaf persons?

_____ Can meeting and function rooms accommodate wheelchairs?

_____ Is parking accessible for the physically handicapped?

_____ Is public transportation available with special provisions for the handicapped?

_____ Does the site permit guide dogs?

_____ Do presenters need any special orientation for adjusting to handicapped participants?

_____ Do any registration procedures need to be modified for the handicapped?

SOURCE: Adapted from Redden, 1976.

Platform Personnel

In designing the conference, the coordinator uses people on the platform. _Presenter_ is the generic term for the person responsible for a session. This title may describe a keynote speaker or a small group leader. The person may not actually present anything but rather only have responsibility for making sure that a session starts and progresses. Other names for this position are speaker, discussion leader, small group leader, and resource person.

One kind of presenter is a *speaker*. This term is used essentially to designate that person who makes a presentation at a general session. For other sessions, the term *resource person* is used. The classification also includes others who may not be making a presentation but are available during a session to respond to questions or to participate in other ways.

The *convener* has responsibility for calling the group to order and facilitating its operation. This person does not make a formal presentation but assists the group in its functioning.

Very Important Persons (VIPs)

Many conferences invite speakers or participants who are in some way in the public spotlight. A VIP may be a public figure, such as an elected official, a stage, screen, or television personality, the author of an important book or play, or someone who is only momentarily in the spotlight, such as a returned hostage.

VIPs must be accorded special treatment. A VIP is usually invited to bring attention to the conference, but some people may see the VIP as an enemy or a target. The rampant terrorism of the mid-1980s has illustrated the need for special security in connection with some VIPs.

The Checklist

At the end of this chapter is a checklist for VIPs. The items that appear on this checklist are discussed here.

Who Decides That a Person Is a VIP?

What is important is in the eye of the beholder, of course, but some people are obviously in this category and the decision is automatic. If there is any doubt, the decision should be made jointly by the sponsor and the coordinator.

Will One Person Be Selected as the Liaison with VIPs?

VIPs usually have a staff who make arrangements for them, and they prefer to deal with one individual on the conference staff. Although it is tempting to be involved with VIPs, the coordinator should probably control his ego needs and *not* be the liaison, since liaison work can be very time consuming. It is advisable, then, for the coordinator to designate a reliable individual to be the liaison. This person need not be on the secretariat or on the design committee but must be in constant contact with the coordinator.

What Special Security Measures May Be Necessary for Each VIP?

Not every VIP will require special security, but the focus here is on those who have such a need. Some special measures are illustrated in the remaining items of this checklist.

Has There Been Any Indication of Possible Disturbance or Terrorism in Connection with a VIP?

A VIP may not evoke disturbances or terrorism at the time of invitation, but by the time of the conference, that condition can change. If a VIP has been invited, the liaison should maintain a watch on the public image of that VIP. A coordinator might want to invite a controversial figure, even when knowing that a disturbance may result. If this is the case, the sponsor must be involved in the decision.

Does the Site Have Any Special Security Personnel or Procedures?

Some sites, such as major hotels, have had experience with security for VIPs. If so, the best course of action may be to rely on them. They have the experience and the personnel. The coordinator, of course, should always investigate the site's security measures.

Will It Be Necessary to Have Liaison with Police at Either the Local or State Level?

Particularly in metropolitan areas, or where crowds are expected, the local police should be involved early in the planning. Some localities rely on state police and the relationship should be clarified.

Do Any VIPs Receive Secret Service Protection?

Some VIPs receive constant protection from the Secret Service. If so, this agency will inform the coordinator of the exact steps to be taken. They should be consulted as soon as the VIP has agreed to attend the conference. In many cases, the agency initiates the contact with the coordinator or sponsor.

Will Professional Advice Be Needed to Provide Security for VIPs?

If the VIP is not protected by the Secret Service, it is still possible to obtain professional help, such as security consultants. This help can be expensive, but this is part of the cost incurred when inviting some VIPs.

Will a Room Sweep Be Required?

A room sweep is an electronic analysis of the room (and possibly adjoining rooms and spaces) that detects the presence of bombs and similar destructive devices. If a room sweep is made, it means that the room and its environs must be inaccessible to everyone until the VIP arrives. That can mean the loss of a room for a day or more.

*Should There Be Controlled Access to Rooms
in Which VIPs Will Meet or Occupy?*

Even when no sweep is made, it may still be necessary to control access to the room and the general area. Participants may be required to show badges or other identification and to pass through a metal detector. These measures can take a considerable amount of time, so the conference design must allow for them.

Trends

Given advances in electronics, the conference may have to be redefined to include such areas as teleconferencing and computer conferencing.

Teleconferencing has two meanings. The older meaning pertains to telephone conference calls, in which several people communicate on the same phone line at the same time. One or more people, speaking from different places, may talk to a large group or to several groups in scattered locations. In this form of teleconferencing, it is possible to have two-way oral communication. If needed, the presenters can be supplemented by visual aids, handouts, and other materials.

The more recent and well-known version of the teleconference uses television as the conference medium. A closed-circuit arrangement is generally employed and can utilize satellites for broader coverage. This too can be a conference with people in various locations who not only talk to each other but see each other. Visual aids are easily introduced into such situations. Generally, it is one-way communication, but the technology exists for two-way verbal and visual communication.

Computer conferencing has been evolving for several years. As the technology in this field changes so rapidly, it is difficult to predict what it will be like even in the next few years. In the mid-1980s it has still not gathered enough momentum to be a significant factor, but the trend should not be overlooked. This type of conference requires that each participant have a computer and a modem (for telephone transmission and receiving). The participants, in some organized fashion, type their inputs and send it to a central (mainframe) computer. From this, the other participants can receive the information and make any written comments they wish. The process can include an electronic bulletin board, a local area network (LAN), or some other type of file server. At present, it is a relatively slow process that fails when it is intended to replace a regular conference. It has advantages when it links people in various time zones who can come on line whenever they wish.

There has been an increase in the number of regional conferences, most being sponsored by public seminar sponsors and membership sponsors. Many large national conferences (over five thousand participants) sponsored by membership organizations are having problems because they are limited to only a few cities. The logistics involved can sometimes exceed the revenue, which is a factor for the membership sponsor. A large conference can also be discouraging for the participant, who may feel lost and have difficulty relating to a large number of people. Many people prefer a smaller conference.

It is expected that the economy will be a factor in conferences. Just how much, and in what direction, is difficult to say. Even during the recession of the early 1980s, both the number of conferences and the number of participants increased.

The impact of technology is always difficult to determine. We seem to be experiencing the "high-tech/high-touch" phenomena described by Naisbitt in his book, *Megatrends:* As more technology appears in the workplace, we have an increased need for relating to others; as a result, the conference field should grow.

Preparing for the Conference

Many readers will be familiar with Parkinson's Law, as modified here: "Conference preparation will take up all of the time allotted to it." This is true for many of the tasks in conference preparation, and for other tasks it is not how long they will take, but when they should be started.

In a logical progression (1) a sponsor decides to have a conference, (2) a coordinator is selected or hired, (3) a design committee is appointed, (4) goals or purposes are agreed on, (5) a site is chosen, (6) presenters are selected, (7) marketing is done, and (8) the conference is conducted. However, specific conferences differ according to their size, the structure of the sponsoring organization, and the like. Therefore, developing a standard order of tasks is almost impossible.

Item 1 will generally be the first step, and may happen by habit (a membership sponsor has a conference each year) rather than by considered decision. By the time the new officers appear, some of the decisions will already have been made. The sponsor (the organization) does not change, but the elected officers do. The coordinator may have been selected before the new officers were elected. It is customary for the coordinator to be selected by the new administration, but this is not always possible. Similarly, with an employer sponsor, the annual marketing conference may already be on track after a new marketing director has been named.

In the case of a large conference, the site is probably selected years before the coordinator is chosen. In other situations, the design committee is designated before the coordinator. Indeed, one of the first tasks of the design committee can be to select the coordinator. The presenters may be selected before the site, but changes are frequently made when a particular presenter does not want to come to that site. When does marketing begin? It depends on the selection of the site, presenters, and other variables. This does not mean that a time line (that is, the chronological order in which activities are to be accomplished) should not be established, because due dates have to be agreed on and distributed so that all concerned know what they are. One way to do this with any size conference is with a status chart (see Figure 2).

The coordinator should assume responsibility for developing and filling in this chart, although such actual maintenance can be a secretariat function. The chart shows only major headings, but it may also be necessary to have subheadings or subordinate charts. Paperwork should be kept to a minimum. This chart should focus on what is supposed to happen when and what has been accomplished.

Figure 2. Status Chart.

Title of Conference: _____

Date: _____ **Venue:** _____

Coordinator: _____

As of: _____
        (date)

Activity	Start Date	Completion Date	Responsibility	Condition	Check-Off
Conference design committee					
Site selection					
Marketing					
Budget					
Speakers					
Resource people					
Transportation					
Exhibitions					
Registration					
Meeting room logistics					
Audiovisual					
Public relations					
Recognition events					
Entertainment					
Food functions					
Related events					
Evaluation and follow-up					
Operations (implementation)					
Participant book					
Companions					

SOURCE: *The Comprehensive Guide to Successful Conferences and Meetings* by Leonard Nadler and Zeace Nadler. San Francisco: Jossey-Bass. Copyright © 1987. Permission to reproduce hereby granted.

The coordinator should provide copies of this chart to the design committee before any meetings and to the sponsor, as needed. It should be continually reviewed by the coordinator. At first, weekly reviews may be sufficient. Later, as the date of the conference draws near, the reviews should increase until they take place at least once every day.

- *Activity.* Each activity should be reviewed to make sure it is relevant for the particular conference. As needed, items should be deleted or added.
- *Start date.* This is the date when actual work should begin on that particular activity.
- *Completion date.* This is the date when all work on that activity must be completed.
- *Responsibility.* The name of a specific person should be placed next to each item. As responsibilities change (and they usually do in the planning stages of a conference), the names should change. No name should be placed on this chart without the individual's agreement.
- *Condition.* This crucial column should change regularly as the work progresses. It provides immediate information for the coordinator and others on the most recent status of each activity.
- *Check-off.* An entry in this column signifies the work on that activity is completed. Only the coordinator should be permitted to initial in this column.

Periodically, the chart should be replaced with a blank version and redone. The previous ones should be retained; if something goes wrong, it will then be possible to backtrack and see what happened. The "old" reports will also be valuable as a history of how the conference was planned.

CHECKLIST FOR VERY IMPORTANT PERSONS (VIPs)

_____ Who decides that a person is a VIP?

_____ Will one person be selected as the liaison with VIPs?

_____ What special security measures may be necessary for each VIP?

_____ Has there been any indication of possible disturbance or terrorism in connection with a VIP?

_____ Does the site have any special security personnel or procedures?

_____ Will it be necessary to have liaison with police at either the local or state level?

_____ Do any VIPs receive Secret Service protection?

_____ Will professional advice be needed to provide security for VIPs?

_____ Will a room sweep be required?

_____ Should there be controlled access to rooms in which VIPs will meet or occupy?

SOURCE: *The Comprehensive Guide to Successful Conferences and Meetings* by Leonard Nadler and Zeace Nadler. San Francisco: Jossey-Bass. Copyright © 1987. Permission to reproduce hereby granted.

Chapter 2

Designing the Conference

CHECKLIST FOR DESIGN COMMITTEE

Purpose

_____ Does the design committee have a specific purpose?

_____ Has the mandate of the design committee been stated in writing?

_____ Have the operational areas of the design committee been specifically designated?

_____ Has the relationship between the design committee and the coordinator been clarified?

_____ Is it clear to whom the design committee is responsible?

_____ Is there a sunset time for the design committee?

Selection

_____ Must design committee members belong to the sponsoring organization?

_____ Will the members be volunteers or will they be assigned?

_____ Has a process been established for selecting design committee members?

Operations

_____ Does the design committee have a budget?

_____ Are design committee members expected to visit the site?

_____ How often will the design committee meet?

_____ Will the design committee plan the evaluation?

_____ Can interpersonal factors be expected to arise in the design committee?

_____ Will the experience of the design committee be recorded for future conferences?

SOURCE: _The Comprehensive Guide to Successful Conferences and Meetings_ by Leonard Nadler and Zeace Nadler. San Francisco: Jossey-Bass. Copyright © 1987. Permission to reproduce hereby granted.

Participants leave a well-designed conference commenting on how well everything went and how easy it must be to design and implement a conference. The sponsor is also pleased and wonders why such a simple job took so much time, energy, and resources. As with a good stage production, the audience only sees what is up front; they are not aware of the thought, planning, and drive that went into making the production flow so easily.

Throughout this book, the term *designing* will be used to mean the process of bringing together all the elements involved in producing a successful conference. Other terms for the process, particularly *planning,* are also popular. Although a good deal of planning is required, planning alone is not sufficient. The coordinator and the design committee must be able to *design,* a process that includes planning but also goes far beyond it.

This chapter covers the elements involved in designing a conference, indicating some of the pitfalls and many of the opportunities. Designing a conference is not an exact science, nor simply a sequential process. It is a mixture of art, conjuring, gazing into a crystal ball and, for some, praying.

Design Factors

Three major factors should be considered in designing a conference: purpose, participants, design. These three factors must be completely congruent if a conference is to be successful.

Purpose. A conference must have a purpose. As discussed in Chapter One, it may be as simple as a required annual ritual, but most conferences have other purposes as well. A membership sponsor conference may be held to bring the members together, but it will also usually include some content, based on an identified purpose. An employer sponsor generally has specific objectives that can be stated. A public seminar sponsor must be able to state its purpose very clearly in order to attract the public for which the conference has been designed. Sponsors sometimes use the phrase "expected outcomes"; membership sponsor conferences use that terminology to enable their members to plan for their participation in the conference.

Participants. What kind of participants does the sponsor want? For both the employer sponsor and the public seminar sponsor, the design process usually starts with the purpose and then the appropriate participants are identified. In the case of the membership sponsor, these two factors (purpose and participants) are sometimes reversed: Given the kinds of participants that are expected to come to this conference, what conference purpose will encourage them to attend? Whichever comes first, it is important that purpose and participants are congruent.

Design. The design of a conference must reflect the purpose and participants. Although this may seem obvious, a sponsor sometimes starts with the design. This can happen when the sponsor has attended a conference, found it worthwhile, gives the coordinator that design, and tells the coordinator to develop the goals and identify the participants to implement that design. Fortunately, this does not happen too often, but it does happen.

Duration is a design factor. The authors once designed a successful three-day conference for a sponsor but were then asked to redesign it into a one-day conference. The sponsor said that the participants (managers and executives) generally did not want to be away from their offices for three consecutive days, but instead preferred three separate one-day conferences. Accordingly, the goal was modified to reflect what could be accomplished in this time format.

Religious preference is often overlooked in the design process. Christian participants may react negatively to a design that schedules sessions for Sunday morning. Jewish participants may need a special design for a conference scheduled on Friday night and Saturday (Nadler and Edelman, 1967).

The Design Committee

Most conferences are designed by some kind of committee, usually because so much work is involved that no one person can do it all. The design committee is a group, usually from the sponsoring organization, which has some responsibility for the conference. The specific responsibilities are discussed as part of the checklist.

For a small conference, the coordinator can work with a small design committee, but as the size of the conference increases, it may be necessary to increase the size of the design committee. This can lead to many problems, particularly in assembling all the members for each meeting. An alternative is to use subcommittees, each reporting to a member of the design committee. This may require some special training for the design committee members on how to delegate and control several small groups or subcommittees.

The Checklist

Purpose

Does the Design Committee Have a Specific Purpose?

It should. Too often, a design committee is formed because the sponsor has always used a design committee, but that is not a sufficient reason. One purpose for having a design committee is to be sure that the conference represents the thinking and planning of more than one individual. For the membership sponsor, the design committee provides for the involvement of members, which avoids a conference that is only staff-driven. There may not be complete agreement on this arrangement, and it should be clarified as a reason for having a design committee.

Has the Mandate of the Design Committee Been Stated in Writing?

The mandate of the design committee need not be a long statement and should avoid legalistic terminology, but having a written statement minimizes conflicts with the coordinator and among the committee members. Indeed, an external coordinator might want to see the written statement before agreeing to accept the assignment.

Have the Operational Areas of the Design Committee Been Specifically Designated?

The operational areas presented in Figure 3 are not meant to be all inclusive; this list may be expanded or shortened. What is essential is that the areas be stated specifically so as to avoid conflict that could interfere with the design process. To illustrate the importance of this step, a design committee for a membership sponsor had worked diligently to design a conference that would involve about two thousand participants. They carefully sequenced various sessions, paying particular attention to the methods to be used by presenters. For this conference, the design committee wanted sessions that provided for participant involvement. When the conference was held, the members of the design committee were horrified to find that room setups were arranged theater-style, thereby limiting the possibilities for participant involvement. When they questioned the coordinator, they were told that the site had a charge for resetting rooms, so for cost reasons the coordinator had decided to use theater setups for most of the rooms, most of the days!

Has the Relationship Between the Design Committee and the Coordinator Been Clarified?

Sometimes the sponsor designates one of the members of the design committee as the coordinator. This is acceptable if the individual has the competency to serve as the coordinator. More common, however, is a coordinator who is not a committee member. The coordinator must devote much more time to design

Figure 3. Responsibilities of the Sponsor, Coordinator, and Design Committee.

Issues	Sponsor	Coordinator	Design Committee
Objectives of the conference			
Site selection			
Identification of participants			
Duration of the conference			
Dates of the conference			
Coordination of resources			
Selection of resource people			
Budget approval			

Key: **MR** = **Make recommendations**
    R   = **React**
    D   = **Decide**
    NA = **Not applicable**

SOURCE: *The Comprehensive Guide to Successful Conferences and Meetings* by Leonard Nadler and Zeace Nadler. San Francisco: Jossey-Bass. Copyright © 1987. Permission to reproduce hereby granted.

than the design committee. In many cases, the conference is the coordinator's major or sole project but only a part-time assignment for those on the design committee.

The design committee has three major functions on design issues—make recommendations, react, or decide (see Figure 3). Although these functions can lead to confusion and conflict, they need not be a problem if sufficient attention is paid to these functions in stating the purpose of the design committee. Clarifying these functions also provides guidelines for the coordinator and the sponsor.

A design committee is asked to make recommendations, but it should be understood that these recommendations will not automatically be accepted. This allows the design committee to be creative in their recommendations without limiting themselves to the considerations for execution.

On other issues the design committee is asked to react to material presented by the coordinator. Again, reaction should not necessarily lead to decision making by the design committee. The value of the design committee is its ability to react to some of the plans of the coordinator and the wishes of the sponsor without having the responsibility for implementation.

On some issues, however, the sponsor has delegated decision-making power to the design committee rather than to the coordinator; when this is the case, the coordinator must agree to abide by these decisions and be prepared to implement them.

It must be clear, for each issue, who has responsibility for making the decision. The instrument shown in Figure 3 can be used to clarify the relationship among the sponsor, coordinator, and design committee. The coordinator starts by reviewing the issues and adding others as appropriate. Then, the coordinator should mark the appropriate key in each box. Every box should be marked and be reviewed with the sponsor.

Is It Clear to Whom the Design Committee Is Responsible?

This is, in some situations, a political question. For a membership sponsor, the design committee is usually composed of members (volunteers) who may feel that their prime responsibility is to the members of the organization when it should be to the coordinator. If the coordinator is a staff person in a voluntary organization, the typical conflicts of volunteer versus staff can be expected to surface.

The question is much more difficult for an employer sponsor. The responsibility of the design committee, which is probably composed of employees, will reflect the usual relationships in that organization. When the coordinator is internal, that person's position in the organization may automatically answer the question. When the coordinator is external, the question of responsibility may be determined by the position of the person who has contracted for the external coordinator and by the level of the people on the design committee.

Is There a Sunset Time for the Design Committee?

The term *sunset* refers to a specific time when the design committee is to be dissolved, unless some specific action extends it. The design committee should be organized early enough to accomplish the tasks set for it. At what point, however, is their work finished? Typically when all the planning work has been completed, usually some time before the conference is scheduled to open. If possible, a specific sunset date should be announced in advance. The design committee should not be involved during the conference, since that puts the design committee members in the position of defending their previous actions. During the conference the coordinator may work with a steering committee, discussed in Chapter Twenty.

Selection

Must Design Committee Members Belong to the Sponsoring Organization?

At least some of the members of the design committee should be members of the sponsoring organization, but in some situations the sponsor might find it advantageous to involve outsiders as well. A membership sponsor, for example, may appoint nonmembers to the design committee when appointment is considered especially prestigious. However, appointing nonmembers can convey the message that the organization does not have a sufficient number of members with the interest or competence to serve on the design committee. A public seminar sponsor can acquire outside opinions and inputs by organizing ad hoc (temporary) subcommittees that report to the design committee.

An employer sponsor might use outside people who do not belong to the sponsoring organization, depending on the objectives of the conference. A public seminar sponsor might also use people who do not belong to the sponsoring organization, in order to get ideas and to involve others. This is particularly applicable to a government-agency or community organization–sponsored conference that affects many people outside the organization.

Will the Members Be Volunteers or Will They Be Assigned?

In the case of a membership sponsor, the design committee is almost always composed of volunteers. The design committee might include some assigned staff members, but that is not generally a good practice. In an employer sponsor situation, the design committee members are usually assigned, although there might be some latitude. A for-profit public seminar sponsor commonly assigns some internal staff to the design committee but might seek some outside people who are generally not volunteers. A nonprofit public seminar sponsor usually has a design committee composed of a mixture of people who have been requested to join the committee (a form of assignment) and those who are volunteers.

Has a Process Been Established for Selecting Design Committee Members?

The selection process can be expected to reflect the philosophy of the organization. A membership sponsor that encourages volunteer participation usually makes open announcements, encouraging people to volunteer for the design committee. A membership sponsor that is tightly controlled, usually by the staff, tends to select design committee members who can be expected to conform to staff directions.

With an employer sponsor or public seminar sponsor, the process of selection depends on the purpose of the conference and the expected participants. For these sponsors, the process can be expected to follow the usual patterns for allocating committee assignments.

Operations

Does the Design Committee Have a Budget?

A design committee usually costs money to operate, and even before the members are selected, consideration should be given to budget. Anticipated expenses include at least travel, food and lodging, and communications. The amount and extent of these expenses depend on many variables, particularly the type of sponsor.

A membership sponsor generally expects volunteer members to pay for most of their own expenses. In some instances, this is made a condition for appointment to the design committee, although this limits the pool from which the design committee can be selected and favors those who have expense accounts or can otherwise be reimbursed, or have sufficient personal funds.

An employer sponsor usually has a budget for the conference, and that budget will provide funds, if needed, for the design committee. The for-profit public seminar sponsor needs to make similar budgetary provisions. A nonprofit public seminar sponsor tends to seek outside funding for the design committee, and, depending on the sponsor, the topic, and the expected participants, various funding sources can be approached to provide the budget for the design committee.

Are Design Committee Members Expected to Visit the Site?

Sometimes the conference site is selected before the design committee is appointed; other times, site selection is one of the tasks of the design committee (see Chapter Five). If the latter case, this task should be stated before the design committee is selected. For a national membership sponsor, the geographic location of a site may change from year to year; if the design committee is expected to participate in site selection, this task can involve time and money for several trips. If the site was selected before the design committee was formed, it is still helpful for the design committee to inspect the actual venue. Usually, only one such visit is necessary, but it is extremely helpful.

How Often Will the Design Committee Meet?

If the design committee is involved in many areas, several meetings might be required. At the outset, the coordinator and/or sponsor should at least be able to estimate the number of meetings for prospective design committee members. Those who are being considered for membership on the design committee need this information to plan their schedules.

When screening people for the design committee, it should be clearly stated that they are expected to attend every meeting—so they need to know what this entails. It is extremely disruptive to hold design committee meetings with only some members present. Inevitably, the work of the design committee is slowed considerably as previously absent members are brought up-to-date or take exception to recommendations or decisions that were made in their absence.

Will the Design Committee Plan the Evaluation?

Evaluation of the conference is a difficult task and generally beyond the scope of the design committee, but planning the evaluation should be done early in the design process. If the design committee is to plan the evaluation, it is necessary either to select one or more members of the design committee with this skill or to identify another resource to plan the evaluation.

Depending on the type of organization, a membership sponsor may assign a subgroup of the design committee to plan and implement the evaluation. An employer sponsor usually finds a resource within their own human resource development department, if they have one. The for-profit public seminar sponsor usually has that competence internally, as it is one that they frequently use, but a nonprofit public seminar sponsor may have to contract out for evaluation. For a full discussion of evaluation, see Chapter Nineteen.

Can Interpersonal Factors Be Expected to Arise in the Design Committee?

Yes, interpersonal factors, usually producing conflict, commonly arise at some time in the design process, so the coordinator and the design committee should be aware of the possibility. The coordinator particularly should have interpersonal and small group skills to cope with the anticipated problems. In one case known to the authors, a membership sponsor (professional society) conference was being designed by a coordinator and a design committee, the latter coming from one of the constituent bodies within the membership sponsor. Just one month prior to the conference, we were called in to act as consultants because the design committee and the coordinator had spent most of the preceding ten months in conflict! The coordinator had been selected by the executive committee of the membership sponsor, while the design committee members were selected to represent the different groups within the membership sponsor. Aside from selecting the site, they had not agreed on any other part of the design. Even the site presented a problem: The design committee had estimated that 1,600 participants would attend, but the site could only accommodate 850! Before we began to assist with the design, we encouraged the group to confront the conflicts that had blocked their work during the prior months. After that we were able to help them with their design problems.

If interpersonal problems are anticipated, it is helpful to obtain the services of an external observer who is skilled in group process and can avoid involvement in the design process.

Will the Experience of the Design Committee Be Recorded for Future Conferences?

If the sponsor is considering presenting more conferences, the work of the design committee should be recorded. This historical perspective can be important in selecting design committee members for the next conference. The most common method is to use a member of the secretariat to take notes, which should summarize the outcomes of the meetings rather than describe in detail how the design committee got to that point.

Another technique is to ask each member of the design committee to prepare a brief final report, including areas in which they felt the design committee had worked effectively and those areas where they were not as effective. In addition, after the last design committee meeting, but before the conference starts, the design committee members should be asked for their recommendations for the next design committee. The focus of these recommendations should be on operations, not on membership.

The Flow of the Conference

A well-designed conference has a natural flow that starts in the design phase. When possible, a conference should have a theme that relates to the goals and missions of the sponsor. An employer sponsor might have the theme "Looking to the Future." A membership sponsor's theme might be "Our Organization (or Focus) and World Hunger." The theme is usually stated as dramatically as possible in order to attract attention, as well as to communicate the focus of the conference.

The theme is then captured in a logo, a pictorial depiction of the theme. For "Looking to the Future," the logo could be a futuristic design. A "World Hunger" theme might be an empty food plate. Sometimes, the logo is an acronym of the theme or some other nonpictorial presentation. (Themes and logos are covered in more detail in Chapter Twelve.)

Both the theme and logo contribute to climate-setting, which is reinforced by marketing techniques. The important time for climate-setting occurs when participants arrive. Consideration must be given to airport reception, site reception, registration, signs, opening session, and amenities.

The next step in the process is the scheduling of sessions and events and activities. Consideration must be given to arrival times, opening events, participant expectations, relationship to theme, and the variety of sessions.

Finally, the climax! A conference should not be allowed to fade away or close with a whimper. The closing must be as exciting as the opening but for a different purpose. It is important that the participants leave in an "up" frame of mind, particularly if they are going to return to the sponsor's next conference.

Design Possibilities

There are an almost infinite number of conference designs, and we are presenting those that have proved most useful. You can use these as they are presented or generate variations of your own.

Every conference must have at least one general session, a gathering of all participants in one room at the same time. General sessions usually open and close the conference, although they can also be held at other times. The general session is sometimes called a *plenary session,* a term in common usage in many parts of the world and at international meetings. Usually, there is a speaker at the general session (sometimes called the keynote speaker), but this is not absolutely necessary. A general session could have a media presentation, a skit, or some other form of stimulating activity. (More general discussion of sessions follows in later chapters.)

The most prevalent sessions at a conference are the *concurrent sessions,* the designation used when two or more sessions are scheduled at the same time. In large conferences, the number of concurrent sessions can range from 20 to 200 or more, while a small conference may only have two or three. Generally, concurrent sessions do not relate directly to a previous session, although they should relate to the theme and objectives of the conference. Concurrent sessions can employ a wide variety of methods and techniques; they need not be only speeches and reading of papers. This book offers many suggestions on the different types of activities that can be designed for concurrent sessions.

Breakout sessions appear, at first glance, to be the same as concurrent sessions, but they are actually much different. Although some people use this term to mean any small group session, this book defines the term as a small group session that follows a general session and that allows the participants to discuss the topic of the general session in a different way or in depth. These sessions may use group leaders, a set of questions, an agenda, or leave the participants on their own. Provision may be made to share the discussions of the breakout sessions in another general session, where reports from the breakout groups are presented. Another pattern is to ask the breakout groups to submit reports that become part of the general report of the conference.

A concurrent session may also become a *repeat session* when the assigned room is not large enough to hold the expected number of participants. When there are concurrent sessions, participants can attend only one concurrent session in each time period, of course, and therefore may have to miss sessions in which they have an interest. This need can sometimes be accommodated by repeating some of the concurrent sessions. It is also possible to provide a repeat session that was not originally planned. For example, when a concurrent session draws a much larger audience than anticipated, or after a concurrent session it becomes obvious that participants have increased interest in that presenter or topic, the coordinator and the steering committee may still consider a repeat session.

At a conference, most sessions are open to all participants. A variation is the *prerequisite session,* although it is infrequently used as part of a design. Attendance at a particular session is limited to those who meet some prior qualification, which could be attendance at a more basic session at an earlier conference or having some credentials, such as being a medical doctor.

As some participants may have a specific interest, it is sometimes desirable to use a *track design*—a series of sessions designed around a particular area. For example, a membership sponsor conference may design one track for officers of the organization with clearly identified concurrent sessions that are part of that track.

An informal type of session with no presenter or agenda is the *cracker barrel session,* a term that was derived from an earlier period when a group of men would sit around a barrel of crackers in the local general store and talk. Similar sessions can be designed for a conference without the actual cracker barrel. In some conferences, soft drinks and coffee/tea might be provided.

Some conferences plan off-site *field trips* that are conducted during the conference. They are included for a variety of purposes: to see a facility related to the theme of the conference, for a recreational break, to visit an historical site, and so on. Depending on the purpose, the results of the field trip can be shared upon return or at a later time during the conference. (See Chapter Fourteen for further discussion.)

In addition to sessions, other activities take place during the conference that can be important for participants. *Exhibitions* are offered in a special section of the site, so that exhibitors can show their products and services. The number of exhibits can range from a single table to several hundred booths (see Chapter Ten).

Special Interests

Particularly in large conferences, it can be expected that there will be groups with special interests. A large membership sponsor conference, especially a professional society or association, may be used by nonmembers for their own purposes. An employer can use this opportunity to conduct a smaller conference. Some companies and organizations hold their own public seminar sponsor conferences (usually labeled workshops) just prior to or immediately after a membership sponsor conference.

When possible, all conference-related activities should be built into the conference design, although this task might prove cumbersome, raise some political issues, and usually entails working with additional design committees. However, if they are not made part of the design, they can detract from the conference. One large membership sponsor national conference (of about two thousand participants) was immediately preceded by four small conferences. At first, this seemed like a good idea, as it might bring additional participants to the main conference. Over the years, however, that has not happened. Instead, participants attend the smaller conferences, but most of them leave before the main conference begins. In addition, some of the preconferences have run past the opening of the main conference, which has reduced the number of participants at the opening session of the main conference.

There are other drawbacks to preconferences. Because some participants have already been on site for three or four days, they may become fatigued before the main conference begins. Early arrivals have occupied most of the rooms in the hotel selected as the conference hotel, so new arrivals may have to accept accommodations in other hotels, some of which may be some distance from the conference site. A better approach is to incorporate special interest groups as part of the total conference. Arrangements can be made for them to meet during the conference. They can also be given special attention through the track session approach described above.

Strategies and Aids

General, breakout, and concurrent sessions can be conducted in a variety of formats, using numerous strategies and aids. The following list contains some popular media used in sessions to enhance presentations.

Audiotape	Handout
Audiovisual (AV) aids	Magnetic board
Cable television	Newsprint
Chalkboard	Opaque projector
Closed-circuit TV (CCTV)	Overhead projector
Film	Slides
Filmstrip	Videocassette
Flannel board	Videocassette recorder (VCR)
Flipchart	White board

Descriptions of some other formats, strategies, and aids follow, arranged in alphabetical order.

- *Alter ego.* One participant observes another and then provides immediate or delayed feedback on the other's actions or style of communicating.
- *Annotated reading list.* A list of readings on a particular subject, characterized by short descriptions, explanations, or evaluations of the entries. This is a useful aid in preparing participants who have only limited knowledge of the conference topics or issues.
- *Audience reaction team.* A small group of participants (usually not more than five) is selected to listen to the speaker and then ask questions. They sit on the platform with the speaker or in the audience. If they are expected to ask questions during the presentation, they are best positioned on the platform to the side of the speaker. If they are to ask questions at the end of the presentation, they can sit with the audience and come to the platform at the end of the speech. This strategy guarantees some interaction with the participants.
- *Bibliography.* A list of publications and nonprinted resources that relate to the specific topic of a conference, meeting, or learning experience. The list should contain sufficient information for the participant to obtain a desired resource. A bibliography can be placed separately in the participant packet or included in the participant book.
- *Brainstorming.* Encourages the generation of ideas without a following evaluation. Can also be used in conjunction with problem solving and various forms of creative thinking. Emphasis is on ideas, not on solutions, presented in a free-wheeling and nonjudgmental atmosphere.
- *Buzz group.* A large group of participants divided into small units, usually of no more than six participants, meeting simultaneously. The purpose of the group is to react to a topic or a charge given to them. Emphasis is on ideas, as time is usually limited to ten minutes or less. Provision must be made for feedback. Can be used in a general session with an unlimited number of participants.
- *Case study.* An oral or written account of an event, incident, or situation used to develop critical thinking skills and to attain new perceptions of concepts and issues. Can be used in concurrent sessions.
- *Clinic.* A session, or part of a session, in which the participants react to some common experience they have shared earlier, such as a field trip, or to a unique experience of one or part of the group.

• *Colloquy.* A modification of the panel that uses six to eight persons—half representing the audience, half serving as resource persons or experts. They engage in discussion, usually under the guidance of a moderator.

• *Confrontation, search, and coping (CSC).* A three-part experience in which the participant (1) is faced with a problem or a need (confrontation), (2) is responsible for seeking a solution (search), and (3) applies the solution to the problem (cope). Can be part of a conference design but requires a great deal in the way of preparation and resources.

• *Contract* (by participants). A written document developed by the participant that contains the objectives, methods of reaching them, and evaluation. Although it can be time consuming, it can result in improved participation at a small conference. The contract must be carefully developed and can be included in the participant book or the participant packet.

• *Creative thinking.* Generates fresh patterns, new relationships, unconventional kinds of thinking. Can be used in small groups concerned with listing new ideas or new ways of thinking.

• *Debate.* Two individuals, or teams, take opposing sides of a clearly specified issue. Participants observe, unless other strategies are used for involvement. Requires a high level of oral ability and stage presence.

• *Demonstration.* A presentation that shows how to perform a task or procedure. Can be a live presentation or a prepared media, such as film or videocassette. Should be brief and allow for interaction with the participants.

• *Dialogue.* A conversation between two individuals in front of the participants. Those engaged in the dialogue are usually invited presenters or participants, discussing an assigned topic. They need not present opposing views but should explore the topic in some depth, based on prior learning or experience.

• *Dyad.* Another name for a pair, when two participants work together or talk together. The dyad can remain in the room, or move to another convenient place. Usually, some form of feedback is required when using a dyad.

• *Exercise.* A structured experience, usually using some form of instrumentation or guide sheet. An exercise may be used to introduce a new topic, for skill practice, review, or evaluation. Effective with small groups or when a large group can be conveniently broken into small groups.

• *Feedback mechanisms.* A response system (mechanical or nonmechanical) that provides feedback on how a session is going. If mechanical systems are not available, one alternative is to provide colored cards that participants hold up as appropriate. White can mean that "all is going well," red that "you have lost me," and blue, "I have a question."

• *Fishbowl.* A discussion group that is divided into two segments—an inner circle that discusses an issue and an outer group that observes. Members of the outer group may "tap in" or exchange places with a member of the inner group. Commonly used in groups of twenty or fewer.

• *Forum.* A type of question-and-answer period. Can be used after a formal presentation, when all the participants are encouraged to ask questions of the presenter(s). Interaction is between the participants and the presenter(s).

• *In-basket.* A simulated, reinforcing exercise in which the participant responds to a collection of memos, directives, and problems that force the participant to prioritize, make decisions, and handle the difficulties that might be faced in a real work situation.

• *Interview*. A strategy for using a presenter without that person making a speech. The presenter is asked questions by an interviewer while the participants listen. The questions may be spontaneous or prepared in advance. Likewise, the presenter may respond spontaneously or prepare answers to questions received in advance.

• *Lecture*. A one-way presentation in which a speaker addresses the audience (participants), although it can be supplemented with other strategies. The lecture has been much maligned, as some lecturers do not know how to focus a strictly oral presentation so that it is a stimulating experience. The lecture should be limited in time and content.

• *Listening groups*. Participants are divided into several groups, each of which is assigned the task of listening to an assigned part of a speech, demonstration, panel, or other type of presentation. Each listening group is then provided with time to report or process their task.

• *Observation*. The participant observes and reports on an action or incident. Can be used in connection with exhibitions and field trips.

• *Panel*. A group of several persons having a purposeful conversation on an assigned topic in the presence of participants.

• *Project*. A specially assigned task in which the participants work independently or in small groups on an assignment, such as producing a report or a position paper.

• *Question*. An inquiry designed to test, stimulate thought, or clarify.

• *Readings*. Assigned readings in textbooks, manuals, periodicals and other printed media, followed by some form of feedback. This strategy is usually part of preconference work in that texts, papers from resource people, or documents must be distributed to participants before or during the conference.

• *Role play*. Interaction among two or more individuals on a given topic or situation. Often used to give participants the opportunity to practice previously presented material. Has many variations including multiple role play and role reversal. Requires skilled person to administer.

• *Seminar*. Each participant is expected to be at a required level and to participate actively. A resource person is utilized to facilitate interaction, but all the participants are responsible for interaction during the seminar.

• *Simulation*. Participants experience an actual situation without incurring the risk associated with the real-life situation.

• *Skit*. A short, rehearsed, dramatic presentation, involving two or more people, usually acted from a prepared script. It dramatizes an incident that illustrates a problem or situation.

• *Still pictures*. Photographs usually offered in a sequence to illustrate a point or show the participants a view that would not ordinarily be seen.

• *Symposium*. A series of related speeches by several people qualified to speak with authority on different phases of the same topic or closely related topics.

• *Workbook*. A book of questions or written exercises that provides space on which the participant can write. It can highlight items that the participant should be looking for during the conference, or it can provide material for

participants to take home at the end of the conference. It can also be part of the participant book.
- *Work group.* A group whose participants interact with the purpose of producing a product. Each participant should be highly involved in the process and the product.

Chapter 3

Four Useful Designs

The four designs presented in this chapter provide a sampling of the range of conference design possibilities available. Regardless of the design used, every event should be numbered for easy reference. The use of a numbering system clarifies relationships among the events for all the different people and groups involved with designing and implementing the conference.

The four examples presented in this chapter are:

- Example A: One-Day Design
- Example B: Three-Day Design
- Example C: Five-Day Design
- Example D: Three-Day Design—Facilitating

Throughout the rest of the book, reference will be made to these designs, citing the Example letter.

Example A: One-Day Design

This is a design for a one-day conference for about fifty participants. Most one-day conferences are held for participants living or working in nearby communities. The site is typically a hotel that has a sufficient number of meeting rooms. A sample matrix is shown in Figure 4. Note that the starting times for each event are listed in the form common in the United States. In many parts of the world, and in the military, a twenty-four-hour clock is used (for example, 1:00 P.M. becomes 1300 hours). The notation used should depend on the practice of the sponsor and the participants.

Event 1. Registration is scheduled for 8:30 A.M.; participants are expected to eat breakfast and to arrive at the site by that time. (The time might have to be altered, depending on the traffic pattern and availability of public

Figure 4. Example A: Design for a One-Day Conference.

Event Number	Time	Activity	Location
1	8:30 A.M.	Registration	Lobby
2	9:00 A.M.	General session	Room
3	9:45 A.M.	Concurrent sessions	See Figure 5
4	10:30 A.M.	Break	Lobby
5	10:45 A.M.	Concurrent sessions	See Figure 5
6	11:30 A.M.	Free	
7	12:00 Noon	Lunch	Room
8	1:30 P.M.	Workshops I	See Figure 6
9	2:30 P.M.	Concurrent sessions	See Figure 5
10	3:15 P.M.	Break	
11	3:30 P.M.	Workshops II	See Figure 6
12	4:30 P.M.	Free	
13	5:00 P.M.	General session	Room
14	6:00 P.M.	Reception	Room

SOURCE: *The Comprehensive Guide to Successful Conferences and Meetings* by Leonard Nadler and Zeace Nadler. San Francisco: Jossey-Bass. Copyright © 1987. Permission to reproduce hereby granted.

transportation near the site.) A half-hour is provided for registration to allow the participants to arrive in a staggered pattern. This particular design assumes that most of the participants are preregistered so the secretariat does not expect any rush during the registration period.

Event 2. The general session opens the conference and is planned to take no more than thirty-five minutes. The next sessions start at 9:45 A.M., allowing no more than ten minutes for participants to move from the general session room to the concurrent session rooms.

Event 3. This event begins the concurrent sessions. A plan for these sessions is shown in Figure 5. Note that each session starts with the number 3, a technique that enables all concerned to see immediately the connection between the specific session and what is in the same time block of the matrix. Many variations are possible, but whatever system is used, it must be clear to participants. With a three-digit system, it is possible to have up to ninety-nine concurrent sessions. When nine or fewer sessions are expected, the numbers could range from 30 to 39.

Event 4. A number is also assigned to the break between events to allow for control over the break. A member of the secretariat should have responsibility for the break, and using the number avoids any ambiguity as to which break, when it is scheduled, and so on. A break is an integral part of the conference; it is scheduled at particular times for specific reasons. In this design it serves several purposes. After an hour-and-a-half of continuous events most participants will need refreshments, rest rooms, or just time to stretch their legs.

Event 5. This is the second set of concurrent sessions (see Figure 5). In this design, no repeat sessions are held in this time slot, but provision is made for them at a later time in the day.

Event 6. This free time, or white space, allows participants to engage in a variety of activities without having to miss sessions. If the site is a downtown area, which is a common practice for one-day sessions, some participants may want to use this opportunity to do some shopping or to socialize with other participants, and if free time is not provided, they may have to miss a session in order to meet. There are those who want some sort of change just prior to lunch.

Event 7. This particular design schedules lunch for all participants in one room. When lunch is not provided at the conference, the matrix would list "Lunch—on your own" or something similar instead of a room number or name. The duration of lunch depends on many factors. If the group is eating together, the time allotted for serving will vary, depending on several factors (see Chapter Nine). If there is a luncheon speaker, two hours are usually allocated for lunch. If there is not a luncheon speaker, the participants may use this time for other activities. If the participants are to make their own plans for lunch, the coordinator should disseminate information or make suggestions to help participants choose restaurants with good food and quick service.

Event 8. The sessions after lunch present a challenge, as participants at that time tend to be sluggish. A workshop, which involves participants in activities that require their input and output, can solve this problem. A plan for workshops is shown in Figure 6. Note the use of recorders, who are participants previously selected and briefed for their task of taking notes on the outcomes of the group work.

Of the many kinds of workshops, this one is designed to produce a brief report, based on material in the general session and the two previous concurrent sessions. The results of the workshop are shared during Event 13.

Figure 5. Plan for Concurrent Sessions Used in One-Day Design.

Event 3   9:45 A.M.   Concurrent Sessions

Session Number	Topic	Resource Person	Room
301			
302			
303			
304			

Event 5   10:45 A.M.   Concurrent Sessions

Session Number	Topic	Resource Person	Room
501			
502			
503			
504			

Event 9   2:30 P.M.   Concurrent Sessions

Session Number	Topic	Resource Person	Room
901			
902	(Repeat Session 302)		
903			
904	(Repeat Session 304)		

SOURCE: *The Comprehensive Guide to Successful Conferences and Meetings* by Leonard Nadler and Zeace Nadler. San Francisco: Jossey-Bass. Copyright © 1987. Permission to reproduce hereby granted.

Figure 6. Plan for Workshops Used in One-Day Design.

Event 8   1:30 P.M.   Workshops I

Workshop Number	Leader	Recorder	Room
801			
802			
803			
804			
805			
806			

Event 11   3:30 P.M.   Workshops II

Workshop Number	Leader	Recorder	Room
1101			
1102			
1103			
1104			
1105			
1106			

SOURCE: *The Comprehensive Guide to Successful Conferences and Meetings* by Leonard Nadler and Zeace Nadler. San Francisco: Jossey-Bass. Copyright © 1987. Permission to reproduce hereby granted.

Event 9. Another series of concurrent sessions are designed to give some participants an opportunity to attend some of the sessions they have missed earlier, since they could not possibly attend all of the earlier concurrent sessions. This design provides for two sessions to be repeated during this time slot (see Figure 5).

Event 10. Break time.

Event 11. A second series of workshops are scheduled so that participants can either return to the workshops in Event 8 or form new workshop groups. The decision should be based on the content and expected outcomes.

Event 12. The free time is inserted here partly for the same reasons as Event 6 and partly to provide time for special tasks required of some participants, such as workshop reports. Although these reports can be prepared after the conference, this design integrates preparation into the workshop, so that the reports can be shared while the conference is in progress. The recorders have previously been instructed to meet in a designated room during this period. Under the guidance of selected resource people, the recorders' information is gathered for presentation at the following general session. As only a half-hour has been allocated for this task, data gathering should be carefully planned.

Event 13. In this design the final session of the day has two purposes. The first is to share the reports from the work groups. It is anticipated that participants will remain to hear their own group's report and to learn of the work of the other groups. The second purpose is to serve as the closing session. It does not require a speaker, but some kind of positive closing statements are usually presented.

Event 14. The reception is usually an optional activity. Although not all participants are expected to attend, many do in order to avoid the commuter problems of rush hour. Some employer-sponsored receptions may not really be optional. If upper-level company personnel are expected to attend, others are also expected to attend. A for-profit public seminar sponsor generally uses a reception at the end of the day as a marketing device. Conference personnel mix with the participants to gather unofficial evaluations of the day and to answer questions about other public seminars offered by the sponsor.

Example B: Three-Day Design

The design shown in Figure 7 was used for a three-day conference with 600 participants, although the design could have accommodated up to 1,000 participants. The sponsor was an international membership sponsor. The sponsor did not hold an accompanying exhibition but a literature table was utilized. Specific reference is made to the site (Washington, D.C.), since some of the same type of resources are available in other cities.

Event 1. Registration started at 2:00 P.M. It also included an orientation session, offered in half-hour segments as shown in Figure 8. The decision to provide this orientation was made for two reasons. First, Washington is an exciting city with a great deal to offer. In a sense, it is a city constantly being built and rebuilt so that even those participants who had visited this city several years before would be unfamiliar with new buildings, monuments, and other attractions.

Figure 7. Example B: Design for a Three-Day Conference.

Time	Event Number	Monday	Event Number	Tuesday	Event Number	Wednesday	Event Number	Thursday
7:30 A.M.			4	Breakfast	12	Breakfast	20	Breakfast
9:00 A.M.			5	General session	13	General session	21	General session
10:00 A.M.			6	Break	14	Break	22	Break
10:30 A.M.			7	Breakout and concurrent sessions	15	Breakout and concurrent sessions	23	Breakout and concurrent sessions
							24	Free
12:00 Noon			8	Lunch	16	Lunch	25	Lunch
2:00 P.M.	1	Registration and orientation	9	Concurrent	17	Concurrent		
4:00 P.M.			10	Free	18	Free		
6:00 P.M.	2	Opening banquet			19	Reception		
8:00 P.M.	3	Orientation	11	Dinner and cultural evening				

SOURCE: *The Comprehensive Guide to Successful Conferences and Meetings* by Leonard Nadler and Zeace Nadler. San Francisco: Jossey-Bass. Copyright © 1987. Permission to reproduce hereby granted.

Figure 8. Plan for Orientation Session Used in Three-Day Design.

Event 1

Room:

Time	Topic	Language	Leader
2:00 P.M.	Washington	English	
2:30 P.M.	Conference	English	
3:00 P.M.	Washington	Spanish	
3:30 P.M.	Conference	Spanish	
4:00 P.M.	Washington	English	
4:30 P.M.	Conference	English	
5:00 P.M.	Washington	Spanish	
5:30 P.M.	Conference	Spanish	

SOURCE: *The Comprehensive Guide to Successful Conferences and Meetings* by Leonard Nadler and Zeace Nadler. San Francisco: Jossey-Bass. Copyright © 1987. Permission to reproduce hereby granted.

Second, this conference included participants from other countries. Although the language of the conference was English, it was anticipated that a significant number of Spanish-speaking participants would attend.

Event 2. The opening event was a banquet. The president of the membership sponsor gave a brief speech, followed by dinner and then a speech by a keynote speaker of international reputation.

Event 3. The starting time for this event actually depended on when Event 2 was finished. This was another opportunity for orientation for those who might have missed the earlier ones. The form, however, was much different. A common room was set aside where participants and presenters could meet informally. During dinner an announcement was made that anybody having questions or needing any kind of help could come to the common room. The common room, at that time, was staffed by the secretariat as well as by volunteers, representatives from sightseeing companies, and a travel agent. Literature about Washington was available, and the secretariat staff (local people) answered questions about the design of the conference, events, and related areas. This event also provided an opportunity for participants to meet others whom they had not seen since the previous conference, the year before.

Event 4. A continental buffet breakfast was provided each morning, so that participants and presenters could easily mingle.

Event 5. Given the nature of the organization and the participants, it was decided to use a special form of general session: Each general session covered a different topic and presented three speakers, each representing a different point of view and a different part of the world. A different moderator was used each day to indicate the variety of groups and countries represented by the participants.

Event 6. This was a break during which coffee and tea were available.

Event 7. This event provided for both breakout sessions and concurrent sessions. The breakouts were based on the presentations made during the general session. Each of the three speakers conducted a breakout session for those who wanted to engage in further discussion of their material. The concurrent sessions were based on subjects other than those covered in the general sessions.

Event 8. Lunch was provided as part of the conference, without a program. Buffet-style service offered a variety of foods to satisfy wide-ranging religious and personal preferences.

Event 9. Different concurrent sessions than those provided in Event 7 were offered.

Event 10. Free time (white space) was provided at this time to allow participants to visit various monuments, museums, and other interesting sites, many of which were open in the evening. Another reason was to give participants time to purchase gifts for family and friends. By making this time available, it was hoped that participants would not take time from other events. It worked; attendance at other sessions was good.

Event 11. This membership sponsor had traditionally provided a cultural evening as part of its annual conference. In this conference, the cultural evening started with dinner and was followed by an entertainer (Theodore Bikel) who sang in many different languages. This event reflected the pluralistic society of the United States and met the needs of participants from other countries who wanted to hear their own folk songs.

Events 12-18. The events of the second day paralleled the first day's events (4-11).

Event 19. This reception invited participants and representatives from various international organizations located in Washington.

Events 20–23. Similar to same time slots on first and second days.

Event 24. This free time was provided for participants who would be taking afternoon flights and needed to pack and check out before lunch. Another intent was to provide a break from the sessions so that participants would be ready for the final luncheon with an outstanding speaker, a United Nations official who had been carefully selected for his subject matter and delivery style. His planned presence was mentioned frequently throughout the conference.

Event 25. Lunch was scheduled a half-hour later than on the previous two days, and announcements about this were made during the general sessions on Wednesday and Thursday. Also, at those times, participants were told when the lunch would conclude so they could plan for their departure.

Example C: Five-Day Conference

This example of a five-day conference by a membership sponsor is typical of conferences offered by professional societies. The program is designed for as many as two thousand participants. The site is a conference/convention center with hotels nearby. It is an annual event for the membership sponsor; about 75 percent of the participants attended the previous year's conference. Most of the participants have preregistered. Figure 9 shows the design for participants. (Another program for companions is discussed in Chapter Eleven.)

Event 1. The registration period formally opens at 10:00 A.M. Preregistered participants can pick up their packets in the usual fashion (see Chapter Seventeen), but provision is also made for registering on site. Although the membership meeting and orientation are conducted from 2:00 to 6:00 P.M., the registration area remains open until 5:30 P.M.

Event 2. This annual membership meeting is mainly a formality, as the actual administration of the membership sponsor is handled throughout the year. This meeting is held to satisfy the sponsor's legal requirement to have one meeting a year. Only a few items are actually voted on during the meeting.

Event 3. The orientation session is provided for those who want to know more about how the conference is designed so they can choose appropriate sessions. Volunteers, carefully selected and trained, are available to answer questions.

Event 4. The opening of the conference uses a general session and a keynote speaker. Announcements are made, but kept to a minimum.

Event 5. This is a national organization, but it is organized on a regional basis. This event provides an opportunity for participants to meet others from their own region. Because the event is held in large adjoining rooms, participants have the opportunity to mix and mingle and meet participants from other regions as well. Tickets are provided in registration

Figure 9. Example C: Design for a Five-Day Conference.

Time	Event Number	Sunday	Event Number	Monday	Event Number	Tuesday	Event Number	Wednesday	Event Number	Thursday
8:00 A.M.			6	General session	13	General session	20	A) Special interest groups B) Field trip	26	Concurrent sessions
9:00 A.M.										
10:00 A.M.	1	Registration (to 5:30 P.M.)	7	Break	14	Break			27	Break
			8	A) Concurrent B) Breakout	15	Concurrent sessions			28	General session (closing)
12:00 P.M.			9	Free	16	Exhibition opening and lunch	21	Exhibition and lunch		
2:00 P.M.	2	Membership meeting	10	Concurrent sessions	17	Concurrent	22	Concurrent sessions		
4:00 P.M.	3	Orientation	11	A) Special interest groups B) Film festival	18	Exhibition	23	Exhibition		
6:00 P.M.	4	Opening—general session			19	A) Film festival B) Poster sessions	24	Free		
7:00 P.M.	5	Regional socials	12	Cracker barrel sessions			25	Banquet and recognition night		
8:00 P.M.										

SOURCE: *The Comprehensive Guide to Successful Conferences and Meetings* by Leonard Nadler and Zeace Nadler. San Francisco: Jossey-Bass. Copyright © 1987. Permission to reproduce hereby granted.

packets for two free drinks; after that, it is a cash bar. Finger foods (pretzels, cheese, and the like) are provided at strategically placed tables. Each social can provide food typical of its region, which encourages participants to explore the various rooms.

Event 6. Participants have breakfast on their own at their own expense. The conference day starts with a general session at which a speaker presents a talk based on the theme of the day. The general session also provides time for some brief announcements. Changes in schedules are communicated by a daily newsletter, which is distributed at the entrance to the general session.

Event 7. Break. Beverages are provided at various stations away from the general session room, to facilitate participants moving on to the next event.

Event 8. Breakout sessions are provided for those who want to pursue the general session topic further. The speaker, with the coordinator, has prepared questions for the breakout sessions. Volunteer group leaders can meet with the speaker at a special breakfast to discuss their roles. At the same time, a series of concurrent sessions are presented on topics that relate to the theme of the day, but not directly based on the general session presentation.

Event 9. On this day lunch for participants is "on their own" (the matrix uses the word *free* to communicate this).

Event 10. Concurrent sessions, including about 10 percent repeat sessions from Event 8.

Event 11. The membership sponsor includes a variety of special interest groups, and each has designed a particular session for this time period. As not all participants are involved in special interest groups, a film festival shows selected films in different rooms. The films are provided by the exhibitors at no charge, but they are not allowed to make any "pitch" or distribute any literature during these showings. An interesting part of this event is that only participants who have actually used the films are allowed to show them.

Event 12. Several rooms and conveners are available for initiating cracker-barrel discussions, and participants are free to wander in and out. Presentations of any kind are discouraged by the convener. As these start at 7:00 P.M., it is anticipated that most participants will the leave the site and will be at their hotels and restaurants. A cracker-barrel session will end when nobody is left in the room, and it is anticipated that some of the cracker-barrel groups will opt to go out to dinner together.

Events 13 and 14. General session and break, as on Monday.

Event 15. Concurrent sessions; about 10 percent repeat sessions.

Event 16. At this grand opening of the exhibition area, lunch is provided, courtesy of the exhibitors. Note that in this design, the exhibition is not placed against any other events. The reasons for this, and the various options, are discussed in Chapter Ten. The exhibition area closes at 2:00 P.M.

Event 17. Concurrent sessions, with about 10 percent repeats.

Event 18. The exhibition hall is open again.

Event 19. A film festival similar to the one described in Event 11 is offered. In addition, poster sessions in a designated place to which participants will have been invited to bring materials that they want to post. Participants are invited to browse through the area, stopping as they wish, to talk to a participant who has posted something of interest. Exhibitors are *not* allowed to exhibit products as part of the poster sessions.

Event 20. Special interest groups have three-and-a-half hours for one or more sessions, and others may go on a field trip organized in conjunction with the theme of the conference. Field trip transportation is arranged so that participants can be back at their hotels by 11:00 A.M. to allow time to freshen up and arrive at the conference site by 11:30 A.M.

Event 21. Lunch is again provided by the exhibitors in the exhibit area.

Event 22. Concurrent sessions, with about 10 percent repeats.

Event 23. The exhibition area is open for the last time until 6:00 P.M. Closing activities are designed to attract the maximum number of participants to the exhibit area.

Event 24. Free, to allow time for participants to prepare for the evening banquet.

Event 25. The grand banquet of the conference offers no main speaker but rather brief comments, as appropriate. Recognition is given to those who have served the organization as volunteers in the past year, and the newly elected leadership is presented with all the ritual connected with turning the gavel over to the new president.

Event 26. Because these concurrent sessions follow the evening festivities, attendance is usually light. The sessions include about 25 percent repeats.

Event 27. Break.

Event 28. The closing general session presents some announcements but no major speaker. It is staged to be as fast moving and active as possible. Some information about next year's conference is provided, including a professionally produced film available from the local conventions and visitors bureau.

Appropriate mementos from next year's site are distributed to those who attend this session.

Example D: A Facilitating Conference

We have presented three of the more traditional designs, but the conference presented in this section utilizes a different approach. Part of the conference is designed to allow the participants to make choices. This particular design has been used by several for-profit public seminar sponsors, with the number of participants ranging from twenty to seventy-five. One version of this design (Nadler, 1977) used two coordinators, but we will refer to only one coordinator who worked with a small design committee.

For this design, the facilitators were seventeen special individuals, leaders in the field, who agreed to be part of this design. They agreed to attend the entire conference and to work within the design as described below. As they were leaders in the field, they were also told that they would be in demand and would have to agree to meet and talk with participants informally. The participants received some information during the marketing phase but learned about the flow of the design (see Figure 10) during Event 2B.

Event 1A. At this session, the coordinator walked the facilitators through the design, which consisted of two types of activities. First, each facilitator was to prepare a presentation of one-and-a-half hours on a topic of their choosing. Second, each would meet with one or more participants in informal resource sessions, where they would just sit and talk together.

Event 1B. The conference accepted preregistration, but final registration took place during this period. As part of climate-setting, a common room was established where the participants could meet informally.

Event 2. A short reception was held during which the facilitators and participants could easily mix. A plated dinner was served, and facilitators were encouraged to sit with the participants rather than with each other, although no attempt was made to stage this. After dinner, a member of the design committee delivered a brief welcoming speech to set the climate, followed by a presentation by the coordinator. The design shown in Figure 10 was presented, using an overhead projector. The coordinator described the various forms that the participants were to use in order to trigger sessions.

Event 3. At breakfast, seating was assigned so that each table had at least one facilitator and some had two. The objective was to encourage participant–facilitator interaction during breakfast.

Event 4. Half of the facilitators made presentations during concurrent sessions, and the participants were free to choose among sessions.

Event 5. Break.

Event 6. The other half of the facilitators delivered their presentations at this time. After this event, no facilitator made a planned presentation unless

Figure 10. Example D: A Facilitating Conference.

Time	Event Number	Sunday	Event Number	Monday	Event Number	Tuesday	Event Number	Wednesday
7:30 A.M.			3	Breakfast	13	Breakfast	23	Breakfast
8:30 A.M.			4	Facilitators—presentations	14	Facilitators—presentations/resources	24	To be planned by facilitators and participants
10:00 A.M.			5	Break	15	Break		
10:30 A.M.			6	Facilitators—presentations	16	Conference review session		
12:00 Noon			7	Lunch	17	Lunch Topic tables	25	Closing
2:00 P.M.	1	A) Facilitator planning B) Registration	8	Participant—presentations	18	Facilitators—presentations/resources		
3:30 P.M.			9	Break	19	Break		
4:00 P.M.			10	Facilitator—resource	20	Facilitator planning session		
5:30 P.M.			11	A) Free for participants B) Facilitators—planning	21	Free		
6:00 P.M.	2	A) Reception and dinner B) Explanation of how conference will work			22	Dinner and speaker		
8:00 P.M.			12	Beer and conversation				
8:30 P.M.								

SOURCE: *The Comprehensive Guide to Successful Conferences and Meetings* by Leonard Nadler and Zeace Nadler. San Francisco: Jossey-Bass. Copyright © 1987. Permission to reproduce hereby granted.

specifically requested to do so by the participants. Such sessions were to be repeats of the previously presented concurrent sessions.

Event 7. Lunch was served and again the facilitators sat at assigned tables, recognizing that some of the participants might not have come to breakfast.

Event 8. Because the participants were also experts in the field, they were also asked to prepare presentations. Those who did (very few) were scheduled into this event.

Event 9. Break.

Event 10. In this event, the facilitator served as a resource, that is, there were no planned presentations. Instead, participants could choose to meet with whichever of the facilitators they chose. The participants were asked to fill out a card, indicating the facilitator with whom they wanted to meet. A note was posted on the bulletin board that "Facilitator A will be in Room 320 during this event." Any participants who wished could go to that room. The facilitators were asked to let participants direct the conversation.

Event 11A. The participants were free. Transportation was provided by the site to the downtown area. The common room was available for those who wished to meet there, or to just sit there.

Event 11B. While the participants engaged in whatever activities they desired, the facilitators met to review the progress of the conference. The sponsor also used this time to give a dinner for the facilitators, the coordinator, and the design committee as a sign of appreciation for their work. The dinner was held off site to avoid any possibility that participants might inadvertently intrude.

Event 12. The common room was set up with large tables, kegs of beer, bottles of soft drinks, and bowls of pretzels. The facilitators were transported back to the site for this event.

Event 13. Breakfast, once again with facilitators at assigned tables.

Event 14. Participants completely controlled this event. Facilitators either made repeat presentations or were available as resources, depending on the cards submitted by participants to the secretariat.

Event 15. Break.

Event 16. Participants evaluated the conference thus far. They were told that the information they submitted would be used during Event 20 in order to plan Event 24.

Event 17. By this time, the participants had already had ample opportunities to meet the facilitators, so this lunch was organized around topics previously suggested by the participants. These topics were made into signs and placed on the tables. Some tables had no designated topics for those who desired more general discussion.

Event 18. Similar to Event 14, facilitators either made repeat presentations or were available as resources. Their activities were again triggered by participants' cards.

Event 19. Break.

Event 20. This session used the participant data gathered during Event 16 to plan Event 24, and the opinions of the facilitators were solicited at this time.

Event 21. Free time, designed to allow everyone to freshen up for the dinner.

Event 22. During the planning phase, the sponsor urged the use of a speaker. The coordinator and design committee suggested that this would be counterproductive, feeling that the participants should be in control of the process of the conference by this time. The sponsor overruled the coordinator, and the speaker chosen by the sponsor was used at this event.

Event 23. This last, buffet-style breakfast was completely unstructured; participants and facilitators were free to sit wherever and with whomever they pleased.

Event 24. This session, planned by the facilitators based on input from the participants, was mainly a repeat of earlier sessions offered by the facilitators.

Event 25. The closing was kept informal except for oral and written evaluations.

Chapter 4

Handling Related Events
and Activities

CHECKLIST FOR RELATED EVENTS

Buddy System

_____ Are we familiar with the buddy system?

_____ Would a buddy system be advisable for this conference?

_____ Do we have criteria for matching buddies?

_____ Have we a plan for matching?

_____ Will buddies need any administrative support?

Temporary Conference Groups (TCGs)

_____ Are we familiar with a TCG?

_____ Would TCGs be helpful at this conference?

_____ Have we developed a mechanism for organizing TCGs?

_____ Do the TCGs have a relationship to the conference design?

_____ Is administrative support needed for TCGs?

Mixers

_____ Are we familiar with mixers?

_____ When should mixers be used?

_____ Will the mixers relate to the conference design?

Lounge Areas

_____ Are lounge areas important?

_____ Will lounge areas be available?

_____ When will lounge areas be available?

Focused Activity Rooms

_____ Do we need focused activity rooms?

_____ Will the rooms be staffed?

_____ When should the rooms be open?

Sports and Recreation Events

_____ Should sports and recreation events be scheduled as part of the conference?

_____ What sports and recreation events would be suitable for the participants?

_____ What sports and recreation events are available at the site?

_____ What sports and recreation events can be reached from the site?

Cultural Activities

_____ Will any cultural events be scheduled as part of the conference?

_____ Are cultural events available at the site or at a reasonable distance from the site?

_____ Will the coordinator purchase tickets for outside events?

Home Hospitality

_____ Is home hospitality appropriate for this conference?

_____ Will home hospitality be arranged?

_____ Will support be needed to implement home hospitality?

_____ Does home hospitality relate to the conference design?

Resource Center

_____ Will a resource center be arranged for this conference?

_____ Will participants be charged for use of the resource center?

_____ What are the sources of materials for the resource center?

_____ Will we have a job exchange?

Recognition

_____ Will recognition be given and, if so, to whom?

_____ Will volunteers be recognized?

_____ Is it appropriate to recognize the secretariat?

_____ Will we recognize old-timers?

_____ Will first-timers receive special recognition?

_____ Will the design committee receive special recognition?

_____ When will recognition take place?

_____ How will people be recognized?

_____ What kinds of gifts are appropriate, and who should receive them?

_____ Will an official conference photographer record the events?

SOURCE: _The Comprehensive Guide to Successful Conferences and Meetings_ by Leonard Nadler and Zeace Nadler. San Francisco: Jossey-Bass. Copyright © 1987. Permission to reproduce hereby granted.

Other events and activities can be added to the basic conference design. These events and activities may not be essential to every conference, but the coordinator and the design committee should at least consider them. When a decision is made to include them, they should receive the same attention, budget consideration, and administrative support as any other event in the conference.

Related events and activities cover a wide spectrum. Some, such as a major banquet, should appear in the matrix, while others merely provide interesting alternatives for participants and need not be listed.

The Checklist

Buddy System

Are We Familiar with the Buddy System?

The buddy system matches individual participants so each has someone to relate to at the conference. It can be used in any size conference but is particularly helpful in a large one. It is a one-on-one system, though the number of buddies could be as high as five. Having more than five buddies requires a great deal of organization and administrative support and therefore can be counterproductive. (A variation of the buddy system for larger groups is discussed below, under temporary conference groups.)

Essentially, the buddy system is a temporary relationship, but we have known some to continue and flourish.

Would a Buddy System Be Advisable for This Conference?

Before making a decision to use the buddy system, consideration must be given to the participants and the design. If the participants are unlikely to know each other, the buddy system provides a mechanism for an immediate relationship. The buddy system is especially useful when two distinct groups attend a conference, as in international conferences when participants from the host country are matched with buddies from foreign countries.

Do We Have Criteria for Matching Buddies?

Many criteria can be used for matching buddies, and each must be explored in terms of the purpose of using this technique and the participants involved. One popular approach is to match old and new participants (in terms of attendance at previous conferences) or old and new members. Geography can be another criterion, matching people from different states or regions of the United States. An employer sponsor might want to match employees from different divisions of the company or different installations. If the conference is designed to facilitate relationships across levels of the organizational hierarchy, the match could be between a high-level manager and a lower-level manager (for example, a vice president with a mail room supervisor). Male-female matching must be approached cautiously but may sometimes be appropriate.

Have We a Plan for Matching?

There are many ways to arrange for the matching. The particular technique to use would depend upon the purpose of the kind of climate setting that was desired. Perhaps the simplest technique is to give two participants the same number and instructions to search for each other. In the course of the search, they will meet other people and, indeed, may never find their buddy; however, they will achieve the purpose of the experience—to meet other participants. As the objective of this experience is to encourage participants to meet other people, awarding prizes to those who find their buddies should be avoided.

For a small conference, another fairly simple approach is to post a list of paired names. Participants search for their buddy by looking at the name badges of other participants. This technique also stimulates interaction.

Will Buddies Need Any Administrative Support?

After the initial planning and implementation, no further administrative support should be needed or desired. The meeting, and any further relationship that develops, should be strictly up to the participants. Some participants may not feel comfortable seeking out a buddy and should not be penalized or forced to take part in the experience.

Temporary Conference Groups (TCGs)

Are We Familiar with a TCG?

A temporary conference group (TCG) is a small group (usually ten or fewer participants) who meet as a subgroup during the conference and afterward if they wish. The emphasis, however, is on *temporary,* and participants should recognize that they are not committing to anything beyond the conference.

Figure 11. Information About Temporary Conference Groups (Part A).

We are planning to organize temporary conference groups (TCGs) as an extra service during this conference. These groups are strictly *voluntary* and offer you the opportunity to meet with other participants in a small group during the conference. After receiving your request (Part B), the secretariat will form groups of people with common objectives. When you come to the registration area to pick up your packet, you will be given information about when and where your TCG will have its first meeting. After that, any subsequent meetings will be arranged by you and your group.

If you are interested, complete Part B of this form and return it to the address indicated. If you have any questions, please do not hesitate to call [name of secretariat person] at [phone number].

SOURCE: *The Comprehensive Guide to Successful Conferences and Meetings* by Leonard Nadler and Zeace Nadler. San Francisco: Jossey-Bass. Copyright © 1987. Permission to reproduce hereby granted.

Although this group activity is voluntary, members of the group should plan to meet several times during the conference. Individual members should be permitted to drop out of the group without any penalty or stigma. A conference may start with several temporary conference groups, but very few may last for the life of the conference. This is perfectly acceptable, for a TCG should exist only as long as it meets a need; when the group no longer feels the need, it should be allowed to quietly disappear.

Would TCGs Be Helpful at This Conference?

One criterion to use is the number of participants. A conference of twenty-five or fewer participants would probably not benefit from TCGs. Larger conferences, however, such as those of a membership sponsor, usually benefit from some form of TCG, since it provides an immediate primary reference group for the participants.

Conferences commonly place some pressure on participants, who find themselves caught up in a rapidly moving series of events. Frequently they need to meet with other participants, just to check out their impressions, reactions, and information. The TCG provides this opportunity.

A conference may consist of people of different races, creeds, colors, sexes, professions, and geographical locations. Too often, participants interact only with people just like themselves. They lose the exciting opportunity of mixing with different kinds of people. Just sitting in large sessions with other people does not allow for personal interaction with others, but the temporary conference group can meet that need.

Have We Developed a Mechanism for Organizing TCGs?

It takes time and effort to organize TCGs. If there is the possibility of many TCGs, they should be organized before the conference; if there are only a few groups, they can be organized during registration.

Organization of TCGs can begin during preregistration. Either as part of the registration form or registration acknowledgment, a form should be sent to all participants (see Figure 11). When Part B of the form is returned (see Figure 12), it should be given to the member of the secretariat who is

Figure 12. Temporary Conference Group Registration Form (Part B).

I would like to be part of a temporary conference group. My objectives for this group are: _____

_____

_____

If possible, I would like to be with people who:

Have attended a previous conference   Yes _____ No _____

Are from (geographical area) _____

Have experience in _____

Are interested in _____

Can converse in (language) _____

Other _____

I do not have any special choices: _____

Name: _____

Position: _____

Address: _____
                (department, division, or unit)

_____
                (organization)

_____
                (street or P.O. box)

_____
       (city)   (state)   (zip code)

Telephone (home): _____

Telephone (office): _____ (ext) _____

SOURCE: *The Comprehensive Guide to Successful Conferences and Meetings* by Leonard Nadler and Zeace Nadler. San Francisco: Jossey-Bass. Copyright © 1987. Permission to reproduce hereby granted.

Figure 13. Instructions for Temporary Conference Group Conveners.

To: _____

From: _____
                        (secretariat member's name)

Thank you for agreeing to be the convener for Temporary Conference Group (TCG) Number _____

Attached is a copy of the instructions given to the members of your TCG. As you were previously notified, your function is just to get the group started. The following could be the agenda for the first meeting, but the specific agenda is up to your group.
1. Introductions
2. How do we expect this group to help us at this conference?
3. Any other thoughts or questions?
4. When should we meet again, and where?

As the convener,
You should *not:*
    a. Chair the meeting
    b. Give direction
You *should:*
    a. Be a regular member of the group
    b. Be the liaison with the secretariat if anything special is needed, such as a meeting room or easel

SOURCE: *The Comprehensive Guide to Successful Conferences and Meetings* by Leonard Nadler and Zeace Nadler. San Francisco: Jossey-Bass. Copyright © 1987. Permission to reproduce hereby granted.

responsible for organizing temporary conference groups. To the extent possible, the groups should be organized to reflect the objectives and interests of the participants.

Each group needs a convener, that is, someone to start the group's activities. The sponsor is probably the best source for identifying participants who can serve in this capacity. The coordinator should contact those suggested, discuss the temporary conference group with them, and compile a list of those who agree to serve as conveners. Prior to registration, the conveners should receive an Instructions for Conveners form (Figure 13).

The instructions for TCG participants (Figure 14) should be included in their registration material. Obviously, not all participants will elect to be part of a temporary conference group, so care should be taken that the instructions go only to the appropriate people.

A common problem is to find space for the initial meetings. Depending on the site, some temporary conference groups might meet in sleeping rooms or a lounge area. It is best not to put the burden of finding space on the convener or the participants, since they cannot be expected to be familiar with the site.

Figure 14. Instructions for Temporary Group Members.

Temporary Conference Group Number: _____

To: _____
(participant's name)

Your convener is: _____

Your first meeting is scheduled for:

      Date: _____

      Day: _____

      Time: _____

      Place: _____

Other members of your group are:

_____   _____

_____   _____

_____   _____

_____   _____

_____   _____

SOURCE: *The Comprehensive Guide to Successful Conferences and Meetings* by Leonard Nadler and Zeace Nadler. San Francisco: Jossey-Bass. Copyright © 1987. Permission to reproduce hereby granted.

Do the TCGs Have a Relationship to the Conference Design?

Temporary conference groups should not be included as part of the regular design, for not all participants want or need to be part of a temporary conference group; it is a voluntary activity. It is necessary, however, to provide time for the meetings. If the conference schedule is tight, the coordinator can recommend that they meet at breakfast or another meal. If white space, or free time, is provided, the groups could meet then. If no time is provided, the participants will get the message that these groups should not be taken too seriously.

It is important to ensure that TCGs do *not* become work groups. TCGs should not be given any assignments, and participants should be encouraged to join work groups whose participants are not in the same TCG.

Is Administrative Support Needed for TCGs?

Before the conference, administrative support is required to organize the TCGs. Once they have started, only some minimal support should be needed, although usually they require none at all.

Mixers

Are We Familiar with Mixers?

Mixers are also known as warm ups, ice breakers, or openers. They are activities designed specifically to facilitate people getting to know each other and legitimizing strangers speaking to each other, thus moving participants immediately into the conference mode and helping them feel comfortable with it. When well done, the mixer sets a warm and accepting climate for the conference. Eitington (1984) describes many types of mixers that are appropriate for conferences of fifty or fewer participants.

When Should Mixers Be Used?

A mixer should have a clear purpose or not be held. If most of the participants already know each other, a mixer may set the wrong climate. Some mixers require special space or movable chairs, and if that is impossible, select a different kind of mixer.

A mixer is particularly appropriate for a membership sponsor conference where individuals frequently seem lost and need direction to become involved. An employer sponsor can also use a mixer to acquaint participants from different parts of the organization who may not know each other. A public seminar sponsor can use a mixer to get participants immediately involved in the conference process.

Will the Mixers Relate to the Conference Design?

Mixers should be built into the conference design, with no other event scheduled at the same time. Several mixers may be held, but all should be offered very early in the conference, preferably before the first session or as part of it.

Lounge Areas

Are Lounge Areas Important?

Lounge areas are similar to common rooms or focus rooms, but are much more relaxed, with no planned activities. (The common room is often very active with many small meetings, displays, and other activities in progress.) During a conference, participants frequently need time to withdraw from the hustle and bustle and pressure that a conference can induce; lounge areas provide a place to do this.

The lounge area also presents an opportunity for meeting people. Cocktail-style tables and chairs should be provided, as well as lounge chairs. If the chairs are heavy, they should be set up in groups of four or five to facilitate informal discussion. Easily movable chairs need not be put into any special configuration.

Once an area has been designated as a lounge area, no sessions of any kind should be scheduled in that area. If breakout sessions or small groups are part of the conference design, they should be provided with space other than the lounge area. Usually, no staff is needed for the area, although it may be desirable to assign a member of the secretariat or a volunteer to that area should any questions arise.

Will Lounge Areas Be Available?

In a hotel, many areas may serve as lounge areas but with an important limitation: The lounge area should be reserved only for the use of conference participants. A hotel rarely designates an area for the exclusive use of one group, but it may do so when it has several lounge areas. Part of a bar or other refreshment service area can be designated as a lounge area, particularly when that area is normally not in use, such as in the morning or early afternoon. If that arrangement is worked out with the hotel, it should clearly specify whether participants will be "encouraged" to purchase drinks or food while in the area. The hotel service personnel may see the participants as customers, rather than as participants using the area for lounge purposes.

In a conference site, it may be possible to set up a room as a lounge area. If so, the room should not be near the exhibition area or the session rooms, since its purpose is to provide a respite for participants.

When Will Lounge Areas Be Available?

The lounge area should be open during specified hours, generally when other conference events are being held. If the lounge area has other functions, such as a bar later in the day, it may have to close earlier. In a hotel, the availability of public space may determine what hours the lounge area can be open to the participants.

If the conference has a common room in addition to the lounge area, the hours can be arranged so that the common room is open when the lounge area is closed. The common room should be the more active facility but can serve some of the purposes of the lounge area, if necessary.

Focused Activity Rooms

Do We Need Focused Activity Rooms?

Participants with special interests frequently want to meet others at the conference with the same interests. Conference sessions fulfill some of this need; another technique is to provide a room where the focus is on a particular area of the total conference design. Focus rooms may be helpful in small or large conferences; even small conferences may not have sufficient time or space within the regular design for meetings of participants with special interests. Large conferences can be expected to have several focus rooms. The total number of focused activity rooms depends on the particular conference and the number of rooms available in the site.

No presentations of any kind should be given in the focused activity room. Rather, activity should be informal so that participants can just drop in and talk to others interested in the same subject. Literature or other information that relates to the focus may be placed in the room. Soft drinks can also be provided; this extra should be strictly controlled, however, so that the focus rooms do not compete with each other.

Will the Rooms Be Staffed?

For most conferences, focus rooms should be staffed by volunteer participants who are interested in that particular focus. They are not expected to be experts, but merely facilitators, greeting participants and handling questions. The staff should be given the basic information to answer questions, and a method for relaying unanswered questions to the leader of that particular focus area or the sponsor.

When Should the Rooms Be Open?

Some coordinators prefer not to schedule related events at the same time as regular sessions. At a large conference, however, a coordinator may find that focused activity rooms help keep down crowding at sessions while still meeting the needs of participants.

When a convention center is used, the focused activity rooms will close at the same time as the center. In a conference center, the rooms can be open to any reasonable time.

Sports and Recreation Events

Should Sports and Recreation Events Be Scheduled as Part of the Conference?

Increased attention to fitness and wellness has created interest in providing participants with sports and recreational activities during conferences. These activities can be designed as part of the conference or as an option in the white space or free time. They meet the needs of participants who regularly exercise and would feel uncomfortable missing this experience during the conference.

Because a certain amount of physical activity heightens awareness, it can energize participants for sessions and other conference events. At no point, however, should participants be forced to take part in sports if they do not feel so inclined. Other forms of recreation, such as a nature walk, can be equally beneficial. It is important to have a variety of possible sports and recreation activities, which participants can use or ignore as they choose.

What Sports and Recreation Events Would Be Suitable for the Participants?

The age and physical condition of the participants are major governing factors. Participants who usually do not engage in competitive sports should not start at the conference. Any competitive sport should be carefully planned and monitored so that the competitive drive does not interfere with behavior at the regular sessions.

If sports and recreation are a significant part of the design, the coordinator should utilize the services of specialists in the human kinetics and leisure fields. These fields have become very sophisticated in the past decade and extend far beyond merely organizing teams for a game.

What Sports and Recreation Events Are Available at the Site?

Some sites, particularly some conference centers, are very proud of their sports and recreation opportunities. When a coordinator selects that site, he is also paying for those facilities and should develop the design so the participants can utilize those facilities. There are no standards for what constitutes sport and recreation facilities, so the coordinator must determine if those that are available at a particular site are appropriate for the participants.

Caution should be exercised if all the sports facilities are out of doors. Inclement weather, at any time of year, would make these opportunities unavailable. Indoor sports and recreational alternatives should always be available.

What Sports and Recreation Events Can Be Reached from the Site?

All of the sports and recreation facilities need not be on site. Some sites have arrangements with nearby golf clubs, tennis courts, and swimming pools to accommodate their guests—your participants. It is important to check out these arrangements, including an interview with the sport or recreation facility. When the opportunities are off site, available transportation must be considered.

Cultural Activities

Will Any Cultural Events Be Scheduled as Part of the Conference?

Cultural events include theater, ballet, concerts, opera, museums, and exhibits. For some participants, the cultural events can be as stimulating as the sports events; for a large conference, both types of events may be required to meet the needs of the largest number of participants. As with sports activities, it is possible to schedule cultural events as part of the design or as an opportunity available during free time.

An international conference usually has some kind of cultural event. This can be a field trip to a nearby landmark, demonstrations of local handicraft, or an exhibition of folk dancing and singing.

Are Cultural Events Available at the Site
or at a Reasonable Distance from the Site?

Many cultural opportunities, such as museums, may be easily reached from the conference site. If appropriate, ground transportation can be provided (see

Chapter Fourteen). The distance, however, should be reasonable, in terms of the attraction. Participants may not be interested in riding for an hour each way to attend a two-hour concert, unless it is in some way unique.

Participants should have all relevant information on the cultural event. We recall a group, in the People's Republic of China, who were involved in a type of conference that went from one city to another. In Beijing, though the participants were tired, they were told that the schedule included a Chinese ballet. As the participants rarely had the opportunity to see Chinese ballet back home, they boarded the bus and rode to the theater. The program started with excerpts from *Swan Lake*! During the intermission, exhausted and unhappy participants asked to leave and return to the hotel. Reluctantly, the coordinator agreed.

It was not until the next morning that the participants learned that they had witnessed the first performance of that ballet in China, in conjunction with the Houston Ballet Company. In addition, after the intermission, the entire program was Chinese ballet! They had not understood the reason for the first part and missed the second part solely because the coordinator had not obtained complete information on the event.

Will the Coordinator Purchase Tickets for Outside Events?

A coordinator can sometimes purchase a block of tickets for sports and cultural events, but this can be risky. The tickets must usually be purchased months in advance, and the coordinator may have to pay for the whole block, no matter how many individual tickets are eventually purchased by the participants (although in some cases it is possible to work out a cancellation agreement).

The block purchase can be valuable when tickets are difficult to get, such as for a hit stage show. The coordinator must determine a method for selling the tickets to participants, usually on a first-come, first-served basis, and the ticket prices, either at the box office rate or at a discount.

Home Hospitality

Is Home Hospitality Appropriate for This Conference?

Home hospitality is an arrangement whereby participants who live near the venue city invite participants from distant cities to visit in their homes during the conference. The purpose of home hospitality is to enable the guest participants to experience the home life of the host participants or to allow for more personal contacts. It is a technique usually more applicable to an international conference but can also be used in a domestic conference in the United States.

The hosts are usually participants, but local clubs, groups, and organizations may also be interested in providing home hospitality for visitors, whether from the United States or abroad. The LCVB can provide information on these groups.

Will Home Hospitality Be Arranged?

The arrangement is mainly a matter of matching up host and guest participants. Unless there are some unusual elements, such as language, it can be done by sign-up sheets. The hosts are asked to indicate how many participants they can accommodate, and the participants simply sign up for the arrangement.

Will Support Be Needed to Implement Home Hospitality?

The major support may be transportation, in the case of hosts who cannot provide their own, but it can usually be arranged through some sort of ground transportation or taxi service.

Does Home Hospitality Relate to the Conference Design?

Home hospitality is usually used in a conference of two days or more. The event should be planned early in the design process to allow time for hosts and guests to make their own arrangements.

Resource Center

Will a Resource Center Be Arranged for This Conference?

Resource center is a generic name for a number of activities that can be combined or offered separately. The purpose is to provide participants with an organized way to share information outside of the regular sessions. For a small conference, it may take the place of an exhibition, and even nonparticipants can provide materials. Only printed materials should be offered, as opposed to sales presentations or product demonstrations.

Even if an exhibition is held, there may still be a need for a resource center; in this case, materials should be provided only by participants, not by exhibitors. Admittedly, that is a hard rule to enforce, as some exhibitors may also be participants.

Before organizing the center, it should be determined whether participants actually have helpful information or materials. The intent of the resource center is to provide an additional benefit to the participants, so those benefits should be readily identifiable. If it appears that conflicts with the purpose of the conference may emerge, it may be judicious not to provide the resource center.

Will Participants Be Charged for Use of the Resource Center?

The resource center should not be viewed as an income producer for the conference. If that is the purpose, it is best to handle it as an exhibition or an exhibit, even though it may be a small one (see Chapter Ten). It may be necessary to charge for displaying materials, however, if the coordinator is charged for storage, space, or security. It may be possible for the coordinator to absorb that cost in the conference budget, as the presence of the resource center might be a factor that brings participants to the conference.

What Are the Sources of Materials for the Resource Center?

The primary source of materials is usually the participants, although external sources should also be considered. A membership sponsor might also use the resource center as a way of providing materials about the organization. An employer sponsor might provide company material to the center, such as product and financial information.

Will We Have a Job Exchange?

The job exchange is a low-key technique to help job-seeking participants and employers get together. A membership sponsor, particularly a professional association, would most likely use a job exchange. It would rarely, if ever, be an official part of an employer sponsor conference, even though a certain amount of job exchange information may be shared informally. It could be arranged for in a public seminar sponsor conference.

The exchange can be handled directly by the secretariat, or arrangements can be made with a search firm. Using a search firm, however, can set a commercial tone that interferes with the theme and tone of the conference. Although some participants may be attending in the hopes of obtaining employment, it would be unusual for a large number of participants to have that as a major objective.

If confidentiality is not a factor, it is simply a matter of compiling files of resumes of those seeking jobs and files of job descriptions of those seeking employees. They are open files, and participants are free to look at them. If it is necessary to provide anonymity for either side, a member of the secretariat must be present to provide files only as requested.

Recognition

Will Recognition Be Given and, If So, to Whom?

Recognition events are held for many reasons but primarily as a way of rewarding individuals or organizations for their contributions to the success of the sponsor or to the specific theme of the conference. For example, a conference on the subject of retirement might honor Senator Claude Pepper for all he has done in that area, as well as using the event to focus on the problems and opportunities of retirement or to highlight positive changes in the retirement laws. When a national figure such as Senator Pepper is involved, recognition is also related to publicity for the conference.

A membership sponsor might decide to recognize a private company that has supported its efforts with funds or services or an outstanding member who has made an important professional contribution. An employer sponsor might recognize exceptional employees, such as salespeople who have performed well. Recognition is often given to high-level officials who are about to retire. A public seminar sponsor might want to recognize people who have achieved a goal related to the theme of the conference.

When the recipients are not participants, they should be given a complimentary registration to the conference so they can take part in the recognition activities and any other part of the conference they wish.

Will Volunteers Be Recognized?

Sometimes it is important to recognize those who have worked behind the scenes to make the conference a success. A membership sponsor usually relies on its own members to work on the design and implementation of a conference. This does not include those volunteers provided by the local convention and visitors bureau, but only those who are members or relatives of members, such as spouses and children. They should be recognized, although not in the same way as the people discussed in the previous question. These volunteers might be given a small token or souvenir, or the coordinator can arrange a small reception for them, attended by some of the officers, so they can express their appreciation. They might also be given a small token as a remembrance of the occasion.

Is It Appropriate to Recognize the Secretariat?

In a well-run and successful conference, participants are usually unaware of the secretariat's hard work behind the scenes. The secretariat for an employer sponsor might be overlooked, as they are expected to work and get paid, but frequently they work above and beyond the call of duty. The membership sponsor secretariat frequently involves many of the staff, who assume extra duties during the planning and implementation phases of a conference.

The secretariat should be recognized but in a different fashion from participants or invited guests. A simple direct method is to use the banquet or final luncheon. The members of the secretariat are asked to stand and receive a round of applause. When their work has been exceptional, a letter from the coordinator (to be included in personnel files) is certainly appropriate.

Will We Recognize Old-Timers?

Participants who have attended many conferences of the sponsor should be recognized for their participation and support. A system can easily be set up to keep track of those participants who have been to ten (or any other number) consecutive conferences. Recognition, no matter how brief, encourages others to join the old-timers' ranks.

Will First-Timers Receive Special Recognition?

At some membership sponsor conferences, first-time attendees are asked to stand and receive a round of applause. In essence, this rewards the wrong behavior. Some special attention might be given to first-timers to help them benefit from the conference, but recognition is probably the wrong technique.

Will the Design Committee Receive Special Recognition?

Most design committee members work very hard and should receive some recognition. Their names, and pictures, can be included in the participants' book, and they might be asked to stand at a general session or other function to be recognized. This kind of recognition may encourage others to volunteer to be on the next design committee.

When Will Recognition Take Place?

The placement of the recognition event within the conference design should be carefully considered. The people or organizations being recognized can be sources of publicity for the conference, so the event may have to be scheduled in such a way as to obtain maximum coverage.

The recognition event can take place at the opening of the conference or at a point early in the program. This can be gratifying to the recipients, since they will receive personal good wishes from other participants during the conference. Obviously, when the recognition comes at the end of the conference, such acknowledgement is less likely to happen. It is also possible to have several recognition events, but quantity tends to diminish impact.

Consideration must also be given to the scheduling of recognition events at previous conferences, because participants may anticipate the recognition event to occur at the same time. The schedule can be changed, but care should be taken to avoid the impression that the recognition event is being downgraded.

How Will People Be Recognized?

Recognition can range from a simple announcement at a general session to the gala event of the conference. Recipients can simply receive a round of applause or be asked to make a speech when accepting the award. Pictures of the recipients can appear in the participant book (see Chapter Eighteen) or blown up and exhibited at various places in the conference area. It is possible to provide recognition for recipients through special badges to be worn during the conference and even taken home so recipients can save and exhibit them.

Whatever form of recognition is selected, it should be relevant to the recipient, the sponsor, and the conference. Good taste is difficult to define objectively but must be used in planning recognition ceremonies. For example, a scantily clad female emerging from a cake is no longer considered an appropriate way to recognize a male recipient.

What Kinds of Gifts Are Appropriate, and Who Should Receive Them?

Traditional recognition awards, such as the proverbial gold watch, have been replaced by more imaginative awards. A plaque or scroll with a special message, for example, can be read aloud at the time of presentation. A membership sponsor can award life memberships with an accompanying certificate. An employer sponsor might award a key to the executive washroom or some similar status symbol. Appropriate gifts for a public seminar sponsor are more difficult to identify, as they would have to relate to the nature of the sponsor and the types of participants.

Gifts should project the image of the organization and satisfy the wishes of the recipients. Budget, of course, is also a factor. A sponsor may want to award an automobile, but for a budget of only $200 a gift certificate for professional books may be a better choice.

Will an Official Conference Photographer Record the Events?

Pictures should be taken of the presentations, and recipients should be given copies as part of their recognition. Some pictures may be used for conference publicity, and all of them should become part of the conference record.

If the sponsor has a publication, the pictures should appear in it. Almost every membership sponsor has a publication that goes to all its members; an employer sponsor can use the pictures in its internal publication.

Chapter 5

Site Selection

CHECKLIST FOR SITE SELECTION

Location

_____ How far is the site from participants?

_____ How is the site positioned in relation to preconference and postconference trips?

_____ What is the climate of the site at the time the conference will be held?

_____ What is the distance between the various hotels and the meeting site?

Past History

_____ Have you used this site previously?

_____ Has the sponsor used this site before?

_____ Do you know others who have used the site?

_____ Is the site part of a chain?

Service Facilities

_____ Is a car rental service provided on site?

_____ What recreational facilities are provided on site?

_____ Does the site have any arrangements with nearby facilities?

_____ Does the site charge any special fees for using the facilities?

_____ Are shops located on site?

Accommodations

_____ What is the total number of rooms available for a specific conference?

_____ Does the site have VIP accommodations?

_____ Do all sleeping rooms have media?

_____ Is a newspaper routinely delivered to each room?

_____ Is the level of housekeeping acceptable?

_____ What amenities are provided in the rooms?

_____ Are some sleeping rooms designated no-smoking rooms?

_____ Is room service available?

_____ How early will rooms be available on arrival?

_____ When is check-out time?

_____ Does the site have express check-out?

Site Personnel

_____ Do the site personnel need special orientation?

_____ Are bellpeople appropriately dressed and responsive?

_____ Are front desk personnel polite and efficient?

_____ Is a concierge available to assist guests?

_____ Are the site personnel unionized, and, if so, what is the current status of the union contract(s)?

Public Areas and Facilities

_____ Are there enough elevators to handle the movement of participants?

_____ Does the site have signs to welcome participants?

_____ Does the site have facilities for the handicapped?

_____ Are hallways and public areas neat and clean?

_____ Are public washrooms plentiful, clean, and well equipped?

_____ Are checkrooms available and staffed?

Financial Factors

_____ What type of financial arrangement does the site have?

_____ Does the site provide complimentary rooms?

_____ Does the site offer an off-season or shoulder rate?

_____ Are rates different on weekdays and weekends?

_____ Is a deposit required?

_____ What is the site's policy on late arrivals?

_____ What type of currency is accepted?

_____ Can credit cards be used?

_____ Are purchase orders acceptable?

_____ What is the cancellation policy?

_____ Does the site overbook?

_____ Are there insurance requirements?

_____ Who has responsibility for property damage?

_____ Does the site have any special charge for utilities, particularly on the days preceding and following the conference?

_____ What is the site's policy on additional charges?

_____ What constitutes late payment?

_____ Can the site guarantee room rates?

_____ What add-ons can be expected?

Other Attractions

_____ Are there local attractions nearby?

_____ Will the participants be interested in the attractions?

_____ Does the site management have any reciprocal arrangements with nearby attractions?

Safety

_____ Are site personnel safety conscious?

_____ Does each room have a smoke alarm and/or sprinkler system?

_____ Does the site have a working fire alarm system?

_____ Does the hotel post evacuation procedures?

_____ Are exits on each floor clearly marked?

_____ Are room keys being used?

_____ Are safe deposit boxes available?

_____ Does the site maintain a security force?

_____ Does the site have a house physician?

_____ How close is the nearest medical facility?

_____ Are site personnel trained in CPR?

General

_____ Does the site provide transportation for site review?

_____ Is the site planning any construction or remodeling?

_____ Are internal communication devices available?

_____ What other activities are booked into the site at the same time?

SOURCE: *The Comprehensive Guide to Successful Conferences and Meetings* by Leonard Nadler and Zeace Nadler. San Francisco: Jossey-Bass. Copyright © 1987. Permission to reproduce hereby granted.

It is not possible to overstate the importance of the conference site, or venue. The physical place—its facilities, ambiance, and personnel—can contribute to the success of a conference or to its failure. Considering its importance, one would think that the coordinator and design committee should be directly involved in site selection, and in many cases they are. In too many situations, however, the site is chosen by others.

This is frequently the case with large conferences (over five thousand participants), since there is a limited availability of sites that can accommodate conferences of this size. New sites are being built for this need, but the number of large conferences is also growing. Therefore, it is not uncommon for the staff of the sponsoring organization to make the site decision three to five years before the conference date and thus years before a coordinator or design committee are chosen.

Types of Sites

The Resources chapter at the end of this book provides information about some specific conference sites. It is also possible to write to a site and request floor plans and related material. Recognize, however, that the site personnel want to "sell" their site so caveat emptor—let the buyer beware. Keep in mind that there are a great many different ways to describe or picture a particular site.

The following types of sites are most often used for conferences. Coordinators in the United States who are researching sites in other countries should check with the Office of Security/Foreign Operations Group of the U.S. State Department regarding safety and security.

Hotels and Motels. Just a few years ago, it was possible to call a facility either a hotel or motel. The difference, essentially, was that the motel was designed for road travelers who could reach their rooms directly from the street. That is no longer the case. Today, motels can be multistoried and may not appear much different from hotels. Hotels may have garages adjacent or in the same building. Therefore, references to hotels in this book include both types of facilities.

Over the years, buildings that once provided only sleeping rooms have found it economically advantageous to offer meeting rooms and other facilities as well. A major problem occurs when a hotel is large enough to house two or more conferences at the same time but can really only provide audiovisual materials, staff time, and meal seating for one group. Depending on how they are furnished, the meeting rooms may be more appropriate for social events than for serious conferences. Ornate chandeliers, limited lighting, dark paneled walls, and the like are not conducive to a businesslike conference atmosphere.

Hotels that want to maximize their conference business typically have on staff an individual designated as conference coordinator (or something similar). Hotel managers have become more flexible in negotiating for some of the sometimes unusual requests of conference coordinators and directors.

Conference and Convention Centers. This is a generic term sometimes used to include any facility that accommodates a conference. The International Association of Conference Centers has defined *conference center* as a facility that (1) receives at least 60 percent of its business from conferences; (2) provides a total meeting environment including functions rooms, equipment, sleeping rooms, dining rooms, and recreation areas; and (3) is staffed with professionals who are prepared to serve coordinators and participants.

It is usually a self-contained unit that can handle small conferences—usually about 400 participants at most. If the conference is large enough, it is sometimes possible to contract for the entire facility, which reduces the conflicts that can occur when several conferences are using a facility at the same time.

A *convention center* is a special building that is designed for large conferences but does not have sleeping rooms and recreation areas. They usually have such unique features as rooms large enough to hold thousands of participants for general sessions and ample space for exhibitions. It has rooms that can be used for food functions (though the food is usually brought in from outside the center). When using a convention center, the coordinator must rely on nearby hotels for sleeping rooms. Depending on the location of the center and the proximity of the hotels, it may be necessary to provide ground transportation (as discussed later in this book).

Universities and Colleges. Whether state owned or private, many of the three thousand colleges and universities in the United States have some kind of conference facility. This can range from a few rooms, to many rooms, to a separate building, and even a separate campus or site.

At some universities, only faculty and student conferences may use the site. Frequently, however, the site is also available to outside groups (for a much higher fee than that a university group is charged). Some of the university facilities are equal to those of commercial conference centers, and universities sometimes provide assistance in implementing conferences.

Ships. Despite frequent changes in Internal Revenue Service regulations, ships are still used for conferences. These are ocean-going, registered vessels that cater to conferences rather than tourists and provide special conference facilities (such as conference rooms and AV equipment) in addition to the usual amenities to be found on a cruise ship. It may be possible to contract for the entire vessel or for only part of the facilities.

Resorts and Theme Parks. Sites such as Las Vegas, Reno, Miami Beach, Disneyland, Disneyworld, Williamsburg, and other places of general or historical interest frequently offer the elements needed for a good conference in addition to the amenities of a resort or park. Sponsors frequently refuse to consider resorts and theme parks as conference sites, because they seem more suited to recreation than a serious meeting.

Public Buildings. Buildings owned and/or operated by the government (federal, state, and local) can sometimes be rented for conferences. They range from the prestigious Smithsonian to undistinguished local halls. If there is interest in such a site, contact the appropriate government unit to explore the possibility.

Among the public buildings most difficult to rent for conferences are schools (kindergarten through secondary or any combination of those grades) that were built with federal funds. These schools are restricted to the types of activities and subject matter that can be conducted on their premises. Nevertheless, if the theme and organization are within the regulations, a school building can be a good site, particularly on weekends or holidays.

In-Company Sites. For an employer sponsor, the company premises may be a possible site. Holding a meeting in the company board room or stockholders' room can contribute to the prestige of the conference and can allow upper-level people to attend who would not be able to travel to an external conference site. Keep in mind, however, that when using company sites, participants may find themselves called out of a session to answer phone calls, see visitors, and the like.

Relationship to Other Aspects of the Conference

The site and the design must be congruent. If the design calls for the use of small rooms, the site must have such rooms available. If the design requires a room with a seating capacity of two thousand for general sessions, such a room must be available. Some sites have both types of rooms; others have only large rooms with removable subdividers to make smaller rooms. Obviously, this means designing for this change or selecting a site that has both sizes available at the same time.

Dates become extremely important when considering ships, resorts and theme parks, and public buildings as possible conference sites, for they are not always available throughout the year.

Duration of the conference can be a factor when using a ship. It is usually not cost-effective to have a two-day conference cruise; a longer duration is required. If a public building (such as a school) is used, two days may be fine, but three days may interfere with the building's normal activities.

The time of year is also a factor. Some facilities are more desirable at certain times than others. During the winter, for example, a ship is not nearly as conducive to a good conference as in other seasons. Of course, the particular itinerary of the ship can make all the difference and could be the determining factor.

Written Reports

If several sites are visited during the selection process, it is important to keep a written record. At first, it may seem possible to recall the differences using the literature and collecting name cards, but after visiting three different sites, the data can be overwhelming. A helpful practice is to take along a small tape recorder. Then, immediately after leaving the facility, dictate your impressions, reactions, unanswered questions, and similar points. It is not necessary to transcribe that material, but it is important to have it available.

If numerous conferences are planned and a facility might be used more than once, a written report is very useful for future coordinators and design committees.

The Checklist

(It will be helpful to use a separate checklist for each site under consideration.)

Location

How Far Is the Site from Participants?

Some conferences are national and others are regional. Some membership sponsors move their conferences to different parts of the country each year because they realize that some participants do not have the time or the money to travel across the continent. By changing the site, they draw some different participants each year and are viewed as not favoring any one particular area.

On the other hand, some sponsors do like to hold their conferences in the same city each year; participants know they will be going to the same city and can budget their time and funds accordingly.

How Is the Site Positioned in Relation to Preconference and Postconference Trips?

Preconference and postconference trips are not usually a concern of the coordinator and therefore might easily be overlooked in site selection. The important question is whether participants expect to have these trips. If so, the site should be located near a major airport that provides good connecting flights.

A preconference trip should logically and comfortably end at the conference site. If a significant number of the participants are expected to take part in a postconference trip, this must be reflected in the design. The trip has the advantage of ensuring that some people who might otherwise leave early will stay for the whole conference. It is preferable to choose a site that allows the participants to leave the conference and start directly on their trip, rather than having to make connections. Sometimes, connecting flights just cannot be avoided, in which case, the trips must take into account how flexible the participants are and how willing they are to accept the additional difficulties.

What Is the Climate of the Site at the Time the Conference Will Be Held?

The geographical location of the site generally determines the climate. Northern sites generally have weather problems during the winter, and southern sites may be uncomfortably warm during the summer. This is not always the case, however. There are times when Alaska is warmer than many parts of Minnesota! The time of year is a significant variable, but the jet stream and other factors can upset normal expectations. One conference in the Philippines, for example, was planned based on information that the typhoon season ended in November. That year there was a typhoon in December!

The effect of the climate on the participants will be tempered by their expectations and preferences. For example, some participants desire a northern site during winter because they like winter sports. If the conference is to be conducted totally indoors in one building or in a connected complex, the outside climate may be only a minor factor. With central heating and air conditioning, the external climate has little effect on an indoor conference.

What Is the Distance Between the Various Hotels and the Meeting Site?

The coordinator does not need to consider this question if the facility selected includes both sleeping and meeting rooms, but the question is vital if a convention center is being considered. Time distance is more important than mileage distance, that is, how long will it take the average participant to get from the conference center to the hotels and vice versa? Considering the profile of the participants and the anticipated climate, is it a reasonable walk, is public transportation efficient and available, or must ground transportation be provided?

Past History

Have You Used This Site Previously?

The emphasis here is on *you* as a coordinator. If you are an external coordinator, you may have used the site previously with the present or another sponsor. If so, you have experience with it and may even know some of the site personnel. Do not count too much on this advantage, however, for turnover is high among personnel in many sites. If you are an internal coordinator, the next question is more appropriate.

Has the Sponsor Used This Site Before?

Records of previous conferences become very useful in answering this question. Both internal and external coordinators should determine whether the sponsor has used this site previously. If so, what was the past experience? Did the sponsor feel it was good? Was there any feedback from the participants? Were the site personnel helpful and cooperative? Has the site changed in any way since its last use by the sponsor?

Do You Know Others Who Have Used the Site?

Even if you or the sponsor have used the site before, it is still a good idea to check with others. Whether you had an excellent experience or a disaster, you should not judge from just one experience. If you used the site more than once, it may not be necessary to check with others.

Information from others is helpful but should be considered only as unevaluated data. Their experiences, good or bad, may reflect personalities, unique conference designs, and the like, which may not be relevant to your situation. Sites in continual use should be able to provide testimonials from satisfied clients or at least their names, addresses, and phone numbers.

Is the Site Part of a Chain?

Many hotels and motels are part of national or international chains, and some of these chains produce elaborate books listing the facilities available at their various sites. These books are helpful, particularly during the initial exploration of sites, even though each facility in a chain may be different. Few chains have a national conference manager or a person in a similar position, but as the number and frequency of conferences increase, such a position may become well established.

Some chains provide unadvertised benefits, depending on how frequently a sponsor or coordinator uses their various sites. The coordinator may find that frequent use makes the job easier, since the chain personnel are familiar with the coordinator's requirements and know that satisfaction may bring in more than a single conference. Conference centers are generally one site, independent facilities (although some companies have recently entered the business of managing several conference sites) but may also provide some of the benefits available from a chain operation.

For an international conference, the chain may offer benefits for handling reservations. They might send notices to members or organizations in the countries where the chain has offices or facilities. The chain can also advise on currency regulations, particularly as they pertain to the use of their facilities. Some international chains have special promotional materials about the country where the conference will take place that could be part of the marketing effort. Some of these benefits, and others, are generally available, but do not make this assumption.

Service Facilities

Service facilities are services provided for participants within the facility. Some are managed by site personnel; others are staffed by commercial companies that rent space within the site.

Is a Car Rental Service Provided on Site?

The availability of car rentals is a factor in site selection. Although participants generally do not need cars while attending a conference (and the sponsor may want to discourage car rental because it helps participants leave the conference site), some participants always want the option of renting a car. A rental company may have an office at the site airport, or other location, but it is important to know where the car can be picked up and delivered. For preconference and postconference trips, car rental can be important: The site may be located near some points of interest, such as national parks or historic sites.

What Recreational Facilities Are Provided on Site?

The interest in recreation has been increasing, and more attention is being given to including recreation time in conference design. This is sometimes termed *white space* and may appear as a blank space on the design matrix. If the site has been chosen for its recreation facilities, make use of them. One conference center offered horseback riding free of charge for participants but discontinued the activity after coordinators did not leave enough time for it. Some larger hotels and conference centers have extensive indoor recreational facilities, such as tennis and squash courts, to nullify the effects of inclement weather.

There needs to be a balance between recreation and the conference purposes and design. An Arizona facility had indoor squash courts and outdoor tennis courts that were in constant use by members of the facility, as well as by conference participants. There was no difficulty in scheduling time for those activities. The problem was that conference activities were constantly interrupted by announcements over the public address system: "Mr. Smith, your court is ready. Please proceed to court number six." These messages were repeated numerous times even in the meeting rooms, and there was no way to turn off the system.

Does the Site Have Any Arrangements with Nearby Facilities?

It is not necessary that all the recreational facilities be located at the site. A golf course might be located within a reasonable distance, and the site may have arranged for guest privileges and transportation for participants.

Does the Site Charge Any Special Fees for Using the Facilities?

Special fees may be charged for recreational facilities, but generally these fees can be negotiated for conference participants. During one conference, the coordinator announced the availability of swimming pools at certain hotels and gave the impression that all participants, regardless of where they were staying, could use them. So many participants began to use the pools that the hotel personnel began asking for room keys. Many participants were embarrassed, and this was reflected in their negative behavior during part of the conference.

Are Shops Located on Site?

Most sites have shops that provide basic necessities, such as toilet articles, national newspapers, magazines, and other reading material, snacks, and usually a beauty salon and barber shop. If these items or services are not readily available on site, the participants should be informed where they can be obtained. Frequently, participants can purchase items ranging from bathing suits to ski outfits at nearby clothing stores.

Accommodations

What Is the Total Number of Rooms Available for a Specific Conference?

The total capacity of the site can be determined easily, but a more difficult task is identifying the exact number and types of rooms available for a particular conference. Hotels and motels generally hold a certain number of rooms for vacation and corporate travelers and may also reserve some rooms for other purposes. The coordinator should ask specifically for the number and types of rooms available for the planned dates. The possibilities are generally singles, doubles, and suites; the desirable mix depends on the participants and the design of the conference. If an exhibition is planned, it can be anticipated that exhibitors will want suites to entertain and conduct business.

Does the Site Have VIP Accommodations?

VIPs generally include officers of the sponsoring organization, high-ranking officials of the sponsoring company, public figures who are presenters, and visiting dignitaries. (The coordinator is not generally considered a VIP, even though the facility may treat the coordinator in that fashion.) The VIP accommodations may be a suite or a room that has some special significance. At the Raffles Hotel in Singapore, for example, some rooms are named after famous people who have lived there, and these could be considered VIP accommodations. The site personnel should not assign the VIP accommodations, but rather the coordinator, who knows the politics involved among the VIPs at the conference, is responsible for this task.

Do All Sleeping Rooms Have Media?

The kinds of media being considered here are television and radio. The television should receive regular broadcast transmissions, but it can also receive closed-circuit transmissions, which is an added attraction. The radio would be the conventional one that might receive either AM or FM transmissions, or both.

The radio is not particularly important, but closed-circuit television can transmit conference announcements, information on local attractions, and other relevant information to the participants. It is also possible to send some sessions directly to the participants in their rooms.

At a conference in Miami Beach, several adjacent hotels were used, since no one hotel was large enough to handle the conference. At past conferences of this sponsor, the general sessions were only moderately attended. This year, being in Miami Beach, it was expected that many of the participants would opt for a morning swim. As in the past, the general session speaker was an important person who had been selected a year before the conference. Just a week before the general session, however, this speaker became a controversial national figure and interest escalated. It became obvious that the general session room would not be adequate.

If the sleeping rooms of the various hotels had closed-circuit television, this problem could have been handled easily, but they did not. The coordinator searched for alternatives and found that the hotel bars did have large-size television screens, which could all be put on the same circuit. After the general session room was filled to capacity, volunteers and staff directed the overflow into the bars, which were closed at that hour of the morning. The ambiance may have been distracting to some, but closed-circuit television enabled all the participants to see the session at the same time.

Is a Newspaper Routinely Delivered to Each Room?

Many people routinely read a newspaper every morning and feel their day has not really begun without it. Staying in a different city, they may miss their own local paper but are usually willing to adapt to whatever local press is available. For a business-oriented conference it is not uncommon to have *The Wall Street Journal* or other business paper delivered.

Some hotels deliver newspapers to each room as a regular amenity. In other hotels, it may require a small budgetary provision to pay for this service. Some unusual conference designs may find a newspaper an intrusion. If so, the coordinator would want to assure that there is no delivery.

Is the Level of Housekeeping Acceptable?

A beautifully planned and constructed site can be seriously downgraded by inefficient housekeeping. The only way to determine the level of service is by staying in the facility. Even then, the coordinator must ascertain if special service has been provided or if the level is the same as what is generally provided.

The coordinator should determine housekeeping efficiency by observing public areas. Are ashtrays routinely cleaned? Are the areas clean and free of litter? Have the staff been trained to clean and maintain the areas without inconveniencing the participants? It is disturbing to find a hallway being washed or vacuumed just when a session is ending and participants are moving through that hallway to other sessions.

Certain designs utilize sleeping rooms as meeting rooms. This may be necessary when the design calls for many small breakout rooms or concurrent sessions for eight or fewer participants. If the site cannot provide enough small rooms, sleeping rooms may be preferable to a large meeting room. Using certain sleeping rooms only for meetings presents few problems, although housekeeping may have to provide some extra chairs and possibly remove the beds. If the sleeping rooms are also used for sleeping, it requires careful coordination with the housekeeping department to ensure that the sleeping rooms are made up early enough to be available as meeting rooms. Usually, the housekeeping staff will try to oblige as long as they are notified sufficiently in advance.

What Amenities Are Provided in the Rooms?

Procter & Gamble lists the following popular amenities: shampoo, large bars of soap, toothpaste, hand and body lotion, mouthwash, bath gel, hair conditioner, shoeshine cloth, stationery, cologne/perfume, shower cap, sewing kit, and suntan lotion. These items may not seem significant, but their absence can interfere with the conference. If participants have to shop for some of these items, it means time from conference activities as well as being a distraction. Some of these items may routinely be provided by the facility, but others are available only on special request; if the latter, determine if the site charges extra for them. It may be possible to have a packaged item, such as soap, imprinted with the conference logo. Depending on the quantity, this may not be expensive, and the coordinator may have the cost offset by advertising paid for by an exhibitor.

Other room amenities are on loan, that is, the participant is expected to leave them when checking out. The coordinator, during negotiations, should verify who is to pay for any loan items that are taken by participants. Usually, the hotel charges these items directly to the participants, but the coordinator may want to make some other arrangement.

- *Bathrobes.* In some Japanese hotels, the cotton *yukata* is part of the room amenities, and each hotel has its own distinctive garment. Some robes in American hotels are also attractive, and the hotel sometimes posts a list of prices, should a guest wish to purchase one.
- *Hair dryers.* In the past, the hair dryer was not a room amenity; in some sites one may be obtained only by calling housekeeping. More modern facilities, however, are building them into the room in a special place and with a dedicated outlet. When hair dryers are provided, both male and female participants should be apprised; they will be pleased to leave home an extra piece of personal equipment.

- *Scales.* Increased attention to fitnes has encouraged many sites to provide bathroom scales.
- *Clothing hangers.* In the past, so many guests took hangers with them that many sites installed nonremovable hangers. The coordinator should check with housekeeping to make sure there are enough hangers (including skirt hangers for female participants).
- *Nonallergic pillows.* For a person with allergies, these pillows can be the difference between a good night's sleep and a night of sneezing and coughing. These pillows are available in most hotels, but it is desirable to make sure of this during the site examination.
- *Drawer space.* Drawer space can become a real problem when a conference is five days long or when there are many different types of events and participants have brought several changes of clothing. Although the coordinator cannot usually obtain additional drawer space, the information can be helpful to participants when planning their conference wardrobes.
- *Desks.* Desks can be helpful if participants have to do written work in their rooms.

Are Some Sleeping Rooms Designated No-Smoking Rooms?

Some sites now designate a certain number of rooms, sometimes entire floors, nonsmoking areas. There are good reasons for doing this. It is very important for allergic guests, and, in addition, some sites have found no-smoking rooms to be less costly to maintain than rooms where smoking is allowed. Participants should be notified if such special rooms/floors are available.

Is Room Service Available?

Most hotels have some kind of room service, but the question is, how good it is.

Different countries have different practices, as one would expect. For an international conference held at a prominent hotel in Mexico City, some of the United States and Canadian participants arrived after 10:00 P.M., due to irregular flight schedules. Some called for room service and were told either that none was available or that it was limited to one or two dishes, responses that produced many negative ethnocentric comments. (Generally, Mexican hotel guests do not use room service in the evening.) Actually, since Mexicans eat dinner late, the dining room and restaurants in the hotel were open, and many participants were there eating and socializing. If the North American participants had known that, they would gladly have gone to the restaurant to meet other participants.

How Early Will Rooms Be Available on Arrival?

Checking into a site is frequently a traumatic experience, particularly when participants have traveled long distances, encountered traffic difficulties, delayed flights, and the like. Early check-in will not be a problem if the facility has space, but where space is limited, it is essential that participants realize that early check-in may not be feasible. (Late guaranteed arrivals and sites not honoring reservations are discussed in another question.)

Delays are sometimes unavoidable, yet the coordinator should always discuss check-in time with site personnel. If the check-in time conflicts with expected arrivals, alternatives should be explored. It may be possible to arrange for rooms for a quick wash up, and the concierge can be alerted so that luggage can be stored. The site may provide a free drink or another amenity that at least shows the hotel's concern when the room is not ready.

When Is Check-Out Time?

Most sites have a posted check-out time, which generally varies depending on the number of rooms to be vacated, the number of rooms needed at a given time for incoming guests, and the housekeeping schedule. The participants should be informed of the expected check-out time and how to make arrangements for late check-out.

The check-out time is a factor in design. Too often a design schedules its last session to end at 12:00 noon—the same time as check-out in many sites. If no later check-out time is arranged, some participants are forced to miss the conference closing.

The conference closing sessions and the check-out time should be carefully coordinated, and often a later check-out can be negotiated. Frequently, however, this arrangement is made months in advance when the site is not particularly busy. At the time of the conference, the site may be under pressure because of the arrival of a new group of participants. Check-out, then, should be stated in writing when negotiating for the site.

Many sites, particularly hotels, offer a variety of options. For example, a block of rooms can be held aside for late check-out—particularly important when many of the participants are departing by air. Although check-out time may be 3:00 P.M. (generally the latest time without incurring an additional expense), air departure may not be until 10:00 P.M. What do participants do meanwhile? Because the conference is completed, some believe that this interim is not the responsibility of the coordinator, but for the participants it is still part of the total conference experience. They may view this conference, and any future ones by that sponsor or site, as unfinished until they leave for the airport.

When the coordinator and the site personnel work together, they can find many alternatives to cope with that situation. Arrangements can easily be made for storing baggage in a secure place at the site. The participants could have the option of last-chance shopping or a sightseeing tour that fits within the time available. The site may have some special activity that can be scheduled during that time. Any activities during that time period should be strictly optional, as participants prepare for departure in many different ways.

Does the Site Have Express Check-Out?

Many hotels have express check-out systems. In one common system, guests present a credit card when they check in and just drop off their room keys at check-out time; their bills are sent by mail. Too many hotels, however, still use the traditional check-out procedure, which means long lines and short tempers. To shorten the delay, some sites provide guests with a copy of the bill the evening before check-out. In this way, the guest can review the bill privately and shorten the check-out procedure for everyone. If the hotel has this option, participants should be informed in order to give sufficient notice to the cashier. For an employer sponsor, it is frequently easier to have the site bill the sponsor, and the secretariat can make any financial allocations later.

Site Personnel

Do the Site Personnel Need Special Orientation?

Specific orientations are generally not necessary for conference centers, as they deal only with conferences and handle many of them. If the design is unique in any way, however, a special orientation may be required. For hotels, a special orientation may be necessary, as site personnel change frequently. If it is a well-managed site, the coordinator may only have to work with the conference manager or another designated individual.

A special orientation may cost money, for it takes time, and the site personnel involved in it will not be available for other duties. The special orientation may be added to the bill, or the site manager may find that a special orientation actually provides a training program for various site personnel and may therefore not assess any charge. This charge should be negotiated at the time of site selection.

Are Bellpeople Appropriately Dressed and Responsive?

The doorman and the bellpeople are usually the first site personnel the participants meet. The doorman should be clearly identifiable and knowledgeable. If participants are expected to arrive by car, the doorman should know the exact procedures for taking care of cars, whether parking is on the street, valet, or other type. It is disturbing to the arriving participant to be told, "Oh, just leave your car there. Someone will take care of it."

Hotel bellpeople should help with the luggage. Although motels usually do not provide this service, the site may provide personnel to carry the luggage of handicapped participants; this should be determined during the site visit. (For a thorough discussion of handicapped participants, see Chapter One.)

Bellpeople usually wear some kind of uniform, but at some sites the bellperson is identified only by a name tag. If that is the case, this information should be communicated to the participants to avoid confusion and anxiety.

Are Front Desk Personnel Polite and Efficient?

The front desk personnel are the next people to greet the participants. The coordinator can evaluate their behavior by lingering near the registration desk, listening and observing how they greet and handle incoming guests. Try to be at the desk when they handle groups similar to yours. For example, if the anticipated participants will be arriving by air, observe what happens when the airport bus arrives. We have found the major front desk problem is understaffing, but some sites alleviate this problem by assigning additional personnel to the front desk during a rush. Conference centers may not have a front desk but generally do make some provision for greeting incoming participants. As these practices vary, the coordinator should listen and observe how incoming participants are greeted and processed at these sites as well.

Is a Concierge Available to Assist Guests?

The term *concierge* originated in France but is gaining acceptance in the United States. At one time, a concierge was similar to a bell captain, but today these jobs differ. The concierge, for example, has little to do with luggage but is more concerned with other aspects of the guests' welfare and convenience, such as providing maps, theatre and touring reservations, and information on airline schedules; confirming reservations; arranging ground transportation; and responding to emergency situations. If the facility has a good concierge and the participant group is not too large, some of the responsibilities of the secretariat can be delegated to the concierge.

Are the Site Personnel Unionized, and, If So, What Is the Current Status of the Union Contract(s)?

Unionized site personnel have a substantial effect on some aspects of conference planning.

The coordinator should learn which personnel are unionized and which are not and then be prepared to ask such questions as: What is the status of the contract? When was the last negotiation? When is the contract up for renewal? What will be the status of the contract at the time of the conference? If the contract is due to expire before the conference date, there might be protracted negotiations and even a strike. Although strikes are not common, a strike of even a few hours during a conference can destroy the design and turn the well-planned conference into chaos. Some participants may be union members or sympathizers and refuse to cross a picket line.

If the particular site is a desirable one despite possible union problems, ascertain the general relationship between the union(s) and the site. Ask to speak to the shop steward or other union official. Share your concerns openly. After all, the union does not want to get a bad reputation, be responsible for cancellations, or harm the employer. The issue of unionized personnel is discussed throughout this book, as it is a major factor. This is so important that the Jacob K. Javits Convention Center in New York City in 1986 appointed a labor "czar" for two years to rule on labor disputes. The center has seventeen unions involving staff and suppliers. A labor czar is an important factor in coordinating the bargaining and settlement of disputes that can disrupt or make a conference unworkable.

Public Areas and Facilities

Are There Enough Elevators to Handle the Movement of Participants?

Conferences conducted entirely on one floor present no real problem, but many hotels were built essentially to provide sleeping rooms. When sleeping rooms on the lower floors are converted to meeting rooms, the result can be an elevator crush. As participants attempt to return to their sleeping rooms on the upper floors, they may be confronted with elevators that are partially or totally filled. When meeting rooms are located on several floors of the facility, the problem is exacerbated. Because convention centers typically have only two or three floors and no sleeping rooms, elevators are usually not a problem; vertical movement is handled by escalators or stairs.

Does the Site Have Signs to Welcome Participants?

Many sites now have marquees at or near the entrance of the facility. These signboards generally advertise some aspect of the facility. Motel marquees advertise the food service, in-room movies, or other special features. Generally, at no extra charge, the site manager will replace these commercial notices with one welcoming the participants to the conference; this type of sign also helps the site advertise its availability for conferences.

A welcoming sign makes the participants feel catered to; they also know they have come to the right place. During the conference, participants often have their pictures taken in front of the sign.

Does the Site Have Facilities for the Handicapped?

An increasing number of facilities have special facilities for the handicapped, including ramps, elevators with braille numbers, and so on. (See Chapter One for detailed discussion of these facilities.)

Are Hallways and Public Areas Neat and Clean?

The coordinator can assess the condition of the hallways by walking through them, as the participants will do at the conference. If possible, the coordinator should take walks at different times of the day, looking for obstacles such as low ashtrays or other wall projections that can be significant hazards to the handicapped and large groups of participants.

Are Public Washrooms Plentiful, Clean, and Well Equipped?

The term *public washrooms* encompasses similar terms such as restrooms, toilets, gentlemen and ladies, and powder rooms. The number and distribution of restrooms are factors to consider in relation to the location of meeting rooms and the number of participants expected. As with hallways, several visits may be necessary to determine their usual condition. (A male coordinator should bring a female colleague and vice versa, as the condition of one gender's washroom may not be a fair indication of the other.)

Some exclusive hotels have washroom attendants who expect to be tipped by patrons. In such cases, this information should be communicated to the participants or arrangements should be made for a blanket tip, with the understanding that attendants will not solicit tips from participants (usually by displaying a small sign noting that the gratuity has been taken care of by the sponsor).

Are Checkrooms Available and Staffed?

If the sleeping and meeting rooms are in the same building, or the climate of the site is warm, checkrooms are usually not a factor. If checkrooms are needed, their locations should be established. Hotel checkrooms may be near the meeting rooms, but not necessarily so. Although nothing can be done to move the checkroom, signs showing the location of the checkroom(s) can be helpful. The gratuity question can be handled in the same way as with washrooms.

Financial Factors

What Type of Financial Arrangement Does the Site Have?

Hotels have various plans; the three major types are the European Plan, the American Plan, and the Modified American Plan. The coordinator should ask for specific details as to what is meant by these designations at the particular site.

Does the Site Provide Complimentary Rooms?

Complimentary rooms are provided by the site at no cost to the sponsor. They may be sleeping rooms, meeting rooms, or some combination of both. Almost all facilities provide complimentary rooms, but the number and level of complimentary rooms is a highly negotiable item. It is essential that the final agreement on complimentary rooms be put in writing.

Hotels base the number and level of complimentary rooms on the number of sleeping rooms and the number and type of food functions that the coordinator books. A general rule of thumb (but certainly subject to negotiation) is the allowance of one complimentary sleeping room for each fifty sleeping rooms booked. It is sometimes possible to negotiate that the complimentary sleeping room be a suite that might otherwise not be booked. This arrangement gives the sponsor a suite, allows the facility to fill a vacancy, and reserves regular sleeping rooms for conference participants or other hotel guests.

If the site will be providing meals for the participants, this can be used to negotiate for complimentary rooms and should be determined early enough to be reflected in the design and budget. This negotiation has no rule of thumb, but rather must be negotiated on a case-by-case basis, depending on the number and frequency of meals and breaks.

When complimentary sleeping rooms are negotiated, the coordinator must decide how these rooms are allocated and who receives them; this decision can become a political factor, particularly in the case of a membership sponsor.

For a one-day conference, it is not uncommon for a hotel to negotiate a package that includes the meeting room(s) and the food service; the coordinator must determine if the package is preferable to separate charges for each item. In conference centers, negotiating packages is usually not a factor, and some offer only a total figure for the entire conference, including sleeping rooms, meeting rooms, and meal functions. It is still possible, however, to negotiate some complimentary packages.

Does the Site Offer an Off-Season or Shoulder Rate?

Sites usually charge lower rates (called off-season or shoulder rates) during certain times of the year when they do not expect much business. For example, summer is generally considered off-season in Florida and Hawaii; winter is off-season for many northern sites (but not those that cater to ski patrons). A facility that has outdoor recreational facilities, such as tennis and swimming, would be off-season during those times when weather can interfere with those activities. For some cities, off-season is not a factor of weather. Washington, D.C., for example, is off-season from October to April only because it has a higher tourist level from May to September. If a particular site, or a particular part of the country, is attractive for a conference, consideration should be given to scheduling during the off-season. If the sponsor insists on scheduling during the season, however, this decision must be accommodated.

Are Rates Different on Weekdays and Weekends?

Many sites offer lower rates on weekends than on weekdays. If the coordinator has flexibility, scheduling the conference on a weekend could produce significant financial benefits for the sponsor and the participants.

Is a Deposit Required?

This may seem like a simple matter, but it actually can become very complex. For large conferences, participants' hotel reservations are usually *not* made through the hotel but rather through the local convention and visitors bureau. In some cases, the bureau sends a confirmation, telling the participant which hotel has been reserved, the rate, and the expected time of arrival, but information on deposits may not be included. The bureau apparently expects that either participants know they must send a deposit, or that the hotel, on receiving a copy of the reservation, will inform the participant of the required deposit. Unfortunately, neither is done in many instances, and the participant arrives to find that the room has not been reserved. The coordinator should not get involved in checking on individual deposits but should determine the procedure and, if a deposit is required, ensure that participants get the message.

What Is the Site's Policy on Late Arrivals?

Many sites consider a late arrival to be after 6:00 P.M., but individual sites establish their own times. If late arrival is guaranteed, does the site require advance payment or credit card information? Both practices are in common use and participants should be informed.

What Type of Currency Is Accepted?

Where international reservations are concerned, this can be a bit more complicated. If the site is part of an international chain, a reservation made in one country will presumably be honored in the country where the conference is being held. The coordinator, after checking on the procedure, should determine what kind of confirmation is acceptable to the conference hotel. International reservations also raise the question of foreign exchange, since some hotels accept a check payable in U.S. dollars, but only if it is received early enough to clear before the participant arrives. In some countries, the hotel must be paid in local currency. Given the possible complications, the coordinator should make sure that the participants are informed. An alternative is to place the entire matter in the hands of a responsible travel agent.

Can Credit Cards Be Used?

Although most sites accept credit card payments, a few sites insist on being paid in United States dollars or local currency. The method of payment should be clarified as early as possible and the information communicated to the participants.

Another issue to resolve is which credit cards are accepted. Although the American Express card is acceptable at almost all sites, some hotels in some countries prefer a local credit card, such as VISA, MasterCard, or some similar bank card that is easily handled by a bank in that country or favored in that locality.

Are Purchase Orders Acceptable?

Purchase orders are frequently used by government agencies and occasionally by some private companies. Participants need to know in advance whether a purchase order will be accepted.

What Is the Cancellation Policy?

Each site has its own cancellation policy, which should be negotiated and stipulated in writing. A coordinator may negotiate in good faith for a conference but cancel the conference later for any number of reasons. The site usually has some kind of penalty clause, depending on how much prior notice is given. This is an area that can be lucrative for lawyers but devastating for the coordinator and the site. It is much better to have a clear statement up front, stating the responsibilities of both parties in regard to cancellation and the respective penalties.

It is not always the coordinator who cancels. One large membership sponsor "contracted" for almost all the rooms in a large, major-chain hotel. Quotation marks are used because the coordinator for the membership sponsor neglected to formalize the booking with a signed contract. Publicity was sent out announcing the conference at that specific hotel. About six months prior to the conference, while checking on some details, the coordinator was shocked to find that he did not have a solid booking. Someone in the conference office of the hotel had double booked those dates, and even though the second conference was negotiated much later, it had a signed contract. The site employee had neglected to inform the coordinator of the first conference that the oral agreement would not be binding. The hotel employee was subsequently discharged, but that did not help the coordinator who, on six months' notice, had to find a new booking for a conference of over four thousand participants plus exhibition space. Ultimately, the conference was moved to another city, to less-than-adequate facilities.

Does the Site Overbook?

Very few sites overbook, but it does happen. One New York City hotel negotiated with a coordinator at a time that economic prospects were not good. Consequently, the coordinator had been able to negotiate an extremely favorable room rate. In good faith, participants made reservations and received confirmed registrations. Two years later, when the conference was held, the front desk refused to honor the reservations, saying that there had been an error! The hotel lobby looked like a refugee center, as hundreds of participants milled around or sat—devastated—on their suitcases.

We were presenters at this particular conference and we knew some of the hotel staff. They confided to us that after an upturn in economic conditions, rooms had subsequently been reserved at higher rates, resulting in overbooking. We showed the coordinator a sign at the registration desk that clearly stated if a confirmed registration was not honored, the individual's rights were protected by the City of New York. The notice gave a specific phone number to call. We suggested that the coordinator make use of the number, but the coordinator demurred. Ultimately, all the participants were housed, but many had horror stories to tell. Some had to go by taxi, at their own expense, to nearby hotels. (The law specifically stated that in such a case the overbooked hotel was to pay the taxi fare!) Others were forced to stay at other hotels at much higher rates. As can be imagined, the opening hours of the conference were overshadowed by participants sharing their horror stories!

Overbooking is not always the fault of the facility. Given their experience with no-shows, sites might understandably overbook; the coordinator, however, should know the local laws and what recourse participants have under such circumstances.

Are There Insurance Requirements?

Increasing attention is being paid to insurance coverage for some conference activities. The coordinator cannot assume, however, that the site carries all the necessary insurance. The conference budget might also have to provide for insurance premiums for personal and property loss and damage. Insurance is a specialized area, and the coordinator should seek appropriate legal assistance.

Who Has Responsibility for Property Damage?

Participants sometimes engage in activities that are not part of the design and that can result in property damage to the site. Usually, the site has some insurance for this, but would obviously prefer to collect directly from the sponsor.

　　One coordinator conducted a conference for an employer sponsor at a ski resort. Some participants who did not ski spent their time inside drinking and generally having a riotous time. When the skiers returned, they were bombarded with empty bottles, ash trays, and other paraphernalia. The skiers counterattacked with ski poles, snow, and anything that was not nailed down. (In fact, even some of the nailed-down items were wrenched from their positions and used in the melee.) Fortunately, there were no personal injuries, but the property damage was more than $10,000—a surprisingly low figure considering the extent of the encounter. The coordinator was horrified but was advised by the sponsor to pay; apparently this sort of thing happened every year. Although payment for the damage was not built into the budget, the sponsor provided the funds, having planned ahead of time for this payment.

Does the Site Have Any Special Charge for Utilities,
Particularly on the Days Preceding and Following the Conference?

Generally speaking, the cost of utilities is built into site costs, but some exhibits or demonstrations use equipment that draws inordinate amounts of power. If such is the case, the site may assess an additional charge particularly prior to agreed times for setup and knockdown, or before the conference opens or after it closes.

What Is the Site's Policy on Additional Charges?

If all parties have negotiated effectively, there should not be any additional charges. However, sometimes the site assumes that the coordinator knows about additional charges for certain services, equipment, or space. One way to handle unspoken assumptions is to list all the charges by item and to agree that no additional items can be added. Specific charges should be listed next to each item, but this is not always possible during early negotiations. If any doubts remain, all parties should agree on a minimum-maximum range that can be charged for each stated item.

What Constitutes Late Payment?

The site provides space, renders services, and expects to get paid. Some sites insist on payment at time of completion (check-out time); others allow fifteen or thirty days, though this became less prevalent during the days of double-digit interest rates. All parties should agree on when outstanding bills are to be paid, and the coordinator should not hold back payment to the site until all payments have been received from the participants and exhibitors. This policy can cause some cash flow problems for the coordinator, but that should be taken into account at the time of budgeting and negotiating agreements.

Can the Site Guarantee Room Rates?

At the time of negotiation, each side tries to make the most advantageous financial arrangement. Although the participants usually pay for their sleeping rooms, the rates must be in line with their expectations. One risky approach is to establish a range of rates that will be in effect at the time of the conference. The most desirable approach for all concerned is to have a fixed and guaranteed rate at the time the negotiations are completed.

What Add-Ons Can Be Expected?

In addition to the negotiated rate for sleeping rooms, some add-on costs, such as sales tax and room tax, are generally charged. In recent years, these amounts have increased, and some participants have been caught by surprise. Naturally, the extra charges affect their reaction to the conference, and they complain to the coordinator. (For an employer sponsor, the participants will probably not complain, as the charges will be reimbursed by the sponsor, but the coordinator needs to know the add-on costs anyway for budget purposes.) Generally, the coordinator should inform the participants of all add-on costs. Although tax rates change, the coordinator can inform the participants of the tax rates at the time the conference is announced. The rates may increase, but usually the increase will not be staggering. The taxes can usually be waived for participants from government and nonprofit organizations, on presentation of the required documentation.

Add-on charges for telephone service are more complex and difficult to accept. In recent years, these charges have escalated to the point where they can seriously affect the budget for an employer sponsor conference and the attitude of participants at a public seminar sponsor or membership sponsor conference. A small charge of less than a dollar for local calls has become generally accepted, but for long-distance calls, particularly those that are operator-assisted, the charges can escalate rapidly: It is not unknown for a hotel to add a 50 percent surcharge! All such surcharges should be itemized at the time of confirmation, which would eliminate some hostilities at check-out time.

In many foreign countries, hotels traditionally add about 15 percent to the bill for service, presumably, the replacement for the U.S. practice of tipping. The U.S. participant attending a conference overseas may not be aware of this, tip as usual, and later be aghast at the additional 15 percent.

Preconference information should inform the participant of the tipping practices in the particular country where the conference is being held.

The same holds true for international participants attending a conference in the United States. Unaccustomed to the practice, international participants may not tip, causing some of the site personnel to feel they have been "stiffed." This affects the relationship between the coordinator and the hotel the next time a similar conference is planned.

Other Attractions

Are There Local Attractions Nearby?

Many sites are near unique local attractions. For example, a conference held in Washington, D.C., offers such attractions as monuments, Congress, and the White House. In San Antonio, there is the Alamo. The coordinator should be aware of these attractions, relying on site personnel, the LCVB, local historical societies, and other community and civic groups for such information.

Will the Participants Be Interested in the Attractions?

Interest will depend on the nature of the conference and the particular participants. Generally, for the public seminar sponsor and the employer sponsor the local attractions are secondary. They will only be of significance in an incentive type of conference, where participants are being rewarded. For the membership sponsor, the attractions can be extremely important as an added feature and can make conference attendance more attractive.

If the attractions are of interest, the coordinator should make appropriate plans in the design to provide the time for visiting the attractions. In one conference in Mexico City, the venue was a hotel within walking distance of the world-renowned Anthropological Museum. Recognizing the proximity, the coordinator arranged for one of the conference lunches to be held at the museum, on a day when it was closed to the public. In addition, interested participants were given a special tour of the museum. For a conference in Amsterdam, the coordinator arranged for the opening cocktail party to be held at the Van Gogh Museum. The participants were free to walk through the museum during the party.

Does the Site Management Have Any Reciprocal Arrangements With Nearby Attractions?

The site management may have some special arrangements with local attractions that can inure to the benefit of the coordinator and the participants. The attractions may, for example, provide free transportation or reduced fees for the participants.

Safety

Are Site Personnel Safety Conscious?

Participants are increasingly concerned with safety, which should also be a major concern of the coordinator, who has some implied responsibility for their safety. When exploring different sites, the coordinator should keep safety factors in mind. During negotiations, the coordinator should also request a warranty statement that the site must meet or exceed all applicable safety codes—documentation that could reduce the sponsor's liability in case of an incident that involves a safety code violation.

Does Each Room Have a Smoke Alarm and/or Sprinkler System?

In some localities, alarms and/or sprinklers in each sleeping room of a hotel are mandatory; in other localities, it depends on a variety of factors. For example, the requirement may be that only those facilities built after a certain date need have those safety factors.

Does the Site Have a Working Fire Alarm System?

Just having a fire alarm system is not sufficient; the coordinator should inquire as to when the system was last tested. If the date is in doubt, the local fire department can provide that information. To allay fears and assist participants, the coordinator can obtain a pamphlet on fire safety hints for hotel/motel occupants, which is available from local fire stations, the site, or a state office, such as the Office of Fire Prevention and Control in Albany, New York.

Does the Hotel Post Evacuation Procedures?

In most U.S. hotels, an evacuation plan is posted on the door of the sleeping room or close to it. This plan should be brought to the attention of the participants. The coordinator should also be sure that the secretariat knows of the evacuation plans for the various meeting rooms.

Are Exits on Each Floor Clearly Marked?

Exits are not always clearly marked. For esthetic reasons, exit signs are sometimes placed flush with the doorway rather than projecting out into the hall. During one conference, we left our hotel room to find the hallway blanketed with heavy smoke; we could not see the exit signs. Fortunately, we follow the practice of noting the location of floor exits when we check into our room. We found the exit, and the sign was well lit, but it could only be seen when standing directly in front of it!

Are Room Keys Being Used?

Although the room key is still the most common method of entry, other forms of room access have been developed for security reasons. One newer form gaining wide acceptance is the room card, a computerized card that slips into a slot in the door or the door handle. The code for each room is changed by computer immediately after each check-out.

The coordinator should investigate the arrangements regarding room access. For example, should keys be left at the desk when the participant leaves the room? Although some sites urge this procedure, in many hotels anyone can go to the front desk, ask for a key, and get it! Sites can easily improve room security by requiring personal identification or by giving each guest an ID card at registration time. Both of these measures are helpful, but in most cases participants should retain the key when leaving the room.

Are Safe Deposit Boxes Available?

Most U.S. participants do not make use of safe deposit boxes even though they are generally provided, free of charge, for valuables. Safe deposit boxes do not guarantee safety, but they do minimize risk. (Boxes have been burglarized, and in these cases the site has no financial responsibility. A statement to this effect is usually printed on the form that the participant fills out when requesting the box.) In the United States, participants should be urged to use the boxes if they are carrying large amounts of cash, traveler's checks, jewelry, or a passport. In many countries (including the United States), passports are highly prized by thieves and readily negotiated, and the U.S participant attending an overseas conference should be alerted to this fact.

Does the Site Maintain a Security Force?

The presence of a site security force does not mean that the site is dangerous, just as the absence of such a force does not mean that the site has no security problems. The coordinator should ascertain how the security force operates. Are they in uniform? Do they patrol the halls, or are they stationed in the lobby or at some other location? How can they be contacted in case of a security emergency? Naturally, a site does not want to advertise the extent and nature of its security force, but the coordinator should provide this information to the secretariat office. (Exhibit and equipment security are discussed later in the book.)

Does the Site Have a House Physician?

In the United States, given the aging of our population, this question has become more important. The coordinator must consider the age and health status of participants when selecting a site. Most sites provide some kind of medical service or at least a list of nearby physicians for minor ailments.

How Close Is the Nearest Medical Facility?

The site usually has some plan for emergencies, and a designated person in the secretariat should know how to activate the plan rapidly, how to contact an ambulance service, and the location and status of a nearby hospital or other medical facility.

Are Site Personnel Trained in CPR?

Cardiovascular pulmonary resuscitation (CPR) has saved many lives. The American Red Cross regularly conducts certification courses in this skill, and similar courses are frequently offered by local health facilities. The coordinator should ascertain if any site personnel have been certified in CPR, who they are, and how they can be reached in time of emergency. Consideration should be given to training secretariat personnel in CPR as well.

General

Does the Site Provide Transportation for Site Review?

In most cases, the coordinator should visit the site and review it in terms of the design or the anticipated design. It may also be necessary for the design committee to visit the site. These visits may be paid for out of the conference budget, or, in some instances, the site may cover the cost of transportation. The site visit is a negotiable item, and the site personnel will want to review the number of conferences the coordinator places, as well as the revenue the coordinator may bring to the site through this or other conferences.

Is the Site Planning Any Construction or Remodeling?

The coordinator usually visits the site well before the actual event. What is the future of the site? The management may relate the site's glowing plans for remodeling, but when will that take place? Will extensive work be going on during the conference dates? The coordinator might also investigate the adjacent area to determine if any major construction projects are anticipated during the conference dates. In addition to querying the site personnel about this, the coordinator should also raise that question with the LCVB.

Are Internal Communication Devices Available?

In conference centers and large hotels, communication can be a problem, since the coordinator and various secretariat members must stay in constant contact, yet are separated by large distances. Portable paging devices and small walkie-talkies have made this task much easier. Are they available at the site? If not, what other devices are provided for rapid communication? A loudspeaker paging system may be adequate but also intrudes on conference activities. Does the site have any other devices?

If devices of any kind are provided, do they cost extra or are they complimentary? Some sites provide a limited number of devices at no cost but charge for additional devices. The cost and availability must be known beforehand, so the coordinator can plan for budget and related support.

What Other Activities Are Booked into the Site at the Same Time?

A small site may be booked for only one conference, but larger sites may book several conferences at the same time. One question is whether the site can support the variety and range of conferences they have booked. The coordinator may not be able to determine this easily, but should at least make the attempt. The sponsoring organizations and the themes of the simultaneous conferences should be identified. Picture the plight of a coordinator who discovers too late that her conference on "The Dangers of Smoking" is booked at the same time as a conference for tobacco farmers!

Chapter 6

Meeting and Function Rooms

CHECKLIST FOR FUNCTION ROOMS

Selection and Assignment

_____ Who assigns the rooms?

_____ Has the coordinator actually seen the rooms?

_____ Will the rooms be used by other people who are not conference participants?

Setups

_____ What are the possible room setups that can be used?

_____ Who is the site person responsible for setups?

_____ How is setup communicated to site personnel?

_____ Is the room being used before or after your sessions?

_____ How are the rooms usually set up?

_____ When will the rooms be set up and torn down?

_____ Does the site charge extra for resetting the rooms?

_____ Does the room have a fixed platform?

_____ Will tablecloths (or skirts for tables) be provided?

_____ Will smoking be controlled?

_____ What will be provided for participants?

_____ Does the sponsor want a banner or sign in the room?

_____ Will the presenter need a work table?

Traffic and Room Control

_____ Where will signs indicating the location of the rooms be placed?

_____ What kind of signs will be needed outside the rooms?

_____ Will room monitors be used?

_____ What is the maximum number of people permitted in the room?

General Session Room

_____ When and for how long will the room be available?

_____ Is any activity scheduled before the general session?

_____ Will any seats be reserved?

_____ Does the room have a balcony?

_____ Is a bandstand needed for musicians?

_____ Is the stage fixed or erected?

_____ Does the room have curtains?

_____ Are the AV screens fixed or portable?

_____ Does the room have a projection booth?

_____ Who controls the lighting?

_____ Will headsets be required for other languages?

102

Physical Factors

_____ Are there pictures on the walls?

_____ Does the room contain posts?

_____ Do chandeliers hang from the ceiling?

_____ Are mirrors located in the room?

_____ Will there be any seasonal decorations?

_____ Is the room height appropriate?

_____ Can air conditioning be controlled in the room?

_____ Can the room phone be turned off?

_____ Can the sound system in the room be controlled?

_____ Does the room allow easy entry and exit?

_____ Will a cloakroom be needed?

_____ Does the room contain a lectern with controls that can be operated by the presenter?

_____ Can the room accommodate the required equipment?

_____ Will microphones be needed, and, if so, what kind and how many?

_____ Will the session be taped?

_____ What kinds of aisles, and how many, should be provided?

_____ Can noise in or outside the room disrupt the session?

_____ Does the room color contribute to participant comfort?

_____ Is the shape of the room appropriate?

_____ What is the source of lighting and how is it controlled?

_____ Is the room carpeted and/or wallpapered?

_____ What kinds of chairs are available?

_____ Does the room have any acoustical peculiarities?

_____ If the room has movable walls, are they soundproof?

_____ How often will rooms be cleaned?

_____ Where will necessary materials needed for sessions be stored?

SOURCE: *The Comprehensive Guide to Successful Conferences and Meetings* by Leonard Nadler and Zeace Nadler. San Francisco: Jossey-Bass. Copyright © 1987. Permission to reproduce hereby granted.

This chapter focuses on the rooms used for general, concurrent, and other types of sessions. These rooms, commonly called function rooms, may be used for other events, and the reader should refer to the appropriate chapter for discussion of these rooms when used for these events.

Relation to Site Selection

Selection of function rooms has a direct relationship to site selection (Chapter Five). For large conferences of over three thousand participants, sites are usually booked years in advance, before any design work has been done. When the site has been selected before the conference has been designed, the coordinator's primary responsibilty is to make sure that the design fits the physical aspects of the site. The checklist in this chapter will serve as a guide for this task. The ideal, of course, is to investigate and examine the site's function rooms before site selection; in this regard, this chapter will be particularly helpful.

Few facilities have everything a coordinator wants. Sometimes a coordinator gets lucky and finds a good match between the conference events and the site's function rooms. Communication between the coordinator and site personnel is extremely important. The coordinator may get better results by talking about general outcomes than by making specific requests. For example, instead of requesting drapes to keep light out, a coordinator should discuss the need for a room to be used for showing films. The site personnel may be able to offer new alternatives unknown to the coordinator.

Relation to Design

The term *rooms* may pertain to an immense auditorium or a small room that can hold only five chairs. It is also possible to use a sleeping room as a function room, depending on the participants and the design. For one conference, arrangements were made with housekeeping to clean certain sleeping rooms early, so they could be used as meeting rooms. We later learned that some participants from the Middle East were very uncomfortable about meeting in someone else's bedroom. In their countries, a bed that has been occupied by a man and wife is considered their "marriage" bed, even when it is outside their home. They felt that a nonfamily person should not sit on this bed, yet that is what the participants were being asked to do!

The number and location of the rooms should be related to the design, flow, and "traffic" of the conference. Many sessions use audiovisual (AV) materials, so function rooms must be discussed in that context, particularly the physical factors that must be considered for AV presentations.

Types of Rooms

Almost every conference has some kind of general session. The size, ambiance, and equipment of the general session room must all be related to the number of participants and the purpose of that general session.

Most rooms will be used for concurrent or breakout sessions, including workshops and similar variations of concurrent sessions. These rooms may need to hold from ten to several hundred participants.

A difficult task is trying to match the available rooms with the overall design and the specific sessions. Some variables can be controlled, such as the equipment or room setup required by a presenter, but other crucial factors, such as the number of participants who will attend each session, are unknown at the time rooms are selected.

The Checklist

Selection and Assignment

Who Assigns the Rooms?

All room assignments should be coordinated by one individual—the coordinator, a member of the secretariat, a member of the design committee, or a person designated by the coordinator to have that responsibility. No changes should be considered or promised without first checking with that person (whom we will refer to as the coordinator, even though a different person may be responsible).

The actual assignment of rooms depends on how the conference planning group is organized and the complexity of the conference. For a small conference that needs only a few rooms of approximately the same type, the secretariat can make the assignment. If participants are assigned to small groups (as in Example A: One-Day Conference described in Chapter Three), the exact numbers of participants are known and room assignment is not a difficult task, unless the rooms are on different floors of the site or in different buildings. In this case, attention must be given to handicapped or older participants who may not be able to move too rapidly or climb too many stairs.

Assigning rooms for larger conferences requires political skills. Some presenters, when asked how many participants they expect to attend their sessions, suggest astronomical numbers. If the coordinator thinks the number is inflated, perhaps a reflection of the presenter's ego, he must assign a smaller room at the risk of antagonizing the presenter.

When participants are able to decide at the conference which sessions they will attend, estimating the number of particpants for each session becomes educated guesswork. In 1970 a conference of two thousand participants featured a session entitled "Management by Objectives." At that time, the design committee felt that the topic was not of great interest and scheduled a room that could hold 100 participants. Before the doors opened, over 100 participants were waiting in line! It was too late to do anything about the room then, except to announce that the session would be repeated the following day in a larger room.

Has the Coordinator Actually Seen the Rooms?

A coordinator should not rely solely on the site's diagrams of the function rooms. Some sites also supply photographs, which can be helpful for initial site selection but are less useful in making specific room assignments. The coordinator or another responsible person should actually examine *every* room. This inspection should have been done during site selection, but if the site was selected years ago, changes may warrant another inspection (although this can be costly if the site is located far away). A walk-through should take place before rooms are assigned. Most coordinators like to see the rooms in use, because it enables them to evaluate some of the items that appear later on this checklist.

The coordinator should walk through the conference design at the facility, inspecting the room layouts and names, a task that should be done before the participants' book goes to press. This book contains room assignments; changing rooms later means an additional printing cost and possible participant confusion.

Will the Rooms Be Used by Other People
Who Are Not Conference Participants?

This information is important in assigning rooms. If the coordinator does not have exclusive control of a room, perhaps an alternate room can be identified. If that option is not possible, the coordinator should note carefully which rooms are totally available and which are not. Others may leave the room in a condition that requires cleaning and resetting, both of which take time.

Setups

What Are the Possible Room Setups That Can Be Used?

Setups refer to the seating arrangements in function rooms. Setting up rooms is an extremely important task that frequently does not receive enough attention. Presenters are sometimes asked to choose a setup and plan their sessions accordingly. If they arrive to find a different setup, the results can be disastrous. If the site does not present any choices, do not raise expectations by asking the presenter to select the setup.

The seating arrangements shown in Figures 15-30 are generally for sessions that do not require special arrangements for AV or other devices. Given the extensive variety of possibilities, it is not feasible to include all variations.

These setups use rectangular tables that seat two participants at each table—the table commonly found in most sites. Longer tables are sometimes available, but the two-seaters are shown in all the diagrams for the purpose of comparing the setup. Chairs are by no means standard in size or configuration. The number of participants that can be accommodated at a table will vary, depending on the type of chairs used. Ceiling height, room color, outside windows, AV equipment, and local fire laws restricting room occupancy may also require different ways of using space.

The setups shown are for sessions of thirty or fewer participants. Some can be increased by varying the arrangement but at the cost of losing eye contact and reducing the space for each participant. A small conference of thirty or fewer participants can easily use some of these setups for a general session.

The presenter is signified by the letter P. Some presenters may prefer different positions within a particular setup, and this issue should be clarified before setup instructions are given to site personnel.

The U shape (Figure 15) can be enlarged by adding more tables, or can be made smaller by removing tables but retaining the shape. This setup allows all the participants to see the presenter but does not allow them to readily see each other.

The square/rectangle setup (Figure 16) is essentially a closed U shape. It accommodates more participants in the same space but requires that the presenter sit with the participants. This setup can be desirable for some presentations but requires special skills on the part of the presenter. Because the presenter has more eye contact with those directly across the square, he or she will tend to have more interaction with these participants than with the others, unless the presenter makes a determined effort to include others in discussions.

The T shape (Figure 17) is most suited to small groups. One row of tables, with participants seated opposite each other, may replace two rows shown in the figure. The top of the T, where the presenter sits, should not extend too far beyond the tables. The board of directors setup (Figure 18) closely resembles the T setup; the essential difference is that in the directors setup, the presenter is seated at the same table with the participants. This may be necessary when the room has one very long table or several tables that are too heavy to be readily moved.

The E shape (Figure 19) is an extension of the T and can seat many more participants. The limitation is that participants cannot readily see each other, and the presenter either has to stand or sit on a platform to have eye contact with the participants. An alternative, if space allows, is the open E, or spokes setup (Figure 20). As with the regular E, participants can be on one or both sides of the tables.

The classroom arrangement (Figure 21), among the most common setups, is helpful when participants are expected to work with printed materials during the session. The presenter can see all the participants, but most participants can only see the backs of heads, which does not encourage participant interaction. The closed tables setup (Figure 22), a classroom setup without the middle aisle, may be necessary when many participants must be seated in a small space; the arrangement does not, however, allow much movement among the participants. A variation is the herringbone or classroom V shape (Figure 23), which does allow for some eye contact among the participants.

The difference between the V shape and the inverted V shape is where the presenter is placed (Figure 24). The V is used to allow participants to see each other and therefore increase interaction. It also allows the presenter to readily see each participant. If a presenter feels uncomfortable apart from the participants, he or she might choose the inverted V. The presenter sits at the same table with the participants but may have some difficulty seeing all of them, depending on the acuteness of the angle.

A variation of the V setup is the diamond shape (Figure 25). The presenter can be at any corner of the diamond. The hexagon (Figure 26), a variation on the diamond, is useful for larger groups than can be accommodated by the diamond shape. The presenter can see most of the participants, and most of the participants can see each other. Smaller groups can be accommodated with a triangle shape (Figure 27). The presenter can sit almost anywhere but usually at one of the points of the triangle. In this setup, the presenter cannot easily see two-thirds of the participants.

Round tables (Figure 28), like those used for meal functions, come in various sizes, but most provide seating for eight to ten people. For a small group of ten or fewer participants, the round table may be most appropriate, particularly if the room can hold only one table. In a large room, multiple round tables (Figure 29) may be used, though the presenter must stand or be seated on a platform in order to see and be seen.

When panels are used (Figure 30), some of these configurations are also useful. The panel usually sits in front of the participants; with large groups, the panel may be raised on a platform.

Who Is the Site Person Responsible for Setups?

Site units responsible for setting up rooms are known by such titles as housekeeping, banquets, maintenance, and service. During site visits, the coordinator must identify the person who is responsible for setups and, just

Figure 15. U Shape.

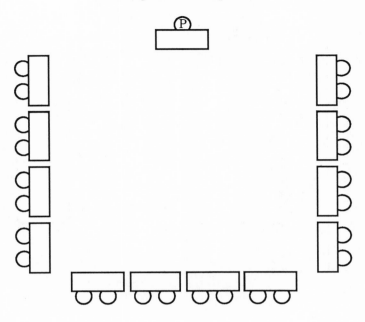

Figure 16. Square/Rectangle.

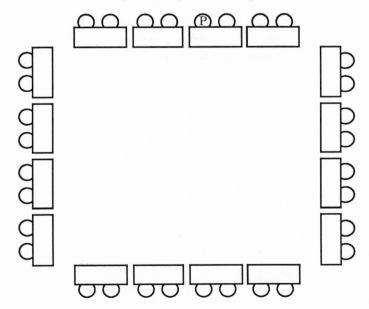

SOURCE: *The Comprehensive Guide to Successful Conferences and Meetings* by Leonard Nadler and Zeace Nadler. San Francisco: Jossey-Bass. Copyright © 1987. Permission to reproduce hereby granted.

Figure 17. T Shape.

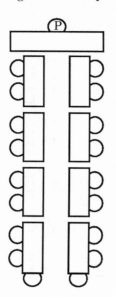

Figure 18. Director-Board.

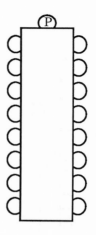

Figure 19. E Shape.

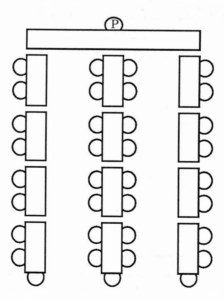

Figure 20. Open E or Spoke.

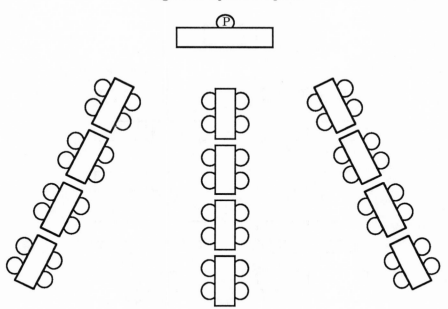

SOURCE: *The Comprehensive Guide to Successful Conferences and Meetings* by Leonard Nadler and Zeace Nadler. San Francisco: Jossey-Bass. Copyright © 1987. Permission to reproduce hereby granted.

Figure 21. Classroom.

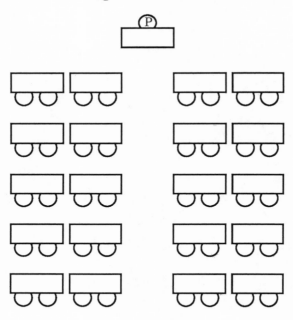

Figure 22. Closed Tables.

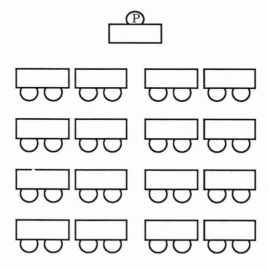

SOURCE: *The Comprehensive Guide to Successful Conferences and Meetings* by Leonard Nadler and Zeace Nadler. San Francisco: Jossey-Bass. Copyright © 1987. Permission to reproduce hereby granted.

Figure 23. Herringbone or Classroom V Shape.

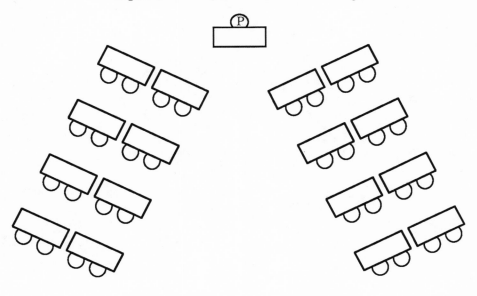

Figure 24. V Shape and Inverted V.

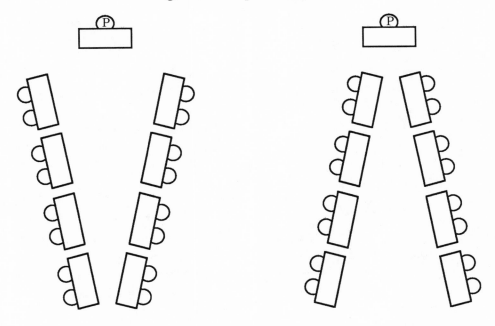

Figure 25. Diamond.

Figure 26. Hexagon.

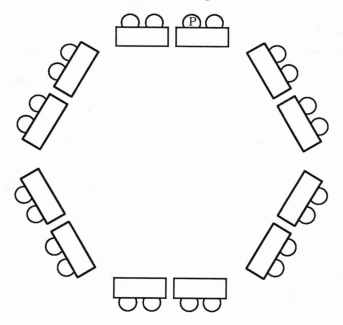

SOURCE: *The Comprehensive Guide to Successful Conferences and Meetings* by Leonard Nadler and Zeace Nadler. San Francisco: Jossey-Bass. Copyright © 1987. Permission to reproduce hereby granted.

Figure 27. Triangle.

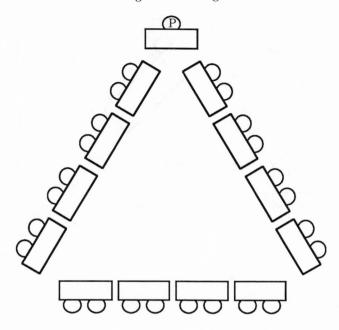

Figure 28. Round Table.

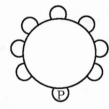

Figure 29. Multiple Round Tables.

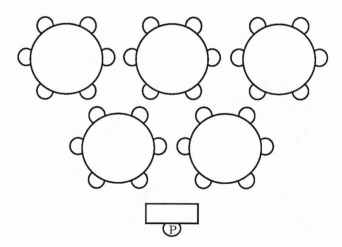

SOURCE: *The Comprehensive Guide to Successful Conferences and Meetings* by Leonard Nadler and Zeace Nadler. San Francisco: Jossey-Bass. Copyright © 1987. Permission to reproduce hereby granted.

Figure 30. Panel Setups (M represents moderator).

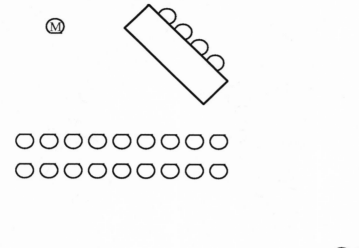

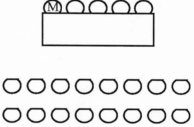

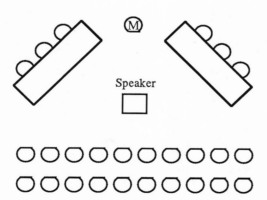

SOURCE: *The Comprehensive Guide to Successful Conferences and Meetings* by Leonard Nadler and Zeace Nadler. San Francisco: Jossey-Bass. Copyright © 1987. Permission to reproduce hereby granted.

before the conference starts, verify that the same person is actually on site. Unfortunately, the coordinator sometimes discovers during setup that the site personnel are being supervised by an individual who is not on the site at the time! The supervisor's absence makes it virtually impossible to change any instructions being followed by the setup workers.

How Is Setup Communicated to Site Personnel?

The room setups should be stated in writing. Using diagrams, such as the ones in this chapter, the coordinator should note the room numbers for each setup. (This safeguard is reinforced by the staging book discussed in a later chapter.)

Avoid the use of terminology to describe the setups, for this differs from one site to another. Instead use a diagram that approximates as closely as possible the actual room. Some advise drawing diagrams to scale, but that is generally more detailed than is necessary and entails a great deal of work.

Is the Room Being Used Before or After Your Sessions?

A coordinator usually books rooms, assuming that no one else will be using that room on the same day. However, particularly in hotels, rooms used by conferences during the day may be rented to other organizations and functions in the evening. When that is the case, materials and equipment must be removed from the room, and the room is reset as required for the morning session. These tasks should not be taken for granted. The coordinator should verify the arrangement with appropriate site personnel and assign a member of the secretariat to inspect room setups early in the morning. The reverse can also happen when a coordinator is using certain rooms that are available to others during the day for evening sessions only.

How Are Rooms Usually Set Up?

Some sites set up all rooms in a particular way (usually theater style), and any variations may require additional room setup charges. Some conference designs can fit into that setup with no problem. If the design calls for any other setup, the site may be reluctant to change or may not have the appropriate furniture. If possible, this should have been worked out during negotiations for site selection, but at that time the coordinator may not have known the required setups.

When Will the Rooms Be Set Up and Torn Down?

Labor charges and practices vary in different parts of the United States and in different countries. At some sites, room setups are done the evening before. Other sites assign a crew to come in early for setup, but sites have different definitions of early. Site personnel should specify the exact time of an early setup. This is particularly important when the event requires equipment or materials.

Usually, a coordinator does not pay much attention to the time for tearing down the room, but it can be a problem. A session can end at 5:00 P.M., but it will usually take the participants another fifteen to twenty minutes to empty the room, depending on the number of participants and the availability of exits. At 5:01 P.M. the site may send a crew into the room to begin tearing it down. They certainly have the right to do so, but unless this has been negotiated beforehand, further interaction between the presenter and the participants must be cut short.

Does the Site Charge Extra for Resetting the Rooms?

The site's policy may be to set the room any way the coordinator requests, but it stays in that setup for the whole day; any resetting requires an extra charge. A coordinator must consider that possibility when assigning rooms. In addition, the coordinator must consider the time required to reset a room. The coordinator may be willing to pay the extra charge but must allow sufficient time for the site personnel to reset. Before offering room setup alternatives to presenters, a coordinator should consider the time and cost factors.

Does the Room Have a Fixed Platform?

A platform (also called a dais or stage) is usually a temporary piece of equipment. Generally, it consists of separate sections that can be set up in any fashion desired. However, some rooms, such as rooms used for dances and parties, have a fixed platform. Generally, the fixed platform is not a problem, but it should be examined. Of course, a coordinator might want a fixed platform for certain events.

Will Tablecloths (or Skirts for Tables) Be Provided?

Generally, a tablecloth lies on top of a table or hangs slightly over the ends, while a skirt extends from the top of the table to the floor. It is possible to have a tablecloth without a skirt, but it is unusual to have a skirt without a tablecloth. The skirt is desirable when the presenters are seated at a table on a platform. Women particularly tend to feel uncomfortable on the platform when the table is not skirted.

Tablecloths can be provided for both the presenter's table and those used by the participants. One frequently overlooked problem is the cloth material or fabric. Some people are allergic to certain fabrics, particularly a green felt-like material commonly provided by sites. This cloth (or the dye) causes itching and should be avoided.

Will Smoking Be Controlled?

Smoking in function rooms is a controversial issue and will probably remain one for several years. A coordinator should not allow personal preference to determine the policy in this area. More sites are prohibiting smoking in public areas, and when that is the law or practice of the site, the coordinator has no options.

If the site permits smoking, however, it is important to provide an alternative, such as a nonsmoking area. Before assigning separate smoking and nonsmoking areas, the coordinator should check the air flow and the ventilation system in the room. Nonsmoking areas should be placed so that smoke is carried in the opposite direction. The site personnel should be able to advise on this for individual rooms. It is also important that the presenter be consulted about whether smoking should be allowed during the presentation.

The smoking policy for function rooms should be clearly stated in the participants' book. This will avoid, or at least minimize, problems that might arise. Signs should be posted to reinforce the policy, and site personnel should be alerted when setting up the rooms. The tendency is to put ashtrays on all tables or chairs, a practice that communicates that smoking is permitted in all areas of the room.

What Will Be Provided for Participants?

Participants may need some items to facilitate their participation and add to their comfort during a session. Some items discussed below are provided by sites but must be requested. Some are provided at no charge, but there may be a charge for others.

If writing materials, such as pads that carry the logo and name of the conference, as well as pens or pencils, are not in the participants' packets, a coordinator may wish to provide them. A site, particularly a hotel, might provide those materials at no charge since they see it as advertising.

Whether to provide drinking water is not as simple a decision as might first be thought. Some communities do not put water on the table unless specifically requested. Should the water have ice? If so, when should it be put out? It certainly should not be placed on the tables while the session is in progress. Will the participants be provided with paper cups or glasses? That may be a decision that depends on the level of the participants and their expectations. In some parts of the world, it is customary to provide bottled water. Should water be placed on each table or just at water stations in one or a few places in the room? The answers to some of these questions depend on the type of room setup, the anticipated needs of the participants, and the design of the session.

For some setups, particularly where participants are expected to interact, name tents are desirable. These can be produced before the conference, or the participants can make them out as needed. Usually, they are pieces of white cardboard that can be folded in half to make a tent, hence the name. Participants write their names, or other information, on one side or both. The hotel may provide these, or a coordinator may have some printed with the name or logo of the conference.

Some sites place lozenges, mints, or candies at each participant position at a table. This will generally carry the name of the site and it is expected that participants will take them with them. These are apparently replacing matchbooks, which are less in evidence since people are not smoking.

Does the Sponsor Want a Banner or Sign in the Room?

Name recognition can be important for all types of sponsors. The coordinator should determine whether the sponsor wants signs or banners in function rooms. These can be placed across the front wall of the room or attached to the lectern.

Will the Presenter Need a Work Table?

As can be seen in Figures 15–30, most presenters usually sit at a table with participants and at a table on a stage. Some presenters, however, may wish to be peripatetic but still have a base of operations. A small table, strategically placed, can hold the presenter's outline, materials, a watch, and other items. The need for this size table must be determined before setup as sites cannot always meet this need on short notice. Sites have large rectangular or round tables, but they less frequently have small card or cocktail tables that will be used by the presenter.

Traffic and Room Control

Where Will Signs Indicating the Location of the Rooms Be Placed?

When many rooms are being used, participants can easily become confused. Some sites use room numbers and others use room names, but neither assures that participants will find the room. Diagrams and floor plans may be included in the participant packet, but not all participants are adept at deciphering these diagrams. Signs should be placed at strategic points, indicating the direction to and location of the rooms in use. When rooms are not in use, the signs should be taken down. The signs should be on each floor near the elevators and at any points where corridors intersect.

What Kind of Signs Will Be Needed Outside the Rooms?

A sign should be placed outside of each session room. If the site does not have signholders built into the door or the wall adjacent to the entrance, an easel sign or similar device should be used. The sign should indicate the room name, the number of the session, the name of the presenter, the topic, and the opening and closing time. To reduce the work load, some secretariats prepare a sign listing all the sessions in that room for a morning, an afternoon, or the whole day. Although this saves time, it can be confusing.

Will Room Monitors Be Used?

Room monitors perform a variety of functions for each session room. When they are used, they should be informed about the various aspects of traffic and room control discussed in this section.

What Is the Maximum Number of People Permitted in the Room?

In many U.S. cities, the fire department posts a notice stating the maximum room capacity, and this regulation should be strictly followed for the safety of all concerned. During a conference, it is not unusual to find at least one session that will not accommodate all the participants who want to attend, and it takes a strong monitor to resist their pressure.

The maximum number of participants may also be a reflection of a design that limits the number of participants. The presenter's wishes should be adhered to and not changed without sufficient advance notice to that presenter.

General Session Room

This section deals with any room that is used for a general session, that is, when all the participants are expected to be in the same room at the same time. Depending on the conference, general session rooms must accommodate from ten to ten thousand participants. The greater the number, the larger the space needed for the general session and the more important the need for coordinated planning. The following questions concern general sessions of fifty or more participants.

When and for How Long Will the Room Be Available?

Many facilities, particularly hotels, have a large room that is used for general sessions as well as for other functions, such as receptions, banquets, meals, and the like. If space is limited, the same room may be required for both breakfast and for the general session. It is possible to do this, but it will probably mean that the tables will not be cleared and the speaker will have to deal with the clatter of cutlery and dishes as participants move in their seats.

Is Any Activity Scheduled Before the General Session?

Many participants attend a general session, and it usually will take some time for all of them to enter the room. Those who come early can get restless; appropriate music, either by a live band or recorded music over the loudspeaker system, can ease the waiting. Another possibility is a pertinent, climate-setting media show, although darkening the room may hamper participants' ability to find their seats.

Will Any Seats Be Reserved?

Free seating is the rule for general sessions. Special seats may be reserved for VIPs or visiting dignitaries, and this should be noted by appropriate markings or barricade tapes (yellow tapes about two inches wide). Seats might also be reserved for presenters and the sponsor's officers.

Does the Room Have a Balcony?

Large auditoriums, such as those in conference centers, frequently have balconies. In order to fill the main floor area before the balcony, the balconies may be closed off until the person in charge of the general session signifies otherwise. Some hotel balconies have many entrances; if access is not controlled, nonpaying nonparticipants can easily enter and attend a well-publicized general session given by a celebrity speaker.

Is a Bandstand Needed for Musicians?

If musicians are used before, during, or after the general session, adequate provision must be made for them, perhaps a stage or bandstand to the side of the presenter's platform.

Is the Stage Fixed or Erected?

Large general session rooms usually require a platform for the speaker. An auditorium probably has a fixed stage, but a room used for a variety of purposes will probably need a portable stage. Stages are composed of various materials; the exact dimensions and construction should be selected on the basis of the number of people who will be on the stage and the amount of movement that will be taking place.

Does the Room Have Curtains?

General session rooms have many different kinds of stage and window curtains. A session design calling for opening the curtains may require the use of site personnel.

Large windows with panoramic views can prove distracting; in these rooms the drapes should be closed before any participants enter the room. Some motorized drapes can only be opened or closed by site personnel; this should be checked out carefully when making arrangements for the general session.

Are AV Screens Fixed or Portable?

Large auditoriums usually have fixed AV screens, which is not necessarily an advantage. One facility had two fixed screens, strategically placed so they could be seen easily from any point in the vast auditorium. The problem was that one had never been lowered in the three-year history of that facility, and the other could not be raised! AV screens should always be checked out during site selection.

Portable screens should be set up before any participants enter the room. The room should be checked carefully to make sure that the screens can be seen from all seats.

Does the Room Have a Projection Booth?

Large auditoriums often have a projection room or booth, which should be inspected to make sure it is functioning and relevant to a particular general session. If not, it may require setting up the AV equipment on the floor of the general session room. If you plan to use the projection room, be sure that it will be accessible when needed.

Who Controls the Lighting?

The form and extent of artificial lighting must be considered in terms of the design of the session. The simplest situation would be where the lights are on when the participants enter and are turned off after they leave. The session design, however, may require that spotlights be used or that lights be turned up or down at particular times. If the site has a complex lighting system, an electrician usually handles the function. This means some kind of scripting, so that the electrician knows when to adjust the lights; a complex script may require a rehearsal. The coordinator should determine whether the electricians are unionized, as this factor may affect costs and usage.

Will Headsets Be Required for Other Languages?

If interpreters are to be used during the general session, the room should have the necessary equipment. The coordinator should determine the kind of equipment available and how it will be used. It is very important to use professional interpreters, not just a bilingual person. Interpreting is a complex skill that goes beyond just knowing two languages.

Coordinators commonly overlook interpreting equipment, resulting in a consecutive interpretation presentation, that is, the presenter must wait while a few sentences are interpreted before going on. In essence, the time for the presentation is doubled. Simultaneous interpreting requires functioning headsets that are connected to each seat or distributed separately at the entrance to the general session room. Time must be allowed for the participants to pick up their headsets before the general session and to return them at its conclusion.

Physical Factors

Many of the physical factors of the room cannot be changed, but the coordinator should know about them anyway; some can be modified by a different room setup. For example, distracting wall murals behind the presenter can be neutralized by moving the position of the presenter.

Are There Pictures on the Walls?

Conference centers rarely put pictures on walls of meeting rooms, but hotels are very likely to have them because the rooms are used for a variety of purposes. The site personnel might be willing to remove the pictures if given sufficient notice and if the pictures are not permanently affixed to the wall.

Does the Room Contain Posts?

Some hotel function rooms might have posts, particularly if the facility was built essentially as a hotel and only later modified to be used as a conference site. Some conference centers, strangely enough, also have posts in function rooms! This reemphasizes the fact that a coordinator cannot rely solely on the statements of site personnel but rather should visit the specific rooms to be used and compare the planned setup against the reality of the room. Even then, some site personnel may need a specific diagram, such as those shown in Figures 15–30, to know where to place the presenter and the participants.

Do Chandeliers Hang from the Ceiling?

Low-hanging and ornate chandeliers are rarely found in a conference center, but they are common in hotels, particularly when the room is used for banquets, receptions, and similar social affairs. A major problem with a chandelier is that it can interfere with AV projection.

In one hotel, we found that the chandelier was made of seashells that moved and vibrated when the heating system came on. They tinkled musically and harmoniously, but that kind of accompaniment was not wanted during a session. The conference was held in winter, so we had to work out something. While the session was in progress, the system was turned off, and the room was quiet but cold. During the breaks, when the room was empty, the heat was turned on and the sound of the shells was not a bother.

Are Mirrors Located in the Room?

Mirrors are sometimes used to make a small room appear larger. In one hotel, the rectangular shape of the room required that the presenter be placed against one of the end walls, both of which had mirrors. This meant that the participants would face the presenter but see themselves! As the presenter was using AV equipment, we repositioned the screen so that it blocked most of the mirror.

Will There Be Any Seasonal Decorations?

At Christmas time, many hotels are used for parties, and the rooms may be ornately decorated with tinsel, smiling Santa Clauses, and blinking lights. The coordinator can do little about the tinsel, but Santa's lights should be turned off, as heretical as that sounds. A coordinator must be extremely careful in selecting a site for a conference that will take place any time from Thanksgiving through the New Year's Day.

Other holidays must also be considered. A hotel may use decorations for a local holiday, college homecoming or reunion, or other special event. A coordinator should take into account that other bookings require special decorations and schedule accordingly.

Is the Room Height Appropriate?

For most sessions, room height is not particularly significant, but it is important when using AV equipment, since a low ceiling can interfere with projection. Some rooms have a low ceiling, particularly basement rooms that were converted from some other purpose. Some participants may feel psychologically cramped. On the other hand, rooms with very high ceilings, such as ballrooms or rooms with balconies, may require that presenters use amplification.

Can Air Conditioning Be Controlled in the Room?

Air conditioning is a necessity in many rooms. If there are many participants in the room, some air circulation is required. Site personnel usually set the room cooler than normal before people enter, knowing that body heat will raise the temperature; thus, the first participants entering the room can be expected to complain of the cold. No one temperature will please everyone; different participants might set the thermostat at their own comfort level. Most sites now equip function rooms with thermostats that cannot be changed without a special tool. The presenter or room monitor should be the only ones to contact the site engineering department if the thermostat is to be changed.

Can the Room Phone Be Turned Off?

Many hotel session rooms contain a phone that can be both a convenience and an annoyance. It is convenient if rapid contact must be made with the secretariat or site personnel. Once the session starts, it can be an annoyance if it rings. Many of these phones are installed with a jack and so are easy to disconnect. If the phone is permanently installed, however, the secretariat should inform the switchboard that no calls are to be placed to the room. In these days of high technology, however, the calls may not go through a switchboard, but directly from the caller to the room. Any calls to the room are probably a wrong number!

If the phones cannot be disconnected, either manually or through the switchboard, the monitor or another person should be stationed near the phone. If it rings during a session, it should *not* be answered; instead, the receiver should just be lifted to stop the ringing and immediately replaced. If it is a wrong number, the caller will try again, and hopefully the call will go to another phone. If someone is trying to reach the room during a session, the caller will get the message after two or three disconnects. Another option is to replace the bell with a flashing light, which can be covered if it proves disruptive.

Can the Sound System in the Room Be Controlled?

Sound systems are found in many hotel function rooms as a way of providing music and announcements from a single source. The sound can usually be turned off with a switch located in the room or in a service area just outside the room. If a central unit controls the system, the person in charge of this unit should be informed about the rooms in use and when music or announcements should be turned off. This kind of system can be advantageous, however, if all the rooms are wired and are being used by the same coordinator. The sound system can announce the start and end of sessions, the opening of the exhibition, and make general announcements.

Does the Room Allow Easy Entry and Exit?

Many rooms used for receptions have several doors. If one session closely follows another in the same room, one door can be marked "entry only" and the other "exit only." A monitor can expedite this movement. The entry and exit should be checked for easy use by handicapped participants, particularly those in wheelchairs. The corridors should be examined in terms of traffic flow when several rooms empty at the same time; it may be desirable to move some sessions to other rooms to ease the traffic flow.

Will a Cloakroom Be Needed?

Cloakrooms may be needed in a convention center when the participants stay at different hotels. The weather, of course, is an important factor. If heavy outer garments are not necessary, a cloakroom might not be needed. Some cloakrooms are only staffed at certain times or when a coordinator pays for that service. No cloakroom might mean using chairs in session rooms for clothing, which reduces the planned seating space.

Does the Room Contain a Lectern with Controls That Can Be Operated by the Presenter?

Lecterns or podiums can be various sizes and be equipped with different types of controls. They can be full pedestals or smaller portable lecterns that are placed on top of a table. Lecterns can range from simple stands for presenters' notes to sophisticated electronic panels that control lights, sound, drapes, projection, audiotapes, and almost any other aspect of the room, except the temperature. Some lecterns even have built-in clocks and warning lights so the presenter does not go over allotted time. Some presenters do not use a lectern but rather choose to be peripatetic, moving across (or around) the room in order to have closer physical contact with the participants.

Can the Room Accommodate the Required Equipment?

In addition to AV equipment, a presenter may have a model or mock-up, charts and graphs, or actual working equipment. The secretariat should ascertain that information when presenters are notified of acceptance. The specific room for each presenter using equipment should be checked by the coordinator for possible changes to a different room than initially planned.

Will Microphones Be Needed, and, If So, What Kind and How Many?

If microphones are not required, no additional questions need be asked. If microphones are required, it is not just a matter of requesting one. A coordinator should explore the basis for need, the wishes of the presenter, and the availability of equipment. All these factors are interrelated. In the same room, one presenter might want to use microphone and another might feel that microphone distances the participants and will only use it when absolutely necessary.

Of the several types of microphones, the most common is the fixed microphone, usually attached to a stand or lectern. It is usually possible for the presenter to remove the microphone from its fixed position and use it as a portable microphone if it has sufficient wire. A table microphone is generally fixed in a holder on a table, but it also can sometimes be removed from its stand and used in a portable fashion. The coordinator must know before setup if the presenter intends to remove a microphone from its fixed position in order to make the appropriate preparations.

Another possibility is the lavaliere microphone, which is worn around the neck or clipped to the presenter's tie, blouse, or jacket. Mobility is limited only by the length of the cord. The lavaliere microphone frees up the presenter's hands for AV presentations or other tasks. It can also be helpful for panel discussions: Panel members and the moderator can talk to each other and the participants without having to hand a microphone back and forth.

A wireless microphone sends a signal that is transmitted to the loudspeakers in the room. However, a wireless microphone requires special equipment and has some limitations. In some sites, it may send signals that interfere with other sessions and may also receive unwanted signals. Also, a large room may contain "cold zones" where transmission is weak or impossible.

Some large sessions use aisle (or audience) microphones for audience participation. Another approach is to take a microphone to a participant. This can be done if the cord is long enough, or by using a wireless microphone.

Whatever types of microphones are used, someone should be assigned to verify before the session begins that the microphones are appropriate to the session, in sufficient number and placement, and in working order.

Will the Session Be Taped?

Some sessions are either audio- or videotaped. Audiotaping is usually done through the existing microphone system or by adding special microphones just for taping. Videotaping is more complicated. The equipment may require special electrical outlets, which may not be available in the room. If the room has sliding doors, for example, those doors do not contain outlets. Additional wiring may have to be provided for special lights and for special positioning of the camera. The entire setup must be completed before participants enter the room, which means that the room must be available for some time prior to the session.

What Kinds of Aisles, and How Many, Should Be Provided?

Aisles are a safety factor, as well as part of the design. Some jurisdictions have regulations on how much aisle space must be provided in relation to seating— regulations should be checked with the site personnel when discussing room setups. If participants are going to use the microphones, the aisles should be readily accessible and the microphones strategically placed.

Can Noise in or Outside the Room Disrupt the Session?

Among the significant complaints from both presenters and participants is disruptive noise during a session. The coordinator should at least walk through the rooms, listening for noises that could prove distracting. Some of them can be eliminated or reduced with the cooperation of site personnel.

One annoying source of noise is the heating or air conditioning system. Noisy, centrally controlled systems are difficult to remedy, but if the controls are in the room, consider sacrificing some amount of comfort for the benefit of noise reduction. If the source of noise is in adjoining rooms, give careful consideration as to which types of sessions should be assigned there. A workshop session, for example, might not be particularly disrupted by a film soundtrack in an adjacent room.

If noise from corridors might be a problem, the coordinator should check with the site personnel as to when and how these corridors will be used. Careful scheduling, on both sides, can be effective.

External sources of noise, such as airplanes, construction, or rush-hour traffic, may be beyond anyone's control. It might be possible, however, to schedule the room during periods when external noise is at a minimum.

Does the Room Color Contribute to Participant Comfort?

Room color should be considered when scheduling sessions. Generally, room colors evoke certain emotional responses. For example, white is viewed as cold or sterile, dark colors are fatiguing, and red elicits excitement. These are only generalizations, of course, and the reactions of individuals will vary. If given options, however, try to match the color to the type of session. A workshop might prove more stimulating in a red room than in a white one, while lectures should not be conducted in a dark-colored room.

Is the Shape of the Room Appropriate?

As with colors, the coordinator should recognize how the room relates to design and assign accordingly. The shape should be related to the possible room setups discussed earlier in this chapter. If possible, a classroom setup should not be placed in a square room. A long, narrow room might not be able to accommodate a V or wheel shape setup.

What Is the Source of Lighting and How Is It Controlled?

Conference centers tend to have better lighting than many hotels, unless the hotel has been built specifically for conferences. The walls of some function rooms have sconces, which are wonderful for receptions and dinners but rarely provide sufficient light for sessions. If the session will primarily show films such lighting would not present problems.

Although many coordinators prefer fluorescent light, incandescent lights with dimmer switches are particularly helpful when using AV equipment. Some rooms have one switch for the entire room; others have numerous switches. If control of the lights is necessary (as when using AV), the presenter or the monitor should control them. The controls might be on the lectern but more commonly are on the wall. It may require some time to learn which switches control which lights or banks of lights and this should be done before the participants enter the room.

Is the Room Carpeted and/or Wallpapered?

Carpeting and wallpapering are usually outside the control of a coordinator, but these items should be considered when selecting and assigning rooms. The preference should be for carpets of a solid shade, not too light or too dark. Avoid carpets with floral, striped, or startling designs or vivid colors. They may be desirable for some events but seldom for conference sessions. The same general criteria can be applied to wallpaper. In some locations, the wallpaper reflects local history or landmarks. For example, in Boston the wallpaper might portray scenes of Bunker Hill, Paul Revere, or Concord and Lexington, which can be very distracting.

What Kinds of Chairs Are Available?

There are so many kinds of chairs that it is impossible to discuss them all. Unless they are bolted to the floor, chairs are movable and one kind can be replaced by another—if they are available at the site. The coordinator should at least explore alternatives when needed.

Chairs with wheels are especially useful when participants are seated close together as in a directors or T setup. An auditorium can be set up with interlocking chairs, which are good for maintaining the consistency of rows but can be a hindrance if the presenter intends to break up the audience into small groups.

Does the Room Have Any Acoustical Peculiarities?

Acoustics are seldom a problem in small rooms but can be a significant problem in large rooms, particularly ones with balconies. The use of microphones and loudspeakers can overcome most acoustical problems, but some may still remain. The coordinator should test the acoustics by placing people in different parts of the room; if any of them cannot hear well, that area should be blocked off or the sound system somehow improved.

If the Room Has Movable Walls, Are They Soundproof?

Many sites use movable walls to create several small rooms out of one very large room. Movable walls provide an element of flexibility that can be helpful—or problematical. Site personnel frequently tell coordinators that the walls are soundproof; the coordinator discovers the exaggeration only after the conference has begun. If possible, a coordinator should visit a conference session held in a room with movable walls. Each room that might be used should be visited, for each has different acoustical possibilities. If no session is in progress, bring along a portable radio, turn it up to what would be presenter volume and go into the adjoining room to test the acoustic bleed.

When setting up rooms that are separated by movable walls, place the presenters back to back; in other words, the loudspeakers in each room should point away from the adjoining room rather than toward it.

How Often Will Rooms Be Cleaned?

If rooms are being used all day, they can get dirty and messy. Check with the site to determine when the rooms will be cleaned. They could be cleaned once in the morning and once in the afternoon, usually during breaks. If there is time between sessions, some minimal cleaning, such as emptying ashtrays and refilling the water pitchers, could be done. Rooms are usually not used during lunch time, so cleaning could be done at that time. The site probably has some schedule for this. The design and session schedule should be checked against the cleaning schedule. It may be desirable to make some minor changes to assure that the rooms will be cleaned. During the conference, the secretariat should spot check the rooms to ascertain if they are being cleaned.

Where Will Necessary Materials Needed for Sessions Be Stored?

The materials being discussed here are handouts, slides, and similar items that a presenter will be using during a session. When a presenter brings these materials, the secretariat does not need to be involved. If the materials are to be reproduced by the secretariat, they must be stored in an appropriate place so they can be transported to the room before the session begins. For a small conference, this does not present a significant problem, as there will probably not be many materials.

A larger conference having many sessions and resource people may require a special room where all the materials can be placed before being delivered to the specific meeting rooms. This may require provision for transportation if there are many materials for concurrent sessions. If more than one building is being used, the problem is exacerbated, so it is important to identify appropriate location(s) that allow easy access and delivery of the materials.

Chapter 7

Presenters and Speakers

CHECKLIST FOR PRESENTERS: SPEAKERS AND RESOURCE PEOPLE

Exploration

_____ Who will be responsible for maintaining the Presenter Control Worksheet?

_____ Why is this speaker being considered?

_____ Does the speaker understand the type of speech that is expected?

_____ Is this presenter a controversial figure?

_____ Will presenters require an honorarium or fee?

_____ Who has final approval of a presenter?

_____ Has the proposed presenter been monitored or previewed?

_____ Have references been requested and checked?

_____ Are preview tapes available?

_____ Has the presenter been interviewed?

Invitation

_____ Has the presenter been given information about the purpose of the conference?

_____ Does the presenter know the reason for the invitation?

_____ Will the presenter be assigned a topic or allowed to select the topic?

_____ Will a form be used to "call for papers" or to solicit information from prospective presenters?

_____ At what point will the presenter and topic be approved?

_____ Is the presenter available at the day and time designated?

_____ Does the presenter agree with the amount of time allotted?

_____ Does the presenter know how the event/session will relate to the rest of the conference program?

_____ Can the presenter be given some idea of the size of the audience?

_____ What can the presenter be told about the composition of the audience?

_____ Do both parties agree to fees, expenses, and related factors?

_____ Have possible formats been discussed with the presenter?

_____ Will someone meet with the presenter before the conference?

After Presenter Accepts

_____ What information is needed for marketing the conference?

_____ What information is needed for the participant book?

_____ Have due dates been established for the presenters' materials?

Preparation

_____ Has the presenter given permission to tape?

_____ Will copies of the presentation be made available?

_____ Will the presenter need special equipment?

_____ Has the presenter been asked to provide a bio and a photograph?

134

_____ Will a companion be coming with the presenter?

_____ Who will make the sleeping room reservation for the presenter?

_____ How will transportation arrangements be made?

_____ When can final confirmation from the presenter be expected?

_____ Are any special security arrangements required?

_____ What is the back-up arrangement for the presenter?

_____ How will last-minute, on-site emergencies be handled?

_____ Will provision be made for deaf and blind participants?

_____ What will be in the presenter's kit?

On-Site

_____ Will hosts be assigned to the presenters?

_____ What materials should be given to the presenter?

_____ Will there be a rehearsal with the presenter?

_____ Who is responsible for handling payment and/or reimbursement?

_____ Will presenters be able to attend other parts of the conference?

_____ Will the presenter need local transportation?

_____ Has a "ready room" been provided for presenters?

At Time of Presentation

_____ Has the room been set up as agreed on?

_____ Will this presenter be talking in conjunction with a meal activity?

_____ Have "during-the-session" factors been planned?

_____ Has the introduction of the presenter been planned?

_____ Are any special seating arrangements required for the speaker or introducer?

After the Session or Event

_____ When will the presenter have to leave?

_____ Will the presenter require transportation to the airport?

_____ Are there any special media arrangements?

_____ Will the participants have an opportunity to meet with the presenter?

Follow-Up

_____ Who will send the presenter a letter of appreciation?

_____ Will copies of publicity be sent to the presenter?

_____ Will comments and/or evaluation forms be sent to the presenters?

_____ Will someone write a memo for the historical file?

SOURCE: *The Comprehensive Guide to Successful Conferences and Meetings* by Leonard Nadler and Zeace Nadler. San Francisco: Jossey-Bass. Copyright © 1987. Permission to reproduce hereby granted.

Presenters may be categorized into two main groups—speakers and resource people. Speakers make presentations at general sessions; those who make presentations at other sessions, such as concurrent sessions, breakout sessions, and workshops, are referred to as resource people.

Speakers—General Sessions

There are various kinds of general sessions. The opening general session is designed as the official opening of a conference. (Sometimes a conference can be opened by other activities, but the usual practice is to open with a general session.) The speaker at the opening general session is typically referred to as the *keynoter,* the person who sets the tone for the entire conference with an opening address. The keynoter for an employer-sponsor conference might be a high-level company officer, a government official, an author, or another dignitary whose work, achievements, status, or public speaking ability fits in with the theme of the conference.

The keynoter for a membership sponsor might be the ranking elected officer of the organization if the officer has speechmaking talent; if not the official might be asked only to make some brief welcoming remarks and then introduce the keynoter. The choice of a public seminar keynoter varies greatly, depending on the nature of the specific sponsor and the purpose of the conference.

General sessions may also be held during a conference. The examples of conference designs presented in Chapter Three show how general sessions may be used. In Example B, Events 5, 13, and 21 are general sessions designed to provide a stimulus for the day through the use of a panel. In Example C, Events 6 and 13 are designed to encourage all participants to arrive at 8:00 A.M. and begin the day together—a good technique for a large conference, where it is desirable to give the participants a feeling of belonging to one organization.

A general session need not present a speech. The general sessions in Example B used panel discussions, which were followed by breakout sessions to enable participants to probe the content in more depth and to talk to the members of the panel at greater length. The panel members assisted in planning and structuring those breakout sessions.

A multimedia presentation is another alternative for a general session. The general session (Event 4) in Example C could be used as a forum for reporting the year's activities to the membership through the use of multimedia. At a later session, possibly Event 13, multimedia could be used as a way of introducing the new officers of the membership sponsor, with a focus on their goals for the year.

Small conferences can employ many variations, such as starting with some form of needs analysis or a review of the objectives of the conference.

A general session can also be used as the closing session, which helps to end the conference on a positive note. In Example A, Event 13 (general session) is purposely placed at the end of the day to encourage the participants to stay for the entire day and to provide participants' feedback from the day's workshops. In Example B, Event 25 (lunch and speaker) is the closing general session. In Example C, the closing general session (Event 28) affords a link to the next year's conference. In Example D, Event 25 was used for evaluation purposes as well as a formal closing.

Some international and government conferences have very formal openings and closings. Conferences sponsored by the United Nations, for example, are not considered open until the appropriate official or dignitary announces, "I declare this conference open," and the same holds for the close of the conference. The formal statement is required whether the conference has twenty or two thousand participants.

Resource People

Resource people refer to those who have some kind of responsibility for a session or an event. These are not people who are part of the secretariat, but people who are involved in the content rather than the logistics. The workshop leaders of Events 8 and 11 in Example A are resource persons. In Example C (Event 12), the cracker barrel session of the participant who has responsibility for opening, overseeing, and closing the session is a resource person. The same applies to Events 11B and 19A (the film festival). A resource person probably would not be needed for Event 19B (poster session), as the secretariat can handle the logistics of this event. (If participants must be screened for this event, a resource person would be required.) In Example D, all facilitators are resource people.

The Checklist

Exploration

The questions in this section should be reviewed before negotiations start and throughout the exploration period. The exploration, selection, and invitation

Figure 31. Presenter Control Worksheet.

Speaker name: _____

Address: _____

_____

Telephone: work ( ) _____

home ( ) _____

(as appropriate)

Organization: _____

Division: _____

Control person: _____

Conference event: _____

Title of presentation (for brochure copy): _____

_____

_____

Date of presentation: _____

Time: from _____ to _____

Financial Arrangements:

Type	Yes	No	Amount	Comments
Honorarium or fee				
Travel reimbursement				
Accommodations				
Other				

Forms:

Item	Date Sent	Date Received	Comments
Travel reservation			
Hotel reservation			
AV requirements			
Policy statements			

Figure 31. Presenter Control Worksheet, Cont'd.

Item	Date Sent	Date Received	Comments
Speaker information			
Companion			
Other			

Support:

Function	Name	Date Invited	Date Accepted	Comments
Host				
Introducer				
Handout materials				

SOURCE: *The Comprehensive Guide to Successful Conferences and Meetings* by Leonard Nadler and Zeace Nadler. San Francisco: Jossey-Bass. Copyright © 1987. Permission to reproduce hereby granted.

of presenters may be done by the coordinator, design committee members, or the sponsor; it is also possible to delegate these tasks to a member of the secretariat or to a consultant. In the following discussion, the coordinator is identified as the responsible person with the understanding that this may not be the case in all situations.

Who Will Be Responsible for Maintaining the Presenter Control Worksheet?

The coordinator, the design committee, and the secretariat should have a good deal of information about each presenter. The identification, selection, and preparation of presenters is a complicated process, and some formal control is absolutely essential, particularly when the conference needs many presenters. The Presenter Control Worksheet, shown in Figure 31, is one formal method of control.

The worksheet should be kept in a specific place, one that is known to all. (If confidentiality is required, necessary clearance or permission measures can be implemented.) Each presenter should have a designated control person who is responsible for keeping the worksheets current.

Why Is This Speaker Being Considered?

Speakers may be invited for many reasons. For a general session, should the speaker be informative, inspirational, or humorous? It may be possible to find a speaker who can be all three, but what is the major objective of that particular general session?

A speaker might be an expert on a particular topic or the author of a new book related to the theme of the conference. A speaker might be considered just because the sponsor suggested that person. No matter what the reason, it should be clearly understood by everyone involved in identifying and selecting speakers.

Does the Speaker Understand the Type of Speech That Is Expected?

A speaker may have an excellent reputation for being a humorist, which was perhaps the reason for the invitation. If that speaker wants to use a different approach, or wants to project a different image, this general session is probably not the time or the place to do it. Everyone concerned should understand what is expected of the speaker.

Is This Presenter a Controversial Figure?

Controversial figures are sometimes needed for a conference, depending on the nature of the controversy. Usually, a person who is controversial because he or she has broken the law would not be considered appropriate. Think back, however, to the days of the civil rights activists. Martin Luther King, Jr., violated the law many times with his acts of civil disobedience yet would have been a very appropriate selection for some conferences. When a controversial figure is being considered, the coordinator owes it to the sponsor and the design committee to make that known. The sponsor particularly should have final approval of any controversial presenters who are under consideration.

Will Presenters Require an Honorarium or Fee?

Not all presenters require an honorarium, fee, or other form of compensation. Keynote speakers, however, are almost always paid. After all, they have been asked to speak because of their status in the community or society. Many demands are made on their time, and they allocate some of that time based on the fee involved. Fees can range from $100 to over $10,000 for a one-hour talk if the speaker is very prominent.

Some speakers are represented by agents, and others are available for direct negotiation. Agents are very experienced in fee negotiation and generally use written contracts. The coordinator is cautioned to read the speaker's contract carefully before signing. In addition to the deposit (discussed in Chapter Sixteen), the contract may include other expenses or penalties for cancellation or changes. Working through an agent has benefits, however. Agents are experienced and want to protect their reputations. They can be helpful in clarifying many of the points that less experienced people can overlook.

The sponsor may have a strict policy on fees, and if so, that should be clearly understood by the coordinator. We recall one membership-sponsor conference where the coordinator negotiated with one of the sponsor's own members, who had an international reputation. The member agreed to be the keynote speaker for about half of his usual fee. The coordinator was elated, but the sponsor promptly told the coordinator that it was against association policy to pay any speaker's fee to its own members!

Payment for resource people varies greatly. Resource people for a for-profit public seminar sponsor are generally paid, and a nonprofit public seminar sponsor may also pay resource people. An employer sponsor almost always pays when the resource person is not an employee.

After a fee is negotiated, it should be noted on the Presenter Control Worksheet. For an international presenter, the type of currency should also be noted, whether in the currency of the country of venue, the sponsor's home country (if different), the presenter's country, or some other financial arrangement.

Who Has Final Approval of a Presenter?

Even though no formal invitation has yet been proffered, it is important to know who has final approval of a presenter. If the sponsor is to have final approval, it is necessary to agree on this during the exploration phase. Otherwise, the coordinator may start negotiating with a presenter who is later rejected by the sponsor, and the negotiations will have been a waste of time. If the design committee has final approval, perhaps it should not recommend presenters so it does not have to defend its own recommendations.

Has the Proposed Presenter Been Monitored or Previewed?

Some presenters are so well known that no preview is necessary. In general, however, the speaker should be observed in action by the coordinator or a member of the design committee. Of course, the differences in conference objectives, venue, and participants should be taken into account: The observed speaking engagement may be much different from the one under consideration. It is usually not as important to monitor or preview resource people, unless they are being considered for an unusual technique or a controversial topic.

Have References Been Requested and Checked?

References may be provided by the presenter of someone who has observed that presenter in action. The reference may ask for evaluation data or just the location and date of the similar presentation. If the presenter has not previously presented that topic, the reference may refer to the presenter's general ability. It is not enough merely to obtain the references; they should also be checked. Checking references may be a delicate matter and not always necessary, but when it is required by the nature of the situation or the presenter, it should be handled politely and professionally.

Are Preview Tapes Available?

Some speakers and resource people have tapes of their past presentations or prepare tapes specifically for marketing purposes. The matter of which tape is being previewed should be clear, so that it can be reviewed in the proper context. A tape made specifically for preview purposes may not fully indicate how the presenter functions in front of a live audience. Likewise, a tape before a live audience may not adequately indicate how that presenter would function in front of your audience. Despite their limitations, preview tapes are a helpful source of data on presenter performance.

Has the Presenter Been Interviewed?

Before seeking a personal interview, the coordinator should have a clear idea of its purpose, since a personal interview takes time and other resources, particularly when the presenter lives in a different city. In addition, a potential presenter may not be willing to spend time on an interview without some compensation. However, a personal interview—particularly with a speaker— can have many benefits. The most obvious is that it is possible to find out more about that speaker than appears on a bio sheet or publicity release. The interview can also be used to discuss the purpose of the conference, the prospective participants, topic, content, and delivery. It may also be necessary to interview resource people, particularly in the case of a design that calls for them to be knowledgeable about a topic or theme.

Invitation

Has the Presenter Been Given Information
About the Purpose of the Conference?

When inviting a presenter, information should be provided about the purpose of the conference. Some presenters have prepared (or "canned") speeches that may be wonderful, but not for this conference. The more the prospective presenter knows about the purpose of the conference, the greater the possibility of a good match.

Does the Presenter Know the Reason for the Invitation?

The coordinator knows the reason for inviting the presenter, but does the presenter know? As discussed earlier, a speaker may be under consideration for many different reasons and should know what is expected. Resource people should also be give this necessary information. The presentation-skills reasons may be the same as for speakers, but it is also possible that the resource person has special small-group skills, or is an expert on a topic of interest to a particular group of participants.

It is not unusual for a presenter to be invited because of a recommen- dation from another source. Someone in the sponsoring organization may have heard the presenter at another conference or may have read the presenter's book. This latter situation must be handled cautiously, because a good author is not necessarily a good presenter.

Will the Presenter Be Assigned a Topic or Allowed to Select the Topic?

Which comes first, the topic or the presenter? If the presenter is chosen first, presumably he will be allowed to select, or at least recommend, the topic. The presenter should not be given complete latitude in selecting a topic, of course, because some topics may be inappropriate for these particular participants. The presenter cannot be expected to know these topics, so it is the responsibility of the coordinator to provide this information. Indeed, after hearing some of these taboo areas, the presenter may choose not to accept the invitation. On the other hand, after discussion, the presenter might suggest a topic that would be of great interest but had not previously been considered.

The other approach is to select a topic and then search for a presenter who can handle that topic in the manner expected by the coordinator. In this case, the coordinator should inform the prospective presenter as to which approach stimulated the invitation.

Will a Form Be Used to "Call for Papers" or to Solicit Information from Prospective Presenters?

Thus far, the discussion has focused on inviting specific presenters, but another approach known as a "call for papers" or a "request for proposal" may be used. This method is seldom employed for speakers but is a common practice for resource people. The "call for papers" is usually associated with a professional sponsor where papers are actually read. Although this practice has changed, some coordinators still use the term *call for papers,* which often confuses resource people. Figure 32 shows the Request for Proposal form, which can be used for screening prospective resource people. It includes more detail than may be needed for a particular conference, but all the items on the form are important.

This form should be accompanied by information about the purpose of the conference, any special instructions relevant to resource people, and should indicate where the form is to be sent and the name of a contact person who will respond to inquiries. For a small conference, the contact person is usually the coordinator; a larger conference that receives many completed forms typically assigns a knowledgeable member of the secretariat to that task.

Item 3 on the form provides for up to two presenters, usually the maximum number for a session. In the case of a panel, the moderator can be considered the prime correspondent and identify the panel members under Item 7.

Item 4 requires only a brief description at this time, as opposed to longer publicity or promotional copy. Item 5 is important since sessions can be presented at various levels, requiring differences in experience and/or knowledge of the participants. Some presenters might be very specific, requiring that the participants must have a given number of years in the field, a specific license or certification, or a specified academic degree. Some sessions

Figure 32. Request for Proposal.

Instructions: Please fill out this form as completely as possible. Selection will be primarily based on the information you provide here. If you have any questions, call _____(name and phone of contact person)_____.

In this space, the coordinator should provide information about:
- Conference theme
- Dates of the conference
- Objectives and/or purpose
- Anticipated number of participants
- Topics being sought
- Final date for submission
- Special instructions on typing or printing of proposal, number of copies, exact address for submission, and attachments.

1. Proposed title of session: _____

_____

2. Type of session:

   General _____ Concurrent _____ Breakout _____

3. Presenter(s):

   (If more than one, list as A and B. The person listed as A will be considered the prime correspondent.)

   A. Name: _____

      Address: _____

                     _____

      Telephone: work ___(   )_____

                  home ___(   )_____

      Organization: _____

      Division: _____

   B. Name: _____

      Address: _____

                     _____

      Telephone: work ___(   )_____

                  home ___(   )_____

      Organization: _____

      Division: _____

Figure 32. Request for Proposal, Cont'd.

4. Brief description of the session in fifty words or less. (If you are selected, you will be asked to revise this description for preconference publicity and for the participant book.)

5. Indicate the type of participant to whom your session will be directed.

    A. No experience or knowledge   _____

    B. Some experience or knowledge   _____

    C. Very knowledgeable and experienced   _____

6. How will the participants benefit from attending your session?

7. Briefly describe the techniques/methods you will use to conduct this session.

8. What special requirements will you have as to room setup and audiovisual materials?

9. Have you previously conducted this or a similar presentation?

    Yes _____ No _____

    A. If "Yes," please provide the following for reference:

        1. _____
           (name)   (organization/title)   (phone)

        2. _____

        3. _____

Figure 32. Request for Proposal, Cont'd.

B. If "No," why do you want to offer this session?

_____

_____

_____

10. **Preferred scheduling:**

A. **The conference will be held on the dates indicated above.**

What date do you prefer?   _____

A.M. _____   P.M. _____

11. **Financial arrangements:**

(This section will vary with each sponsor. In some cases, the policy statement of the sponsor can be provided. In others, the following may be used:)

Are you requesting any of the following?

A. Honorarium/fee $ _____

B. Travel $ _____

C. Accommodations $ _____

D. Other (please specify) $ _____

12. **Taping and publications:**

A. If you are selected, will you grant permission for taping (audio or video) of your session?   Yes _____   No _____

B. If you have a prepared paper, will we have permission to publish it as part of the conference proceedings?   Yes _____   No _____

13. **Any special comments or questions?**

SOURCE: *The Comprehensive Guide to Successful Conferences and Meetings* by Leonard Nadler and Zeace Nadler. San Francisco: Jossey-Bass. Copyright © 1987. Permission to reproduce hereby granted.

might also require a prerequisite session, that is, a session at an earlier conference that is the basis for this advanced session.

Item 6 forces the proposer to think of outcomes. If the proposal is accepted, this information can also be helpful in marketing. Items 7 and 8 can also be used for marketing. Some participants want interactive sessions, while others are looking for sessions where they can be passive. This information helps the coordinator provide an effective mix of concurrent sessions.

Item 9, asking for references, was discussed earlier in this chapter. For Item 10, scheduling, some exact time blocks can be requested if a general matrix has been developed.

Item 11, regarding financial arrangements, must be handled very carefully. Some coordinators prefer not to include it on the form at all (for doing so implies that some kind of payment or reimbursement will be made) but rather to negotiate each financial arrangement individually, as the need arises. This policy can lead to dissatisfaction, however, when resource people receive different financial benefits due to their negotiation skill. Presenters have canceled just prior to the conference when this information came to their attention.

Item 12, on taping and/or publishing the presentation, can be a factor in selection. Item 13, additional space for comments, frequently produces significant responses: Prospective presenters feel that they are doing more than just filling in blanks; they might actually influence the design of the conference.

At What Point Will the Presenter and Topic Be Approved?

A specific time should be established for approving the proposals, which must be related to the earlier question of "who will approve." After the final date, some changes may emerge as the result of new topics or new presenters, but at some point, final approval and decisions must be made.

Changes are inevitable. A particular presenter may be approved, but not her topic, requiring further negotiation. After reviewing a proposal, it may be decided that a topic is excellent, but not that presenter and, in those cases, the coordinator may have to find a different presenter.

Is the Presenter Available at the Day and Time Designated?

The needs of the design must be balanced against availability of presenters. Speakers are usually selected for a particular general session, and the design may not have any flexibility regarding the day and time of these sessions. If the speaker is being sought as the keynoter or as the closing speaker, for example, scheduling those speakers for a different general session is not acceptable. If general sessions are placed within the design, as in Example B, Events 5, 13, and 21 (see Chapter Three), it may be possible to switch a speaker from one general session to another during the design process, but that would depend on the flow of the conference.

There is usually more flexibility with resource people, particularly those doing concurrent sessions. Unless there is some particular flow in the design that dictates otherwise, there is a good deal of latitude available in assigning resource people to days and times. Of course, a one-day conference does not offer as much flexibility as one that is several days in length.

Does the Presenter Agree with the Amount of Time Allotted?

There is nothing magical about the allocation of time, although there are some guidelines. A general session is usually about ninety minutes, with the speaker limited to forty-five minutes to one hour, depending on the type of presentation. In a smaller general session of fifty or fewer participants, time can be provided for the speaker to interact with them. Larger groups make interaction more difficult but this does not eliminate the possibility altogether. Concurrent and breakout sessions generally run up to ninety minutes without a break. If they go beyond that time, a break at the hour or halfway point is desirable.

The design may dictate the allotted time, and in this situation the presenter must agree to the available time. If the design is flexible, discussion with the presenter is advisable. Hopefully, by the end of the discussion, both the coordinator and presenter should feel comfortable with the time allotted.

Does the Presenter Know How the Event/Session Will Relate to the Rest of the Conference Program?

When negotiating with presenters, the coordinator needs to have enough of the design defined so that the presenter can relate to the rest of the conference. The presenter's major concerns are knowing what other sessions will be held at the same time and who will be the presenters at other events. However, the coordinator may want to keep this information confidential to avoid complications. In a large membership sponsor conference, for example, there is generally competition to get on the program, and the coordinator can expect to receive many more proposals than there are spots available. As making final selections can be a political issue, no presenter is given any information on other presenters until all have been selected and notified.

Can the Presenter Be Given Some Idea of the Size of the Audience?

The size of the audience influences the presenter's preparations. For example, a speaker is expected to use a different form of delivery for an audience of five thousand than for one of fifty participants. It is usually possible to give speakers some idea of audience size at their general sessions; audience size is generally equal to the total number of registered participants minus a certain percentage who do not attend general sessions.

It is more difficult to provide this information to resource people, for the design usually calls for concurrent (competing) sessions. Even a pre-conference survey can only provide some vague indication of the number who will attend any session. For large conferences, session attendance can be controlled by tickets, which allow a coordinator to know the largest possible number who may attend. Experience has shown, however, that not all ticket holders necessarily attend the session. For resource people, a range can be indicated because a room must be assigned, and this automatically limits the maximum number, if fire laws and space considerations are complied with.

What Can the Presenter Be Told About the Composition of the Audience?

Some speakers (such as dignitaries or authors) may be unfamiliar with the particular sponsor or expected participants. In the early stages of design, the coordinator should develop a profile of expected participants and share this information with the speaker. As the time of the conference nears and the coordinator receives preregistrations, this profile may be verified or contradicted. If the participant profile does change, the coordinator should share the new data with the speaker.

In the Request for Proposal, the resource person is asked to describe the type of participant to whom a session would be directed (see Figure 32, Item 5). As the design and planning proceed, the coordinator may discover from the responses that the desired type of participant will not be available for that session. This information should be shared with the resource person who is planning a session.

Do Both Parties Agree to Fees, Expenses, and Related Factors?

Before final agreement and confirmation, all elements should be rechecked and the coordinator should determine that there is agreement. It is not suggested that any of the parties are trying to manipulate or obtain unwarranted advantages, only that it is realistic to expect that there can be changes during the time of negotiation that may have been missed by either of the parties. A final check on total agreement is a good practice.

Have Possible Formats Been Discussed with the Presenter?

The presenter may choose from many different formats. Besides or in addition to a speech, speakers can also use an audience reaction panel or a question-and-answer period. The speaker might use an interview format or audiovisual materials as the basis for a general session. (Chapter Eight contains a thorough discussion of audiovisual formats.) Speakers who have been selected more because of their expertise than their public speaking skills might welcome the assistance of someone who can help them in choosing a format.

Resource people, because of the nature of their sessions, have even more possibilities. The coordinator cannot assume that all resource people are equally knowledgeable about the range of available techniques.

If the coordinator is not competent to discuss formats with presenters, she could call in a consultant specializing in this area. That consultant would be a temporary contract person and designated as such in the budget. It should be a short-term relationship structured so that the consultant does not conflict with the coordinator or slip into the coordinator's role.

Will Someone Meet with the Presenter Before the Conference?

Although it is good practice to meet with each general session speaker sometime before the conference, it is not always necessary or possible to meet with each resource person. If the design requires special functions or roles from the resource person, however, a meeting is helpful. In Example A, resource people are expected to function as workshop leaders in Events 8 and 11, organize their reports during Event 12, and later deliver a brief presentation in Event 13. In cases like these, the coordinator should brief these resource people prior to the conference or arrange a briefing breakfast on the first morning of the conference.

After Presenter Accepts

What Information Is Needed for Marketing the Conference?

The identities of the presenters are important for marketing activities for most conferences. After the presenters have accepted, the titles and descriptions of the sessions should be refined with the help of each presenter. To simplify the process, the coordinator can ask each presenter for a revision of the original proposal, which should then be edited for clarity and consistency. Another approach is to edit or rewrite the material in the original proposal and then send it to the presenters for their approval. Not all of this material will be utilized in marketing, but most of it will be used as the basis for marketing information.

What Information Is Needed for the Participant Book?

It is not too early to begin preparing material for the participant book— verifying the title, descriptions of the sessions, names and titles of presenters, time of presentation, and related material. See Chapter Eighteen for a thorough discussion of the participant book.

Have Due Dates Been Established for the Presenters' Materials?

The presenters should have some idea of when they must submit various kinds of material. Many of these items will be discussed in the remainder of this checklist. The intent here is to ensure that everybody knows that a master calendar must be established to bring together all those due dates from various pieces that are related to presenters and are part of conference planning.

Preparation

Has the Presenter Given Permission to Tape?

Not all sessions need to be taped, but there seems to be an increasing trend in that direction. Legally, a release form must be signed by the presenter to allow for taping.

Will Copies of the Presentation Be Made Available?

Some presenters deliver a printed speech word for word and make copies of the speech available to the media in order to avoid being misquoted. Other presenters deliver a written speech but not on a word-for-word basis, so the copy that is distributed may not be what was actually said. And still other presenters work from an outline, modifying the presentation based on the audience and other factors and supplementing the presentation with audiovisual materials or printed handouts. The sponsor may plan to publish conference proceedings, which requires written material about each presentation, such as the actual speech, an outline provided by the presenter, or notes taken by an observer and reviewed by the presenter.

If some kind of printed material on the session is to be made available, who has the responsibility for providing it? The presenter may be required to provide sufficient copies for all participants; if the secretariat is to provide copies, it is necessary to have a budget item for that. A deadline must be established so that reproduction can proceed in an orderly fashion and provision made for storing, shipping, and distribution.

Will the Presenter Need Special Equipment?

It is necessary to determine the special equipment needed by each presenter, and that information will have been gathered from the Request for Proposal (Figure 32). This form is usually submitted many months before the proposal is accepted, however, and new equipment needs may have arisen in the meantime. A final date should be established for presenters to make additional equipment requests; after that time, such requests should be accepted only in exceptional circumstances. See Chapter Eight for detailed description of audiovisual equipment.

Has the Presenter Been Asked to Provide a Bio and a Photograph?

The biographical data for each presenter can be used for many purposes. To avoid confusion and unnecessary paperwork, the coordinator should determine the minimum information needed. The request for this data can be sent to the presenters in the form of a questionnaire or form.

The same information should be requested from each presenter in order to avoid competition among them, to discourage the submission of numerous pages of biographical material, and to elicit the appropriate information for publicity and the participant book.

The coordinator should not request a presenter's photograph unless it will be used. When a black-and-white photo is needed, the coordinator should request (1) the specific size desired (usually 5″ x 7″), (2) the type of print (usually glossy), (3) the date the photo was taken, and (4) the presenter's name clearly printed on the back.

Will a Companion Be Coming with the Presenter?

When a resource person brings a companion, it is generally at his own expense, although this can be negotiated. If it is agreed that the conference will assume some responsibility for the companion, it is important to obtain at least the name of the companion and the relationship to the resource person. The latter may influence such arrangements as sleeping rooms: In some cities in the United States, a man and a woman may not register for the same room when they have different names—even if they are married. Embarrassment can be avoided if this matter is explored before check-in time.

The situation can be even more complex when international presenters are used. In some countries, the wife never takes the husband's name; in others, no family names are used at all. If unsure what to do about room accommodations, the coordinator should check with the presenter's embassy.

Some companions want to be left almost entirely on their own, while others expect special treatment, such as assistance with shopping or sightseeing. The coordinator must explore each case on an individual basis. A detailed discussion of companions is presented in Chapter Eleven.

Who Will Make the Sleeping Room Reservation for the Presenter?

If presenters are to be reimbursed for their sleeping room expenses, it is to the coordinator's advantage to make the room arrangements. This allows for more block booking of sleeping rooms at the site and puts the coordinator in a better negotiating position with the hotel. It also reduces the paperwork for this item, as the rooms can be billed to the conference master account. If the presenters are to make their own arrangements, that should be specified. It is common practice to make room arrangements for a speaker; less common for resource people.

How Will Transportation Arrangements Be Made?

The above discussion on sleeping rooms is generally applicable to transportation arrangements. If a specific airline carrier or travel agent has been arranged for the conference, the same advantages of negotiation and billing apply. The kinds of air travel permissible through this arrangement should be stipulated in an agreement because the carrier or travel agent may be handling participant travel as well as that of presenters. The airline or agent may have different contact persons for each category as well as different allowances or conditions that should be clarified before the first phone call is received from a presenter or a participant. Secretariats that handle transportation for presenters must be knowledgeable in the area of transportation, particularly air transportation.

Estimating the cost of air travel is precarious since rates change so rapidly and drastically. If presenters are to make their own arrangements, they should be told the maximum amount of reimbursement possible. (Some presenters may wish to add on personal or business travel, and others have their own travel agents with whom they prefer to work.) What the presenter must submit for reimbursement (the actual ticket carbon or a copy) should be clarified. The presenter may be doing additional travel, part of which is reimbursable from another source that also requires the ticket carbon, and if this is not clarified at the outset, it will be resolved ultimately, but only after unnecessary paperwork, phone calls, and confusion.

When Can Final Confirmation from the Presenter Be Expected?

Up to this point we have been examining this preparation process from the viewpoint of the coordinator, but the presenter must also be considered. Whether resource people are asked to submit proposals or are invited to be on the conference program, it is probable that there has been a time lag between proposal or invitation and acceptance, and during that time there can be some changes. In almost all cases, a check should be made to determine whether they are still interested and available. Too many coordinators work on the assumption that notifying the resource people of acceptance mades it binding on both sides. Obviously, it is a good idea to ask presenters to confirm that they are still available.

Are Any Special Security Arrangements Required?

Although security is discussed in detail in other chapters, the item is included on this checklist so it is not overlooked. The list of presenters should be reviewed to determine if any special kinds of security arrangements may be required.

What Is the Back-Up Arrangement for the Presenter?

The recurring nightmare of many coordinators is the no-show—the session is ready to start and the resource person is nowhere to be found. Fortunately, no-shows are rare, but they must be considered in the early stages of planning. The coordinator can establish checkpoints to determine if the resource person has arrived. A no-show at those points can be readily dealt with if there has been some planning for that contingency. For sessions using resource people, a no-show generally means a canceled session; if concurrent sessions have been scheduled, no-shows do not present any significant problems.

The more crucial situation is when a speaker does not show up at a general session, since usually only one speaker has been scheduled for a general session and that speaker has been the focus of publicity. The participants expect that specific speaker, and the coordinator can do little at that point, unless some prior arrangements have been made. If the speaker gives some notice, no matter how brief, it may be possible to present the speaker via phone line supplemented with slides or via a videotape.

When the speaker does not or cannot give notice, the coordinator must have alternatives prepared. A membership-sponsor conference may have a participant qualified to be a replacement who is prepared to step in, similar to an understudy in the theater. For an employer-sponsor conference, the speaker himself will usually find a replacement, though the coordinator may not be informed until the day of the speech. A for-profit public seminar sponsor usually has other speakers who are capable of "pinch hitting"; a nonprofit public seminar sponsor may have some difficulty, depending on the type of speaker who is not able to attei .

How Will Last-Minute, On-Site Emergencies Be Handled?

The coordinator should always consider the "what if" possibilities. What if a presenter arrives late, materials are lost, a presenter arrives but becomes ill, or a presenter develops laryngitis? These are some of the most common emergencies, but a coordinator should consider any others that might arise at a specific conference.

The late arrival of a presenter due to uncontrollable factors is probably the most common emergency. In Example B (see Chapter Three) the luncheon speaker for Event 25 was a United Nations official who only had to fly from New York to Washington, so no difficulties were anticipated. The morning of his presentation, however, he notified the secretariat that the United Nations Secretary-General had called a special meeting that he had to attend. He would probably arrive a little late.

To plan for this possibility, several events were changed slightly. An announcement was made at the general session (Event 21) that the free time (Event 24) would be extended by a half-hour, which would allow some participants to check out. The hotel was asked to delay the luncheon service for a half-hour. The coordinator, a staff member, and the president of the membership sponsor stood at the door of the hotel to greet the late arriving speaker. They shared the tension and discussed other alternatives, such as using a different speaker if the invited one did not show up. Fortunately, only fifteen minutes late, the speaker arrived!

Another common emergency is materials lost on airline flights. The materials might be located and reshipped to the site but arrive after the session has been completed. In most cases, it is not possible to replicate the material in time and at a reasonable cost. The secretariat might have some substitute materials, or some transparencies or flip charts can be made on the spot. If the resource person has masters or clean copy, reproduction of handouts may be possible though expensive. In general, coordinators should suggest that presenters carry their materials in their carry-on baggage.

A presenter who becomes ill just before the presentation is a double emergency. Appropriate medical attention should be provided, while at the same time the coordinator should seek alternatives in case the presenter is unable to conduct the session. Depending on the nature and degree of the illness, the presenter might be able to recommend a participant who can step in, or the coordinator may be able to locate a substitute who can arrive in time to handle the session.

Will Provision Be Made for Deaf and Blind Participants?

In general, handicapped participants do not present any problem for presenters, though they should be informed if some participants will be handicapped in order to prepare appropriately.

Blind participants do not need any special attention during presentations unless visual aids are used; sometimes these aids can be presented in braille, or a participant or member of the secretariat can read or describe the visuals to the blind participant. People who are selected or volunteer for this task should have some experience or instruction in handling this responsibility. Local associations can be helpful in providing such training or even in providing qualified aides when many visuals are used in the presentation. If interpreting equipment is available, it can be used to reduce the possibility of interfering with other participants.

Deaf or partially deaf participants can be assisted, depending on the nature of the disability. Deaf people can participate through the use of signers and sign language. If possible, check with deaf participants before the conference to determine their needs. Partial deafness is becoming a more common condition as the graying of the population continues. Depending on need, cost, and availability, an earphone system, similar to the kind used in theaters, should be considered for conferences where many older people are among the participants.

Presenters who have worked with interpreters will have little difficulty dealing with someone signing while they are presenting, but others will require at least a briefing on how to work in that situation. It can be disconcerting to a presenter who relies on eye contact to find that the participants are looking at someone else. A presenter who works with small groups is used to the "buzz" that emanates from them, but a group of deaf people can be working with a very low noise volume.

What Will Be in the Presenter's Kit?

Most of the material in this section should be assembled into a presenter's kit, which can be sent out at the time a presenter is confirmed or soon after. The items must reflect the particular conference but would include most of the items shown in Figure 33.

Two items in the presenter's kit require special mention. The contact person for a small conference might be either the coordinator or a specific member of the secretariat. For a larger conference with many presenters, it is not advisable to have the coordinator function in that capacity. Instead, a specific member of the secretariat should be assigned to the presenters, and any requests for information, communications, and correspondence should go directly to that secretariat member. For some conferences, the contact person should be a professional colleague rather than an administrative person, which is a decision the coordinator must make.

Sponsor policies, the second item, include specific policies about some issues that should be communicated to presenters in the presenter's kit. An employer sponsor may consider certain topics, words, or phrases taboo. A membership sponsor may have a policy regarding sexist language. Depending on the sponsor and the purpose of the conference, the sponsor may have a policy against "selling from the platform."

On-Site

Will Hosts Be Assigned to the Presenters?

A host can be assigned to meet the presenter on arrival—a particularly crucial element for international conferences. In some situations hosts can be

Figure 33. Presenter Kit.

_____ Travel information and request form

_____ AV requirements

_____ Participant description

_____ Tape permission form

_____ Contact person in secretariat

_____ Sponsor policies

_____ Housing information and request form

_____ Expense forms

_____ Session materials

_____ Conference registration form

SOURCE: *The Comprehensive Guide to Successful Conferences and Meetings* by Leonard Nadler and Zeace Nadler. San Francisco: Jossey-Bass. Copyright © 1987. Permission to reproduce hereby granted.

considered cordial; in others they are mandatory. In some countries, entry of certain foreign nationals is permitted only when a qualified national of the host country meets and accepts responsibility for that foreigner at the airport.

To be safe, all international presenters should be met on arrival. Astonishingly, many presenters forget to obtain the necessary visas to enter a country even though that information was sent to them in the presenter's kit. Less experienced presenters sometimes think that the legal aspects will be handled by the secretariat. The host may be able to assist in obtaining the required visa, if one is not held by the presenter at the time of entry.

In the United States, meeting the speaker at the airport is a sign of respect and should be done unless the speaker decides otherwise. For the coordinator, it provides a checkpoint to know that the speaker has actually arrived!

During the conference, the speaker might retain the same host who handled airport reception or be assigned a different host. Resource people might also be assigned hosts, depending on the number of resource people, their status in relation to the sponsor, and the resources available to the coordinator.

What Materials Should Be Given to the Presenter?

The materials given to presenters on arrival depend on the particular conference. Each presenter should receive a participant packet (see Chapter Eighteen). In addition, depending on the financial arrangements, each presenter should receive the various function tickets that are available to the participants.

Will There Be a Rehearsal with the Presenter?

No matter how experienced the speaker, the coordinator should still consider a rehearsal, which does not necessarily entail a full dress rehearsal, but rather a walk through of the session. The speaker can see the room, test the sound equipment, ascertain if the lighting is appropriate, work the lectern, and make sure any special equipment is functioning correctly. The rehearsal or walk through must be coordinated with the site, as it can mean extra charges for use of the hall and personnel. The coordinator should also ensure that the site makes no significant changes in either the room or personnel after the rehearsal.

Resource people generally do not need a rehearsal, but they should be invited to visit the room they will be using and to become familiar with it.

Who Is Responsible for Handling Payment and/or Reimbursement?

It may seem a bit early to be thinking about payment or reimbursement for presenters, but forms may need signing, and this can be done while the presenters are at the conference rather than incurring the additional work and expense of correspondence after the conference. It is helpful if presenters can meet the person who will be handling their account since it makes a financial transaction somewhat less impersonal. It also allows for asking questions on the spot rather than becoming involved in protracted negotiations after the conference. In some situations, it may even be possible to make payments or reimbursements at the conference, a policy that is generally appreciated by presenters and that can result in less work for the secretariat after the conference.

Will Presenters Be Able to Attend Other Parts of the Conference?

Some presenters arrive just in time for their own sessions and leave right after them. Although some have good reasons for this, others do not stay longer because no one has made provision for them to attend other sessions or to take part in other events. Potential participants might be encouraged to attend if they knew the presenters would stay for the entire conference, even for a one-day conference.

In an employer sponsor conference, the presenter may not be part of the sponsoring organization, but might still be invited to attend some of the other sessions. Caution should be exercised if the presenter is considered an outsider; some kind of approval or clearance may be required.

At a membership sponsor conference, a presenter who is not a member might benefit from attending other sessions and the exhibition. This could be considered one of the attractions that encourages a presenter to be on the program.

Will the Presenter Need Local Transportation?

One form of local transportation that is usually provided for speakers is shuttle service to and from an airport or railroad station. Similar transportation for resource people would depend on their numbers, status, and need.

Sometimes local transportation is provided to ensure that speakers arrive at their sessions on time. A limousine can be hired or a volunteer selected from among the participants or the secretariat.

Has a "Ready Room" Been Provided for Presenters?

The ready room is the room where all presenters should be advised to report either upon arrival at the site or at some designated time prior to their appearance on the program. One way to reinforce this is to have registration for presenters in this room rather than in the regular registration area. A member of the secretariat should be on duty at all times and be prepared to provide the coordinator with a status report on which presenters have checked in and which have not. This report serves as an early warning signal about potential problems or no-shows.

The location of the ready room is important and should be carefully selected. The ready room should be located wherever most of the sessions are being held, whether in a headquarters hotel or a conference center.

Presenters should be encouraged to visit the room and spend some time in it. Coffee and other amenities might be offered, and an information board can keep the presenters up-to-date on the events at the conference. Presenters whose materials have been reproduced by the secretariat should be able to see them before their session. All of these materials can be placed in the ready room or just a sample set to be examined by the presenter at time of check-in. Access to this room should be monitored, and admission should be limited to presenters, hosts, moderators, and other people directly related to the purpose of the room.

At Time of Presentation

Has the Room Been Set Up as Agreed On?

It is very disconcerting to a presenter, after providing information to the coordinator about the room setup, to arrive for a session and find that the room is not as requested. There can be a good reason for the difference, and this should have been communicated to the presenter, but that is not always possible. Presenters should check, in the ready room, to verify that the room is set up as requested. If there have been any changes, the person staffing the ready room should be able to explain them. Frequently, the wrong setup is merely a result of miscommunication with the housekeeping or maintenance staff. When correcting room setups, presenters should not be permitted to give directions to the site staff. Directions should come only from the coordinator or the secretariat staff member who has the proper authority. Resetting rooms can become costly if not controlled.

Will This Presenter Be Talking in Conjunction with a Meal Activity?

When presenters may speak in connection with a meal (luncheon or dinner speakers, for example), the event must be carefully coordinated with the food service manager. The starting and stopping times should be agreed upon, and thought should be given to possible emergencies. Other related factors are discussed in detail in Chapter Nine.

Have "During-the-Session" Factors Been Planned?

Minor items sometimes interfere with a smooth-running session. A final check should be made to determine whether physical factors are satisfactory: water pitchers and glasses, smoking/no-smoking signs, placement of ashtrays, a clock, audiovisual equipment, and the like.

Has the Introduction of the Presenter Been Planned?

Every presenter should be introduced. The type of introduction varies, but generally the introduction should be kept to a minimum. The participants are already in the room, so there is no need to "sell" the presenter to them. They should already have read the biographical information about the presenter in the participant book and probably do not need to know any more.

The function of the introducer is just to provide some kind of official opening of the session. The introducer should meet the presenter before the session, if only briefly. A negative, but all too frequent, introduction is, "I have never heard our presenter before, but I understand she is a great gal who does an outstanding job." Another troublesome note is sounded when the introducer, who has just met the presenter, wants to show that they are old friends. The late Gordon Lippitt, who was a general session speaker at many conferences, used to wince when introduced as "Gordie," a name he detested and one that his friends never used.

The introducer should check the planned introduction with the presenter well in advance of the session rather than a minute or two before; serious omissions or errors might take longer than a few minutes to correct.

At the end of the session, the introducer is expected merely to thank the presenter and make any necessary announcements. Too often the introducer gets "microphonitis," an affliction that occurs when certain people get in front of a microphone and an audience and cannot resist making a speech even though that is not their function.

Are Any Special Seating Arrangements Required for the Speaker or Introducer?

General sessions for large conferences must be carefully staged. Certain questions must be answered before the session, such as: Where will the speaker be prior to the introduction—off-stage or on? Will anyone else be on-stage during the speech? Should the introducer stay on stage?

After the Session or Event

When Will the Presenter Have to Leave?

Resource people do not generally rush away after their presentations. On the other hand, it is a bonus when a speaker remains after the speech and even attends some of the other events.

The length of the speaker's speech should have been determined beforehand, but suppose the general session starts late. Will the speaker be prepared to stay after a given point on the clock? It depends, in part, on the negotiation with the speaker.

Late-starting sessions are less of a problem with resource people, but they too can be very busy people, with limited available time. When the presenters check in, their departure time or commitments should be verified.

Will the Presenter Require Transportation to the Airport?

A presenter may be on a tight schedule and have to get to the airport very soon after the presentation has been completed, with little time to spare. Tight scheduling might be considered the presenter's concern, but it is also the problem of the coordinator, who wants that presenter to do the best job possible; if the presenter is worried about transportation to the airport, that concern can influence her performance. It may be a simple matter for the secretariat to arrange transportation, while the presenter might have difficulty trying to work something out. The benefits to the conference will far outweigh the slight additional work for the secretariat.

Are There Any Special Media Arrangements?

Chapter Thirteen includes discussion of public relations and media activities that relate to particular types of presentations.

Will the Participants Have an Opportunity to Meet with the Presenter?

Many participants appreciate the opportunity to meet a celebrity presenter off stage. These meetings are better arranged after the presentation than before it. If the conference has only a few presenters, they can be invited to a reception specifically in their honor; if there are many presenters, attention should probably be focused on the speakers rather than the resource people.

In Example A (see Chapter Three), the reception (Event 14) was planned so that the participants could meet with the general session speakers. In Example B, the general session panelists were also participants throughout the conference. In Example D, several events were designed for this purpose: During two breakfasts (Events 3 and 13), the presenters sat at different tables so participants could meet them informally. Event 7 (lunch) and Event 12 (beer and conversation) were designed for the same purpose.

Follow-Up

Who Will Send the Presenter a Letter of Appreciation?

All the presenters should receive letters of appreciation for their contribution to the success of the conference. The letter is usually drafted by the coordinator, produced by the secretariat, and signed by a high-level official in the sponsoring organization. It is also appropriate to send a letter to the employers of some presenters or other designated persons. To avoid any embarrassment or misunderstanding, the presenter should be asked for the name, title, and address of the person to whom the letter of appreciation should be sent.

Will Copies of Publicity Be Sent to the Presenter?

Frequently, the interviews and reviews of the conference presenters do not appear until after the conference has closed. The presenters have dispersed and have no way of knowing if a review was published or the tape of their interview ever appeared on TV. The secretariat should maintain files on publicity or use a clipping service, which tracks media stories on a variety of subjects. Sharing this publicity with the presenters is just another way of saying "thank you."

Will Comments and/or Evaluation Forms Be Sent to the Presenters?

Session evaluations by participants are a common conference procedure, and sometimes these evaluations are shared with the presenters. With the use of a computer, it is relatively simple to produce evaluation results for each presenter, but the question is whether to do it. Most good presenters have strong ego needs, which is partly why they are good presenters. They welcome good, helpful feedback. If the intention is to share this information, the decision must be made early enough so it can be part of evaluation planning. See Chapter Nineteen for a thorough discussion of evaluation.

Will Someone Write a Memo for the Historical File?

At many points in this book we suggest maintaining some kind of documentation on the conference, and an important item of the documentation is a write-up on the presenters. This information should be considered confidential and released only with the permission of the coordinator or the sponsor. The file has two purposes. First, someone else in the sponsoring organization, other than the coordinator for this conference, may consider using the presenter in the future, and it can save time and energy if information on the presenter—even unevaluated information—is readily available. Second, the file can be used to provide solid information for a reference for the presenter.

The personal impressions of the coordinator or the secretariat on working with the presenter might be included in the file, but these notations should be monitored before they go into the file since they could be embarrassing or harmful to all concerned. The file should include the early negotiations with each presenter, the proposal forms they submitted, relevant correspondence, the results of financial negotiations, and the evaluation of the presenter's session.

Chapter 8

———◆◆◆———

Use of Audiovisuals

CHECKLIST FOR AUDIOVISUAL EQUIPMENT

Site Factors

_____ Does the site have an AV manager?

_____ Has the coordinator conducted a walk-through of the facility for AV purposes?

_____ Will someone from the secretariat meet the electrician and engineer before the conference?

_____ Who sets up the AV equipment?

_____ When will the final AV setup be completed?

_____ Does the session monitor have a list of emergency numbers for AV problems?

_____ Is the equipment insured?

Rental

_____ Does the site have an AV supplier?

_____ Which AV items are available?

_____ How are costs calculated?

_____ What is the cancellation policy?

_____ What support does the AV supplier provide for maintenance problems?

The Room

_____ Will all participants have an adequate and unobstructed view of the screen or monitor?

_____ Are the physical aspects of the room acceptable?

_____ Are AV facilities built into the room?

_____ Can the site provide a diagram of electrical features?

_____ What is the stated capacity of the room?

_____ Does the room have a platform?

_____ Is the ceiling height adequate for the projectors?

_____ Can a pocket be formed around an aisle projector?

Rehearsals

_____ Are rehearsals necessary?

_____ How will feedback from the rehearsals be used?

_____ Do rehearsals cost extra?

Equipment

_____ What equipment is needed?

_____ What auxiliary equipment may be needed?

_____ What supplies and tools should be on hand?

_____ What is the condition of the available equipment?

_____ Are the loudspeakers fixed or movable?

Personnel

_____ Is someone responsible for AV security?

_____ Who will be the projectionist?

SOURCE: *The Comprehensive Guide to Successful Conferences and Meetings* by Leonard Nadler and Zeace Nadler. San Francisco: Jossey-Bass. Copyright © 1987. Permission to reproduce hereby granted.

Almost all conferences use some kind of audiovisual (AV) aids. The aid may be a device as simple as a bulletin board or as sophisticated as two-way communication via satellite. AV equipment is used to supplement a presentation, in place of a live presentation, for entertainment, and other purposes. Exhibitors also make extensive use of AV in the exhibition area. A list of the more frequently used AV items can be found in Figure 34 and will be discussed later, but for now, some basic definitions. *Audio* is something that can be heard by the participants, *visual* is what can be seen. They can each be used separately, but when combined, they are referred to as *audiovisual*. In general usage, it is customary to refer to AV without making a distinction.

At membership sponsor conferences, presentations are commonly audiotaped or videotaped and sold to participants and the general public. Written permission must be obtained from the presenter—some presenters may agree only if they can receive a royalty or some other form of remuneration.

Major problems arise in terms of what the taping does to the presentation, since the presentation is for the participants and not for some unseen audience. Presenters being taped may play to the unseen audience rather than to the participants in the room. When audio is used, only the spoken part of the presentation is used. If slides or transparencies are used and do not accompany the audiotape, the purchaser, who was not present, will have no idea of what was shown. The presenter can, of course, cope with this by repeating what is being projected, but this is contrary to the preferred use of visuals with an audience.

Videotaping becomes even more complicated. If a high-quality tape is to be produced, the presenter may have to limit movements and almost ignore the participants. The limitations of lighting and focusing can severely inhibit the usual behavior of a presenter. The participants will readily see this and can resent having paid their money to enable the sponsor to produce a marketable item.

Taping has some benefits, in addition to the financial, for through this medium, participants can "attend" more sessions than they could otherwise during a conference. We may someday reach the point where many parts of conferences are presented on tape, leaving more time for personal interaction among participants.

Rent or Buy?

Some sites, particularly conference centers, provide AV equipment as part of their package. The availability of specific items and cost factors should be negotiated at the time of site selection.

When equipment is needed, the rent or buy question must be explored. Purchasing represents a significant expenditure that should then be amortized over the useful life of the equipment. Occasional use of a piece of equipment seldom justifies its purchase. When the sponsor or coordinator produces conferences in several cities, the cost of shipping and insurance generally outweighs the benefits of purchase. The sponsor may already own the necessary AV equipment, but if the sponsor and the conference are not located in the same city the same objection to shipping costs must be considered.

The Checklist

Site Factors

Does the Site Have an AV Manager?

Sites are becoming increasingly involved in supplying AV equipment, either through an outside contractor or through their own in-house equipment and personnel, usually working under an AV manager. The coordinator must investigate whether the site AV manager is just a booking agent for the equipment or is qualified to advise and assist with AV equipment. If qualified, the site AV manager can be a very valuable resource.

Has the Coordinator Conducted a Walk-Through of the Facility for AV Purposes?

During site selection, some consideration should have been given to the conference's AV requirements and the site's AV resources. After the basic conference design has been completed, another walk-through is desirable, this time to review the whole facility in terms of the AV requirements that have been identified during the design stage. Rooms that cannot be darkened, for example, should be noted, and sessions utilizing film projection should not be scheduled for those rooms.

Will Someone from the Secretariat Meet the Electrician and Engineer Before the Conference?

About a week before the conference, a member of the secretariat should meet with certain site personnel, such as the electrician or engineer. The AV requirements should be reviewed in terms of placement and control to avoid overloads or inappropriate locations.

Who Sets Up the AV Equipment?

AV setup includes delivering the equipment to the proper room or location, taping wires with safety tape, ensuring that all equipment is working, and checking the projector to make sure that it has the right lens for the room.

Who physically sets up depends on the source of the equipment. If the coordinator provides the equipment, the coordinator usually handles the setup, unless prohibited by a supplier or union contract or license requirement. Regardless of the source of the equipment, site personnel may still set up or supervise the setup to avoid accidents and damage to site property.

When Will the Final AV Setup Be Completed?

The final setup time depends on the complexity of the AV equipment being used and the availability of the room. A general session may be utilizing sophisticated or complicated equipment, such as multimedia or multiscreen projection, which takes much more time to set up than an overhead projector. If a function is scheduled in the same room just prior to the session, there may not be sufficient time to set up. A detailed schedule should be developed that indicates the amount of setup time needed in each room.

Does the Session Monitor Have a List of Emergency Numbers for AV Problems?

Emergencies can occur during a session and the session monitor (see Chapter Twenty) should have a specific number to call—usually the secretariat—if help is needed. When several emergencies erupt at the same time, the secretariat, as the control point, can decide which has priority. If some emergencies should be directed immediately to site personnel, the names and telephone numbers should be specified.

Some breakdowns (such as a burned-out bulb) can be handled by the monitor, so spares should accompany the equipment if possible. Participants should not be allowed to do any emergency repairs, no matter how simple, and the same holds true for presenters. A broken film, for example, is worth an emergency call to the secretariat, while the presenter continues with the presentation. Some equipment breakdowns are better handled by replacing the equipment and repairing it later outside the session room.

Is the Equipment Insured?

Equipment should be insured. If site equipment is being used, insurance is the responsibility of the site. Even if the coordinator's equipment is being used, it may still be covered by the site insurance policy. Insurance should be verified beforehand, so that some form of coverage is always in force.

Rental

Does the Site Have an AV Supplier?

Some sites offer a choice of several AV suppliers for a particular type of equipment; others insist that only one particular supplier be used (because the company has proven reliable and knows the policies of the site). Although an in-house supplier usually has competitive prices, the coordinator should check this during site negotiations. If the supplier has inordinately high charges, this matter should be discussed with the site personnel during negotiations. When a conference design calls for extensive use of AV equipment, the costs can be a significant factor in site selection.

Which AV Items Are Available?

A particular supplier may specialize in only some AV items. The supplier should provide a printed list that describes all of its equipment and supplies; if a coordinator wants other items, they should be cleared with site personnel. There may be valid reasons why some items are not on the list. One site, for example, does not allow the use of masking tape on the walls, and they extended this to prohibit the use of newsprint, since masking tape is used to attach the newsprint to the walls.

How Are Costs Calculated?

The supplier should be able to present an itemized list of charges for the AV equipment. The coordinator should certainly review the basis for the calculations, as well as the exact amount to be charged.

The charge might be made by the *day,* in which case the exact definition of "day" should be stated. Is it a certain number of hours, and if so, what hours are they? If the coordinator does not explore this matter, she may find later that a day is 9:00 A.M. to 5:00 P.M., and any use outside these hours generates an additional fee. If the times are as noted, when does the clock start running? For a 9:00 A.M. session, for example, AV equipment has to be on site before that time. Does the charge start when the equipment leaves the supplier, arrives at the site, or is in actual use? The same applies to the end of the day.

If charges are made by the *hour,* the same cautions should be exercised. Suppliers usually have an hourly charge when the AV equipment is stored at the site; although this reduces travel time, the other questions must still be clarified.

Quotes on AV equipment rental charges might not include delivery and pickup. The coordinator should also check if an outside firm can cart equipment through the site, or if this can only be done by site personnel.

At the last moment, a coordinator may need additional AV equipment. Can the equipment be supplied at the quoted rates or will a premium charge be added when AV equipment is requested without prior notification?

What Is the Cancellation Policy?

After contracting for AV equipment, a coordinator may want to cancel some or all of the items for various reasons: the conference is canceled, a presenter changes the design of a session or is not able to attend, and the like. If possible, the coordinator should have some cancellation feature built into the contract for these contingencies. Some amount will probably have to be paid, but perhaps something can be saved.

What Support Does the AV Supplier Provide for Maintenance Problems?

Once in operation, many things can go wrong with AV equipment. Many suppliers say they will immediately replace the faulty equipment, and the coordinator should ask how this is to be accomplished. In practice, replacement equipment may actually be available only during certain hours or only at the supplier's place of business. If so, the coordinator should negotiate for additional equipment to be provided at the conference site. If the AV contract is large enough, the supplier will probably agree without question or charge.

The Room

Will All Participants Have an Adequate
and Unobstructed View of the Screen or Monitor?

If AV equipment is used, the results must be clearly seen by all the participants. The only real way to know if the placement is right is to test it, but that is generally difficult because of time and expense. Therefore, a coordinator may have to settle for exploring the possibilities on paper and discussing placement with site personnel, who can be very helpful if the coordinator has a clear idea of what is desired. A small session of twenty-five people may have some flexibility, depending on the size and configuration of the room. A session of 100 participants, on the other hand, may not have many options in a particular room. For a general session, more than one screen may be required.

In addition to taking into account convenience for the participants, the coordinator must also consider utility for the presenter. For example, the presenter may want to be positioned at an overhead projector to write on the transparencies.

Are the Physical Aspects of the Room Acceptable?

Each room has its own peculiarities, which must be examined in terms of AV equipment use. A room with columns is usually considered unsuitable for AV equipment, yet not always: The poles may merely reduce the number of acceptable seats and therefore only limit the number of participants who can attend that session. It may even be possible to set up the projector and screen so that the columns are only a minimal limitation. The same can be said for other obstructions, such as overhead fixtures, mirrors, and windows.

(Windows can be a problem if a film or slide projector is being used that requires that the room be entirely dark.) Before either accepting or rejecting a room for AV equipment, the coordinator should see the room and test the equipment in the room, if possible.

Are AV Facilities Built into the Room?

Rooms in some sites, particularly conference centers, have built-in AV capabilities and usually contain some sophisticated equipment. A large room may even have a projection booth, which can reduce AV noise. On the other hand, nonsite employees are usually not permitted in the projection booth, which might incur an additional personnel expense.

Built-in TV monitors can be used for a variety of purposes, including videocassettes or tape, closed-circuit TV, and regular broadcast TV. Most monitors are fairly small and can serve only about fifteen to twenty people, so additional monitors will be required for larger audiences.

Can the Site Provide a Diagram of Electrical Features?

The electrical features of a room are extremely important in using AV equipment since most projectors require some control over lighting. It is not always necessary to black out a room, so dimmers can be helpful; unfortunately, most rooms were planned so that all the lights are either on or off. If the room has separate switches for different banks of lights, they may not be congruent with the setup. Switches can be used separately to dim the lights on the right- and left-hand sides of the rooms, but not the back and front. That is not helpful for AV purposes.

When using an overhead projector, the room should not be blacked out. If the ceiling lights are directly over the screen, it should be moved before the participants come to the room. Armed with an electrical diagram showing overhead lights, the coordinator can recommend screen placement for the setup crew.

The location of electrical outlets should also be known before setup because additional extension cords may be necessary. With careful planning, it may be possible to set up the room in a way that limits the amount of wire that must be taped to the floor. Advances in technology require more electricity than was previously the case with AV equipment. For a multimedia presentation, for example, the type and adequacy of the electrical current should be determined. The coordinator is not expected to be an electrical expert but should at least be able to ask questions about the adequacy and location of the electrical supply in relation to the equipment.

What Is the Stated Capacity of the Room?

Sites often provide a floor diagram that indicates the capacity of the room for different setups, but when AV equipment is being used, the setup diagrams may have to be altered. The capacity of the room can be changed significantly, depending on the type and position of the equipment.

Does the Room Have a Platform?

A few rooms have permanent platforms. For a general session or a concurrent session with a large participant audience, a permanent platform allows for an AV screen to be placed above the heads of the participants. For a large session in a room with no platform, one should be requested.

Is the Ceiling Height Adequate for the Projectors?

Low ceilings can present a problem. Projectors beam their images in a widening angle. If the ceiling is too low, the screen also has to be lowered, and the participants might have difficulty seeing it.

Can a Pocket Be Formed Around an Aisle Projector?

Frequently, projectors are set up in the aisles (though the projector and screen can sometimes be angled from one corner of the room to the other). When the projector is placed in the aisle, chairs should be removed so there is space around the projector. This pocket allows participants to move without upsetting the projector or causing any safety hazards and provides some space for the projectionist, who should have a "reserved" seat next to the equipment. When the chairs are fastened to the floor or to each other, it may be difficult to provide the pocket, a fact that should be considered when setting up the room.

Rehearsals

Are Rehearsals Necessary?

Although most presenters do not request or need rehearsals, a general session speaker may wish to test equipment, transparencies, or slides and get a feel for the room. The coordinator should also be interested in how the specific equipment projects the transparencies or slides in a particular room. For a general session or banquet where AV equipment will be used, a rehearsal may be necessary to test scripted lighting and projection cues and to ensure that all personnel involved know exactly how to follow the script. Depending on the complexity of the equipment, it may even be desirable to conduct a dress rehearsal using the presenters or stand-ins and the same technicians who will service the function.

How Will Feedback from the Rehearsals Be Used?

Rehearsals are also intended to test the equipment. After a rehearsal, it may be apparent that some of the slides and transparencies must be redone or discarded or the staging may have to be changed. New possibilities may emerge that can improve the session or that suggest different AV possibilities.

Do Rehearsals Cost Extra?

Rehearsals cost money, particularly when site personnel and equipment are involved, though for a large general session the money is almost always well spent. The speaker should not have to apologize for the projector or the material being projected.

Equipment

What Equipment Is Needed?

A wide range of basic AV equipment is available, as shown in Figure 34. Although the coordinator can become an AV authority only with hands-on experience with equipment and supplies, the following discussion provides a brief introduction to AV equipment.

The most common projectors use movie film. Sixteen millimeter (mm) is the most common size of film. Almost all 16 mm are commercially produced, though it is possible for an individual to produce a film. The 8 mm film, generally used for silent home movies, can also be used for some conferences. The old 8 mm was replaced by Super Eight, which projects a larger image and can be either sound or silent. Most projectors are self-loading, which eliminates the chore of opening the projector and looping the film over special sprockets. The film needs only to be placed at a given point, and it automatically feeds into the appropriate places in the projector.

The film loop projector uses 16 mm film loaded in a special cartridge so that it loops or repeats itself. Automatic-load projectors cannot usually handle these special cartridges, as the film cannot be taken out of the cartridge, but some projectors can handle both loop film and standard film.

A filmstrip projector uses 35 mm film that is not cut into individual frames. The strip is loaded into a special carrier in front of the lens and is advanced, a frame at a time, either manually or electronically. It can be coupled with a tape recorder that contains an electronic signal to advance the film at selected points in the narration.

The overhead projector (sometimes called a vu-graph) is one of the most frequently used pieces of equipment. It is a flat plate, usually glass, on which a transparency can be placed. Light beams up through the glass and then projects through a lens fixed above the glass onto a screen or a similar clear surface. The bulb and the lens determine whether or not the room must be darkened, but in most situations the overhead projector can be used in regular light or with minimal dimming. The presenter can face the participants while writing on the transparencies. One of the biggest problems is "keystoning," or projecting an image that is not square or rectangular but resembles a keystone—wide at the top and narrow at the bottom. This can generally be handled by putting the projector on a table of appropriate height, or moving it back from the screen.

The opaque projector has slipped into disuse but may return to popularity. This projector is a very large piece of equipment that can project

Figure 34. Basic AV Equipment.

Projectors	Other
_____ 16 mm sound	_____ Audiotape recorder
_____ 8 mm sound (Super 8)	_____ Board
_____ 8 mm sound	_____ Easel
_____ 8 mm silent	_____ Screen(s)
_____ Film loop projector	_____ Video camera
_____ Filmstrip projector	_____ Videocassette recorder (VCR)
_____ Overhead projector	_____ Video monitor
_____ Opaque projector	
_____ Slide projector (size of slides)	

SOURCE: *The Comprehensive Guide to Successful Conferences and Meetings* by Leonard Nadler and Zeace Nadler. San Francisco: Jossey-Bass. Copyright © 1987. Permission to reproduce hereby granted.

directly from printed material, such as a book page or a drawing. The opaque projector is still useful, though large, heavy, and noisy.

The computer video projector, which picks up an image from a computer screen and projects it onto a large-size screen, will probably proliferate in the coming years. This projector needs a computer in order to function, of course, so additional equipment and sources of electrical power are needed.

The slide projector has not changed significantly over the years, except that today it uses 35 mm slides almost exclusively, as opposed to different sizes and glass slides in earlier years. A variety of projectors are available, most of them using devices holding several slides.

Other types of AV equipment include the audiotape recorder, which was once a massive piece of equipment but is currently available in cassette models that are not much larger than a pack of playing cards. Larger equipment, with reel-to-reel tape, is still used for broadcast quality or when splicing is desired. A small recorder can be used, even for a large audience, by either electronically feeding it through a public address system, or manually placing a microphone near the recorder during playback, although that may introduce noise into the system and can be difficult to hear.

Many kinds of boards are available: (1) the familiar chalkboard; (2) the white board, which has a specially coated surface requiring special felt-tip pens and which can be erased by an ordinary felt eraser or a damp cloth, can also be used as a projection screen, depending on the amount of light emitted from the projector and the surface of the board; (3) the magnetic board on which items can be placed with magnets; (4) the bulletin board; and (5) a new variation of the white board with an attached copier that can immediately produce multiple copies of what has been written on the board. At this time, the board is available from Xerox (Conference Copier) or Okidata, but it can be expected that other companies will also produce this new technology.

An easel (sometimes called an A frame) may be used to hold a flip chart or other previously prepared material. If the presenter or participants are expected to write on the paper, it should be firmly mounted with a solid back.

Projected material generally requires a screen, which may be fixed or portable and comes in various sizes and qualities. Portable screens usually roll up into a metal carrying case, which can be turned into a stand for the screen. Unfortunately, some people damage the screens when they roll them back into the metal case; the coordinator should always check the screens for tears and rips before the presentation.

Advances in video technology are continually influencing the field. Not long ago, the video camera was a large device that had to be supported by a stand and required an electrical outlet or generator. This camera was replaced by the bulky hand-held cameras that still required electrical connection. That, in turn, was replaced by the portable, lightweight camera with its own power source. The playback is done through a videocassette recorder (VCR), which is also portable and easy to use, and a video monitor, such as a common TV set. The size of the screens should be appropriate for the number of participants who will be viewing them. A VCR projector, similar to the computer video projector, may also be used for viewing purposes.

The video camera and screen can be used in another fashion. One of the authors was a keynote speaker at a conference held in the Royal Dublin Society in Ireland. Approximately six hundred people would sit in a long, narrow, and poorly lit room, and the speaker wondered how well he would be seen and heard. Fortunately, he was the closing general session speaker, so he could observe the other general sessions. A video camera was focused on the speaker, and the speaker's image was projected onto a large screen on the center of the stage. The image was actually larger than life-size and easily seen throughout the room.

What Auxiliary Equipment May Be Needed?

Other necessary items may be provided by the site or by the supplier. If so, they can be checked off on Figure 35. These items may also be provided by the coordinator and placed in a special AV control room or in the secretariat room under the control of a designated person. Predicting the number of each item needed is almost impossible. Whatever *might* be needed should be brought. Do not rely on being able to purchase an item at the site.

Adapters, also called wall adapters, are small plugs that enable hookups between equipment and from equipment to wall outlets or extension cords. The most common are the three-hole adapters that facilitate connections between two-pronged plugs and three-hole outlets, and vice versa. Caution should be exercised as some equipment has three prongs for safety reasons. Circumventing the third prong is easy to do, but it is dangerous to the operator and can cause damage to the equipment. Outside of the United States, a variety of outlets can be encountered, including two long thin pins, two short thin pins, two flat blades, and three flat prong blades. In some sites it is not unusual to find two or three different types of outlets in the same room, and

Figure 35. Auxiliary AV Equipment.

_____ Adapters   _____ Pointer, electric

_____ Erasers (chalkboard)   _____ Projection stands

_____ Extension cords   _____ Slide trays

_____ Lectern   _____ Stands, projection

_____ Microphones (type and number)   _____ Sound mixer

_____ Pointer, telescope

SOURCE: *The Comprehensive Guide to Successful Conferences and Meetings* by Leonard Nadler and Zeace Nadler. San Francisco: Jossey-Bass. Copyright © 1987. Permission to reproduce hereby granted.

coordinators working an international conference usually carry a set of the four basic adapters.

When using either a chalk or white board, *erasers* are helpful. A presenter can use a damp cloth, but that is not as convenient to use and must be kept damp.

Extension cords may be needed to reach the available outlets. The cords usually have three prongs and accommodate three-hole plugs, but if not, adapters are required. The cords should not be frayed and, for safety reasons, red cords are preferable.

The site may be able to provide *lecterns* when needed, but the coordinator should have some portable lecterns on hand. Lecterns may be very simple, just to hold the presenter's papers, or may have a built-in amplifying system, reading light, clock, and other features. Some lecterns can be stored flat and then set up when needed.

The most common types of *microphones* should be available in any site that books conferences. A coordinator who conducts many conferences may wish to have a supply of lavaliere microphones since they are not always available. Some sites charge extra for microphones, so having a supply of them can be cost-effective. See Chapter Six for a detailed discussion of microphones.

Some presenters bring their own *pointers,* but it is helpful to have some additional ones on hand. The simplest is the telescope pointer, which is about the size of a ballpoint pen but can be extended to about three feet. It is effective for use in small groups, but for a large group, particularly when the presenter cannot reach the screen, the electric pointer is useful. The pointer, slightly longer than a flashlight but about twice its thickness, can be used with an electrical outlet or batteries and can focus a dot of light or an arrow at any given point on the screen. A more sophisticated pointer is available using a laser beam.

Fixed or portable *projection stands* provide a pedestal for a projector and are usually made of heavy metal. Portable stands fold up to facilitate carrying but are fairly heavy.

Slide trays or *carousels* are used with slide projectors. (Some slide projectors come with special boxes or holders that must be used with that particular model of projector.) The trays range in capacity, and can hold from

Figure 36. Supplies and Tools.

_____ Acetate roll for overhead projector	_____ Fuses
_____ Audiotapes, blank	_____ Labels, adhesive
_____ Basic tools	_____ Marking pens
_____ Bulbs, spare	_____ Masking tape
_____ Chalk (colors)	_____ Transparencies, blank
_____ Clock	_____ Videotapes, blank
_____ Easel paper	

SOURCE: *The Comprehensive Guide to Successful Conferences and Meetings* by Leonard Nadler and Zeace Nadler. San Francisco: Jossey-Bass. Copyright © 1987. Permission to reproduce hereby granted.

one slide to 140 slides. When many slides are to be used, however, the 80-slide carousel is preferred: Presentations rarely have a need for greater capacity than this.

What Supplies and Tools Should Be on Hand?

Some items listed in Figure 36 might be supplied by the site or the AV supplier, but it is still useful to have emergency supplies on hand. Most of their items have an indefinite shelf life but may be difficult to purchase on short notice.

Some overhead projectors have an attachment to allow the use of an *acetate roll*, similar to cellophane sandwich wrap but much heavier. The clear acetate is placed on top of the glass and can be written on. Transparencies can be placed on top of the acetate without diminishing the image projected.

There are two types of *audiotapes*. The most common type is the cassette, a sealed cartridge that can record from fifteen minutes to two hours, depending on the cartridge. Cassettes are relatively inexpensive, and an adequate supply should be on hand. Reel-to-reel audiotape is used for commercial production and therefore need not be included among the type of supplies listed here.

Some *basic tools* are generally useful: screwdrivers (cross point or Phillips and regular in different sizes), pliers (needle nose and regular, expandable), hammer, and flashlight (with extra, fresh batteries). The list can also include such items as film and tape splicers, with accessories, but only if someone in the secretariat is competent to use that equipment.

Spare bulbs should always fit the equipment. As bulbs are withdrawn from this supply, they should be replaced. Before each conference, the equipment should be examined so that the correct bulbs are available.

Cellophane tape is an absolute necessity, as well as a tape dispenser.

Chalk should be available in several colors. Dustless chalks produce less dust, but are quite hard and do not show up clearly on all surfaces. If possible, determine what surfaces will be used and the chalk that works best on them.

A *clock* is a handy item, particularly small, flat clocks with soft alarms for presenters who tend to go over their time limits.

Easel paper, almost mandatory at any conference, comes in different sizes and weights and can be heavy to transport. Heavyweight paper should be selected so that writing will not bleed onto the next sheet; on the other hand, avoid heavy glossy or laminated paper that is difficult to remove from the pad and to post. Although slightly more expensive, perforated pads, which facilitate tearing off pages, are better and in the long run are not really more expensive than the nonperforated pads, since fewer sheets are destroyed when being torn off the pad.

Most projectors use *fuses.* They rarely blow, but when they do, they must be replaced immediately, and a small supply of fuses can turn a crisis into a minor inconvenience.

You will find many uses for several boxes of *adhesive labels,* which can be handy for labeling boxes, slide trays, equipment, and many other purposes.

There are basically two types of *marking pens*—permanent and nonpermanent. If the package or pen has no instructions, assume the ink is permanent and cannot be erased or removed. The difference is significant. When a permanent marker is used on a transparency, that transparency can never be used again in its original form. On the other hand, permanent markers should be used if the material is to be saved for use at a later time, to develop a report, or for other dissemination. Nonpermanent ink looks the same on the transparency but can be removed easily by a damp cloth, and the transparency can be reused. Both types of pens come in a variety of colors and thicknesses.

Masking tape comes in a variety of widths and adheres to almost any surface at normal room temperature. When removed, it can be peeled off without leaving any mark or stain, unless it is left in place for a long period of time.

Slides generally mean 35 mm (or comparable size) mounted in a frame, but some people also use this term to mean transparencies for overhead projectors. It is important to make the distinction to avoid having the wrong material for a designated projector. Presenters invariably have their own slides for a presentation, but a blank slide may be needed to hastily prepare a title slide, or some other message. Blank slides that can be written on with a narrow felt tip pen are available.

The coordinator should have a supply of blank *transparencies,* which are available in standard 8″ x 10″ size in a variety of colors and weights. Very thin transparencies require cardboard frames in order to lay flat, but heavier weights usually do not require a frame.

Videotapes come in two basic formats—VHS and Beta—and the tape must be compatible with the equipment. It is advisable to keep several of each format with the supplies.

What Is the Condition of the Available Equipment?

Regardless of who supplies the equipment, it is always advisable to do a final check. If the equipment is provided by the coordinator, it should be checked when being returned to inventory and checked again before it is released for use. When the equipment comes from other sources, it is important to examine it before the conference opens, even when the site or supplier says that "all our equipment is in A-1 condition." The condition check should take place as close to the opening of the conference as possible, and before delivery to the room. If possible, tag the equipment after inspection to reduce the possibility of substitutions.

Are the Loudspeakers Fixed or Movable?

Loudspeakers can be fixed (built into the room) or portable. Little can be done about placement of fixed speakers, though a sound check is advisable in case any of them are not working. A sound check should also be conducted on portable speakers in case they need to be repositioned. Site personnel sometimes place the speakers on the floor, which causes muffled sound; placing the speakers on tables can take care of that problem. The direction of the speakers should be tested in the particular room, as sound is affected by the decor (drapes, pictures, mirrors), room size and shape, and ceiling height.

Personnel

Is Someone Responsible for AV Security?

Given the cost of AV equipment, it may be necessary to have someone in charge of security, including checking equipment in and out and guarding equipment in an unattended room before or after a session.

Who Will Be the Projectionist?

At a few sites, a union projectionist must be used to run even a regular 16 mm projector. At most conferences, however, a union projectionist is not required.

Chapter 9

Food and Beverage Functions

CHECKLIST FOR FOOD AND BEVERAGE FUNCTIONS

Negotiating

_____ Who will negotiate for food service?

_____ Who will be authorized to sign for food functions?

_____ Have the local food and beverage laws been checked?

_____ When must guarantees be given?

_____ How fixed are the printed menus and costs?

_____ Will special menus be required?

_____ What functions are tied in with food service?

_____ Will theme food functions be held?

_____ What form of service should be used?

_____ What is the sponsor's policy on liquor?

_____ What is the site policy on liquor?

_____ How should the site handle liquor orders during food functions?

_____ Will the menu be rechecked just prior to the food function?

_____ What table centerpieces and other amenities will be provided?

_____ Which rooms will be assigned for the various food functions?

_____ If any food functions are to be held outdoors, what are the back-up alternatives?

_____ How much time will be required for each food function?

Organizing the Food Function

_____ Will tickets be used for food functions?

_____ Can additional tickets be purchased for food functions?

_____ Should assigned seating or free seating be used?

_____ Will VIPs, speakers, and other special individuals or groups be seated at special tables?

_____ What notice should appear in the participant book regarding food functions?

_____ How does table size relate to the purpose of the food function?

_____ Will tables require special settings?

_____ Who will collect tickets for the food functions?

_____ Will there be an invocation?

_____ Who clears all announcements to be made during food functions?

_____ Who will make the announcements at food functions?

_____ Who has the responsibility for controlling environmental factors?

_____ Who will coordinate serving with site personnel?

_____ How will movement to the next event be organized?

Head Table

_____ Will a head table be used?

_____ What configuration should be used?

_____ Where should the head table be located?

_____ Who should be seated at the head table?

_____ Will a microphone or lectern be required?

_____ Will head table people enter together or individually?

_____ How will head table people be introduced?

_____ If meal tickets are required at the head table, how will that be handled?

_____ How will traffic at the head table be controlled?

Receptions

_____ What kinds of receptions should be arranged?

_____ Where will receptions be held?

_____ Does the participant book clearly state when receptions will be held?

_____ Have receptions been planned in relation to other events?

_____ What type of bars and how many will be used?

_____ Who decides what beverages will be served?

_____ How will costs for drinks be calculated?

_____ What kinds of hors d'oeuvres will be served?

_____ Should a package deal be negotiated for drinks and hors d'oeuvres?

_____ What site personnel will be required?

_____ At what point must the site be given a guaranteed minimum?

_____ Will tables and chairs be provided?

_____ What decorations and lighting are appropriate?

_____ Have all agreements been put in writing?

_____ How will the reception be concluded?

Banquet

_____ Will any special decorations be needed?

_____ Who will plan the menu?

_____ Will the national anthem be played?

_____ Who should manage the agenda or cue sheet?

_____ Will the banquet offer music?

Breaks

_____ How will breaks be planned?

_____ Will breaks be considered part of the food function responsibility?

_____ Is it necessary to assign a secretariat member responsibility for breaks?

_____ How long should a break be?

_____ Where will breaks be held?

_____ Will tickets be required?

SOURCE: _The Comprehensive Guide to Successful Conferences and Meetings_ by Leonard Nadler and Zeace Nadler. San Francisco: Jossey-Bass. Copyright © 1987. Permission to reproduce hereby granted.

Just about all conferences have at least one food function, if only a coffee break. Therefore, consideration must be given to determining how food and beverage functions relate to the conference purpose and design, and then to planning and supervising those events.

Importance of Food Functions

It is better to err on the side of too many food functions than too few. Food functions have a psychological effect on the participants, particularly in those countries in which it is important to break bread together. The food functions also serve as a social mechanism in a conference, allowing the participants to get to know each other.

The primary physical benefit of a food function is that it provides the participants with an opportunity to relax. Even if a speaker appears at the food event, the participants experience a change of pace that can have positive physical benefits.

The financial benefits for the participants are obvious: the participants are paying for the food events, albeit indirectly, when they are included in the conference fee.

Relation to Budget and Site Negotiations

Food functions provide leverage for the coordinator when negotiating with a site, unless it is a conference site that does not serve food. Generally, the more meals (and more individuals served), the lower the cost for facilities. Even when all three meals will not be contracted for each day, the coordinator can still point out that the participants are likely to use the restaurants and bars in the site hotel.

Food and beverage functions are a very large element in site negotiations. Functions include breakfast, lunch, dinner, breaks, and receptions, and any number of variations, depending on the design of the conference and the budget.

One variation uses meal coupons or tickets. If the hotel has several restaurants, the ticket could provide a credit of a set amount, with each participant free to pay additional amounts for the more expensive restaurants. This plan provides flexibility and allows each participant to select the restaurants and meals without the coordinator having to make special arrangements. The ticket cost is approximately equal to the charge for food functions, so it is part of the total negotiated package.

The Checklist

Negotiating

Who Will Negotiate for Food Service?

The basic negotiations for food service are usually handled by the coordinator. If the design includes many or complicated food functions, the coordinator usually delegates future negotiations and supervision to a member of the secretariat. All hotels and most conference centers have food service, but that is not the case with all convention centers: Some provide food service, others may arrange for an outside caterer, and still others may not hold any food functions at all in the center.

The coordinator should identify the proper negotiator for the site, which is sometimes difficult because sites use a variety of titles, such as food service manager, banquet manager, sales manager, or food and beverage director, and titles do not always clearly delineate responsibilities. Too often, coordinators make arrangements with the sales department, only to find that the chief chef has other ideas of what is to be served, how, and when. During negotiations, it is frequently best to involve more site personnel rather than fewer.

In addition to negotiating for menus, the coordinator should negotiate for—and inspect—specific rooms. A coordinator may be told that a room holds ten tables and discover later that this arrangement does not allow any space for a buffet option.

Who Will Be Authorized to Sign for Food Functions?

At an early stage of negotiations, agreement must be reached on who can sign for food functions, that is, who represents the coordinator and signs the charge slips for the functions. If possible, that person should be involved in the negotiations and be responsible for the guarantees and for seeing that the agreements are adhered to during the conference.

This is much more than a clerical function, so this person should be carefully chosen. Large sums of money are involved, as well as a significant part of the participants' overall enjoyment of the conference. It does no good to get apologies afterwards for a wrong menu or inadequate service; these factors must be checked out during the function before the charge slip is signed.

Have the Local Food and Beverage Laws Been Checked?

Each locality has its own laws that must be considered during negotiations. Some localities have strict liquor laws for all days of the week; other communities' laws are in force only on Sundays. A locality may require that all food handlers be physically examined and even certified—an important factor if the coordinator schedules a buffet luncheon where the officers of the sponsoring organization will do the serving (a symbolic custom showing that the officers "serve" the members).

In some localities, once food leaves the kitchen it cannot be served again under any circumstances. This restriction can make a buffet extremely expensive and difficult unless individual dietary and religious preferences have been carefully monitored.

When Must Guarantees Be Given?

A guarantee of the number of meals to be served at each function must usually be confirmed with the food service personnel forty-eight hours before the event, though this time can vary from twenty-four hours to a week, depending on the number of meals to be served, the menu, and the capacity of the site. The intent of the guarantee provision is to enable the site to order sufficient food and to assign a sufficient number of people to service the function.

The specific time for guarantees should be established during negotiations and agreed to in writing for each food and beverage function. Some sites allow a certain overage, as much as 10 percent, but are less likely to allow any shortfall once the guarantee time has passed. These factors must be taken into consideration when the coordinator arranges for reservations, sells tickets, or engages in any other activities related to food and beverage functions.

How Fixed Are the Printed Menus and Costs?

During negotiations, the coordinator is usually given some sample menus and they should be considered only as suggestions. A site rarely insists on only a few choices and fixed costs with no possibility of further negotiation. Cost is a major factor, and some costs can be reduced after exploring alternatives. For example, what cost difference results if no salad is served or if the initial fruit salad is replaced by soup? How will the cost differ if an additional vegetable is substituted for dessert? Food service staff are usually willing to explore alternatives, and some have their own suggestions for keeping costs down while providing first-rate meals.

After all the basic costs have been determined, additional costs must be calculated. The two most common are gratuities and taxes. Gratuities are frequently nonnegotiable; the general guideline is 15 percent of the check before taxes. (Some establishments prefer to add the 15 percent after taxes, but the coordinator should balk at paying a gratuity on the tax.) Taxes vary extensively from one place to another and are, of course, nonnegotiable, but the coordinator should make sure that the tax rate is applicable. A nonprofit public seminar sponsor might find that under certain circumstances it is exempt from local taxes.

Will Special Menus Be Required?

The food and beverage area is complicated; when planning and negotiating, the coordinator must consider several factors that might otherwise be overlooked. The participants may have religious preferences: Many Moslems and Jews do not eat pork, Hindus do not eat beef, and some Catholics do not eat meat on Friday, to name only a few.

Some participants have dietary choices, such as vegetarianism or choices of food based on health factors. Some participants may have food allergies (to dairy products, shellfish, and so on), and special menus may have to be provided.

The meal time can be difficult to arrange. Some people need a hearty breakfast, while others require only a cup of coffee. Some people eat their heavy meal at lunch, while others have it later in the day. In the United States, dinner is usually eaten between 6:00 and 8:00 P.M., while in Latin American countries, dinner does not start until 10:00 P.M. Most dining rooms in the United States charge extra when the dining room must remain open that late.

Participants at an international conference do not expect to find their native foods in the host country, but they should not be forced to cope with foods and styles of serving that might be uncomfortable for them.

Special menus do not necessarily mean more expensive menus, just different foods than those being served to most of the other participants.

What Functions Are Tied in with Food Service?

Some functions are specifically tied in with food service, such as a luncheon or dinner speaker. The banquet, of course, is a food function but is more than just a dinner, as will be described below.

Though not too common, food service might be provided at other sessions. Work groups, for example, may function through the noon hour, with special arrangements for lunch to be served in the room so that the groups can continue to work.

Will Theme Food Functions Be Held?

A theme food function is one in which the food, service, decorations, and other related factors are all tied together. For example, a "Winter Sports" function might serve foods that one would find at a winter resort area. The waiters might be appropriately costumed, and the entire room decorated as a ski lodge.

Theme food functions can be more expensive than regular food functions because of the other factors that must be considered but can be well worth the extra expense by providing a stimulating change from the regular conference schedule.

What Form of Service Should Be Used?

There are several different ways to serve meals, and each has its advantages and limitations. The generally agreed upon forms are:

- *Russian:* The food is presented on a serving platter and is taken individually by each diner.
- *French:* The waiter serves from a platter and puts the food on each diner's plate.
- *Plated:* The food is placed on plates in the kitchen, and each individual is given a prepared plate.
- *Buffet (self-service):* Food is placed on a table, and individuals come to the table and serve themselves.
- *Buffet (served):* The food is placed on a table, but certain items, such as meat, are served by waiters.
- *Cafeteria:* The food is behind a protective shield and main dishes are served as requested. Side dishes (salad, bread and butter, desserts) can be taken by the individuals, as desired.

Although the above terms are generally standard, when site personnel use serving terminology ("We will serve French style") the coordinator should be sure there is no misunderstanding as to the type of food, the cost for the service, and the length of time required for serving.

Russian is generally considered the highest level of service, with French coming next. These styles take time and can require additional serving help. Plated service is fairly rapid and allows for portion control in the kitchen. Buffet is a common form for a variety of reasons. At one time, it was considered the most economical serving form since it required very few service staff. But that is not always the case, since it is possible for food costs to exceed labor costs and for food costs to vary more drastically than labor costs. For a small group, one buffet table can suffice, but when the group is larger than fifty persons, at least two tables should be available. Some coordinators even prefer one table for each twenty-five participants, but that can be expensive. At a self-service buffet people tend to take more food than at a served one, but the served buffet entails the additional cost of help. Arranging for site personnel to serve, however, can speed up the line.

Cafeteria-style is seldom used, as many perceive it as cheap. Also, most sites do not have the special equipment necessary for such service. If the equipment is available, the cafeteria has some of the benefits of the buffet and participants can be served fairly rapidly.

What Is the Sponsor's Policy on Liquor?

The coordinator must determine the sponsor's policy on liquor. A membership sponsor, particularly if it is religiously oriented, may have some specific prohibitions concerning alcoholic beverages. As customs change, even some nonreligious membership sponsors have encouraged less drinking during conferences. Of course, what participants choose to do outside of the organized events is their own concern.

An employer sponsor usually applies the company policy in its conferences. For example, if alcoholic beverages are not permitted on company property, that policy may well be extended to conferences. There are no absolutes on this, so it is necessary for the coordinator to explore policy and practice with each employer sponsor. A for-profit public seminar sponsor often does not have a policy, and therefore the participants are free to decide for themselves, though it may be necessary for this type of sponsor to provide some liquor as part of the conference activity. For a nonprofit public seminar sponsor, policy depends on the source of funds and the nature of the sponsor. For example, if government funds are used, the nonprofit public seminar sponsor cannot use those funds to purchase liquor for the participants.

What Is the Site Policy on Liquor?

In addition to any local laws, the site may have a policy on liquor, including the sale of liquor and also whether or not participants can bring liquor on site. On the other hand, some sites sell setups (ice, mixers, and other drink ingredients), encouraging the participants to bring their own liquor.

How Should the Site Handle Liquor Orders During Food Functions?

At some sites, waiters ask participants for their drink orders before serving. When that is the practice, a decision should be made during negotiations whether the individual participants or the conference budget will pay for those drinks. In either case, the participants and the site personnel should be informed before any food function starts.

If the participants are to pay, waiters should be advised not to push drinks. Nonalcoholic beverages should also be available. If the drinks are charged to the conference budget, is there any limit on the number of drinks? At one conference, the first drink was provided as a courtesy by the sponsor, but subsequent drinks were to be paid for by the individual participants. The participants did not know this, however, and some readily responded to the waiters' queries regarding refills and additional drinks. At the conclusion of the meal, the participants were astonished to receive bar bills and complained loudly and bitterly to the coordinator, who did not have sufficient funds to handle the expense. The resulting negative feelings could have been avoided by more clarity during negotiations and more effective communication of the facts to all concerned.

Wine served during a meal can give rise to problems. When a carafe of wine is placed on each table, some tables will want more than others. If cost is not a significant factor, additional carafes of wine can be provided, up to a certain limit agreed on during negotiations, or additional carafes can be charged to those tables ordering them. Another possibility is to instruct the waiters to share the wine among tables as the need arises. Whatever is decided, instructions should be given to the waiters, with the direction that they share that information with the participants, as necessary. Surprises, concerning liquor, should be kept to a minimum.

Will the Menu Be Rechecked Just Prior to the Food Function?

The menus should be fixed during negotiations, unless the negotiations take place many months before the conference. In that case it is helpful if exact menus can be decided at some time closer to the opening of the conference. Even then, the coordinator should still seek some flexibility. After the initial negotiations, the coordinator should be able to provide additional food functions without repeating menus. The prices of some foods could change drastically, and the site might welcome some menu changes that would be beneficial to all concerned.

As receptions usually precede a food function, a change in the number of receptions or quantity of food served should be reflected in menu changes, if the site is willing. Receptions, as discussed later in this chapter, provide some food, but the major emphasis is on liquor. The food served at receptions, however, may be upgraded in type and quantity when the reception is funded from other sources, such as exhibitors. The exhibitors may be receiving a response at the exhibition that is above their expectations and therefore wish to show their appreciation by providing more food than originally planned. Additional receptions might be offered by collateral sponsors, as in the case for a nonprofit public seminar sponsor.

What Table Centerpieces and Other Amenities Will Be Provided?

Each site uses different forms of table decorations, which range from condiments to a floral centerpiece with matching napkins and tablecloths and individual name cards. The specifics should be explored by the coordinator during negotiation and then checked during setup. Some sites refer to a basic setup, but that will vary from site to site so the coordinator must ask for specifics. Some items may be automatically included in the cost of the food function, while others are an extra expense. Extras for each food function are stipulated in the contract or agreement and are reflected in the staging book (see Chapter Twenty).

Which Rooms Will Be Assigned for the Various Food Functions?

The rooms for some food functions are automatically determined by the size of the group. A large conference requires some form of ballroom, while smaller conferences can be accommodated in regular function rooms. If possible, the coordinator should seek rooms that are located away from the session rooms. The participants will be able to get some exercise as they move from a session room to a food function room. On the other hand, it does take time for such a movement, particularly if many participants are involved. The time required for movements to food function rooms between sessions (usually lunches) should be taken into account during design.

The coordinator should always visit food function rooms to see if they are appropriate. Size and shape may be a factor if a luncheon or dinner speaker is planned. The room setup may be good for the waiters, but the tables too close for the comfort of the participants.

If Any Food Functions Are to Be Held Outdoors, What Are the Back-Up Alternatives?

In some climates, it may be attractive to hold some food functions outdoors, in a special picnic area or around the swimming pool, for example. The possibility of bad weather should be taken into account by agreeing where, when, and how the function can be moved indoors. It should not be left as a unilateral decision by the site personnel; some refuse to make any adjustments once the tables have been set and the fires lit! We have seen barbecues continued in the rain, with the site personnel wearing raincoats while the participants scurried in and out of buildings to grab paper plates of food, much of which was lost on the way.

How Much Time Will Be Required for Each Food Function?

Food functions take time. When the function precedes a session or another event, a closing time should be announced beforehand. In Example B (see Chapter Three), Events 4, 12, and 20 are breakfasts starting at 7:30 A.M., followed by a general session at 9:00 A.M. It should be announced that serving will stop at 8:30 A.M., so that participants can get to the general session on time. If serving continues until 9:00 A.M., some participants will not make the general session.

The amount of time required for a food function is governed by several factors, such as the serving style, discussed earlier in this chapter, and the distance between the food function room and the session rooms. If a program is tied in with a food function, it will obviously take longer for that event than one where the main activity is just eating. Time must also be allowed, both before and after food functions, for people to refresh themselves, visit the rest rooms, and take care of personal matters.

Organizing the Food Function

Will Tickets Be Used for Food Functions?

A small conference may not need to use tickets for food functions, but can rely on participants knowing each other or showing their conference badges to obtain food. As the number of participants increases, tighter controls are required, for the site will charge based on the actual number of meals served or the guarantee, whichever is larger. The coordinator can control this factor by issuing tickets and then having the count verified during the food function. It is not unusual for the actual numbers of meals served to be fewer than the number of tickets provided to participants, but the coordinator usually must pay for at least the guarantee. In some situations, such as when the participants are selecting from a regular menu, the site may be willing to allow for 10 percent less than the guarantee, but that must be stipulated during negotiations.

Can Additional Tickets Be Purchased for Food Functions?

Some food functions are coupled with other events, such as banquets, recognition, an outstanding speaker, or entertainment. It can be anticipated, particularly for a membership-sponsor conference, that there will be requests for additional tickets. How these requests are handled depends on how the conference fee has been determined (see Chapter Sixteen).

One technique is to incorporate the charge for the food functions into the total fee for the conference, so as to decrease the need for additional food function tickets later. (A few participants might want to invite a local friend who is not attending the conference, or an exhibitor might want to reward booth personnel, but that should be the extent of it.) The fee can also include selected food functions for participants' companions, if desired.

If the conference fee covers only the core sessions, other events (such as food functions) are considered extra and participants purchase tickets for those events on an individual basis. The location for purchasing tickets should be clearly designated. It is usually the registration area but can just as easily be located in the exhibition area or at a special service desk in the common room. A specific time should be announced for the closing of ticket sales so that the site can be notified of the guarantee.

Should Assigned Seating or Free Seating Be Used?

The most common form of seating arrangement is free seating, whereby participants sit wherever they wish. If any reserved seats are to be used, that fact should be announced and the seats or tables clearly marked. Participants could be allowed to reserve seats through sign-up sheets or special banquet tickets.

In Example D (see Chapter Three), Events 3, 7, and 13 were food functions where facilitators (presenters) were seated at different tables; therefore, their seats had to be designated beforehand. Event 17 was a luncheon, with different topics for each table, so signs had to be posted on the tables and the participants notified of the assignment.

Will VIPs, Speakers, and Other Special Individuals or Groups Be Seated at Special Tables?

A policy of reserved tables should be the result of design political factors. The membership sponsor may wish to honor the officers or may decide that it is better politically for the officers to sit with the members rather than with each other. An employer sponsor might want to seat high-level company officials together, particularly when an outside speaker of some note is present. A for-profit public seminar sponsor might want to seat certain groups or individuals together for marketing purposes, and a nonprofit public seminar sponsor might make table arrangements to reflect certain groups of sponsors or participants.

What Notice Should Appear in the Participant Book Regarding Food Functions?

If a conference matrix is included in the participant book, the food functions should be clearly shown in their proper sequence, as shown in the examples in Chapter Three. In addition, the food functions should be listed with specific descriptions, and if numerous food functions are planned, the listing should be separate from other conference information. In addition to the days and times, information should be provided about any unusual factors, such as those noted in Example D above. Any entertainment or dancing should also be noted, so that participants can plan which clothes to take to the conference. Ticket requirements should be clearly noted, including the latest time to purchase tickets, when that is an option.

How Does Table Size Relate to the Purpose of the Food Function?

Table shape and size may depend on the type of service. French or Russian service almost mandates round tables, usually seating no more than eight to ten people, the specific number governed more by union regulations than other factors. For plated service, it is possible to have rectangular tables seating any number as long as they can be easily reached. For buffet, the table size bears no relation to the serving need.

The table should also be chosen in respect to the kind of interaction that the coordinator is endeavoring to facilitate. Round tables, particularly those seating eight or fewer, encourage discussion among all the participants. (A round table seating ten usually prevents any discussion across the table, however, though three or four people, seated next to each other, can converse easily.) A rectangular table allows for discussion with partners on either side and possibly across the table, depending on the width of the table and the items on it, since it is difficult to talk through flowers, ornaments, and other decorations.

Will Tables Require Special Settings?

Tables may require items besides the normal meal settings. If the function is using assigned seats and many tables, it may be necessary to place numbers on the tables. (The waiters should be instructed to remove these signs when the tables are full and certainly before starting service, unless they are needed to facilitate service.) If the meal is followed by a speaker who is using handouts, it is customary to have those on the table, though that is not always the best way to distribute such material, since it gets in the way of serving; inevitably some of the handouts will be covered with gravy, coffee, butter, and similar souvenirs of the meal, so other methods of distribution, after the meal, should be explored.

Who Will Collect Tickets for the Food Functions?

When tickets are used, the coordinator and site personnel should agree on who will collect the tickets in order to avoid confusion later.

The waiters usually collect the tickets when everyone is seated and serving is about to commence. When the tickets indicate the participants' entree choices (meat, fish, poultry) or special meals (religious, vegetarian, allergic), the tickets are collected as the entree is being served. Some sites do not want to use the waiters' time for that chore, however, and so others pick up the tickets, sometimes even the secretariat. Whatever system is used, it should be agreed to by both parties and the procedure followed exactly.

Will There Be an Invocation?

Traditionally in the United States, many food functions are opened by a prayer known as the invocation. The prayer usually thanks God for the food and asks for guidance in the conference. It is not necessary that the invocation be given by a member of the clergy.

Very few participants object to the idea of having an invocation, but objections may arise about its content. A Christian invocation is certainly appropriate when the sponsor is a Christian organization, but an ecumenical invocation is more appropriate for all other conference food functions.

Who Clears All Announcements to Be Made During Food Functions?

Almost all the participants are present at food functions, so they are frequently utilized for general announcements. If not controlled, however, announcements can get out of hand. A good rule is that announcements must be cleared with the coordinator or a member of the secretariat given this responsibility. At a membership sponsor, where there can be many competing groups, there will be pressure from them to make announcements concerning their groups; this may not be of interest to all the participants. Valuable time may be consumed for announcements of interest or concern to only a few of those at the food function.

Who Will Make the Announcements at Food Functions?

The coordinator or someone delegated the responsibility should clear announcements but another person should make them. Note the use of the singular pronoun—only *one* person should make announcements except in unusual cases. Avoid a procession to the microphone and announcers who may be uncontrollable once they stand in front of the group.

Announcers may be selected for many reasons. For a membership sponsor, selection can be a way of providing recognition for officers. An employer sponsor or public seminar sponsor might call on a status person from the sponsoring organization, even one who is not a regular participant but has joined the group for that food function.

Who Has the Responsibility for Controlling Environmental Factors?

As food functions involve large numbers of participants, environmental factors must be considered. With fifty or more people in the room, plus the serving and other site personnel, ventilation can become a problem. Rather than wait for complaints, a member of the secretariat should monitor the comfort of the participants and communicate with site personnel as needed. It should not be necessary for numerous participants to remove their jackets or to fan themselves with their conference programs before action is taken.

If a program is tied in with the food function, lighting may have to be considered. During the meal, the lights may have been dimmed to provide "atmosphere," but a dim room after a meal does not encourage participants to listen to a speaker so adjustments must be made. If AV equipment is used, someone must monitor the lights. For a small conference, a member of the secretariat might be able to control the lights by switches within or adjacent to the room. For a large conference, it may require the services of an electrician or similar lighting personnel.

Ambient noise is always a potential hazard at a food function. After the dishes are cleared and the participants are keyed up to listen to a speaker, it is annoying to hear the clatter of plates or the chatter of the service personnel coming from the kitchen. A member of the secretariat should be assigned to listen for this type of noise and know exactly what to do to bring the situation under control.

Who Will Coordinate Serving with Site Personnel?

The participant book is often ambiguous when it comes to indicating whether the starting time is the time the doors will open or the time when serving will start and whether this time is exact or approximate. If possible, the book should be precise on this matter; the participants can then decide when they want to show up for the food function.

The time at which service will cease should be obtained by the coordinator from the service captain. Sometimes the waiters will clear the tables while participants are eating dessert, but at other times table-clearing will start after dessert is finished. If a program is scheduled after the meal, the coordinator must know what sequence will be followed and the times allotted; otherwise, the coordinator may be forced to start the program while service is still in progress or, more frequently, while the tables are being cleared. The accompanying confusion does little to help the speaker or the participants.

Other scheduling alternatives are possible. Speakers often complain that they dislike speaking after a large lunch or dinner, when the participants have difficulty staying awake. One variation is to select a lighter than usual menu. Another variation is to serve the appetizers (soup, fruit cup, or salad and bread and butter), and introduce the speaker at this point. After the speaker is finished, service resumes, and after the tables are cleared, the speaker is available for questions from the floor. This might increase the expense of the function, but the extra cost might be negotiable.

How Will Movement to the Next Event Be Organized?

If the food function is the last event of the day, the participants decide when to leave. After the official closing of the dinner, participants may linger, but they soon get the message as site personnel start dismantling the room.

When the food function is a breakfast or lunch followed by other events, the coordinator should plan for other activities to facilitate movement. A brief but stimulating closing announcement can urge them on the way. The use of music, either live or recorded fast music, particularly marching music, encourages people to move more rapidly than they otherwise would. If participants are likely to gather at the exits or in the hallway, "announcers" or "town criers" can encourage them to go on to the next events. The secretariat and perhaps some volunteer participants can circulate through the group urging them to move to the next sessions, or at least to clear the room.

Head Table

Will a Head Table Be Used?

A head table is more than just a reserved table. Although head tables are usually used for banquets, they may be used for any food function for formal speeches or as a way of recognizing leaders and important participants or guests.

What Configuration Should Be Used?

A head table can be set up so that everyone in the room can see the people seated there. For a large food function, this may require that the head table be set on a platform, but for a small food function it may only be necessary to place the head table at some reasonable distance from the other tables.

When the head table is on a platform, it should be skirted for the comfort of those sitting at that table. Table decorations should not obscure the vision of those seated at the head table or of others in the room.

Where Should the Head Table Be Located?

The head table should not be located near the entrances or exits to the room. Participants should have an unobstructed view of any speakers.

Who Should Be Seated at the Head Table?

Once again, sponsor politics usually influences the selection of those who will sit at the head table. The sponsor must be involved in selecting those to be seated at the head table, but the coordinator can assist by asking pertinent questions. For example, has a head table been utilized in the past, and, if so, who was seated at it? Is it necessary to select the same participants again or those participants who hold the same office in the organization? What is the purpose of the head table at this conference?

When several food functions utilize head tables, the questions should be asked for each of them, as the answers could be different for each function. If only one food function uses a head table, the decision can be more difficult, for participants have only one opportunity to be seated there.

The seating order must be considered. Generally, the center seats are considered the most prestigious, with diminishing status from those points to the right and left ends of the table. The food function speaker usually sits at the center of the table or in one of the two center seats. The introducer for the session, sometimes called a chairman, should be seated next to the speaker. Beyond that, seating protocol depends on the specific situation; the goal should be a balance between both sides of the table so that each side contains important people.

Will a Microphone or Lectern Be Required?

As a head table is usually used with a large group, a microphone or lectern may be required, particularly if there is to be a speech. A common mistake is to leave the lectern in the middle of the table during the entire meal. This blocks vision and is a barrier during the meal, even though it will not be used until the meal is completed. If a lectern is to be used, it should be placed under the table or at the rear of the platform until needed. When the time arrives for announcements or speeches, the act of placing the lectern on the table provides a strong visual signal to the participants. (If the presentation is to be recorded, it may be necessary to place microphones on the table before the meal starts.)

A standing lectern at the end of the table may be another option. At the end of the meal, the introducer moves to the lectern, which signals the start of the program.

Some speakers with an informal style dislike lecterns, and their wishes should be respected to the extent possible.

Will Head Table People Enter Together or Individually?

How head table people move to their positions should be planned carefully, as it sets the climate for the session. The first decision is whether they should enter individually or as a group. Entering as a group, they communicate a more formal atmosphere to the session than if they enter individually, particularly if they gather beforehand, line up in relation to how they will be sitting, and walk to their seats accompanied by appropriate music.

Individual entrances can be confusing if not handled in an organized fashion. The head table will fill up slowly, and the participants have no signal for a formal opening. Name cards may be placed so individuals can find their seats, but individuals may have to read several cards until they find their own. When some head table individuals take their seats before the others, they can become very uncomfortable, sitting in full view of the participants with nothing to do but wait.

How Will Head Table People Be Introduced?

People seated at a head table should be introduced. Their arrival at the head table could be used as the time for introductions. The introducer comes up first, and then each person comes forward as their name is called. (Of course, they should be waiting in the "wings" in the proper order.) The introducer uses the same brief format in introducing each person emphasizing why they are at the head table. In a large room, spotlights may be used to emphasize the introduction.

Another technique is to make the introductions between courses. At that time, serving should stop so all attention can be focused on the head table. Those at the head table should be advised on how to acknowledge the introduction—by standing, waving, being picked up by a spotlight, and so on. The method of acknowledgment should be the same for all.

Similarly, the participants should be advised on whether to hold all applause until introductions have been completed. It is customary *not* to introduce the speaker at that time, but instead wait for a more complete introduction later.

If Meal Tickets Are Required at the Head Table, How Will That Be Handled?

If meal tickets are required, special consideration should be given to the head table. If all those at the head table are participants, they are responsible for their own meal tickets and should be so advised. In the case when there are nonparticipant "guests," meal tickets should be handled by the introducer or given to the guests individually. Speakers are not considered guests for they have already been given a complimentary registration, which includes the tickets for the food functions; it may only be necessary to remind them to bring along the proper ticket.

How Will Traffic at the Head Table Be Controlled?

As the head table contains important people, some participants and presenters will probably want to meet them to renew acquaintances or just to be seen talking to them. To the extent possible, the coordinator should have a policy to govern the situation. For example, only those seated at the head table and the servers should be allowed on the platform or in the head table area during the meal. After the meal, the head table people could be asked to move onto the floor so they are available. It is not necessary to make an announcement about that; just concluding the function will probably suffice.

Receptions

What Kinds of Receptions Should Be Arranged?

A reception almost always serves liquor, but food service depends on the desires and the budget of the sponsor. (Some people still refer to receptions as cocktail parties, which is a misnomer, for cocktails may not even be served!) A small conference might have a reception one evening, hosted by an employer sponsor or, as the case may be, by a for-profit public seminar sponsor. The more participants, the more complicated the arrangements.

This discussion focuses mainly on the receptions that are an official part of the main conference and under the control of the coordinator. During the conference, other receptions may be held by various subgroups or by exhibitors, and the coordinator need not become involved in them; the hosts for those receptions must make their own arrangements with the site.

A large membership sponsor conference might arrange a reception for the participants, hosted by the officers of the organization, or special receptions, such as one for international participants, though special receptions sometimes engender ill will in those participants who are not invited.

Receptions can range from one-drink affairs to those that provide all the liquor and hors d'oeuvres that the participants can consume. They can be held in one room or a variety of rooms within the site.

Where Will Receptions Be Held?

As with other functions, the coordinator must negotiate with the site for the space. A small conference may possibly be held in a suite that is under the control of the coordinator. Suites in some sites can easily accommodate fifty participants for a reception.

Special room arrangements should be made during negotiations, even if the coordinator has to guess at the number of attendees. The room must be able to accommodate the bar(s), food stations, tables and chairs (perhaps), and the participants. Depending on the size of the conference, the space required may be one large room, several large rooms, or even a ballroom.

Does the Participant Book Clearly State When Receptions Will Be Held?

A reception may be an important factor in attracting participants to a conference, so dissemination of specific reception information is important. The receptions might even be mentioned in the marketing efforts related to the conference. If all participants are invited to the reception, they should know exactly when it will be held in order to prepare and dress appropriately and to keep their schedule open for that time slot.

Have Receptions Been Planned in Relation to Other Events?

Receptions are generally held in the late afternoon or evening, at the close of the conference day, before an evening event (dinner, banquet, entertainment), after one of those events, or in place of those events. Given the numerous possibilities, receptions should be carefully scheduled and adequately publicized.

Planning the reception in relation to other conference events will be reflected in the type of reception, provision for beverages and food, and the timing. When the reception is scheduled from 6:00 to 8:00 P.M., the coordinator can expect that more food will be consumed than at a reception that is scheduled earlier or later, unless a banquet is scheduled after the reception. When a reception is followed by a banquet, the coordinator can assume that less food will be consumed, but perhaps more liquor.

What Type of Bars and How Many Will Be Used?

The terminology for the type of bar should be understood by all concerned. An *open bar* is one that is hosted, and someone other than the participants is paying for the drinks. A *cash bar* is just the opposite: Participants pay the bartender or attendant for their drinks with either cash or tickets. With a *combination bar,* participants are given some free tickets but then must purchase tickets for additional drinks.

   A ratio of one bartender for every fifty participants is suggested, even though this can produce lines of participants waiting to be served. If more than one bartender is needed, the coordinator should insist on separate stations located in different parts of the room. The coordinator should discuss the placement of the bar(s) with site personnel. In most cases, the bar should be positioned away from the door and at the far side of the room. A bar should not be set up next to a stage, so a side wall may be preferable. If the budget for hors d'oeuvres is limited, the bar should not be set up near the hors d'oeuvres as that will increase consumption.

Who Decides What Beverages Will Be Served?

The coordinator—not the site personnel—should select the beverages. Some participants prefer certain brands of liquor and eschew others. If sodas are provided, some should be diet. As discussed in the food section of this checklist, some participants will not drink alcohol or caffeine for religious or other reasons, and fruit juices should be provided for them.

   Someone should always check on beverage arrangements before the reception. A coordinator hosting a reception for international participants felt that she had sufficiently underscored the need for nonalcoholic beverages to the site personnel. They assured her that they were familiar with the problem and would have alternatives to liquor. Imagine her amazement, fifteen minutes before the reception was to begin, to find that the site personnel's alternative to liquor was beer! It took a great deal of last-minute arrangements to procure soda, and the promised fruit juices never did arrive during the reception.

How Will Costs for Drinks Be Calculated?

Here we find vast areas of confusion and lack of agreement. Charges based on a *per drink* basis are probably the most costly for a coordinator sponsoring an open bar. A *per bottle* charge is cheaper but much more complicated, depending on how a bottle or a used bottle is defined. The most common usage is that a used bottle is one that has been opened and therefore is charged to the coordinator. For a large reception, many bottles may be opened, some barely used, but the coordinator is still charged for the bottle. In those situations, some coordinators inventory all the bottles available and a count of those charged to the reception. To avoid confusion, once a bottle is opened it should be stamped with the logo of the conference or some other distinguishing mark. This all takes time, but the alternative is an outrageously high liquor bill. Bottles that have been charged to the conference account should be turned over to the coordinator who can then use them in a hospitality suite or for other conference-related activity.

The per bottle or per drink charge will be reflected in the size of the drinks. As can be expected, bartenders will tend to put less liquor in a glass when the charge is by the drink, but considerably more per glass when the charge is by the bottle. The coordinator can try to control liquor content through negotiations with the appropriate captain, but it is difficult, if not impossible, to police this.

When using the per bottle arrangement, the coordinator must also determine the costs for setups, mixes, and other elements utilized by a bartender. Though obviously not as costly as the liquor, they can mount up to a sizable charge for a large or long reception.

What Kinds of Hors D'oeuvres Will Be Served?

It is not absolutely essential to serve hors d'oeuvres at a reception, but participants usually expect some food if only bowls of potato chips and pretzels, both of which make them thirsty for more drinks! Various factors should be considered when hors d'oeuvres are to be provided, and cost is probably the most crucial one. When a coordinator does not have any cost problems, receptions are very easy to arrange. Here are some tips on how to provide hors d'oeuvres without undue cost.

- To reduce individual consumption, do not provide plates, as this will encourage participants to take several hors d'oeuvres at one time. Some people might load up a napkin, but that would still be less than they might put on a plate.
- Avoid shrimp, since they are expensive and large quantities are rapidly consumed. When the budget allows, shrimp can be prepared in many interesting ways to enhance the hors d'oeuvres available.
- Hot hors d'oeuvres can be served from chafing dishes or by waiters carrying them around on platters. Hot tables can be less costly, depending on the number of waiters required, but some foods (such as cream sauces) cannot sit on the table for long without separating or looking withered and depressing. Experienced site personnel should know which foods are at their peak in quality and appearance.
- Although it may take extra help and time, it is advisable not to put out all the hors d'oeuvres at once but rather to stagger them over the time allotted to the reception.
- When using an open bar, avoid salty hors d'oeuvres, as they increase drink consumption. (When using a cash bar, the coordinator may find the site personnel offering salty hors d'oeuvres at little or no charge, since they know they will make it up in the increased drink orders.) Preference for

raw vegetables and fruit has increased, and these foods generally receive a good response. A creative food manager at the site can make very interesting arrangements of raw vegetables and dips.

- The amount of hors d'oeuvres provided depends on the specific hors d'oeuvres selected. There is no one good way to calculate the amount. Some coordinators calculate that a male eats six hors d'oeuvres an hour, while a female eats four. This is a difficult figure to accept, for it must depend, in part, on the hors d'oeuvres. Six shrimp an hour is very little for those who like shrimp. Also, the range and availability of hors d'oeuvres influence consumption. Participants tend to eat fewer hors d'oeuvres when the reception is followed by a dinner or banquet. Music and entertainment during the reception also produce a lower consumption rate of hors d'oeuvres.

Should a Package Deal Be Negotiated for Drinks and Hors D'oeuvres?

At some sites, a package deal for the whole reception may be arranged. Agreement must be reached on the type of bar, number of hors d'oeuvres per participant, decorations, and all the other factors that contribute to a successful reception. An amount is negotiated based on the duration of the reception and the number of participants. This relieves the coordinator of the need to examine each detail or to wonder whether there will be enough hors d'oeuvres.

What Site Personnel Will Be Required?

At some sites, a minimum number of personnel are provided for a reception of a given number of participants, but a coordinator may find that the reception is understaffed. For example, the site may supply too few bartenders; after all, the participants are not going to take their business elsewhere if they have to wait on lines, particularly with an open or combination bar.

For a reception that goes over a half-hour, attendants will be needed to remove used glasses and hors d'oeuvre plates. If waiters are serving the hors d'oeuvres, the site should provide enough waiters so that all the hors d'oeuvres are not consumed by those closest to the service doors.

At What Point Must the Site Be Given a Guaranteed Minimum?

The site will want a guarantee on the number of participants at some point prior to the reception. The amount of lead time required will depend on the type of bar, how the hors d'oeuvres will be served, and the number of participants anticipated. The site personnel must prepare the hors d'oeuvres, and arrange for staff and supplies.

The coordinator for a small conference may find that only a few hours' lead time is required, depending on the selection of hors d'oeuvres. As the number of participants increases, the lead time required depends on the flexibility of the site personnel and their ability to handle large receptions. Of course, the lead time will also relate to the number of other receptions in progress at the same time.

Will Tables and Chairs Be Provided?

Tables and chairs are usually not provided at a reception because one purpose of such an event is to encourage people to mingle. In addition, participants tend to eat more hors d'oeuvres when they have a place to put their full plates or napkins.

Despite these reasons, it may still be advisable to have some tables and chairs, particularly if the participants are elderly and cannot comfortably spend the entire reception on their feet.

What Decorations and Lighting Are Appropriate?

The ambiance of a reception must not be too austere, even if the coordinator has a limited budget. It is not too expensive to provide napkins and tablecloths with the logo of the conference. If the budget is sufficient, ice carvings and other decorations can contribute to a more attractive atmosphere.

Have All Agreements Been Put in Writing?

As a reception consists of so many variables and involves many people, the arrangements must be put in writing. Some sites have regular checklists or other forms that are very useful and represent what is available at that particular site. Many sites do not have such lists, so the coordinator must rely on her memory of other receptions. The coordinator should keep copies of reception agreements as they can be extremely valuable for future planning and negotiations.

How Will the Reception Be Concluded?

A reception starts slowly as people drift into the room, and that is completely acceptable. Without an organized finale, however, the reception can wind down to a slow death, rather than end on an upbeat note. If another event follows the reception (banquet, dinner, or speaker), the participants should be given sufficient notice so they can refresh themselves before the next event. A brief announcement can bring the reception to a positive closing. It should thank those present for attending, and express the desire to see them at the next event, which will start in a certain number of minutes.

If no event follows, the same approach can be used, except to add such phrasing as "see you tomorrow morning for breakfast," "have a good evening," "see you next year," or whatever is appropriate.

When music and entertainment are provided, the traditional "Good Night Ladies," "Auld Lang Syne," or other appropriate musical numbers, communicates the closing very effectively.

Banquet

A banquet differs from a dinner in that (1) it is more formal, (2) serving tends to be more elaborate, (3)) the menu is a bit more extensive and more varied, and (4) it is accompanied by some kind of program. Some items applying to a banquet have already been discussed in other sections of this checklist. The following discussion focuses on items that are particularly relevant for a banquet.

Will Any Special Decorations Be Needed?

Special decorations can change an ordinary dinner into a banquet and make it a gala event. Banners and other items concerning the sponsor should be in clear evidence. Centerpieces can be coordinated with the banquet or conference theme and can be awarded to someone at each table, such as the person who has traveled farthest to attend the conference or the person who has attended the most conferences in the past five years.

The decorations can be seasonal (for example, flags and other symbols for a banquet held on July 3rd or 4th) or regional (for example, American Indian symbols for a conference held in the Southwest). The coordinator should work with site personnel, who are accustomed to providing decorations most appropriate for the conference and the food function.

Who Will Plan the Menu?

Additional attention should be given to the banquet menu, so that it will be perceptibly different from menus at the other food functions. As receptions usually precede a banquet, the menu should be coordinated with any food served at the reception. For example, if shrimp is served at the reception, the banquet menu should not include a shrimp cocktail.

Will the National Anthem Be Played?

The coordinator may choose to open a formal banquet with the national anthem if musicians or a good singer are available. The anthem should not be started until all participants are on their feet. Serving and all other movement should be suspended until the anthem is completed.

For an international conference, the anthem's political implications should be considered. Usually, playing the anthem of the host country presents no problems unless the conference is political in purpose.

Who Should Manage the Agenda or Cue Sheet?

A banquet has a series of events that must be coordinated by using an agenda or cue sheet. This sheet can be developed by the coordinator, but at the time of the banquet the coordinator will probably be busy with other things and should delegate the management of the banquet to a member of the secretariat.

The particular items on the agenda should reflect the purpose and goal of the banquet and the conference. A brief opening or a formal welcome to all in the room might start the banquet. This can be followed by a few comments by a leader of the sponsoring organization, including any necessary introduction to the sequence of events for the function, such as dancing, entertainment, speeches, or other parts of the program. Any invocation should be offered at this time, followed by the food service.

After dinner, any announcements should be kept brief, since too many or irrelevant announcements can spoil the banquet atmosphere. To signal the end of the meal, a benediction might be offered, using the same guidelines for invocations discussed earlier in this chapter. Then, the planned program begins: speaker, AV presentation, recognition, entertainment, or dancing.

Will the Banquet Offer Music?

Musicians can be used for more than just dancing. Musicians can play as people enter the room, to set the mood for the banquet. The musicians can play the national anthem. During introductions of head table or other dignitaries, the musicians can play appropriate music, which should be cleared with the coordinator to avoid embarrassment. Music can be provided for dancing or for interludes between courses. At the end of the banquet, music can set a pleasant mood as the participants leave.

If live music is too expensive for the conference budget, carefully selected prerecorded music is a viable alternative.

Breaks

How Will Breaks Be Planned?

Session breaks are built into the conference design. Even a very small conference has breaks, though they may not be printed on the matrix if they do not require any significant amount of negotiation or administration. The general rule is that participants should not stay in one place for more than one-and-a-half to two hours without some kind of break. The type and length of break depend on the other parts of the design. It is common to have breaks between sessions where participants are going from one room to another. The break allows for participant movement, as well as for refreshments.

The term *coffee break* is common, although a variety of beverages are usually provided, including tea, decaffeinated coffee, and fruit juice, sometimes supplemented by Danish, sweet rolls, cookies, fruit, or other snack items. Some coordinators have experimented with such foods as yogurt, buttermilk, and similar natural or health-oriented items. Others have opted, particularly in the afternoon, for ice cream, sodas (diet and regular), and fruit bars. The chosen items should relate to the participants and their expectations.

With increased emphasis on fitness, a recreation break, when participants are encouraged to walk or engage in some other forms of exercise, is another alternative. (The recreation break should not be confused with a recreation period, which is an event in itself.)

Will Breaks Be Considered Part of the Food Function Responsibility?

As most breaks involve some form of food, they should be considered part of food and beverage activity and negotiated for at the same time as site selection.

The breaks can be a significant budget item and are all part of what the coordinator is paying to use the site.

The general rule is that coffee should be ordered by the gallon rather than the cup. The price difference can be significant, and the coordinator should explore both possibilities with the site personnel. The other food items should also be priced, since cost usually determines what can be provided to the participants.

A problem that sometimes arises is that in some sites the food functions (meals) are handled by one group of personnel, while the food provided at breaks is handled by another. This split function may be convenient for the site, but the coordinator must negotiate from the strength of the total package in order to get the best price.

Is It Necessary to Assign a Secretariat Member Responsibility for Breaks?

The answer is an unequivocal "Yes!" Many things can go wrong with breaks, particularly when the site is serving several conferences at the same time. As can be seen in the sample designs in Chapter Three, the breaks are assigned numbers like any other event, and someone must have responsibility for that event, just as for other events.

The responsible secretariat member should have a specific site counterpart who can be contacted immediately in case of an error, such as too few cups or lack of decaffeinated coffee. Another common problem is the timing of the breaks. All too frequently, the setup for the breaks may be too early, too late, or in the wrong place. Given the limited time available to the participants, it is essential that the breaks be on schedule, as planned.

How Long Should a Break Be?

Except for a conference of under fifteen participants, breaks should be at least fifteen minutes. Time must be allowed for participants to leave the session room, visit rest rooms, obtain their beverage and other items, eat and drink, and return to the same room or proceed to another room.

A break that runs longer than thirty minutes can disrupt the flow of the conference; therefore, breaks should range from fifteen to thirty minutes. If service is inadequate, the participants should not be penalized by cutting the break short. It is sometimes helpful to use some kind of signal to let the participants know when the break is over.

For a small conference, the signal may only need to be a designated person calling out that the break is over. When the group is large, the signal could be flipping the light switch, a bell, or music. For very large conferences, the town crier, a person dressed in that old-fashioned costume with a bull horn, can be used as a signal, if this fits with the tone of the conference.

Handicapped participants may have difficulty during the break if they must move to another floor or to a part of the site that does not have ramps or other facilities for them. Blind participants usually have to move slower than sighted participants. If the break is too short, it can be a significant inconvenience.

Where Will Breaks Be Held?

The location of a break should relate to the purpose of the break, what is being served, the space available, and the participants' convenience. At a small conference, the break can be set up in the same room as the session unless setting up would prove disruptive. In some sites, it may be advantageous to use an adjoining room, particularly when the participants must return to the original room at the end of the break. (Of course, with this plan they have only a limited opportunity for a stretch or short walk.) If participants move on to different rooms, the break can be used as a way of facilitating movement with break stations at various places. It may be necessary to have several stations, which entails more food, of course, and the accompanying costs.

At some conference sites in scenic settings, breaks can be held on the lawn or another outdoor location, weather permitting. Recognize, however, that this may require participants who are highly motivated to return indoors after the break.

Will Tickets Be Required?

A small conference, with only one or two break stations, will usually not require tickets of any kind. A large conference with many break stations may require tickets to limit freeloaders, who somehow manage to gain access to the site while a conference is in progress. This matter should be discussed with the site personnel, since it is sometimes simpler to allow for the freeloaders rather than go to the trouble of providing and collecting tickets.

Chapter 10

Coordinating Exhibitions

CHECKLIST FOR EXHIBITIONS

Planning

_____ Why have an exhibition?

_____ Who will be the exhibition manager?

_____ Will the exhibition have a separate budget?

_____ Has the sponsor offered an exhibition in the past?

_____ Does the site have exhibition facilities?

_____ How much should be charged for each booth?

_____ How many booths will be available?

_____ What complimentary booths will be provided?

_____ Who will prepare the floor plan?

_____ How many complimentary registrations will be given to each exhibitor?

_____ Will exhibitors get preregistration mailing lists?

_____ What are some of the legal issues?

_____ Who assigns booths?

_____ Will a separate exhibitors book be produced?

_____ What is the relationship between the exhibitors book and the participant book?

_____ Will any restrictions be placed on hospitality suites?

_____ Who will develop the formal contract?

Relation to Design

_____ How does the exhibition relate to the purpose and design of the conference?

_____ How does the product/service of the exhibitor relate to the purpose of the conference?

_____ How many days/hours will the exhibition be open?

_____ Will walk-ins be permitted?

_____ Will exhibitors participate in the conference?

_____ Will meals be provided in the exhibit area?

Marketing

_____ Why should an organization exhibit?

_____ Who will prepare marketing materials?

_____ How will a marketing list be developed?

_____ What kinds of mailings will go out to prospective exhibitors?

Selecting Exhibitors

_____ How will applicants be screened?

_____ Has the interested exhibitor participated in the past?

_____ Why does the exhibitor want to participate this time?

_____ Does the exhibitor's product or service relate to the anticipated participants?

_____ Do the exhibitors agree to the restrictions that will be imposed?

_____ Do the exhibitors agree on what constitutes good taste?

_____ When will exhibitors be notified about acceptance?

_____ What payments will be required from exhibitors?

_____ What insurance should exhibitors have?

_____ How will space be assigned?

_____ Who has final approval of exhibitors?

Relation to Site

_____ Who is the specific site contact person responsible for exhibitions, and what is the experience of the individual and the site?

_____ What are the local rules, regulations, and laws?

_____ Where is the exhibition area located?

_____ What are the existing union contracts?

_____ Does the site have an official contractor?

_____ Who has the information for floor plans?

_____ Will the participants have easy access to the exhibition area?

_____ Will entry and exit at the exhibition area be monitored?

_____ Will the site provide security?

_____ Will the exhibit area be shared with other exhibitions?

_____ Who provides the basic signs?

Setup

_____ When will the space be available, and are there any special move-in costs?

_____ How many exhibitor personnel will be allowed in the hall?

_____ Will nonexhibitor personnel be excluded from the hall?

_____ How do exhibitors get necessary equipment and services for a booth?

_____ Who is responsible for empty carton removal?

_____ Will exhibitors be seeking local employees?

_____ How will registration of exhibitors be handled?

During the Conference

_____ When should exhibitors complete registration?

_____ Will the exhibition stage a grand opening?

_____ How will participants be directed to the exhibit area?

_____ Will participants be provided with a plastic card?

_____ What is expected of booth personnel?

_____ Are exhibitors aware that they are responsible for the local personnel staffing their booths?

_____ How will the exhibition be monitored?

_____ What form of closing ceremony will be held?

Knockdown

_____ Do the exhibitors know the latest time for clearing their materials?

_____ Do exhibitors know their responsibility for the condition of the area after they leave?

Follow-Up

_____ Will exhibitors receive a set of mailing labels of participants?

_____ Will an evaluation of the exhibition be conducted?

SOURCE: *The Comprehensive Guide to Successful Conferences and Meetings* by Leonard Nadler and Zeace Nadler. San Francisco: Jossey-Bass. Copyright © 1987. Permission to reproduce hereby granted.

An exhibition is the part of a conference where exhibitors show their products and services to the participants in exhibits, which are usually in the form of booths. An exhibition can range from one literature table to one thousand booths. As a supplement to the conference, the exhibition must be related to the conference and integrated with it at all points. (An exhibition that does not accompany a conference is called a trade show, which is not covered in this book.)

A booth is a designated space rented by an exhibitor from the sponsor. The dimensions vary, but basic dimensions are usually ten feet on each side. Two typical exhibition layouts are shown in Figures 37 and 38. In addition, some large exhibitions use several halls, and the booths are planned accordingly.

Exhibitors Committee

Not all exhibitions can benefit from an exhibitors committee. When a conference contains only a small exhibition, a committee is probably unnecessary. Likewise, a conference that will only be conducted once will not need an exhibitors committee. The need for an exhibitors committee should be explored by a coordinator before implementing one.

The exhibitors committee should not be part of the sponsor's organization nor under the coordinator but rather a group organized by the exhibitors for specific repetitive exhibitions. The exhibitors should have their own mechanism for running the committee and for electing their own officers. A representative of the exhibitors committee should be on the design committee, and a representative of the coordinator should be an observer at the exhibitors committee meetings.

The exhibitors committee can have many functions, depending on the nature of the exhibition and the interest of the exhibitors. To avoid conflict,

Figure 37. Typical Layout of Exhibit Area.

Entrance ——————————— Entrance ———————

Aisle 1

| 101 | | Aisle 1 | | 120 |
| 102 | | | | 121 |

	104	105	106	107	108	109	110	111	112	113	114	115	116	117	118	119	

| 103 | 104 | 105 | 106 | 107 | 108 | 109 | 110 | 111 | 112 | 113 | 114 | 115 | 116 | 117 | 118 | 119 | 122 |
| 201 | 205 | 207 | 209 | 211 | 213 | 215 | 217 | 219 | 221 | 223 | 225 | 227 | 229 | 231 | 233 | 235 | 237 |

| 202 | | | 238 |
| 203 | | Aisle 2 | 239 |

| 204 | 206 | 208 | 210 | 212 | 214 | 216 | 218 | 220 | 222 | 224 | 226 | 228 | 230 | 232 | 234 | 236 | 240 |
| 301 | 305 | 307 | 309 | 311 | 313 | 315 | 317 | 319 | 321 | 323 | 325 | 327 | 329 | 331 | 333 | 335 | 337 |

| 302 | | | 338 |
| 303 | | Aisle 3 | 339 |

| 304 | 306 | 308 | 310 | 312 | 314 | 316 | 318 | 320 | 322 | 324 | 326 | 328 | 330 | 332 | 334 | 336 | 340 |
| 401 | 405 | 407 | 409 | 411 | 413 | 415 | 417 | 419 | 421 | 423 | 425 | 427 | 429 | 431 | 433 | 435 | 436 |

| 402 | | Aisle 4 | 437 |

Food service and lounge area

SOURCE: *The Comprehensive Guide to Successful Conferences and Meetings* by Leonard Nadler and Zeace Nadler. San Francisco: Jossey-Bass. Copyright © 1987. Permission to reproduce hereby granted.

Figure 38. Typical Layout of Exhibit Area with Islands.

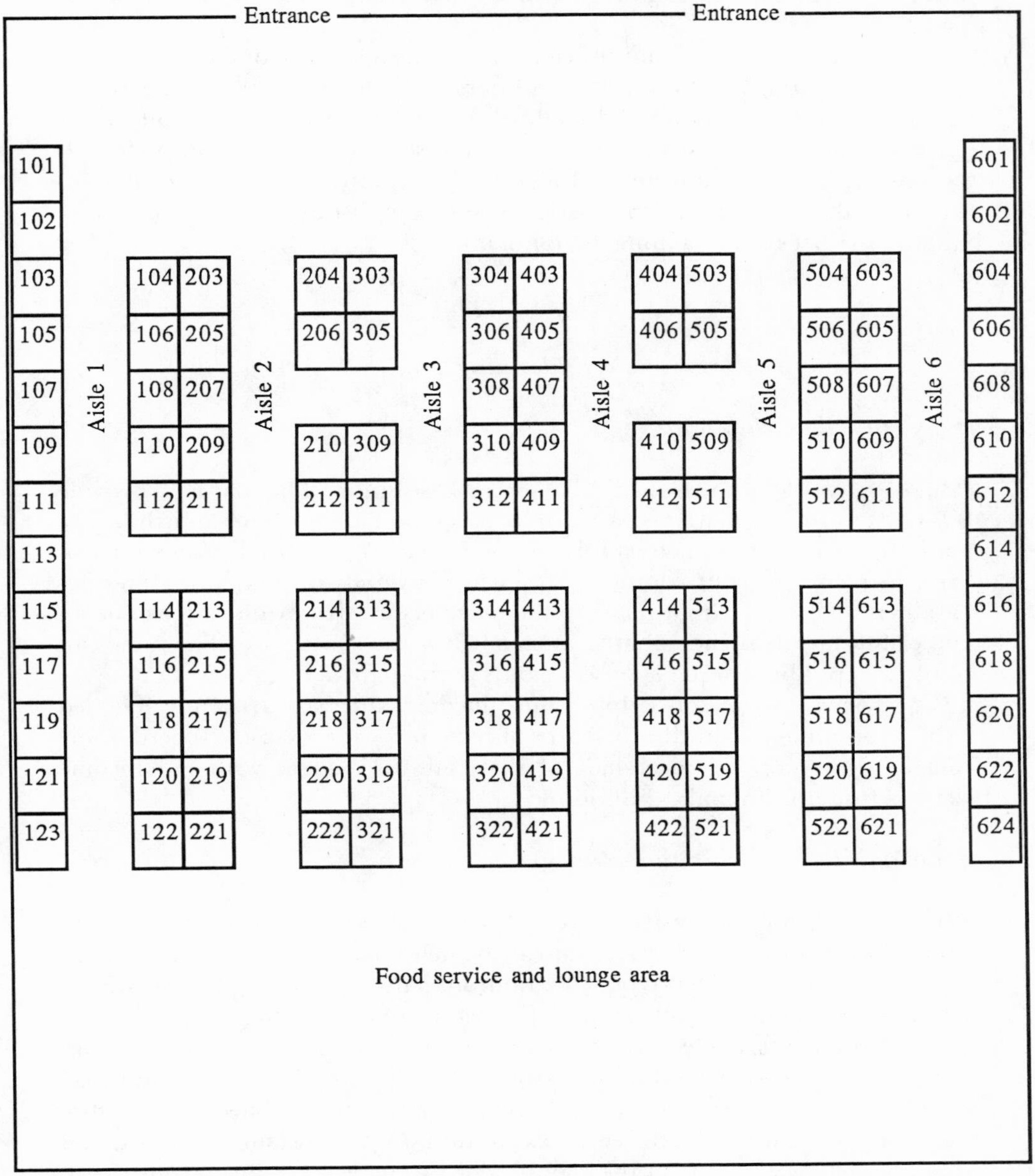

SOURCE: *The Comprehensive Guide to Successful Conferences and Meetings* by Leonard Nadler and Zeace Nadler. San Francisco: Jossey-Bass. Copyright © 1987. Permission to reproduce hereby granted.

the committee might be provided with a worksheet similar to the one shown in Figure 3, so they will know in which areas they can recommend, react, or decide.

The exhibitors committee can (1) provide a coordinator with feedback on past exhibitions and what the exhibitors desire for exhibitions; (2) develop criteria for booth selection and establish the ground rules for exhibitors; (3) review the design and suggest the exhibition schedule they would prefer; (4) make suggestions for improving traffic to the exhibition area and the flow of traffic in the area; and (5) reconcile some of the disputes and conflicts that might arise between or among exhibitors.

The Checklist

Planning

Why Have an Exhibition?

There are two major reasons for having an exhibition. The first is to provide a service to the participants. An employer sponsor might hold an exhibition to show its new products to employees or dealers. A membership sponsor can serve its members by providing a place where a variety of companies can offer products and services that relate to the membership. An exhibition can be an important factor in encouraging attendance at the conference. The same can apply to a public seminar sponsor and its participants.

The second reason is to produce income, since an efficiently handled exhibition can be a significant source of income for the sponsor. Indeed, some membership sponsors meet half of their annual budget with the income derived from the annual exhibition.

Who Will Be the Exhibition Manager?

When an exhibition consists of only a few tables set up near the function rooms, a member of the secretariat can be delegated the managerial responsibility for such a limited type of exhibition. This type of exhibition usually consists of brochures or other printed materials that are being made available to the participants, and exhibitors will not provide any staff, just the materials.

As the size of the exhibition grows, however, a specific person must act as the exhibition manager; for some exhibitions, it may be necessary to hire a person who can handle the entire exhibition. In that instance, it is essential that the manager be part of the coordinator's team and not just a consultant. The exhibition should supplement the conference, not compete with it.

Will the Exhibition Have a Separate Budget?

The budget for a small exhibition may be included in the overall conference budget, but a separate exhibition budget may be desirable for a large exhibition. The general guidelines will be the same as budgeting for a conference (see Chapter Sixteen), but some of the specifics will be different, depending on how the exhibition is organized.

Has the Sponsor Offered an Exhibition in the Past?

The design of an exhibition must start with what has happened in the past. If a membership sponsor has never had an exhibition, the membership may be curious as to why one is being considered now. Rather than allow rumors to proliferate, a clear and positive statement should be sent to the members. Sponsors other than membership sponsors do not have to justify an exhibition.

How will the present exhibition differ from past exhibitions? The only real difference might be size: Exhibitions seem to be growing larger, and new conference facilities are providing more space for exhibitions. Convention centers are also providing more space for large exhibitions.

Does the Site Have Exhibition Facilities?

Exhibitions should be coordinated with site selection. It is desirable to have the sessions in the same building as the exhibition. Some hotels advertise that they have exhibition areas available, but a coordinator should examine this claim closely: Where is the space located, and is it real exhibition space or merely public access space that will have to be blocked off during the exhibition?

How Much Should Be Charged for Each Booth?

The sponsor rents all the space from the site and then establishes booth charges. Usually, the charge is based on the total cost to the conference budget for the space, expenses, and related factors. The number of booths is calculated based on the basic 10′ x 10′ or similar size. The charge for the booth must reflect the sponsor's past exhibitions. It is difficult for a sponsor to raise the rate drastically from one conference to another, and it is unusual for rates to go down! The exhibitor expects the rate to be higher, depending on size and location of a booth, but within reason.

Referring to Figure 37, the cost will be the same for almost all booths. Because the corner booths receive more traffic, the rate would be somewhat higher for booths 101–104, and 201–206, and other booths in corner locations. The booths directly opposite the entrances (106–109 and 114–117) also receive heavier traffic, and therefore exhibitors recognize that they will have to pay more for these locations.

In the layout shown in Figure 38, "islands" have been created (such as the one created by booths 204, 206, 303, and 305), which can be expected to receive more traffic than booths in the middle of an aisle, so here also the rate would be higher. In that configuration, it is not unusual for an exhibitor to want adjacent booths, such as 406 and 505, and combine them into one large booth.

Booth charges must be decided fairly early in the planning stage, since these amounts become part of the marketing package that will be discussed later in this chapter. A tentative net figure must be calculated for budget purposes.

How Many Booths Will Be Available?

A small conference may only have a few booths, which may actually not be booths at all but tables that have been prepared to be used for exhibits. A larger exhibit area may have some limitations. The total floor space may not be usable for booths because of pillars or curved walls. Some space will probably be allocated to food and beverage service, particularly if lunch is to be served in the exhibition area. Though this space cannot be used for exhibits, it does keep the participants in the area. It may be decided to provide lounge space— an area where participants can sit down and relax—placed away from the entrances so that participants must pass booths in order to reach that area. The site itself may require that space be allocated for a snack bar where participants can purchase sandwiches and beverages. Not until all these factors are considered is it possible to calculate the maximum number of booths available for exhibits.

What Complimentary Booths Will Be Provided?

Exhibitions usually contain several complimentary booths. The sponsor may want one, particularly a membership organization, for the purpose of obtaining applications and answering questions about membership. The booth can also be used to exhibit some of the publications and other services of the sponsor.

The LCVB might be given a complimentary booth to provide participants with information about the city and local attractions. This booth would probably be placed outside the exhibition area so LCVB personnel can be available to answer questions even when the exhibition is closed.

Reciprocity can be a factor. The sponsor could trade a booth for similar space at the exhibition of another sponsor. Sponsors sometimes donate a booth to a local civic or social organization.

Who Will Prepare the Floor Plan?

The site personnel may prepare the exhibition floor plan, but they need information from the exhibition manager or from someone designated by the coordinator. The floor plan is very important because it can be costly or even impossible to make changes. The floor plan becomes part of marketing, is announced to many different people, and becomes part of the agreement between the coordinator and the site. It may still be possible to have further negotiations, should either more or less space be required.

How Many Complimentary Registrations Will Be Given to Each Exhibitor?

Exhibitor personnel frequently attend sessions and functions to mix with participants and become familiar with their concerns. At least one complimentary registration is usually given to each booth; the "comp" usually includes all functions and has been figured into the cost of the booth. Some exhibitors may bring additional personnel so provision should be made for an exhibitor to purchase additional registrations.

Will Exhibitors Get Preregistration Mailing Lists?

For many conferences, preregistration is an important factor, and special rates are established to encourage preregistration (see Chapter Sixteen). The list of preregistered participants can be useful to exhibitors and can be part of the marketing package. With this list, an exhibitor can send promotional material to participants, indicating its booth number and special products or services that the exhibitor will display. An exhibitor can include a card in the mailings to preregistered participants, offering a prize, gift, or a souvenir to participants who bring the card to the booth during exhibition hours. The purpose, of course, is to encourage the participant to come to their specific booths and this technique has proven to be very successful.

What Are Some of the Legal Issues?

Site personnel and the LCVB should be able to answer questions about the local legalities. If possible, the exhibition manager should send all applicable legal material to exhibitors as part of the marketing package.

At some conferences, exhibitors are only permitted to show their products and services but cannot take orders; at others, exhibitors are allowed to take orders for future delivery. At some sites, some items, such as books, may be sold on the spot, but these sales can have many implications, depending on local and state laws. Frequently, local authorities frown on selling by conference exhibitors who are not part of the community and do not pay business taxes.

When direct sales are permitted, local and state sales taxes may have to be collected from the buyer. Although the sponsor is not doing the selling, by renting the space to the exhibitor, it can be construed that the sponsor is a party to the transaction. Exhibitors need to have all this information in planning how they will exhibit. Generally, these factors are ignored and frequently nothing happens, but when it does, it can be costly and embarrassing.

Federal tax implications depend on the sponsor. Most membership sponsors have nonprofit status under the Internal Revenue Code, so income from a conference is not considered taxable. However, the IRS has at times ruled that the income from an exhibition can be considered taxable income. When planning an exhibition, a coordinator should consult with a qualified lawyer or tax adviser to determine how the exhibition will affect the sponsor's tax status, if at all.

Who Assigns Booths?

Although the actual assigning of booths occurs later in the process, all parties should agree during the planning stage on responsibility: Will the final decision be made by the coordinator, the exhibition manager, or the exhibitors committee? Some exhibitors always ask this question early in the process, and the coordinator should be able to give them an answer.

Will a Separate Exhibitors Book Be Produced?

For some exhibitions, it is desirable to prepare an exhibitors book. For a large exhibition, the book would include the exhibition floor plans, such as the ones presented in Figures 37 and 38, while for a small exhibition, these diagrams might show the names of the exhibitors instead of booth numbers.

The book should also list the names of exhibitors in alphabetical order. (For an international exhibition, the list might also be classified by country or region.) The listing can also include the names of booth personnel and each exhibitor's major products and products that will be shown at the exhibition. Each exhibitor should receive the same space in the book or an amount of space equivalent to the booth space rented on the exhibition floor. The book can be prepared as a take-home piece, containing a great deal of helpful information for both participants and exhibitors.

The book can be funded by estimating the cost and then including it in the booth rental price so the book pays for itself. The book might also be an income-producing item if exhibitors place ads and pay for their listings. Ads should be limited to exhibitors. If ads must be solicited from nonexhibitors, the cost should be such that it encourages a company to exhibit and advertise, rather than just advertise.

What Is the Relationship Between the Exhibitors Book and the Participant Book?

The exhibitors book may be part of the participant book. In this case, different colored pages should be used for each section so the exhibition pages can be readily identified. This greatly facilitates the participants' use of the book. Ads may be accepted in a combined book, but the book may get too large and participants may not wish to carry it every day. Daily session listings may be required (see Chapter Eighteen), which would result in the relevant exhibition information not being carried by the participants. However, a separate exhibitors book might also be seen by participants as extra baggage to be left in their sleeping rooms. If the book has been designed as a take-home piece, this may not be a problem, but it needs to be supplemented by something more convenient that the participants can use at the exhibition (such as one or two sheets showing the booth layout and list of exhibitors). It is also desirable to hang layout blow-ups at strategic places in the exhibition hall, so that participants can readily locate booths in which they are particularly interested.

Will Any Restrictions Be Placed on Hospitality Suites?

Exhibitors usually prefer to hold a hospitality suite in the headquarters hotel, though this preference puts them in direct competition with the coordinator who may need suites for conference purposes. A membership sponsor usually seeks such a suite for its officers, and an employer sponsor might want such a suite for its upper-level company officers. If the hotel has sufficient suites, no problem results. Exhibitors can always use another hotel, as long as it is located nearby and has suites available.

Who Will Develop the Formal Contract?

Much of what is discussed in this chapter forms the basis for the contract that exhibitors must sign when renting a booth. Exhibitors also want to know what else they get with the booth or what extras they may have to pay. Some of that information will come from later sections of this chapter and some of it has already been discussed. A sponsor who has used exhibitions previously probably has some form of contract, but it should be reviewed by qualified legal personnel in light of any changes or differences in the current exhibition and any changes due to location or laws.

Relation to Design

How Does the Exhibition Relate to the Purpose and Design of the Conference?

An exhibition should be an extension of the conference and related directly to it. A one-day conference might have an exhibition, but it would obviously be very limited. If it is necessary to have one, in the case of an employer sponsor introducing a new product, workshop sessions might be replaced by an exhibition, or the workshops might be held in the exhibition area, where participants can actually use the product, such as a computer.

How Many Days/Hours Will the Exhibition Be Open?

This is one of the most difficult questions to answer and reflects the competition between the events and the exhibition. Exhibitors, of course, prefer nonopposing time, that is, no other events for the time the exhibition is open.

Two days of Example C (see Chapter Three) are shown in Figure 39. Note that Event 16 is actually the opening of the exhibition, followed by lunch in the exhibition area. The exhibition closes during Event 17 and then reopens—unopposed—for Event 18. The same pattern is planned for Events 21-23.

Although some exhibitors prefer to have the exhibition stay open during Event 17, most do not prefer that arrangement, since it means that the exhibit would be open from 11:30 A.M. to 6:00 P.M.—an extremely long time for the personnel who must staff the booth; most exhibitors would rather have the split. During Event 17 (2:00 to 4:00 P.M.), as presently designed, the exhibitors can either rest or hold individual meetings in their hospitality suites.

No pattern can possibly please everyone. A compromise might be to have the exhibition remain open during Event 22 (concurrent sessions). The resource people presenting those sessions may object, but they cannot exert the

Figure 39. Design for a Five-Day Conference (Example C) (Partial).

Time	Event Number	Wednesday	Event Number	Thursday
8:00 A.M.	13	General session	20	A) Special interest groups
9:00 A.M.				B) Field trip
	14	Break		
10:00 A.M.	15	Concurrent sessions		
12:00 P.M.	16	Exhibition opening and lunch	21	Exhibition and lunch
2:00 P.M.	17	Concurrent sessions	22	Concurrent sessions
4:00 P.M.	18	Exhibition	23	Exhibition
6:00 P.M.	19	A) Film festival	24	Free
7:00 P.M.		B) Poster sessions	25	Banquet and recognition night
8:00 P.M.				

NOTE: See Chapter Three for complete design of all five days.

SOURCE: *The Comprehensive Guide to Successful Conferences and Meetings* by Leonard Nadler and Zeace Nadler. San Francisco: Jossey-Bass. Copyright © 1987. Permission to reproduce hereby granted.

same pressure on a coordinator as the exhibitors can. There is no one best way to allocate time between sessions and exhibits. The best that can be hoped for is to negotiate and be prepared for trade-offs.

Will Walk-Ins Be Permitted?

Walk-ins, people wanting to attend the exhibition only, can be disruptive and require additional security to make sure that those paying only to attend the exhibition do not also attend other events. Most exhibitors, on the other hand, welcome walk-ins, as this policy allows exhibitors to reach more potential consumers. It is not a major issue but one that does need to be addressed. See Chapter Sixteen for a more detailed discussion of walk-ins.

Will Exhibitors Participate in the Conference?

Exhibitors can participate in the conference, but caution should be exercised so they do not distort the conference. Participants resent attending a session that is actually an extension of an exhibit. That comes under the heading of "selling from the platform," which is usually forbidden at a membership sponsor conference, though frequently permitted in some for-profit public seminar sponsor conferences, where the participants have been alerted to that practice ahead of time.

Exhibitors can relate to the conference in certain ways that are beneficial for all concerned. An AV supplier, for example, might make equipment available to presenters at little or no cost, reducing the expense for the coordinator. To reward the exhibitor, a sign might be posted at the session noting that "Equipment for this session has been provided by Exhibitor X, Booth 101." The coordinator should be very open and fair about this procedure: If several exhibitors are handling the same equipment, each should be given the opportunity to provide equipment and receive recognition.

Many exhibitors have films that they show at their booths. When films are important to the participants, special viewing booths can be set up in the exhibition area and each exhibitor allotted a time when their films will be screened.

A "film festival," such as the one shown in Event 19A (Figure 39) is part of the conference, not the exhibition, and should be controlled by the coordinator. An effective way to set it up is to allow showings only by participants who have actually used the films. It is the responsibility of the exhibitor to identify such a participant and to make the film available. Exhibitor personnel may attend, but discussion should be limited to participants.

Will Meals Be Provided in the Exhibit Area?

Some exhibitors deplore food and drink in the exhibition area, as it can result in damage to some of the items they are exhibiting. Generally, however, exhibitors do not mind paying for a lunch that is served in the exhibition area. (For psychological reasons, a coordinator may not tell exhibitors they are paying for the lunch, but merely include the cost of the lunch in the price for a booth.) This allows the coordinator to provide free meals to participants, which contributes to increased traffic in the exhibit area.

As shown in Figures 37 and 38, the serving area should be at the rear of the exhibition hall so that participants have to walk through the exhibits to obtain lunch. There must also be a place where participants can sit down and eat. When not in use, this area can be used as a lounge attached to the exhibit area. These factors must be negotiated with the site.

Marketing

Why Should an Organization Exhibit?

Exhibitions must be marketed because exhibitors are approached by many different coordinators with invitations to exhibit at various conferences.

Considering the competition, exhibitors must have good reasons to exhibit at one conference rather than another. Therefore, it is necessary for a coordinator to develop a well-organized campaign to reach and convince potential exhibitors. As with other aspects of conference work, a coordinator may wish to engage the services of professionals, in this case those who are experienced in marketing exhibitions. Some sponsors who offer many conferences have their own in-house exhibition marketing personnel.

No matter which approach is used, an individual should be designated as the marketing manager for the exhibition to provide one focal point for marketing and for responding to interested parties. For a small exhibition, the exhibition manager and the marketing manager may be the same person, though for a large conference the task may require two separate people or units. It is also possible, for a small conference, to assign exhibition marketing to the person or group that is marketing for participants.

Why should an organization or company exhibit at a particular conference? There are many good reasons, and sometimes a marketing approach will focus on one or two of them, while at other times all the reasons discussed here will be emphasized in the marketing plan.

1. An exhibition provides an exhibitor with potential new clients and customers. Even if an organization has participated in previous exhibitions of that sponsor, there are always different participants. Some of the previous participants will not attend this time, while there will be others who are participants for the first time and are, therefore, new prospects.

    A nationwide company may turn its sales leads over to its regional or local office. On the other hand, local companies will probably not exhibit at a conference drawing participants from outside its geographical area, for few of the participants will be potential sales leads.

2. An exhibitor may actually want to sell its product at the exhibition, if selling is permitted at the site. Actually, making direct sales is usually one of the less important reasons for an exhibitor to participate in an exhibition, though it can be a major reason for taking part in a trade show. Some exhibitors are quite disappointed when they compare the cost of exhibiting with the actual sales at the exhibition, not realizing that an exhibition is not the place to make significant sales but a place to do significant marketing to produce future sales.

3. An exhibition can be a good way to introduce a new product and to provide significant exposure for it. Some companies time such an introduction to coincide with an important exhibition so they can reach a large potential market and gain immediate feedback on the product.

4. Companies are very interested in consumer feedback, and some exhibitors choose conferences where the participants are their past or present customers. The exhibition atmosphere is neutral territory and is conducive to a face-to-face exchange.

5. Exhibitors can benefit from a mailing list of all participants. Informing potential exhibitors that such a list will be available is good marketing strategy.

6. An exhibitor may participate just to enhance its image (sometimes referred to as "missionary work" or "name recognition"). The objective is to keep the name of the company in evidence before actual and potential consumers. The exhibitor may not actually show any specific product, but wants the participants to remember the name of the organization and what it has to offer.
7. Exhibitors want to know what their competitors are offering, and the exhibition provides an excellent opportunity for visiting competitors' booths and seeing not only what they are offering but how they are offering it.

Who Will Prepare Marketing Materials?

Marketing is an expensive proposition, so a coordinator wants to be sure that the return on exhibition marketing will warrant the expense. If the exhibition has only a limited number of booths and a number of exhibitors who traditionally participate, marketing may be very low key. A letter can be sent to past exhibitors to remind them of the forthcoming exhibition and another letter sent to a few potential exhibitors in case additional booths become available.

For large exhibitions, a coordinator cannot risk losing exhibitors, so all previous and potential exhibitors are contacted with a kit of materials that "sell" the exhibition. The contents of the kit are discussed later in the chapter.

The marketing materials should be developed by the exhibition manager, the marketing manager, or a marketing consultant. The coordinator must review the materials before production, to make sure that they reflect the image of the conference and correctly represent the relationship between the conference and the exhibition.

How Will a Marketing List Be Developed?

Marketing should be focused on those exhibitors whose products and services bear a direct relationship to the theme of the conference and the interest of the participants. The first source for marketing is a list of organizations that have exhibited in the sponsor's prior exhibitions. If these exhibitors were pleased with the results of their previous participation, they will be eager to exhibit again and they will expect to be notified first for the next exhibition. (Notification is sometimes handled at the current exhibition to inform exhibitors of the time and place of the next.) They may also be provided with a request or contract form so they can be among the first to sign up, accruing the attendant benefits including booth selection.

Unless all booths are sold out in this manner, marketing lists need to be developed to reach out to new exhibitors. Although past exhibitors rarely provide the names of competitors, they might provide the names of companies with products that supplement theirs. For example, an exhibitor of films might provide names of companies that supply screens and projectors.

As the exhibition is, in part, a service to the participants, the participants themselves may have suggestions. A letter could go out to potential participants as part of the marketing plan to this group, asking for suggestions of exhibitors that they would like to see at the next conference. Participants can provide general product areas (for example, video disk), the names of companies that might exhibit, and, in some cases, even the name of the person to be contacted.

A coordinator, with help from others, should contact exhibitors who are related to the theme of the conference and the interest of the participants but who may not realize how they could benefit from exhibiting. One source is commercial mailing lists, which can sometimes be purchased from the same sources that provide potential participant mailing lists. A few sources are listed in the Resources.

Because many coordinators are competing for the same participants and exhibitors, one marketing approach is to obtain the list of exhibitors at similar conferences and exhibitions. These exhibitors may not be familiar with the exhibition and do not realize the benefits to be gained from participation.

What Kinds of Mailings Will Go Out to Prospective Exhibitors?

The nature and content of the mailings to potential exhibitors will depend on the sponsor's previous experience, the kind and amount of exhibit space available, and the exhibitors' anticipated need for information. Exhibitors cannot make a decision without sufficient information. If the mailing does not provide sufficient information, the exhibitor will have to phone or write the coordinator or just not respond at all.

The mailing is the face of the exhibition, projecting the competency of the coordinator and the image of the sponsor. The material must be professional and comprehensive. Some exhibitor kits are more expensive to produce than similar kits for participants. The contents of the kit should provide answers to all possible questions from potential exhibitors (see Figure 40).

Potential exhibitors want information about the sponsor. Even if they have exhibited previously, any new directions or policies would be important for exhibitors to know. A mailing going to new exhibitors should include a brochure or other material describing the sponsor.

Exhibitors need to know the dates of the conference and the exhibition. Some conferences start before the exhibition opens and continue after it closes—a generally accepted practice to achieve maximum participation in the exhibition (see Example C in Chapter Three). From this information, exhibitors can determine if they have any conflicts and identify personnel and products for the date(s) of the exhibition. Obviously, it is important to get this information to exhibitors as early as possible.

Exhibitors want to know the theme of the conference, since this helps them to decide if it is to their interests to exhibit. The kit should explain the meaning of the theme and underscore why potential exhibitors with particular products and services should exhibit.

From the conference matrix, exhibitors will be able to see exactly how the exhibition relates to the conference. For the initial marketing effort, it will

Figure 40. Contents for Exhibitors Kit.

_____ Information about sponsor	_____ Procedures
_____ Dates of conference and exhibition	_____ Payment and financial policies
_____ Theme of the conference	_____ Order forms
_____ The conference matrix	_____ Shipping and drayage
_____ Participants: number and profile	_____ Setup labor
_____ Why an exhibitor should participate	_____ Utilities
_____ The exhibition hall layout	_____ Exhibitors book
_____ Union regulations	_____ Contact person

SOURCE: *The Comprehensive Guide to Successful Conferences and Meetings* by Leonard Nadler and Zeace Nadler. San Francisco: Jossey-Bass. Copyright © 1987. Permission to reproduce hereby granted.

probably not be possible to list the individual sessions or presenters, but this is not really necessary: Exhibitors are more concerned with how much time will be available for exhibits and how those time blocks relate to other events.

The probable number and profile of participants should be provided, even though the number of participants is, of course, only an estimate. If the kit contains unrealistic figures, the exhibition will lose credibility in the future. The profile of the participants should highlight why they are potential consumers for the products and services of the exhibitors being contacted.

A strong case should be made for why an exhibitor should participate in this exhibition (see discussion on this question earlier in this chapter).

Exhibitors need to see the exhibition hall layout in order to request a particular booth and to understand the extent of the exhibition and the number of available booths. (This number should also be as realistic as possible, though it may be necessary to subtract or add a few booths later.)

The procedure for applying for booth space should be spelled out clearly, and the forms that the exhibitors must fill out should also be clear and simple. The agreement form projects an image to the potential exhibitor, and if it is clear and well-designed, it communicates that the exhibition will be as well. A registration form should be developed for exhibitors that will include all the pertinent information, especially how soon they can expect to be notified about the acceptance of their application for a booth.

Payment and financial policies should be clear and specific. The price per booth should be clearly stated, as well as what that price includes. Any additional costs should also appear on the order form. It is customary to ask for a deposit with the registration form and to specify the date for final payment and accepted method of payment—whether by check or purchase order. A closing date for the receipt of applications should be clearly noted on the registration form, including information about the exhibition's policy on the refund of deposits.

Well-planned order forms should be enclosed, listing booth items available and their prices. The order forms need not be returned to the coordinator at the same time as the registration since, in some situations, the order forms will be sent directly to a site contractor. The order forms should inform the exhibitor as to what furniture will be provided, if any. In some sites, it is customary to provide one chair and a small table for each booth, with additional chairs and tables available at a cost. The booth usually has no decorations aside from a backdrop or a wall that separates it from other booths. Exhibitors may want other kinds of decorations or furniture—such as floor lamps, floral displays, bookshelves, or additional carpeting—but they will have to pay for them. The coordinator usually supplies a small sign giving the name of the exhibitor and the booth number; for a large exhibition with several aisles, the exhibition usually pays for signs indicating the aisle number. Any additional booth signs are typically at the expense of the exhibitors.

A significant expense item for exhibitors is shipping and drayage—the costs for sending exhibits and materials from the point of origin to the exhibition site. The exhibitor must coordinate these shipments very carefully to keep costs down for warehousing and trans-shipping. A large exhibition site usually has contacts with shipping and drayage firms. It is important that the order form indicate whether the exhibitor is obligated to use the site's companies or is free to use any company. To make wise decisions, the exhibitor needs to know the rates charged by the contract companies as well as the rates of others in the exhibition city.

Some exhibitors use their own personnel to set up their exhibits, while others hire experienced local people to do the setup. The site or the LCVB can usually provide a roster of them with comparative costs.

Basic utilities, such as lighting for the area, are usually provided free of charge and sometimes include one electrical outlet per booth. If an exhibitor requires additional utilities, they must request and pay for them. If the exhibitor is using AV equipment or computers, special wiring may be needed. A telephone line may have to be installed in order to use a computer modem. In a specific situation, water may be required. The exhibitor must request all these items early enough to allow for the necessary work orders and payment.

Exhibitors need to know the local union regulations. In some cities, exhibitors can employ whom they wish to set up their booths and negotiate for an hourly rate; in others, hiring must be through the union and at specified rates.

Exhibitors should be told about any exhibitors book and informed about the possibility of advertising in it and the costs involved.

The exhibitor should be given the name of a specific contact person on the coordinator's staff. When exhibitors call, they may need an immediate response to a question, in order to make a decision. The way they are handled on the phone will strongly communicate how the exhibition is viewed by the coordinator. A good phone response indicates that the coordinator is prepared to serve the exhibitors. If possible, an 800 number should be used, but a different one than the one supplied to prospective participants.

Selecting Exhibitors

How Will Applicants Be Screened?

If every exhibitor can be accommodated with a booth, the coordinator has no problem, but if applications for exhibit space are refused for whatever reason, conflicts can arise. Though very few conflicts end up in the courts, it is always best to be prepared. One way of minimizing possible misunderstandings is to provide a written statement that lists the criteria and process for accepting applications for exhibition space.

Has the Interested Exhibitor Participated in the Past?

A major factor to consider is past performance. Exhibitors who have participated in previous exhibitions expect some favorable treatment, such as early notice of the exhibition and favorable consideration of their applications. That is good business practice.

Why Does the Exhibitor Want to Participate This Time?

It can sometimes be enlightening to ascertain why an exhibitor wants to be part of the current exhibition. This is particularly of interest when a company exhibited in the distant past, then dropped out of the exhibition, and now wants to return. The company's reasons for returning can furnish important information to a coordinator.

Does the Exhibitor's Product or Service Relate to the Anticipated Participants?

This is a type of fail-safe to ensure that the exhibitor understands the exhibition and the participants. It is not that the coordinator wants to discourage the exhibitor, but it is in the best interests of all that the exhibitor understand the nature of the participants and what to expect.

Do the Exhibitors Agree to the Restrictions That Will Be Imposed?

The exhibition's restrictions should be spelled out. Examples of restrictions include: the hours that the exhibit hall will be closed, when entry will be limited to those with exhibitor badges, and the availability of hospitality suites in the headquarters hotel or the prohibition of hospitality suites in the conference site near the exhibition area. A commonly violated restriction is that no exhibitor literature can be distributed outside of the exhibition area.

Do the Exhibitors Agree on What Constitutes Good Taste?

Good taste, of course, is subjective. For example, some participants may resent an exhibitor utilizing scantily clad female models to draw attention to the exhibitor's booth. Others feel that huckstering loudly as participants pass by is not in good taste. One exhibitor practice that occurs all too often is pasting the company logo on the participants' badges.

When Will Exhibitors Be Notified About Acceptance?

Exhibitors should be notified by the date stated in the exhibitors kit. The date must be early enough so that accepted organizations have time to do the necessary planning and rejected organizations have time for an appeal if they desire. The notification of acceptance need not state which specific booth has been allocated, though that information would be helpful, but exhibitors need to know what the next steps are and when they need to be taken.

What Payments Will Be Required from Exhibitors?

At time of notification, exhibitors should be reminded about financial matters, even though this information has been sent to them earlier and was on the registration form. If any additional payments are due at the time of acceptance, it should be stated clearly. The remaining financial commitments should probably be reiterated, such as balance of payment due date and cancellation clause information.

It is important to give specific instructions as to whom the check should be drawn. In most cases, it will be to the sponsor, but in some situations it will be to some other individual or organization.

What Insurance Should Exhibitors Have?

If they have not been notified earlier, this is the time to inform exhibitors about the need for insurance. They may need liability insurance, product insurance, or insurance for pilferage and robbery. The coordinator need not be specific; exhibition insurance is a specialized area, and experts can offer advice. The coordinator should merely bring the item to the attention of the exhibitors.

How Will Space Be Assigned?

At some point, specific booth assignments must be made. The price differential may automatically limit competition for certain booths, but some booths will be requested by more than one exhibitor regardless of price. An organized system should be used to assign space, and exhibitors should know the system used. Some possibilities are:

- An exhibitors' committee can be permitted to assign booths when two or more exhibitors are competing for the same booths. Although these committees can be considered prejudiced and be accused of restraint of trade, they have received a favorable response in the past.
- Priority can be given to those who have exhibited at a previous conference, particularly the last one. This encourages exhibitors to exhibit at each conference and reduces the marketing costs of the coordinator. If there is

competition between two such exhibitors, giving priority to previous exhibitors can be combined with the next possibility.

- Allocations can be based on date of application receipt, so the earlier an exhibitor applies, the greater the possibility of receiving the requested booth. Frequently, applications are accepted at the close of a current exhibition to exhibit at the next one so current exhibitors obviously have an advantage.
- A point system can include several of these factors. Points are given to each application based on the date it was received, whether it was submitted by a previous exhibitor, and the size of booths previously rented. The point system should be carefully constructed to give equal points to each item or to weight the items differently. For example, more weight (and thus more points) may be given to those who have been recent previous exhibitors than for some of the other items.
- A lottery can allocate space with a random drawing of exhibitor applications and booth numbers and matching them up. It is more likely to work better for the layout in Figure 37, where the booths have approximately equal exposure. (A separate lottery could be held for those who apply for end booths, such as 104 and 119.)

Who Has Final Approval of Exhibitors?

Although recommendations can come from several sources, one person should have final approval. Usually this is the coordinator or some other designated person.

Relation to Site

Many of these items concerning the exhibition site should be completed early in the design phase, as the information is needed for marketing. They are covered here for easy reference.

Who Is the Specific Site Contact Person Responsible for Exhibitions, and What Is the Experience of the Individual and the Site?

There is a level of turnover in the conference field, and the coordinator must investigate the experience of both the general site personnel and the specific contact person. Although large hotels that contain exhibition areas usually have a single contact, a smaller hotel may not have one contact. Instead the coordinator may have to work with the sales office, maintenance people, and a designated contractor. Convention centers almost always have an exhibition contact, and that person should be clearly identified as the site counterpart of the coordinator or the coordinator's exhibition manager.

A site should be inspected while another exhibition is in progress, when the coordinator can talk to the coordinator or exhibition manager of the current exhibition. It is also helpful to ask some of the exhibitors such questions as: Are site personnel helpful? Do exhibitors have any special problems? What would they advise? Exhibitors can be a valuable source of information, particularly while the exhibition is in progress.

What Are the Local Rules, Regulations, and Laws?

Pertinent local laws must be investigated and shared with the exhibitors. The investigation may require that the exhibition manager meet with such local officials as the fire marshal, police captain, or a health inspector. In some situations these officials or their subordinates must visit the exhibition and provide an official certificate or some other form of approval. If these local agencies have been involved from the outset, approval should present no problem.

Where Is the Exhibition Area Located?

The exhibition area may be in the same building where sessions will be held, which is frequently the case when a conference center is chosen. If hotels are used, the exhibition area might be in a different building from the sessions.

In some cities, hotels are built around a conference center, which allows for some sessions to be held in the conference building, while others are in adjacent hotels. The exhibits, however, should all be located in one exhibition area. The hotels may provide access to the conference center building through covered passageways, a highly desirable feature in locations where inclement weather can reduce attendance at some sessions and the exhibition.

What Are the Existing Union Contracts?

Unions frequently insist on certain standards regarding quality of work and safety that are beneficial to the exhibition. As labor is such an important part of setting up, operating, and dismantling an exhibition, it would be foolhardy for a coordinator to ignore the site union relationships and status.

Initially, the coordinator should determine what work can be done only by union members, which unions are involved, the status of the current contracts, and what that status is likely to be at the time of the exhibition. Are there any items currently under negotiation? What can change? Some of this information can be gathered by speaking to the site management, but the coordinator should also ask to speak to union representatives, particularly the shop steward. In general, the unions want to cooperate, for if the site gets a reputation as one that has labor problems, it can mean fewer exhibitions and less work for the union members.

Does the Site Have an Official Contractor?

Some sites have an official contractor, a company that handles most or all of the labor related to an exhibition. In that case, a coordinator must also work with the contractor in establishing relationships and rates. The contractor may also serve as the decorator for the booths, supplying—at a cost—the chairs, tables, rugs, drapings, and other items that make a booth attractive to the participants.

Who Has the Information for Floor Plans?

In order to allocate booth space, lounge areas, and generally plan the exhibition area, specific information is needed about the space. The hall may have different load limitations that restrict heavy exhibit equipment to certain parts of the floor. The hall may also have retaining walls or pillars that limit space. The location and number of entrances may sometimes be altered to suit the exhibition design. Finally, the hall might have fire or safety codes that dictate how some of the space must be used.

Most sites have a scaled floor plan that a coordinator can consult, but it is also important to walk through the area to get a feel of the space. During or immediately after the walk-through, the coordinator should develop the possible floor plan for the exhibition area and, at that time, have it reviewed by the appropriate site personnel to be sure that the plan is completely workable. At the same time, the coordinator should ascertain if the site is contemplating any changes in or near the exhibition area.

Will the Participants Have Easy Access to the Exhibition Area?

Participants should be able to get to the exhibition area without resorting to complicated routes. The Philippine Convention Center, a site that was built mainly for United Nations–type meetings, has outstanding meeting rooms with interpreter booths and well-planned lounge areas. However, at one conference with an accompanying exhibition, participants had to find a specific escalator and staircase combination that were not clearly marked in order to reach the exhibition. By the end of the conference, very few participants had been to the exposition, and the exhibitors were rightly incensed.

Access can also be a problem when a hotel is used for a conference and exhibition. A major hotel, part of an international chain, advertises itself as a conference and exhibition center. The meeting rooms are on the second floor; the exhibition area is on the third floor. Only one narrow staircase connects these two floors. Participants can also reach the third-floor exhibition area by elevator, but only if they go down to the ground floor and take an elevator from there. The result, when we observed a conference and exhibition at that site, was chaos.

The question of access for the physically handicapped, particularly participants in wheelchairs, must also be considered. This is usually much less of a problem in conference centers than in hotels.

Can access be customized for a particular exhibition, that is, can the entrance way be decorated or set up in some fashion that will be attractive and functional? An entrance that relates directly to the exhibition can be much more welcoming to participants.

Will Entry and Exit at the Exhibition Area Be Monitored?

Because very few exhibitions are open to the general public, most will have limited access. Participants will usually have to show their badges to gain entry to the exhibition hall. Exit areas should not be blocked or used as extra entrances for safety reasons.

In one conference center, the entry to the exhibition was closely watched by uniformed guards who checked badges. At the back of the area, an emergency exit was open most of the time, and participants quickly discovered that this exit was closer to the meeting rooms than the planned exit. It did not take long before most of the participants used the emergency exits as an entrance. We observed that process for two days before the door was closed!

Will the Site Provide Security?

Most exhibitions require some kind of security, including uniformed guards, to control entry during and after exhibition hours. Security guards should be given instructions to check anyone who leaves the exhibition area with equipment. In such cases, badges are not enough; skilled thieves can duplicate badges, so additional authorization should be required.

Security may also be necessary during the hours the exhibition is officially closed. Some sites provide twenty-four-hour security protection, which is built into the cost of the space; other sites provide only minimal protection unless the coordinator specifically requests more and pays for it. The site may provide the additional protection or give the coordinator a list of reliable security companies that can provide whatever protection a coordinator thinks is necessary.

Will the Exhibit Area Be Shared with Other Exhibitions?

It is best if a single exhibition can have the entire exhibition area all to itself, but that is not always possible. Particularly in large sites that provide for both trade shows and conferences, it is not unusual to find two exhibitions going on at the same time. Even in a hotel, two small exhibitions may be open at the same time, using adjoining areas. Although a coordinator can get exclusive use of the exhibition area—for an additional cost—simultaneous exhibitions may not be a problem unless some exhibitors' products and services overlap. In any event, a coordinator should check on the possibility that the exhibition area may have to be shared.

Who Provides the Basic Signs?

Depending on the site and size of the exhibition, a few signs may be required or many. The site should provide some signs and may even provide all the necessary ones listed below. As special signs can be expensive, it is best to negotiate this item with the site and include the decision in the agreement.

1. Participants must find the exhibition easily. This may require signs at strategic places, pointing to the exhibition area.
2. A clear, prominent sign should designate the entrance to the exhibition area.
3. A sign informing participants about badges and security provide added authority to the uniformed guards.
4. Once the participants are inside the exhibition, they need aisle signs to identify where they are and locate the booths they want to see.
5. Minimal booth signs identifying the exhibitor's name should be provided, but many exhibitors supplement these with their own larger signs.
6. Participants will also welcome rest room and food service signs.

Setup

Setup, or move-in, refers to the process of entering the exhibition area and arranging or constructing exhibits.

When Will the Space Be Available, and Are There Any Special Move-In Costs?

A coordinator should negotiate for a specific date and time when the exhibitors can move in and begin to set up. The usual allowance is for setting up one day prior to the opening of the exhibition and dismantling no later than twenty-four hours after the exhibition has closed. (This is still, usually, within the time the site is being used for the conference.) Generally, no special costs are involved when exhibitors move in within the allotted time period, though this varies from one facility to another. When a particular exhibitor needs more time, the coordinator should have information as to any extra cost that will be charged to the exhibitor.

How Many Exhibitor Personnel Will Be Allowed in the Hall?

Setup can get quite hectic, with a great deal of movement in the hall and many people, boxes, crates, and cartons strewn all over the floor. For this reason, a limit should be placed on the number of exhibitor personnel allowed in the hall. Although most exhibitors use very few people to set up the exhibit, others see it as a training opportunity and try to include many of their personnel.

Will Nonexhibitor Personnel Be Excluded from the Hall?

Conferences frequently open before exhibit setup begins, and participants wanting to visit with exhibitor personnel before the exhibition opens attempt to gain access to the exhibition area during setup time. Because exhibitor personnel are totally occupied with the setup, they usually prefer not to be disturbed. From the security and safety viewpoint, extra people on the floor present additional risks, so security guards should be advised about that prohibition and provision can be made for participants to leave messages for exhibitors at the entrance. That usually meets everyone's needs.

How Do Exhibitors Get Necessary Equipment and Services for a Booth?

The exhibitors have already placed their orders for the equipment and services they require, but during setup they need to know whom to contact to verify delivery, or about any equipment and service problems. This person should generally *not* be the coordinator or exhibition manager on the coordinator's staff but rather the site exhibition manager or service manager. The location of that manager should be communicated to all the exhibitors.

Who Is Responsible for Empty Carton Removal?

As empty cartons are often needed for reshipping, exhibitors need to know how to mark empty cartons, how they are to be stored, and how they will later be retrieved. Some sites charge extra for storing cartons and then delivering them to the booth at the end of the exhibition.

Will Exhibitors Be Seeking Local Employees?

At some sites, exhibitors may hire local people to assist with setup, and their work may be controlled by union regulations or site restrictions. The availability of temporary personnel should be confirmed with the site and requests for that labor should be coordinated to the degree needed. A coordinator should work with the site and the LCVB on this need.

How Will Registration of Exhibitors Be Handled?

All exhibitors will have preregistered by virtue of having an exhibitor's contract. Some exhibitors might arrive at the start of the conference to meet participants and they should be provided with a special place to pick up their packets, exhibitor's I.D., badges, and other materials. However, most exhibitors can be expected to arrive after the conference has opened, and at that time their registration desk should be adequately staffed and the registration procedures kept to a minimum. Exhibitors should receive all relevant material, including a packet that is similar or identical to that given to participants with such additional material as an application for a booth for next year's exhibition.

During the Conference

When Should Exhibitors Complete Registration?

Exhibitors should pick up their materials at the registration desk before beginning setup. This can be controlled by prohibiting entry of any people into the exhibition area unless they have an exhibitor's badge. If an exhibitor wishes to switch personnel, this should be allowed, as it does not really present any problems for the exhibition or the coordinator. The main point is that the number of exhibitor personnel should be controlled, and all of them, whether permanent or temporary employees, must have an exhibitor's badge.

Will the Exhibition Stage a Grand Opening?

The grand opening of the exhibition should be carefully planned, staged, and compete with no other events. For a membership sponsor and employer sponsor, the appropriate top-level officials should be highly visible. At the grand opening, many more participants will enter the area at one time than during the rest of the exhibition, so provision should be made for the entrance of this increased number through the main entry point. If participants must be admitted through other entry points, the effect of the grand opening will be lessened considerably.

Avoid speeches at the grand opening; participants are there to view the exhibits, not to listen to speeches. The event can be highlighted by music or other fanfare, and it is a good practice to serve lunch in the same area. Lunch should not be served immediately on opening the exhibit, for that conflicts with the main purpose. If the exhibit opens at 11:30 A.M., for example, lunch service might start at 12:00 noon. This reduces the pressure on the lunch service and encourages the participants to first visit the exhibits.

How Will Participants Be Directed to the Exhibit Area?

During the conference, activities should be planned to encourage participants to attend the exhibition. Serving lunch has proven extremely effective, as well as breaks scheduled between sessions to coincide with food and beverage services in the exhibition area. Announcements can be made at general sessions to remind participants of the exhibition. Monitors and hosts can be reminded to make announcements about the exhibition, particularly during sessions followed immediately by exhibition open hours.

Periodic lotteries can be arranged—drawings held for some products or services donated by exhibitors with the proviso that participants must be present in the exhibit area to claim their prizes. The names of the winners can be read on the loudspeaker, but only in the exhibition area. If a participant does not claim a prize within five minutes, another drawing is held, and that process continues until all prizes are claimed or the exhibit closes.

Will Participants Be Provided with a Plastic Card?

This device has gained favor in many exhibitions. Participant packets contain a plastic card, much like the ubiquitous credit card, on which is imprinted the name and mailing address of the participant (obtained from the registration form). Cards are prepared for on-site registrants at the same time as their name badges. Each exhibitor is provided with a machine that makes an imprint from the card. From the imprints, exhibitors can develop their own mailing lists or make notes as to special interests or concerns of participants—a time-saving advantage over handwriting the necessary information or asking for business cards.

What Is Expected of Booth Personnel?

A code of behavior should be established for booth personnel, as some common courtesies appear to be less common during the pressure of an exhibition—for example, removing trash as rapidly as possible. If smoking is permitted in the exhibition area, it is not uncommon to see an exhibitor empty an ashtray into another exhibitor's tray or put the filled ashtray off to the side while surreptitiously acquiring an empty one from a temporarily unstaffed booth.

When not carefully controlled, sound from AV equipment can disrupt other areas and booths. Recently, remote-controlled robots have been used in exhibits to attract participants but are often allowed to wander into aisles, lounges, food service areas, or the booths of other exhibitors; if robots cannot be controlled, they should not be permitted.

Are Exhibitors Aware That They Are Responsible for the Local Personnel Staffing Their Booths?

Exhibitors sometimes hire local personnel to staff their booths. Although most of these temporary employees behave appropriately, some local personnel are completely inexperienced in exhibition behavior. In such cases, the exhibitor should provide training for this staff and be held responsible for their demeanor and behavior. An exhibitor sometimes hires local models, usually female, to attract attention to the booth. This is not necessarily bad, depending on how it is handled. The model can be attractive, without leaving most of her clothing in her hotel room, but exhibitors should caution models about making what could appear to be sexual advances or innuendoes. This practice is usually frowned on as being sexist.

How Will the Exhibition Be Monitored?

An exhibition, like a conference, needs to be constantly monitored to be sure things are going as planned. On-the-spot decisions may be necessary to avoid complications and to meet the objectives of the exhibition. In large exhibition areas, communication and transportation must be considered. The conference staff should be provided with walkie-talkies so that problems with electricity, food, and so on can be communicated and dealt with immediately.

Members of the secretariat and other selected staff should patrol the exhibition area during the open hours. When the exhibition area is large, the site usually provides some form of electrical scooter for its personnel, and one or more of these might be made available to selected individuals on the coordinator's staff.

During the exhibition, specific people should be designated to speak to exhibitors. Membership sponsor officials, for example, can visit exhibitors and ask if they have any problems or suggestions. Even if these visits do nothing more than let the exhibitors know that the highest levels of the sponsoring organization have interest in them, that alone is beneficial. In a few cases, important information may be gathered that should be brought to the attention of the coordinator.

What Form of Closing Ceremony Will Be Held?

As with the conference, the exhibition should not close with a whimper. The plan for closing the exhibition should produce a positive effect, but will leave no doubt about the termination. Lotteries can be scheduled for the closing hours of the exhibition; some exhibitors might welcome this, as it gives them a way to dispose of materials that otherwise would have to be repacked and shipped to another location. It also provides additional advertising for them. The lotteries should be controlled at a central location, rather than several exhibitors doing their own. They can be staged at various times beginning one hour before the exhibit is scheduled to close.

In the last hour of the exhibit, periodic announcements should be made about closing time and, at closing, a bell or some other audible sound should denote that closing. Exhibitors should be advised to stop activities at that point, or as soon thereafter as possible, but they should be encouraged to maintain full operations until closing and not start the knock-down until after the closing signal.

Knockdown

Knockdown (also known as dismantling or move-out) is the act of taking apart exhibits and preparing them for transport out of the exhibition area. In some cases the exhibits will be turned over to a company for shipping, while in others the exhibitors may do the work themselves. Some exhibitors may find it necessary to arrange for temporary warehousing, but they should have made all the necessary arrangements before they arrived.

Do the Exhibitors Know the Latest Time for Clearing Their Materials?

The coordinator and the site will have established the time that the hall must be cleared, and the coordinator must notify the exhibitors of that time. If any exhibitor goes past that time, a financial penalty can be expected and it should be made clear that the exhibitor, not the coordinator, is responsible for that penalty. The site may assess it against the coordinator, since the agreement was written between the site and the sponsor. It is essential that the penalty clauses be clearly understood and that the coordinator polices the situation, so that any penalty charges can be assessed against the appropriate exhibitor.

Do Exhibitors Know Their Responsibility for the Condition of the Area After They Leave?

At some sites, exhibitors merely have to remove their own materials and equipment from the booth, and anything that is left is automatically categorized as garbage for disposal. At other sites, the exhibitors are responsible for leaving the area in the same condition they found it, clean and with everything removed. The coordinator should have notified the exhibitors of the site's policy at the time of acceptance.

Follow-Up

Will Exhibitors Receive a Set of Mailing Labels of Participants?

After the conference, the coordinator should provide any additional services previously agreed on, such as a set of mailing labels of all the participants. After the conference, many exhibitors find it productive to send some kind of follow-up message to all the conference participants. As noted earlier, this could be one of the marketing points, and it is important that the coordinator deliver.

Will an Evaluation of the Exhibition Be Conducted?

The exhibition should be evaluated by a short questionnaire to each exhibitor to determine the level of exhibitor satisfaction or dissatisfaction. This information would probably go to the exhibitors committee, if there is one. It is essential, however, that the results of this evaluation be processed by the coordinator and, perhaps, the sponsor and given to those responsible for the next exhibition.

Chapter 11

———— ·◄►· ————

Planning for Companions

CHECKLIST FOR COMPANIONS

General

_____ Will we allow companions?

_____ What kinds of companions can be expected?

_____ Who will plan the companion program?

_____ Will companions be part of the regular conference?

_____ How will companion fees be determined?

_____ Will the conference make a special marketing effort for companions?

_____ How will companion registration be handled?

_____ Will special sessions be held for companions?

_____ Will the conference provide a special hospitality room for companions?

_____ What is the conference's policy on unregistered companions?

SOURCE: *The Comprehensive Guide to Successful Conferences and Meetings* by Leonard Nadler and Zeace Nadler. San Francisco: Jossey-Bass. Copyright © 1987. Permission to reproduce hereby granted.

The term *companion* needs explaining. The term *wife* was used in the past, when most participants were men and some brought their wives with them to conferences. Then, a series of demographic factors coalesced. By the 1970s women were entering the professional world of work in larger numbers than ever before. Increasingly, conference participants were women, so the term for whoever came with the participant was changed from *wife* to *spouse*.

Through another evolution, the point has been reached where the accompanying person might not be a spouse but a *friend* of either sex. The possible people that can accompany a participant have now proliferated greatly, and what is now needed is an all-inclusive term. There are those who have opted to use *guest*, but this does not clarify who the host is so the term is only used by a few coordinators. The older terms are still in use in some situations, depending on the policy and practice of the sponsor or the reality of the situation.

However, the preferred term is *companion*, that is, anyone who accompanies a participant but is not a participant. Children are not included in this discussion, even though some participants may bring their children, particularly when the conference venue is at or near a theme park. Some companies provide programs for children in conjunction with conferences; if necessary, the coordinator should work with those companies as suppliers to a conference. Companions do *not* include those who accompany participants but have no relation to the conference in any way. For example, a participant might bring someone who does whatever he or she wishes apart from the conference; such a person is not considerd a companion for conference purposes. It is important to make this distinction, particularly for a membership sponsor or public seminar sponsor conference, since it means that the coordinator need not consider that group in any way. An employer sponsor might make special arrangements for spouses during a conference, since sponsors are focusing more attention on the role of the spouse in relation to the work of the participant.

The Checklist

General

Will We Allow Companions?

This important question must have a specific affirmative or negative response. If the answer is negative, there is no need to go any further on this checklist. Coordinators who are considering the question of companions for the first time should definitely review the checklist as an aid to making that decision.

   If the answer is affirmative, another question should follow. Will we merely allow companions, or will we actively encourage participants to bring companions? To allow them to be part of the conference suggests minimal action and, perhaps, that is all that is required for a particular conference. For other conferences, it should include encouraging participants to bring companions and to plan that the experience of the companions will be as positive as that of the participants.

What Kinds of Companions Can Be Expected?

For a large membership sponsor conference, only vague estimates can be developed on the number and kinds of companions who might attend. If the participants are likely to be mostly female, it can be assumed that most of the companions will be male, and vice versa. The age of the companions will probably be similar to that of the participants. It is not possible to guess at the companions' level of schooling or their interests unless there has been some previous experience with them, or if efforts are made to gather that data. Usually, it is not necessary to be that specific in order to draw up a profile of the companions. Reviewing the participants' profile can provide clues to the companions' profile, though external factors can encourage or discourage companions with much different interests than those of the participants.

Who Will Plan the Companion Program?

Once it is agreed that companions will be part of the conference, the planning for them should fall within the purview of the coordinator and the design committee. Sometimes a separate group is given the task of designing activities for the companions, and the result can be chaos. The coordinator should not try to run two conferences, one for the participants and the other for the companions, but one conference that encompasses both groups. If a large number of companions are expected, the design committee can add one member who has specific responsibility for that part of the total program. A companion program manager, similar to an exhibition manager or a conference marketing manager, can be designated and will report to the coordinator.

Will Companions Be Part of the Regular Conference?

There are several ways to plan the companion program. The companions can be considered as a group within the regular conference, can have their own parallel conference, or a combination of both.

If the companions are considered part of the regular conference, they become regular participants and nothing special need be done for them. A membership sponsor or a public seminar sponsor, particularly one that is not professionally oriented, can just open the conference to companions, who can participate to the extent they wish. Assuming that the number of companions is low compared to the number of participants, the presence of the companions will not dilute the sessions or other activities.

An employer sponsor rarely includes companions as regular participants but instead frequently organizes a separate companion program. A membership sponsor and public seminar sponsor might do the same if the substance of the core conference is too technical or of little interest to companions.

A combination of a regular design plus a companions' design in one conference presents problems as well as opportunities. For example, the coordinator must avoid making the companion program so attractive that the regular conference participants want to join it. That applies mainly to sightseeing and tours, which are part of the companions' program but not included in the participants' program.

How Will Companion Fees Be Determined?

A special fee for companions should include all charges for their special program, but if they are allowed to participate in the regular conference program, the charge should be the same as for the regular participants. A special companion program might include some of the conference events (meals, banquets, receptions), charged on some basis to at least recover costs. The customary practice is to include some of those events in the companion fee so they will receive the same tickets as the regular participants. The rationale behind this policy is that since the companions are accompanying participants, they will want to take part in the nonsession events that are provided for the participants.

Will the Conference Make a Special Marketing Effort for Companions?

The extent of the marketing depends on how important it is to the conference to encourage companions. On a cruise ship, companions can reduce the overall cost of the conference and provide participants with partners of their choice for the social activities. Once the sponsor decides to include companions, the reasons for the decision will have implications for marketing strategy.

Too few coordinators attempt special marketing efforts geared to companions, perhaps reflecting the attitude that companions are a necessary nuisance. When companions are only tolerated rather than encouraged, the marketing effort to attract them will obviously be weak. The coordinator who really wants companions to attend should support a special marketing plan, which can be part of the regular marketing effort or a separate marketing plan (such as special mailings to companions through the anticipated participants). Whatever the marketing vehicle chosen, the marketing should go through the participants rather than directly to the companions to avoid any embarrassment or confusion.

How Will Companion Registration Be Handled?

Companion registration can be handled the same way as participant registration, that is, when the preregistered participant picks up the registration packet a packet for a preregistered companion should also be ready. When the participant registers on-site, the companion can do the same; the companion should be encouraged to come to the registration area, complete the forms, and be made to feel part of the conference. Badges of a different color than those provided to participants should be given to companions.

Will Special Sessions Be Held for Companions?

A special program for companions requires careful design, based on the types of companions and their interests. Usually, the coordinator can expect the interests of the companions to be more diverse than those of the participants.

Companion programs may be designed in many ways, depending on the backgrounds of the companions and the budget for the program. Sessions relating to social and physical self-improvement can be designed. Well-planned and -produced fitness sessions have proven successful, though the coordinator must engage a professional for that activity, unless the site provides one. Many companions enjoy current events programs that bring them into touch with new ideas and people that they usually do not encounter. Some fun sessions might be arranged, although caution should be exercised to avoid embarrassment, for one person's fun can be another's misery. Sightseeing and tours should not be ignored, but recognize that they may draw the regular participants as well as the companions.

A frequently overlooked source is presenters already on the program. In the case of speakers, the fee, if any, has already been planned for, and further negotiations might include having the speaker speak to companions for only a slight additional charge. The topic or content of these speeches should not be the same as that for the regular participants. Some presenters might be interested in repeating parts of their sessions for the companions, once again, not in exactly the same way as for the participants but directed to the interests of the companions.

Will the Conference Provide a Special Hospitality Room for Companions?

It is very helpful to provide a special hospitality room at the site for companions, where they can gather any time they wish. The purpose of the room is to provide companions with a place to meet other companions casually and avoid the loneliness that can develop when participants are completely involved in the conference. The room also helps the participants, since they know that their companions need never be alone, and gives them a place to meet their companions after sessions. The hospitality room should never be used for sessions, since that defeats its purpose. When a session is held in the room, everybody in the room is forced either to attend or to leave and the leisurely atmosphere is destroyed.

For such off-site companion activities as sightseeing, the hospitality room provides a departure and arrival point. Light refreshments can be provided all day in lieu of regular breaks. The room should be staffed, particularly to discourage its use by participants or those who have come with participants but have not signed up as companions. The staff can be selected from local volunteers; in many cities, civic groups are interested in this kind of activity, particularly when supported by the LCVB. It is also possible to use a secretariat member for this task, particularly when an employer sponsor is involved.

What Is the Conference's Policy on Unregistered Companions?

A delicate situation arises when participants bring people to the conference who do not register as companions. The cautious approach is to ignore them, which frequently works quite well since most of them do not expect attention or they would have registered as companions. However, sometimes unregistered companions want to participate in events where badges are required, such as entrance to the exhibition hall. Obviously, policy must be determined before such situations arise. Unregistered companions can usually purchase tickets for special events, but attending a general session might present a problem. It can be argued that if the hall is large enough, it does not hurt to seat them in the balcony or another uncrowded area, but it is difficult to make a special exception. If they are permitted entry without badges, why not local friends of participants or local citizenry who have heard about the speaker and want entrance to the hall?

A small conference will probably not pose much of a problem; it becomes a matter of making some individualized arrangements. All conferences, however, should formulate some policy about this issue, even if the coordinator chooses to modify it in a particular case.

Chapter 12

Effective Marketing

CHECKLIST FOR MARKETING

Audiences

_____ Has the major audience been identified?

_____ What is expected from that audience?

_____ What are the expectations of that audience?

Brochures

_____ What style will be used in the brochure?

_____ Should the brochure be personalized or nonpersonalized?

_____ How will the brochures carry the theme and logo?

_____ Does the brochure clearly state the title of the conference?

_____ Which benefits of the conference will the brochure describe?

_____ How much information should the brochure contain about the design of the conference?

_____ Will the brochure contain a registration form?

_____ Will the brochure contain travel and arrival information?

_____ What information should the brochure contain about fees?

_____ Will the brochure also be used for making hotel reservations?

_____ Will a professional be used to prepare the brochure?

_____ Will the brochure contain photos?

_____ Will information about speakers and resource persons arouse interest?

_____ Will the recipient of the brochure know how to respond?

_____ Have you given the recipient a good reason to respond?

_____ Does the recipient have a person to contact for more information?

_____ Can you include any testimonials?

Mailing

_____ How many mailings are planned?

_____ What is the timing of the mailings?

_____ What are the current post office regulations?

_____ Will it make any difference if the envelopes are stamped or metered?

_____ What will be sent by exhibitors?

_____ Have you anticipated the cost and the rate of return?

_____ Should you send individual mailings or combine several?

Mailing Lists

_____ Does the sponsor maintain a house list?

_____ Which lists will you select?

_____ Which other groups or organizations have lists for purchase or exchange?

_____ Do any of the mailing lists need purging?

_____ Should the mailing lists be tested?

_____ Would other forms of marketing bring better results?

Advertising

_____ Will you use a professional advertising agency?

_____ In which publications should you advertise?

_____ What are the alternatives to print advertising?

General

_____ Does the sponsor issue a periodic catalog?

_____ Does the catalog contain material other than conference announcements?

_____ Will telephone calls be used to follow up mailings and advertising?

_____ Are some participants more likely to respond to a handwritten note?

SOURCE: *The Comprehensive Guide to Successful Conferences and Meetings* by Leonard Nadler and Zeace Nadler. San Francisco: Jossey-Bass. Copyright © 1987. Permission to reproduce hereby granted.

W hat if a sponsor offered a conference and nobody came? That is the nightmare that constantly haunts a coordinator. Although the employer sponsor is not generally concerned unless the participants are voluntary (such as dealers and distributors), the public seminar sponsor and membership sponsor have such worries all the time. Imagine the coordinator who has carefully designed and planned a conference. It is the opening session and the speaker waits in the wings, but only 100 people sit in a room set up for 500 participants. What then? At that point, it is too late, but the coordinator can do a great deal before that time to ensure that such horror stories do not come to pass.

No one has yet found *the* formula for marketing success, but some activities have proved reliable. The coordinator needs to learn these techniques and use them appropriately.

Why Market?

Marketing is essential to the success of a conference, at least in terms of registering the number of participants that the sponsor wants. That number will vary depending upon goals, budget, and expected outcomes. At the very beginning of the design process, the coordinator and the sponsor should reach agreement on the minimum and maximum number of participants, otherwise chaos and conflict can result.

For a membership sponsor, marketing has two purposes. The first is to acquire the number of participants the sponsor determines is the goal. The second purpose is to communicate information, since the marketing material can indicate the organization's activity level to the membership; in other words, the marketing material serves as good public relations for the organization. It may even result in signing up additional members who may join the organization just because it has a high profile and level of activity.

When the conference is solely for employees of an employer sponsor organization, marketing is not a significant activity. Marketing is usually done to provide information rather than to encourage employees to attend. For an employer sponsor conference, participants are either selected by management, or it becomes obvious who should attend, given the goals of the conference. On the other hand, when the employer sponsor invites nonemployees, such as distributors or stockholders, these people may need some encouragement. A carefully planned marketing strategy can be the factor that encourages them to attend the conference.

Marketing is a major factor in the planning of for-profit public seminar sponsors. In general, this type of sponsor allots a comparatively large marketing budget for a conference. Besides desiring to generate profits, the public seminar sponsor also wants to enhance its image. Although all those targeted for marketing will not attend the conference, they will receive the message that this sponsor conducts conferences, and they might be interested in a future conference with a different topic.

The nonprofit public seminar sponsor also markets but may not be concerned with profit—even though the coordinator must still plan to work within the available budget. A cost overrun may not be acceptable if the sponsor does not have other funds to cover the loss. When this sponsor conducts a conference for a targeted group, the participants themselves generally know who is expected to attend, much as in the case of the employer sponsor. The marketing, therefore, focuses on information and encouragement. If the conference is conducted for the general public, the marketing effort typically resembles that of the for-profit public seminar sponsor.

The Marketing Approach

The way a conference is marketed reflects the image of the sponsor. Even though most recipients of the marketing material will not attend the conference, they do form an image of the sponsor based on the material, so the coordinator must recognize that both the sponsor and the conference are being marketed.

The mailing pieces and advertisements also serve as climate setting for the conference. Careful thought must be given to the ambiance that the coordinator wants to establish for that particular conference.

A coordinator and sponsor should select a logo that can be used in all marketing materials. The conference logo should be kept in constant view, which may require special stationery, adhesive stickers placed on envelopes and packages, and various other techniques. For almost every conference, a brochure is produced. Designing and producing a brochure requires special skills, and coordinators generally need to rely on experts in those fields.

Needs Analysis

When designing, the coordinator must identify the needs of the sponsor and of the participants. The design committee might do some of this analysis (see Chapter Two), but the part of the analysis that focuses on the needs of prospective participants can also be part of the marketing effort. A needs analysis commonly includes sending a questionnaire to prospective participants and to participants of the sponsor's previous conference. This questionnaire can also be used as a marketing tool. It delivers the first information to the recipients about the conference: dates, site, and some of the early plans. It also involves them in planning the conference, initiating a type of "psychological contract" for some of them.

Needs analyses vary depending on their major purposes. If it is supposed to aid in designing, most of the questions focus on that element; if the major purpose is marketing, the questions should arouse the interest of the prospective participant. A balance is usually required, and the coordinator must decide on the major purpose of a needs analysis before initiating one.

The Checklist

Audiences

Has the Major Audience Been Identified?

The audience—the prospective participants—must be determined by the coordinator and the design committee before any marketing can begin. One approach is to develop a profile of the desired participant including such factors as age, sex, experience, interests, and geographical location. Other items can be added to this list, depending on the particular sponsor and the goals of the conference. In addition to the major audience, peripheral groups (such as potential members of a membership sponsor) might have some interest in the conference.

What Is Expected from That Audience?

The audience should know what is expected of them. Is the particular mailing piece just to pique their interest? Is the advertisement "missionary," that is, merely carrying a message but not expecting them to do anything? This type of advertising is sometimes done early in the marketing program to get the audience's attention and interest and promises more information in the future. The advertising piece (direct mail or print ad) may indicate the dates of the conference and a message "mark your calendar." At that point, the audience should know that this is all you expect from that particular marketing effort.

What Are the Expectations of That Audience?

Put yourself in the place of the recipients: Why should they be interested in your message? What is its value to them? Do they want to receive Continuing Education Unit (CEU) credits? Do they need the conference for their own professional advancement? Will they want to attend because of the conference's social activities? Should they attend because they are members? At this point, you should try to determine the needs and desires of the audience, particularly as they relate to the substance of the conference.

Brochures

What Style Will Be Used in the Brochure?

As used here, the term *brochure* includes leaflets, pamphlets, letters, and other printed material specifically designed to market a particular conference. Although the coordinator may use a professional supplier to produce the brochure, that supplier cannot be expected to be completely familiar with the intended audience—that is the responsibility of the coordinator. Therefore, the coordinator must be able to advise the supplier on the following factors. If the coordinator writes the brochure, the same factors must be considered.

Length. For some audiences, a great deal of detail is needed; for others, just the "bare bones" will do. Brochure length will also be related to the number of pieces to be sent. The first one may be short, but later pieces can be longer, as more information is available and communicated to the anticipated participants.

Simplicity. The marketing piece should avoid long and complicated sentences. Impact is important; the format and sentences should be simple and direct. The general admonition is to use plain language because busy people respond to clear, concise messages.

Jargon. One person's jargon is another person's professional language. It is difficult to avoid buzzwords or cliches, but at the same time the audience expects to see their professional vocabulary in the marketing pieces. Caution must be exercised, however, as some of the audience may resist the piece when they see too many buzzwords.

Grammar. Marketing specialists recommend that the copy should be written in the present tense using active verbs.

Tone. Tone may be defined as the total image conveyed by all the factors described above, plus color and format. These two questions must constantly be asked: What are we trying to communicate to the audience? and What do we expect them to do as a result of seeing this piece?

Sequencing. The material should be organized in such a way that the reader starts at the beginning, is guided through the necessary information, and is led to respond in some way. Response may take the form of sending in a card to get on the mailing list, obtaining additional information, or actually registering for the conference.

Should the Brochure Be Personalized or Nonpersonalized?

Through the use of computers, marketing pieces can be addressed to an individual by name, a technique that generally attracts the reader's attention. Will your audience react positively? The extensive use of the word *you* is a form of personalizing. In general, the brochure should address people as individuals rather than as vague, broad audiences.

How Will the Brochures Carry the Theme and Logo?

The theme is important and should be clearly stated. The logo should also appear prominently, but its size and configuration should be determined by expert brochure designers.

Does the Brochure Clearly State the Title of the Conference?

Ambiguity should be avoided. The theme, site, dates, and sponsor should be clearly stated early in the brochure in a way that is readily apparent to the recipient.

Which Benefits of the Conference Will the Brochure Describe?

Given the competition for people's time and money, the recipient needs to know the expected benefits. Will CEUs or other form of professional accreditation be available? What kinds of take-home materials can they expect to receive? Perhaps the benefit should be stated in the title of the conference, such as, "How to _____." Additional benefits might be meeting other people with similar interests or big-name speakers, or going on special field trips that are not open to the general public. Limited enrollment can be a benefit, particularly for people who dislike large conferences.

How Much Information Should the Brochure Contain About the Design of the Conference?

The brochure might just provide the starting and closing dates, though, for some audiences, a matrix may be preferable. The coordinator must find the delicate balance between giving the recipient enough information to become interested and to make a decision and overwhelming the recipient with more information than can be absorbed. The recipient may want basic information about major events, special functions, and related activities and may want to know how the design relates to the needs of those who will be attending.

If the recipient needs approval from his organization for the time and/or the funds to attend the conference, the recipient will probably show the brochure to the approving source as evidence that the conference is worthwhile. The design, or parts of it, should be understandable by people who are not recipients, but can support the participation of the recipients. The brochure may actually be addressed to a person who is not expected to be a participant, but who functions as a "funnel," that is, a high-level officer of a company, who then recommends that the conference be considered for an employee at a lower level.

Will the Brochure Contain a Registration Form?

If the recipient is expected to respond by registering, the brochure must contain a registration form. One major error made by those who produce brochures is to place the registration form in the wrong place in the brochure. For example, the registration form should be placed so that the other side does not contain information that the participant will want or need to retain. When a self-mailer is used (the brochure has an attached reply card or envelope), the registration form should be on the back of the panel that contains the recipient's address—information that the participant does not need. This layout also provides the coordinator with the recipient's name, which may be different than the one who actually registers. If a tear-out or insert registration sheet is used, a self-addressed envelope (postage-paid, if budget allows) should also be enclosed.

A registration form should provide space for basic information, such as name, title, department, organization, address (with zip code), and phone (with area code). Is other information necessary? Keep the form short, however, a long or complicated form may convey an impression of poor design and planning.

Execute a trial run of the registration form by asking some colleagues to fill it out and then asking for their reactions. A common problem is that some questions on the form have insufficient space for responses. Another problem is that form designers instruct the participant to "type or print," forgetting that the printing of an individual is not necessarily the same size as the print of a typewriter.

Will the Brochure Contain Travel and Arrival Information?

Participants are usually free to make their own travel arrangements, though an employer sponsor may prefer to make all the bookings to obtain available discounts. A public seminar sponsor may offer a package deal that can be an added inducement to participate.

The membership sponsor has several options, and the easiest is to encourage the individual participants to make their own travel arrangements. However, some benefits do derive from block booking (see Chapter Fourteen). If special fares are available, the brochure should specify whom to call, what group number to use, and what options exist.

The brochure should also mention other travel alternatives, such as pre- and post-tours. If the brochure is being sent far in advance of the conference and this information is not yet available, the coordinator may want to determine from the responses how many will want specific travel information. This question could be included on the preregistration form, to be followed up at a later date.

Arrival time can be a personal matter or part of the design. It is helpful to the coordinator to know when the participants will be arriving, particularly for a national conference, when the participants will be arriving from distant locations, and for international conferences. The brochure can suggest arrival times, based on available data. Information can also be provided about movement from the airport to the hotels, parking arrangements, and the availability of public transportation.

What Information Should the Brochure Contain About Fees?

Even if a registration form is not part of the brochure package, conference fees should be stated clearly. Preregistration discounts should be noted with no ambiguity about cut-off dates. Any special group rates must be clearly indicated. Special rates for companions should also be included, particularly important information in these days of two-career couples. For additional information on fees, see Chapters Eleven, Sixteen, and Seventeen.

Will the Brochure Also Be Used for Making Hotel Reservations?

Hotel reservations can be handled through the LCVB, directly with the hotel(s), via the secretariat, or other ways. The brochure should clearly state the options and provide appropriate information.

When reservations are handled by the LCVB or a hotel, the brochure should contain a tear-out sheet or card that can be sent directly to either location. Some hotels provide special return cards that can be inserted in the brochure. If more than one hotel is to be utilized (generally the case when the coordinator has negotiated special conference rates with those hotels), the brochure should contain relevant information on rates and location for each hotel.

Participants in employer sponsor and for-profit public seminar sponsor conferences usually send in reservations to the secretariat. For large conferences, however, the paperwork using this method can become horrendous, and the coordinator will try to utilize one of the two options discussed earlier.

Will a Professional Be Used to Prepare the Brochure?

The coordinator should use carefully selected suppliers to prepare, print, and mail brochures because they have the competency and resources for those specialized tasks. If the job is large, the coordinator should get bids from several suppliers; although reviewing bids takes time, the cost savings—and quality of the supplier chosen—can certainly justify the extra effort.

Before selecting suppliers, the coordinator should request samples of their previous work and a list of references. Obviously, the supplier will provide a list of clients for whom the supplier has performed successfully, and the coordinator should recognize this.

Some coordinators are part of a total conference service organization, which usually has in-house competencies and experience for brochure production. A for-profit public seminar sponsor producing many conferences might find it profitable to build in-house capability. An employer sponsor, if it is large enough, might have units within the organization that can effectively handle the tasks related to brochure production. A large membership sponsor, offering many conferences throughout the year, might build the in-house capability. Most of them, however, rely on outside suppliers.

Will the Brochure Contain Photos?

Adding photos to a brochure can increase cost, but they can attract more participants. The pictures should be relevant and of good quality for they represent, to the potential participants, the level of expertise that they can expect to find at the conference. If the speakers have well-established reputations, the brochure could contain their photos even if their faces are familiar; these photos reinforce the message that the speakers will attend the conference. The same applies to well-known resource people. Care should be taken that the photos are recent and no more than three years old.

When the site is a major attraction, relevant pictures should be included. If theme parks, historical sites, or other public access attractions are located near the site, photos of these locations might be appropriate to include.

Will Information About Speakers and Resource People Arouse Interest?

Speakers and resource people are usually selected because of what they have to say or how they say it (see Chapter Seven). When marquee presenters have agreed to be on the program, information about them should be included in the brochure. The coordinator may courteously ask the presenters for the relevant information and permission to use it. For personal or professional reasons, a presenter may not wish to appear in the brochure, so the coordinator should send copy to presenters for approval.

Will the Recipient of the Brochure Know How to Respond?

The brochure should be explicit about the action expected of the recipient. A direct mail piece should clearly indicate the ways recipients can respond. The response card can be signaled by a special border, type, color, or perforation. A toll free (800) number can be set up to take registrations, answer questions, or provide information. (A contact name makes response even more personal.) Those assigned to the phone must be able to take registrations quickly and pleasantly and to respond to almost any question the participant might ask. If an immediate response is not available, a follow-up procedure should be established, so the participant gets that information by the next workday.

A self-addressed, stamped envelope is always helpful and care should be taken to ensure that the registration form fits comfortably into the envelope and goes directly to the secretariat. If the secretariat is handling more than one conference, the envelope should be coded so that it goes directly to the right person or group.

Have You Given the Recipient a Good Reason to Respond?

The registration form concisely lists the benefits of preregistration, the cut-off date for preregistration, and payment methods. As most participants can be expected to pay by check, the brochure should specify the party to whom the check should be drawn. If credit card payment is acceptable, the acceptable cards should be specified, along with space for the registrant's card number and date of expiration. For an international conference, information should be provided about the acceptable currencies (in some countries, payment is only acceptable in the currency of that country).

The brochure should provide good reasons why the participant should respond. To emphasize these points, the brochure can contain a brief checklist of the benefits, with a statement at the bottom, such as, "If you have checked off eight of these ten items, go to page x and fill out the registration form. You can benefit from this conference!"

Because many people tend to procrastinate, the recipient needs to be provided with a good reason for responding at once. The most obvious one is a reduced rate; a free gift is another possibility. For a membership sponsor, it could be a publication of the sponsor; for a public seminar sponsor, it could be a free ticket to an event apart from the conference.

Can You Include Any Testimonials?

Testimonials from participants in past conferences should be accompanied by the name of the participant's organization, particularly when the name of the organization carries some weight. When testimonials are used, be sure that the person being quoted has agreed. Take the case of the coordinator who receives a nice letter from a participant after a conference. For the next conference, the coordinator quotes from that letter, without checking with the participant. What can happen? Nothing—if the coordinator is lucky. On the other hand, the former participant may demand remuneration for having his name used for promotional purposes.

Mailing

How Many Mailings Are Planned?

Direct mail marketing is a major vehicle for advertising conferences but must compete with the multitude of direct mail pieces that clog our mailboxes. One way to get attention is to have multiple mailings, although no data currently available indicate the optimum number of mailings. Early in the planning, a decision must be made about the number of mailings and how that number relates to the budget. In addition, the coordinator must decide if subsequent mailings will use a different brochure, for that factor also has budget implications.

What Is the Timing of the Mailings?

The timing of the mailing is crucial. The best brochures, arriving at the wrong time, may elicit few responses. An important question is, "How long before the opening of the conference should the recipients receive the first brochure?" For an employer sponsor, the first brochure may merely be a one-page letter announcing the date of the conference, and this letter can arrive from one year to one day before the conference opening. It notifies the recipient to mark that date on the calendar and to begin making the necessary preparations to be away from work.

The for-profit public seminar sponsor also tries to give sufficient advance notice, depending on the expected participants, because some participants may need a year's notice while others can react in a few weeks or months. The membership sponsor needs to time the mailing so that it provides sufficient advance notice but does not conflict with other activities of the membership organization.

To complicate this further, consideration must also be given to the time of year. If the participants are in school systems, for example, notices should not arrive during the first hectic weeks of late August and early September. Likewise, mail that arrives during the summer, at the school, may not receive any attention until October. If the participants are in retail sales, consideration must be given to their busiest times, such as Easter and Christmas. Pieces of mail that arrive during those periods get little or no attention.

If participants are to be drawn from outside the U.S., the timing is very important. International mail, in most countries, does not travel as rapidly as in the U.S. Even first-class mail can take several weeks.

What Are the Current Post Office Regulations?

Because postal regulations and rates are constantly changing, a coordinator is advised to consult with postal officials or suppliers competent in the field of post office regulations.

First-class mail is expensive but may still be cost-effective. Most people seem to respond more positively to that kind of mail. A mailgram communicates urgency but does not allow for as much or as varied copy as a printed brochure. Bulk mail has cost benefits, including an extra discount if the envelopes are batched according to zip codes. A membership sponsor may be able to obtain a special rate as a nonprofit organization. (Local postmasters can advise on this aspect.) Printed matter weighing less than one pound can be sent third class, which costs less but will be delivered more slowly than first class. If time is a factor, first class may be necessary even though it is more expensive.

Mailing costs should be considered when deciding on the paper stock for the brochure, since a small adjustment in weight can produce a significant cost saving for large mailings. For example, making the brochure a self-mailer rather than requiring an envelope can reduce the weight without reducing the impact.

The cost of international mail can be quite high. An alternative is to send all the mail for a country to one individual by air, and then have the contact mail the pieces separately by surface.

Will It Make Any Difference If the Envelopes Are Stamped or Metered?

In the past, metered envelopes were perceived as being less important than those with stamps, but this perception has changed as postage meters are used by so many companies and organizations. A stamped envelope might still receive more attention, particularly if the stamp is attractive. At times, it is even possible to get a commemorative stamp that has a theme related to the conference. For a membership sponsor in the field of conservation, the duck stamps of an earlier year might still be available. Of course, using stamps might raise the cost of preparing the brochures for mailing. A meter is rapid and efficient. If the sponsor has an in-house meter, explore the possibility of including a message (sometimes called a meter ad), which can easily be done with most postage meters.

What Will Be Sent by Exhibitors?

Mailings may be done by other entities. Exhibitors may find it advantageous to mail pieces about the conference in order to invite participants to visit their booths. The pieces may be mailed individually or combined with the exhibitor's other mailings.

Have You Anticipated the Cost and the Rate of Return?

Cost should be calculated in relation to the rate of return, that is, given the number of mailing pieces and the cost, how many participants will register? There is no absolute way to calculate this, but a guess must be made. After doing the projections, the coordinator should ask, "Is this the best way to get a return on our advertising dollar?" Perhaps other marketing alternatives could be more cost-effective than a mailing (see Advertising section below).

Should You Send Individual Mailings or Combine Several?

Cost savings can be obtained by mailing several pieces at one time, but the recipient may feel overwhelmed and throw them all out. This risk has to be weighed against the cost saving of combined mailings.

Mailing Lists

Does the Sponsor Maintain a House List?

Sponsors who offer many conferences probably maintain a house list of past conference participants. The list should also include those who have inquired about conferences even if they have not previously participated.

Which Lists Will You Select?

New suppliers of mailing lists are constantly entering the field and the permutations of lists become almost endless. A sponsor can obtain lists grouped by geographical location, zip code, profession, business classification, subscribers to particular magazines, job titles, telephone numbers, number of employees, net worth rating, sales volume, and so on. The lists may come on sheets, index cards, magnetic tape, or pressure sensitive labels. The costs vary, so the coordinator should do some comparative shopping. Chapter Twenty-One presents a short list of suppliers of mailing lists.

Which Other Groups or Organizations Have Lists for Purchase or Exchange?

In addition to commercial mailing lists, private lists, owned by certain people or organizations, can be used for a one-time rental fee. The coordinator supplies the brochures to the list owner, who mails them to the names on the owner's list and charges the coordinator for the mailing.

Exhibitors frequently make their lists available as it is to their interest to have as large a turnout as possible. In addition, professional societies that do not compete with the sponsor might be willing to share their lists. Publications in the field, both local and national, might also sell their mailing lists. Presenters should not be overlooked as a resource, since they too might be interested in attracting as large an audience as possible.

Do Any of the Mailing Lists Need Purging?

It should not be necessary to purge, or delete, any names from a commercial mailing list as that would have been done by requesting a specific list or a specific breakdown of a list. When lists are obtained from more than one source, duplication can be anticipated. Usually, it is cheaper and more productive to ignore duplications and count it as a bonus that some participants will receive more than one brochure.

Should the Mailing Lists Be Tested?

There are several ways to test a list. One is to purchase only a limited number of names from a list and then analyze the rate of return. If the response is high, by predetermined levels, the rest of the list can be purchased. If the response is low, another list should probably be chosen.

Would Other Forms of Marketing Bring Better Results?

Before making a final commitment to mailings, this question should be asked. One possibility is advertising, as discussed below, and another is contacting key persons in selected organizations and asking them to distribute brochures internally. A membership sponsor may find it more cost-effective to send brochures to their local and regional chapters, which will distribute them at meetings or with their local mailings.

An airline that has been designated as the official carrier for an international conference can sometimes deliver brochures to the countries where it has landing rights at no cost to the coordinator. The coordinator must then make some provision for those brochures to be picked up at each stop and distributed.

Advertising

Will You Use a Professional Advertising Agency?

An employer sponsor or a nonprofit public seminar sponsor would be unlikely to use a professional advertising agency. A membership sponsor might use one, depending on the nature of the organization and the audience it is trying to reach. A for-profit public seminar sponsor may either develop its own in-house advertising capability or select an agency that can handle its kind of business.

An advertising agency can handle numerous marketing functions, and though it charges a fee for such services, it may not be as high as some might think. The work of producing brochures, preparing mailings, and placing advertising takes time, and perhaps more importantly, requires competency and experience. It can be more economical to have these projects handled by a professional advertising agency.

In Which Publications Should You Advertise?

An advertising agency can help select the publications in which to place ads; few advertising agencies, however, have staff who are fully conversant with every sponsor. Therefore, the coordinator may have to make suggestions after the participant profile has been developed. In addition to many other important items, the profile tells the coordinator and the advertising agency the type of publications the participants read. Generally, ads are placed in national publications, but local publications should not be overlooked. The significant number of local newspapers allow for pinpointing participants in specific geographical areas.

What Are the Alternatives to Print Advertising?

Television advertising is extremely expensive, but it might be possible to get some free advertising. The coordinator of a public seminar sponsor conference of general interest, for example, may arrange for one of the keynote speakers to appear on a talk show. The leverage might be the speaker's recent book on the theme of the conference; talk shows frequently book current authors. Radio is much less expensive than television and can be focused regionally or locally. Many radio talk shows are interested in interesting or controversial figures. If such people are going to participate in the conference, their appearance on those talk shows is good advertising. The coordinator might also arrange for announcements to be made at meetings of noncompetitive organizations whose members might be interested.

General

Does the Sponsor Issue a Periodic Catalog?

Sponsors who offer many conferences, usually for-profit public seminar sponsors, frequently produce a catalog that announces their future offerings.

The same practice is also followed by membership sponsors that offer many public seminars (profit) as part of their membership services. Some sponsors have annual catalogs, and others produce them periodically. A sponsor that offers many conferences will probably have an internal coordinator for each conference who must keep an eye on the catalog copy as it raises the expectations of the public. Once the conference is marketed in this fashion, the coordinator is constrained by what appears in the catalog. Presenter changes should be kept to a minimum, and no changes should be made in objectives, content, or methodology.

Does the Catalog Contain Material Other Than Conference Announcements?

The catalog may contain other kinds of information about the sponsor and its products and activities. In competing with others in the organization for catalog space, the coordinator may need to have some political know-how and negotiating skills to get the best coverage.

Will Telephone Calls Be Used to Follow Up Mailings and Advertising?

Technology has changed telephone marketing: Through the use of the computer, it is now possible to have automatic dialing, an initial message on tape, and then a live person for further conversation. Some people resent this kind of marketing, so the coordinator must determine if such marketing is appropriate for the anticipated participants. Telephone marketing is generally unsuccessful for marketing conferences, since it is not possible to provide all the necessary information in a telephone call. Some sponsors, however, have had success in carefully planned telephone marketing. Telephoning may be able to produce a more positive response when used in conjunction with mailings and advertising.

Are Some Participants More Likely to Respond to a Handwritten Note?

A handwritten note can sometimes personalize a brochure. This is time-consuming and would generally not be used by a membership sponsor. When used by an employer sponsor, depending on the work relationships, it could make the conference a command performance—the recipient must attend. A for-profit public seminar sponsor can turn the handwritten note into an important marketing tool, particularly when the sender (the sponsor, coordinator, member of the secretariat, or a member of the design committee) knows the recipient.

Chapter 13

———————◆·◆·◆———————

Public Relations

CHECKLIST FOR PUBLIC RELATIONS

General

_____ Should we be involved in public relations at all?

_____ Who has the authority to make PR policies?

_____ How much coverage is desired?

_____ Will a professional PR agency be used?

_____ Who will prepare and/or clear news releases?

Prior to the Conference

_____ Is the site located in a major area?

_____ Does the site have a PR person?

_____ What are the local media?

_____ What kinds of releases should be sent to the media?

_____ Where should releases be sent?

_____ To whom should releases be sent?

_____ What should a good release contain?

_____ Should photos be sent as part of the news releases?

_____ What information should be sent about award winners and new officers?

_____ Do any special events warrant PR attention?

_____ Who controls the budget for PR?

_____ Who will invite and clear PR people?

_____ What should be in the public relations kit?

_____ What role does the LCVB play in public relations?

_____ Does the site have any contacts with the media?

_____ Will the appropriate trade press be contacted?

_____ Will you contact the presenters for their ideas on PR?

_____ What preparation do presenters and others need for interviews?

Public Relations Room

_____ Has responsibility been assigned for planning the public relations room and related facilities?

_____ What are the physical aspects of the public relations room?

_____ Who is responsible for staffing the PR room?

_____ What staff will be required in the PR room?

During the Conference

_____ How will PR personnel be registered?

_____ Will special briefings be held for PR people?

268

_____ What if additional stories or events emerge during the conference?

_____ Will customized events, such as photo sessions and press conferences, be held?

_____ Does the conference have an official photographer?

_____ Will backgrounders be arranged?

_____ Will texts of speeches and presentations be provided?

After the Conference

_____ Who will send thank-you notes to the people from the media who attended the conference?

_____ Who will analyze the PR activity?

SOURCE: *The Comprehensive Guide to Successful Conferences and Meetings* by Leonard Nadler and Zeace Nadler. San Francisco: Jossey-Bass. Copyright © 1987. Permission to reproduce hereby granted.

According to *Meetings and Conventions* magazine, "In 1984 the American Society of Association Executives (ASAE) and the Gallup Organization conducted a survey of 500 association executives and discovered that nearly 80 percent considered that they were professionally weakest in the areas of publicity and public relations. The executives found publicity—the act of generating coverage by the media—to be perplexing . . . and even intimidating" (February 1986, p. 24). If a similar study were done among coordinators, the results would probably be similar.

Although almost every conference uses some form of public relations, insufficient attention is devoted to this important topic. Public relations goes far beyond mere publicity; it is concerned with transmitting the image of the sponsor and of everyone involved with producing the conference.

First, some terms need to be defined. Today, the *press room* is frequently called the *public relations* room to signify that it is used by more people than newspaper and magazine reporters. *Media* includes print media and electronic media, such as television and radio (*print media* denotes newspapers, consumer magazines, and trade magazines and newsletters).

Make or Buy?

A coordinator can choose to handle public relations (PR) through the secretariat (make). A large employee sponsor, for example, may handle general PR in-house, and with some help from the coordinator, the secretariat can work with the in-house unit. If so, the budget should reflect this decision, because even if done in-house, PR costs money. In the same manner, a public seminar sponsor that offers many conferences may also develop in-house public relations capability. A membership sponsor may have in-house resources, depending on the type of organization and how often it uses PR for some of its other activities.

On the other hand, the decision may be made to use a professional PR organization (buy), which has experience and contacts in this area. The costs of an outside professional can be determined in the early stages of conference planning.

This chapter assumes that, for the most part, PR will be done under the guidance of the coordinator in-house. Most of the questions, however, are equally pertinent when buying that service through a professional PR organization.

The Checklist

General

Should We Be Involved in Public Relations at All?

At the outset, a firm decision must be made as to whether the conference should engage in PR. Entering into PR lightly or tentatively can lead to disaster. Before making a decision, several factors must be considered.

First, PR has a direct relationship to marketing, but each has a different purpose. Marketing is designed to promote the conference in order to encourage attendance (see Chapter Twelve). Public relations, on the other hand, has a broader scope than marketing, for increased attendance is only a part of the total effort. PR is concerned with sponsor image among the general public and the participants. For example, an employee sponsor may wish others to know that it is introducing a new product and is holding a conference for its sales personnel and distributors. A membership sponsor may wish to inform many people about what it is doing for its members through a conference as a way of encouraging others to consider membership in the organization. A public seminar sponsor may want to keep its image as sponsor of many public seminars before a large public, even though only a few may be interested in the particular upcoming seminar.

A coordinator may have been very successful in obtaining well-known speakers or resource people, and through PR informs a broad audience of the drawing power of the conference. Once again, it is not marketing, since the intent is not to push this particular conference, but rather to inform as many people as possible of the kinds of speakers and presenters who take part in this sponsor's conferences.

As with marketing, good PR can also attract participants and can reinforce participants' decisions to attend the conference when they hear about the conference from another source.

Who Has the Authority to Make PR Policies?

Because PR can have an impact beyond one particular conference, a sponsor may wish to retain authority concerning the formulation and development of PR policies. The PR activities based on those policies would be carried out by the coordinator or by someone delegated to do this. When a sponsor gives the coordinator the authority to make PR policy, this should be made clear to everyone concerned.

How Much Coverage Is Desired?

This is, partially, a political decision to be made by the sponsor. Taking the broad view, a sponsor may see the conference as being only a minor affair, but one that should be publicized for other reasons. In most conference planning and implementation, the sponsor expects the coordinator to take the responsibility and to do the work. In the area of public relations, sponsors frequently want to know what is being planned and how it will be carried out. A sponsor may want much more coverage than a conference warrants, but may be willing to provide the additional budget to make that happen.

Will a Professional PR Agency Be Used?

Given the extent of PR coverage desired, the resources of the sponsor, and the available budget, the question may answer itself. Professional PR organizations cost money, perhaps more than is available in the budget for this conference. When a coordinator is considering a PR agency, it is advisable to exercise the usual caution in contracting for any service related to the conference, such as obtaining proposals and references from several agencies and checking the references carefully. These precautions may be very time-consuming, as a PR agency cannot possibly submit a proposal without having a good deal of information about the conference, including most of the elements contained in this book! This means that the coordinator or a member of the secretariat must talk to potential contractors to provide the necessary information. A coordinator may already have a favorite PR agency, based on past experience, in which case the personal relationship, so essential for this activity, will already have been built.

Who Will Prepare and/or Clear News Releases?

Responsibility for preparing news releases (before, during, and after the conference) must be agreed to early in the planning stages, though the actual writing may be delegated. In some organizations, news releases of any kind that relate to the organization must be cleared through a central source.

Prior to the Conference

Is the Site Located in a Major Area?

Some sites are chosen specifically because they are not located in a major urban area; the intent is to have the participants meet in a resort or some other "isolated" environment. Sometimes referred to as "getting off the ranch," this approach means more than just getting out of the office or home but also meeting in a new environment, one with few distractions. With this type of site selection, the emphasis of PR activities would then focus on the local media, as discussed in the next question.

Does the Site Have a PR Person?

Many sites employ their own PR person or have a contract with a PR agency. This entity will not replace the coordinator's PR effort but rather complement the efforts of the coordinator and the secretariat. The site resource is usually familiar with the local resources and outlets, so working together should be to the mutual advantage of the site and the coordinator. When a site has an important conference its reputation is enhanced. Publicizing the conference, it is hoped, will encourage other coordinators to select the site.

What Are the Local Media?

Local can be either mainstream or isolated, but it is used here only to indicate the venue of the conference, not the extent of dissemination. Although located in the same geographical area as the conference, the local media usually do have outlets to national media.

Consideration should be given to the various types of media in the local area. Local radio and TV stations may be part of a national network and, by law, they must carry local programs, and a conference held in their city is in that category. It is also possible that a story that emanates from a local media source may be picked up by national media—in typical occurrence in print media, when a local story is picked up by a national news service and "put on the wire" to its subscribers throughout the country and, in some cases, in other parts of the world.

In some communities and cities, media work is done by stringers, or part-time media people who have other jobs. They are not directly employed by any media, but they have developed a liaison with some media outlets, which count on them for stories.

It is important that a coordinator identify the kinds of stories being sought by the different media. The electronic media and newspapers usually look for stories that are happening right now, while magazines seek more in-depth stories that will not become dated. Daily newspapers and TV have slow news days, and that is when they may use boilerplate, or stories that do not involve a time factor. Because radio and TV are required to make some of their time available for public service announcements, a nonprofit public seminar sponsor should provide audio- or videocassettes of twenty to sixty seconds that could be used.

Most TV and radio stations have talk shows that welcome interesting conference presenters and participants who are visiting the city. Even though some programs may not be shown until after the conference, they are still good public relations for the conference and the sponsor.

What Kinds of Releases Should Be Sent to the Media?

The coordinator, being close to the planning of the conference and perhaps not maintaining an effective amount of objectivity, is probably not the best person to prepare releases. Several aspects of the conference might be newsworthy. The theme of the conference can be important and catch the attention of an editor. The design of the conference may be unique. For example, a general session using multimedia or the use of special technology, such as teleconferencing, can get attention.

The content can be of national concern. During the 1960s in the United States, conferences on minority issues were well received by the media; during the mid-1970s, conferences about energy resources, particularly oil, received attention. In the early 1980s, releases about conferences on the Japanese were sure to get media coverage. Even though a conference might not have international or national impact, it could still be significant for a region or a particular locality.

The site may be a factor. A conference located at an historic site or theme park can merit coverage. Sometimes it is necessary to prepare releases, even though that was not originally planned. In the mid-1980s, a congressional group chose a plush site in the hills of West Virginia to discuss the budget and deficit crisis. Almost immediately the group had to issue press releases to explain why they had chosen that site in light of their objective—reducing costs.

Marquee speakers (see Chapter Twelve) can be important for marketing and newsworthy for public relations. Even after the conference, the fact that a particular speaker was on the program can make a good story for public relations purposes. Resource people may not have the same name recognition as speakers, but they might still be appropriate subjects for publicity. Some may be authors or members of prestigious organizations or companies; others might deliver speeches on topics appropriate for PR releases.

The participants may be newsworthy—for example, visiting dignitaries or others who have done something that will catch the attention of the media.

The exhibition accompanying the conference might have national or international impact. For example, new health or new technology products usually attract the attention of the media.

Some conferences produce decisions or resolutions that affect many people. Even a regional conference may take a stand on an important issue, such as discrimination or gun control, which applies locally and nationally.

Where Should Releases Be Sent?

Published directories provide lists of newspapers, magazines, TV stations, radio stations, and columnists; some of these directories are listed in the Resources section at the end of this book. Media people are always looking for releases even if they use only a small fraction of them. The conference PR person should send releases to many places, even though only a few might be used.

The internal publication of an employer sponsor would probably want first opportunity to print a story about a conference produced by the employer. Similarly, the magazine of a membership sponsor would welcome stories about the conference or papers that might be read at the conference. A release should be sent not only to daily newspapers but also to weekly and regional newspapers, which have had tremendous growth in the United States. The hometown newspapers of presenters or participants might be interested in a story about one of their residents who spoke at or attended a conference.

To Whom Should Releases Be Sent?

Although in some cases it is necessary to send releases to as many media as possible and hope for the best, it is usually better to send them to the attention of a particular individual. This requires that the coordinator have information about each of the media being contacted, and a control sheet should be established for each possible recipient.

The coordinator should have the name of the individual in the media organization; just sending it to "editor" may not get much attention. For organizations with several editors, each with a specialized area, a prior phone call can identify the specific person who should receive the release. Check the mailing address. Magazines, for example, frequently have different addresses for subscriptions, editorial, and advertising, and even the editorial department may have several addresses. If possible, obtain the telephone number of the individual who should receive the release; a direct line is preferable to a switchboard phone number.

The coordinator should make note of deadlines and plan for them, as some media will discard any release arriving after the deadline date. On the control sheet, a record should be kept of the releases sent and the ones that were actually used. This information can be very valuable for future conferences of the sponsor and the coordinator and can be acquired through a commercial clipping service.

What Should a Good Release Contain?

Even the best news release may receive no attention, but a poorly organized release is almost guaranteed rapid disposal. A one-page release is preferable. The top of the page should contain at least the logo, theme, or sponsor of the conference, depending on which would most likely grab the attention of the particular recipient. The desired release date should be clearly indicated, usually any date after it is received, but sometimes the release date should follow an event. For example, a release may be sent before the conference opens publicizing a speech to be delivered a week later at the conference. The coordinator and the speaker may not want the contents divulged until after the speech, and this request is usually respected by the media.

The body of the release should contain the usual information required by the media—who, what, when, where, and why. The bottom of the page should mention whom to contact for further information. It may be helpful to follow up some of the releases with a phone call to determine if the release has been received by the appropriate person.

Should Photos Be Sent as Part of the News Releases?

Photos should be handled judiciously. Radio media, for example, cannot use photos, and by enclosing them the coordinator shows a lack of experience on how to handle public relations.

Photos should be 5″ x 7″ or larger, printed on glossy paper, and black and white, unless the magazine uses color photos.

For the coordinator, an important element of the photo is a graphic representation of the conference, such as a speaker wearing a conference badge or a banner showing the name of the conference or sponsor.

All photos should be captioned on a piece of paper affixed to the bottom of the picture with tape, making sure that removing the tape will not destroy the picture. The essential information, such as names and titles, should be clearly specified. More than one photo can be sent, but sending more than one implies that the editor should choose one, and some editors resent having to do that. In fact, some prefer only a phone number to call should they wish any photos.

What Information Should Be Sent About Award Winners and New Officers?

Award winners may be of interest for publicity. Avoid just giving the name of an award if it does not communicate where it came from or why it is an important award. A release for a hometown newspaper is written differently from a general release: The hometown paper would want such local information as address, position in town, length of residence, family, relatives, and the like. The same material in a general release would be counterproductive. Be equally cautious when writing releases about new officers. Trade and internal publications look for information that would be of interest to their readers; personal information may be insignificant and even counterproductive.

Do Any Special Events Warrant PR Attention?

Special conference events may be obvious to the coordinator but may not be so evident to the media. These events should be brought directly to the attention of the release recipient. The coordinator might send the whole conference matrix but should identify those special events worthy of media attention. The coordinator can enclose a return card to be used if the recipient wants special seating at this event.

Who Controls the Budget for PR?

Public relations costs include preparing releases, providing photos, sending out the materials, contacting media, and other functions discussed in this chapter. One person should prepare the estimate for the budget and be responsible for how that money is spent.

Who Will Invite and Clear PR People?

One person should coordinate the invitations and clear the media people who are expected to attend the conference. Some media rely on releases, but others prefer to send a representative to all or part of the conference. From these invitations, an approved list can be developed. In some cases, such as international meetings of government figures, the media may be present at the entire conference. In these cases, special provision must be made for them, since it is not always possible to know who and how many people will attend. One approach is to send an early release to the media. Then, about three weeks before the opening of the conference, send a follow-up release that includes information about attending the conference, with a reply or preregistration form. About a week before the conference, follow-up phone calls can be made to those media people who were felt to have an interest but have not yet responded. The public relations kit, discussed next, can be part of the invitation, but as the kit can be an expensive item to package and send, one person should authorize sending them.

What Should Be in the Public Relations Kit?

A public relations kit, when sent out before the conference, alerts the media to the possibilities for coverage at the conference. The kit should be well planned, attractive, and useful to the media.

A variety of fact sheets, generally one page, with information about particular presenters, events, or topics are usually included. The sheets should be on conference stationery or at least start with the essential information: logo, conference name, theme, dates, sponsor, and address. The fact sheet information should follow, limited to one item per page, though some brief reference may be made to related items on other fact sheets. At the bottom of the sheet should be the name and phone number of the person in the secretariat to contact for further information.

The kit should contain a preregistration form if it is anticipated that the recipient, or someone from the recipient's organization, will attend. Though only a few will bother to preregister, it will minimize paperwork later and allow for some planning. A special note should indicate that the recipient is not being asked to pay the registration fee or any other charges. If the regular registration form requests information not applicable to the media people, a simple form can be constructed specifically for them. When the secretariat receives the media representative's registration form, the secretariat should produce a badge. The other alternative is to provide for on-site registration and produce a badge at that time. Special badges should be provided for those registered as PR people.

A regular set of function tickets should be provided for meals, receptions, the banquet, or other special functions. Some PR people may refuse to use these, since many organizations have policies forbidding their employees to accept those amenities and in such cases, whoever is on duty in the public relations room should not urge them to accept. According to *The Wall Street Journal*, TV station KDKA in Pittsburgh has a written policy that bans gifts to employees, including amenities over $25, and *The Chicago Tribune* has an unwritten rule that bars reporters from accepting anything that costs more than a key chain! Reporters and editors for the *Bridgeport Post* in Connecticut cannot accept liquor, sports tickets, or other gifts, but *The Post-Gazette* in Pittsburgh lets reporters accept free trips or subsidized travel if it is the only means available to cover an event.

The kit should contain a copy of the participant book and perhaps the other materials that are in the participants' packets. Items such as maps and lists of restaurants need not be included.

Request forms should be enclosed so that public relations personnel can readily request interviews and additional information by checking a box or listing a name or number of a session.

What Role Does the LCVB Play in Public Relations?

The local convention and visitors bureau usually welcomes publicity for conferences held in its area because it helps the community to understand its unique role and may encourage other coordinators to bring their conferences into that area. Some LCVBs have a person on the staff who specializes in publicity while others consider public relations as just one of the duties of staff members. Either way, they will know the local media and can be extremely helpful in making important contacts.

Does the Site Have Any Contacts with the Media?

The site may have one person who does only public relations or several people who do it as an extra function at different times. The site usually welcomes publicity and can be very helpful. If the site is part of a national chain, it may have personnel in the corporate office who are skilled in PR and have ongoing contacts with national media.

Will the Appropriate Trade Press Be Contacted?

The trade press are those publications that relate to the profession or business of the sponsor or to the purpose of the conference. Most membership sponsor organizations subscribe to some kind of trade press, such as professional magazines and newsletters. An employer sponsor invariably is part of some trade or professional group that has publications. A public seminar sponsor investigates the link between the specific conference and the possible trade publications that might be interested.

Will You Contact the Presenters for Their Ideas on PR?

Presenters are often overlooked as a source of PR leads. Many speakers and resource people are interested in having a larger audience for their views than just the participants. The presenters may not only have ideas, but also contacts in the media. The coordinator should designate someone to contact the presenters about PR ideas after they have been selected. Even if they are not able to furnish ideas or contacts, they will appreciate the interest reflected by the request.

What Preparation Do Presenters and Others Need for Interviews?

Interviewees—presenters, participants, or officers in the sponsor's organization—should be prepared. Some of these people may have experience with interviews but may welcome additional help anyway; being interviewed is more complicated than just answering questions.

All interviewees should receive a copy of Figure 41 and the conference PR person should meet (if possible) with those who have limited experience being interviewed. For the most part, all they may need is a little psychological reinforcement. An employer sponsor might want to give its employees more help since the interviewee may be perceived as representing the company. The company may have an in-house PR expert who can advise the interviewee or use a consultant to prepare company executives for effective interviews.

Public Relations Room

Has Responsibility Been Assigned for Planning the Public Relations Room and Related Facilities?

Coordinators who are concerned with design and negotiations may easily overlook the importance of assigning responsibility for the public relations room and other facilities (such as rooms for interviews and press conferences) related to the PR effort. One person, perhaps from the secretariat, should be given prime responsibility for this effort or, in the case of a membership sponsor, a volunteer. The site may also designate a person with that responsibility, and that site person should work closely with conference personnel.

What Are the Physical Aspects of the Public Relations Room?

PR rooms are typically busy, and the people who use it need supplies and equipment (see Figure 42). Some requirements are fairly obvious, but other items need further discussion.

It is difficult to pinpoint how much furniture will be required: Although many public relations people may be invited, it is impossible to know how many will actually attend or will attend at the same time. A minimal number of desks or tables should be provided, with the option of obtaining additional furniture very rapidly should the need arise.

Unless the conference entails spot news, telephones will not be a major concern, but at least one phone should be allocated to the room. Incoming calls should be answered promptly and dealt with accordingly. Requests for PR information should be handled competently and rapidly by the staff member on duty. If the caller is leaving a message for a PR person, the message should be carefully recorded and placed on the bulletin board provided in the room. Outgoing calls can be a problem, particularly when a PR person wants

Figure 41. Information for Interviewees.

Date: _____

To: _____
                   (name of interviewee)

From: _____
                 (secretariat contact)

Subject: Your interview

1. Your interview is scheduled as follows:

   Date: _____

   Place: _____

   Scheduled starting time: _____

   Probable ending time: _____

2. Reconfirm the time and place of your interview with the public relations room about one hour before the scheduled starting time.

3. There will be (number) _____ interviewers.

4. The interviewer(s) are from the following media:

   Radio: (local)   _____   (national)   _____

   TV: (local)   _____   (national)   _____

   Newspaper: (local)   _____   (press service)   _____

   Magazine: (name) _____

   Other: _____

5. Suggestions:
   A. Listen carefully to the questions. If you do not understand, do not hesitate to ask the interviewer for clarification.
   B. Do not get into an argument with the interviewer.
   C. Make your answers direct and to the point of the question. Do not stray off into minor or irrelevant points.
   D. If you need additional information that you do not have at hand, such as statistics or a policy statement, ask the interviewer if you can provide this later. Do not attempt to prove your ability at total recall; instead, ask for the time to get the exact information.
   E. Recognize that everything you say will rarely be reported verbatim; only some statements you make will be used. Choose your words carefully.
   F. For a TV interview, check on whether you will have to arrive early for makeup.

6. If you have any questions about this interview or preparing for it, contact the person indicated above.

Good luck!

SOURCE: *The Comprehensive Guide to Successful Conferences and Meetings* by Leonard Nadler and Zeace Nadler. San Francisco: Jossey-Bass. Copyright © 1987. Permission to reproduce hereby granted.

Figure 42. Physical Aspects of the Public Relations Room.

_____ Furniture

_____ Telephones

_____ Typewriters

_____ Refreshments or food

_____ Bulletin board

_____ Photocopier

_____ Security

_____ Supplies

    _____ typing paper

    _____ carbon paper

    _____ staplers

    _____ paper clips

    _____ mailing envelopes

    _____ conference stationery

    _____ typewriter ribbons

    _____ pencils/pens

    _____ wastebaskets

    _____ ashtrays

SOURCE: *The Comprehensive Guide to Successful Conferences and Meetings* by Leonard Nadler and Zeace Nadler. San Francisco: Jossey-Bass. Copyright © 1987. Permission to reproduce hereby granted.

to make a long-distance call, but the staff person may just have to accept those charges as part of the PR budget. Some people suggest that telephone privacy should be provided in the room, but that is not always possible. If the call requires privacy, the PR person can use a phone outside the room. It is more important to place the telephone where noise will not interfere. It may be possible for the phone company to install the type of cabinet that is used on public telephones.

As some PR people need to type their stories immediately, electric typewriters should be provided in the room. As with furniture, it is difficult to estimate how many typewriters will be needed at any one time. The coordinator should also determine the need for computerized equipment, such as word processors, terminals, and modems. A computer expert and the appropriate telephone company should be consulted.

Authorized people using the PR room should be provided with refreshments, but they do not expect an elaborate setting. Ice water and nonalcoholic beverages should be provided and perhaps coffee, hot water, sweet rolls, cheese and crackers, or other light refreshments.

A bulletin board should be placed in a prominent and accessible place in the room. One part of the board should list notices of interest to PR people, including changes of presenters or topics, additional events, or highlights of the day's program, and another part should be reserved for messages for PR people.

A photocopier can be an expensive item, but one should be provided in the room or nearby. PR people might have little or no use for this item, but it may be useful for the staff if speeches or press releases must be copied in a hurry.

Extra security for the room may not be necessary unless some special or expensive items, such as electric typewriters and computers, are housed there.

Who Is Responsible for Staffing the PR Room?

The basic responsibility rests with the coordinator, though it can be delegated. Given the importance of the room, staffing should be at a high level and not treated as merely providing clerical assistance.

What Staff Will Be Required in the PR Room?

At least one person at all times must have the authority to make such decisions as granting on-the-spot requests for PR status. Although policy on this matter should have been established by the time of the conference, a staff member must put that policy into practice. Requests will be made for interviews and perhaps even a press conference, and the staff person in the room must be able to respond immediately to those requests.

The room can be staffed by the secretariat, volunteers, or employees of the PR firm, if one is being used. Consideration must be given to the anticipated PR activities. When the room is open for many hours, relief staff must be available to handle requests and needs. Someone in the room should be assigned to run errands, obtain additional supplies, locate selected presenters or participants to meet with the press, and so on—not a high-level responsibility, but one that must be anticipated.

During the Conference

How Will PR Personnel Be Registered?

On-site registration should take place in the PR room, not in the general registration area. PR personnel should receive a badge to gain entrance to events, a participant's packet, and the PR kit.

A few stringers attend all kinds of events, hoping to get a story, and it is usually good practice to honor their requests. In addition, PR personnel who are not on the list and have not been previously identified should be registered.

A frequent problem that arises during conferences is how to deal with those people who attempt to obtain complimentary registration by presenting themselves as PR personnel. They may be from a high school or college paper, or some obscure publication that is completely irrelevant to the conference. The decision to allow admittance should depend on the sponsor and the theme of conference. A membership sponsor might see benefits in having these PR people attend, for they can contribute to enhancing the image of the sponsor. An employer sponsor might similarly benefit, particularly if the schools or colleges are potential sources for employee recruitment. Usually, it is better to err on the side of being too permissive than too restrictive.

Will Special Briefings Be Held for PR People?

Most PR people prefer to make their own decisions about whom to interview or what stories might be of interest. If the conference is "heavy" either in content or time, the PR people might appreciate some help in identifying the issues and presenters. The coordinator can arrange for a briefing, which should be an overview of the entire conference, with particular attention to those people or events that would be of interest to the PR people. The briefing can be scheduled for the day before the conference opens or some other convenient time. If many important people are attending over the course of several days, the coordinator might arrange a breakfast briefing for the PR people each morning.

What If Additional Stories or Events Emerge During the Conference?

Before the conference or at registration, the PR people should receive fact sheets and lists of people and events that might be of interest to them. Additional items might arise during the conference, however, and the coordinator and secretariat should be sensitive to these possibilities—for example, a participant who received an award or recognition outside of the conference, who could still be part of a conference-related story. Information about such occurrences can be posted on the bulletin board in the PR room, and a press release can be distributed to PR people at the conference, as well as those who are on the PR list but did not attend.

Will Customized Events, Such As Photo Sessions and Press Conferences, Be Held?

When speakers or resource people have national or international reputations, requests for some customized events can be expected. An appropriate room or background should be provided for still photos and video cameras. All of the people who will be in the pictures should receive ample notice. If the event is intended for TV, a specific time on a particular day may be designated for the event in order to meet broadcast deadlines. The secretariat should give the photographers the exact names of all the people as they will appear in the photo or on the broadcast.

A large press conference may require additional equipment and microphones. Some media personnel may wish to have their own microphones taped to the lectern, and this should be done before the press conference starts. A starting and stopping time should be announced, though the conference can go overtime with the permission of the person conducting the conference. The ground rules should be established, and everyone attending should know ahead of time whether a prepared statement will be read and whether questions and answers will be allowed.

Does the Conference Have an Official Photographer?

Some media people bring their own photographers; others rely on local resources. If the conference has contracted with a photographer, provision can be made to have that photographer's services available to the PR people. Agreement should be reached on whether the expense for the photographer is charged to the conference or to the person requesting the photographer. Usually, the conference absorbs the cost, but some limits should be established. Most PR people will use the photographer judiciously, but some will be indiscriminate and therefore costly. Some sites also have official photographers and might be interested in providing that person or in making a cooperative arrangement.

Will Backgrounders Be Arranged?

A backgrounder is an off-the-record press conference or interview in which the press agrees that the interviewee will not be quoted or cited by name. (In the national and international arena, the backgrounder sometimes becomes the basis for the familiar phrase "according to an informed source.") PR people should be told very explicitly if the interview is a backgrounder, for some will refuse to attend under those conditions. For the most part, media people are very honorable about respecting the limitations of a backgrounder if they have been given adequate notice. Despite the limitation, many media people attend backgrounders since they can provide them with important information, even if they cannot quote the source.

Will Texts of Speeches and Presentations Be Provided?

Not all speeches and presentations will be of general interest, but it is customary to reproduce the speech of a general session speaker and make it available in the PR room. The printed text can become the basis for a follow-up interview where the speaker can focus on points not already included in the printed speech.

After the Conference

Who Will Send Thank-You Notes to the People from the Media Who Attended the Conference?

Thank-you notes should be sent to all media people or their supervisors (including editors) who attended any part of the conference. This is not only good manners, but also contributes to building rapport for the next conference. The note should be signed by a high-level person in the sponsoring organization or by the coordinator. In the note, it is also appropriate to ask for copies or information about any stories or programs that were issued about any part of the conference. In some cases, it may mean paying for videotapes, but it could be well worth the cost.

Who Will Analyze the PR Activity?

The PR activity should be analyzed, probably by a qualified member of the secretariat, and a final conference report issued. The coordinator should not prepare the analysis but should review it carefully. The coordinator may be tempted to ask the person who staffed the PR room to analyze the activity and prepare the report but should avoid the temptation: The PR room staff person may have been too close to the individuals and the activity to analyze the activity objectively, though that person should certainly be one source of data. The analysis should seek information about all aspects of the PR effort: cost, list of contacts, lists of actual attendees, copies of published or aired material about the conference, and any suggestions for improving PR for future conferences.

Chapter 14

Transportation Issues

CHECKLIST FOR TRANSPORTATION

General

_____ How does transportation relate to design?

Individual Air Travel

_____ Will an official carrier be designated?
_____ What benefits will be provided for staff travel?
_____ Will provision be made for airport reception?
_____ Will the conference make VIP travel arrangements?

Group Air Travel

_____ Will there be a group leader?
_____ Will the airline offer a discount for group booking?
_____ What are the requirements for a contract and deposit?
_____ Will the airline provide a special-rate ticket for the leader?
_____ When will the group leader meet the airline and/or airport personnel?
_____ How will the tickets be handled?
_____ Who assigns seats?
_____ Who selects the routing?
_____ Do the participants know the baggage allowances and limitations?
_____ Do all participants have required passports and visas?
_____ Will there be group check-in?
_____ Are any special meals required?
_____ Can the airline make an on-board welcoming announcement?
_____ Do any of the participants have medical problems?
_____ How does the airline provide for the handicapped?
_____ On arrival, who will collect the baggage?
_____ Will the group be returning together?

Airport Transfer

_____ Where is the airport located in relation to the hotels?
_____ Does the site provide courtesy transportation from the airport?
_____ Do participants need information on traveling from the airport to the hotels or site?
_____ Where is the closest public transportation?
_____ Should airport transfer/shuttle service be provided?

Field Trips, Tours, and Sightseeing

_____ Who will negotiate for ground transportation?
_____ Is the company bonded?
_____ What is the track record of the company?
_____ What is the safety record of the carrier?

_____ Does the carrier have all the appropriate licenses?

_____ How are costs calculated?

_____ What is the cancellation fee?

_____ Does the ground transportation contract have a nonperformance stipulation?

_____ Does the carrier have appropriate and adequate insurance coverage?

_____ What is the anticipated load?

_____ How many vehicles will be needed?

_____ What is the legal capacity of each vehicle?

_____ Who will inspect the vehicles?

_____ Should buses be air-conditioned?

_____ Do the buses have facilities for handicapped participants?

_____ Should each bus have sanitary facilities?

_____ If the drivers are unionized, what is the status of the contract?

_____ Are the drivers uniformed?

_____ Does the carrier provide an attendant?

_____ How long is the journey and will there be rest stops?

_____ What time must participants be ready to board?

_____ Will boarding be at one site or several?

_____ Will smoking be allowed?

_____ Is it necessary to provide food and beverages?

_____ Are there any interesting sights along the route?

_____ Will guides be needed?

_____ Do the buses have working microphones?

Shuttle Service

_____ Will a contractor be needed to provide shuttle service?

_____ What transportation is available in and around the site?

_____ Is on-site parking available?

_____ What are the commuting patterns around the site?

_____ How will shuttle pickup and drop-off points and routes be determined?

_____ Will a dispatcher be provided?

_____ Can the buses have special signs?

_____ Can participants leave an event early?

_____ Will special vehicles be required?

Leaving the Conference

_____ How does the conclusion of the conference relate to traffic patterns around the conference site and hotels?

_____ Is it necessary to arrange for group transportation to the airport?

_____ Should car pools be arranged?

SOURCE: _The Comprehensive Guide to Successful Conferences and Meetings_ by Leonard Nadler and Zeace Nadler. San Francisco: Jossey-Bass. Copyright © 1987. Permission to reproduce hereby granted.

Some coordinators prefer to leave the matter of transportation to others, but a coordinator should have a good working knowledge of transportation factors. Many aspects of transportation directly impact on the design and conduct of a conference.

An employer sponsor may have an internal unit that handles company transportation, including conference travel. Some companies have one unit that handles regular company travel and a separate unit for conference travel, but they are finding that combining these two units improves their bargaining position with carriers. Perhaps this restructuring is a mistake: Saving money is desirable, but different competencies are needed to arrange for individual business travel than for conference group travel.

A membership sponsor that conducts many conferences may contract out for travel services, but the coordinator for that conference must still be involved. For small conferences, the membership sponsor might handle all the travel, though that is unusual. For large conferences, most membership sponsors find it better to contract out for part or all of the transportation factors. The for-profit public seminar sponsor usually leaves travel to the individual participants, unless a ship is involved or another carrier that makes group travel more economical and desirable. A nonprofit public seminar sponsor seldom gets involved in air travel but might need ground transportation.

Availability of transportation can also influence site selection (see Chapter Five). Some airlines have special convention personnel and can provide computer printouts of comparative travel costs. To do this, they need such information as the participants' probable departure cities, number of participants, days of the week for departure and return, and dates of the conference. Given that data, they can provide recommendations for cities to be the site of the conference. Transportation is a budget item for a conference. Therefore, a coordinator must be cognizant of the possibilities and the costs.

Suppliers

For transportation, a coordinator should rely on travel professionals, for the field is too complicated and specialized to handle directly. A coordinator must speak to several potential suppliers, get bids, and make comparisons; the caution is to endeavor to identify those that are professional and to avoid those that are incompetent.

Airlines are frequently used in connection with conferences, for passenger traffic, cargo shipments, or both. Increasingly, airlines are developing in-house convention desks staffed with professionals who deal specifically with conference travel. Because participants sometimes travel as a group and sometimes individually, the range of fares is confusing to say the least. Since airline deregulation in 1978, the confusion has reached the point where a coordinator may find that even the convention desk personnel are unsure of what to quote for fares or for conditions of travel. As with many other aspects of conference planning, a written agreement is essential.

The secretariat may have to ship conference material from one city to another, and even though most passenger carriers also handle freight, shipment will probably be arranged in another department of the airline. If possible, discussions should include both passengers and cargo, to obtain more leverage for negotiating rates.

Although railroads are not generally used for conference travel in the United States, they should not be ignored, for a railroad can be an interesting method of travel. The coordinator must determine availability and project into the future: Will the railroad still be operating when it is time for participants to travel to the conference? With deregulation, it is equally easy for a railroad to abandon a route as it is for an airline to do the same thing. If the railroad depends on government funds, as in the case of AMTRAK, what effect will budget cuts have on the schedules and equipment? Despite the limitations, railroads should be considered for conference transportation in some areas of the country.

Travel agent is a generic term and should be viewed cautiously. Agents who have met the standards of the American Society of Travel Agents (ASTA) can be presumed to be more qualified than those who have not met the criteria of that organization. Not all travel agents are equally competent in handling conference travel. Some equate that with group travel, but there are many differences. A coordinator, when considering a travel agent, should ask for a list of conferences that agent has handled and then check the list, particularly for similar conferences and for such factors as number of participants, various points of departure, special fares, and other arrangements.

Auto rental companies are also conference suppliers. Coordinators usually do not arrange for a fleet of rental cars, though that is a possibility for a conference of VIPs. Arrangements can be made with auto rental companies to get special rates for participants who want to rent a car for use during the conference. Some participants may also want to rent cars for pre- or postconference tours.

All of these transportation suppliers—airlines, railroads, travel agents, auto rental companies—should also be considered as possible sources of income. They might advertise in the conference publication. Some of them provide printed material about the city where the conference is being held and using that material reduces the cost of printing for the conference. The airlines and railroads could carry conference-related material at no cost or at reduced charges. A travel agent might share the cost of advertising material and perhaps even use some of their own channels for additional advertising.

The Checklist

In the discussion that follows, the term *participant* includes companions, unless otherwise stated.

General

How Does Transportation Relate to Design?

When many participants are arriving by air, it may be necessary to consider airline schedules when designing the conference. If most flights arrive at midday at the conference city, should registration and the opening general session be scheduled accordingly? If the conference is to start in the morning, participants may have to arrive the day before, and that could mean an additional night of accommodations. The design could be constructed so that the conference opens late in the afternoon or the early evening and concludes a half-day earlier to avoid an extra day of lodging.

If the conference is held on the West Coast and many participants have to come from the Midwest or the East, consideration must be given to the time zone differences. For example, participants returning to National Airport in Washington, D.C., must consider the 10:00 P.M. curfew since planes cannot land after that time. Given the three-hour time difference and the flying time, participants must leave the West Coast fairly early. A conference that is designed to close at 5:00 P.M. in Los Angeles forces the Washington area participant either to leave early and miss the closing or stay for another day.

For an international conference, obviously the relationship between transportation and design becomes even more complicated. If participants are coming from a large distance, the design may have to provide for some early, light activities, to allow for jet lag.

Individual Air Travel

Even when participants travel individually, the coordinator can sometimes make arrangements that benefit them and encourage them to attend. The items discussed below can apply to as few as fifteen participants but are usually more beneficial for larger numbers.

Will an Official Carrier Be Designated?

An official carrier is one that is so designated by the coordinator, and in some cases the designation merely means that the carrier can advertise itself in that manner. For large conferences, it usually means that participants who use the airline can get special rates that are not available to the general public. Major airlines have established convention desks, frequently with an 800 number, which participants call at no charge. The airline usually assigns a special code number to the conference so that when participants call they can immediately be identified with the specific conference. In one instance, a presenter called to make travel arrangements and was told that there were two classifications: VIP and participant. It took a lengthy discussion, and a call to the coordinator, to ascertain that the VIP classification included presenters! A code number could have easily cleared up the confusion. The official carrier may provide literature about the venue, pre- and postconference tours, and other promotional materials.

What Benefits Will Be Provided for Staff Travel?

The coordinator should explore the official carrier's benefits for staff travel. These benefits will depend, in part, on the anticipated number of bookings. Since deregulation, an airline can provide free travel in special cases; at the least, the carrier should offer some special reduced fares for staff, including the coordinator and secretariat, perhaps the design committee, participants from the sponsoring organization, and even presenters.

Will Provision Be Made for Airport Reception?

The official carrier may also assist with participants' arrival, for example, by placing signs at strategic locations to welcome participants. The signs might display the name and dates of the conference and might be written in two or more languages depending on the participants.

   The airline can arrange receptions for international travelers in a variety of ways. The participants could receive messages from the airline ground personnel as they deplane. If needed and available, bilingual personnel can be assigned to a particular conference. Assistance might be provided for passport and customs formalities, and the participants could receive help in converting currency.

   Some airlines provide courtesy buses to take the participants to their hotels or credits to be used on the regular airport buses or taxis.

Will the Conference Make VIP Travel Arrangements?

The designation VIP must first be defined. For most conferences, the VIP group will include the speakers, but for an employer sponsor conference, all the participants might be VIPs.

   Special arrangements can be made with airline personnel for VIPs to proceed to a special room on arrival. Many airports have VIP rooms or lounges or the airline's own club that is usually limited only to those who pay an annual fee.

   Airport check-in procedure, including baggage handling, might be expedited by airline personnel, including special baggage tags or other markings. Boarding can be facilitated, usually by late boarding, which means the VIPs board after all the passengers and so do not have to stand in line or be jostled by other passengers when being seated. If only a few VIPs are part of the group, some airlines assure that the cabin attendants know the names and/or titles of the VIPs and address them personally.

Group Air Travel

Group travel means that the participants depart from the same airport at the same time. A large conference may have many points of departure, but in each case the participants will be traveling as a group. A coordinator should rely on the airline or a travel agent for the arrangements, but the coordinator should at least know what to consider. Some of the items below are automatic with group travel, while others have to be negotiated.

Will There Be a Group Leader?

Not all groups need a group leader, but for international travel, it is very common to have a group leader who travels with the group from predeparture to the end of the trip. That leader can be a designated and qualified participant or a person provided by the travel agent.

Will the Airline Offer a Discount for Group Booking?

Discounts for group booking are common but not applicable during certain times and for certain destinations. A coordinator should assume that group booking will result in financial benefits, but sometimes the benefit may only be a matter of convenience. The coordinator or travel agent should shop among several airlines to get the best possible discount.

What Are the Requirements for a Contract and Deposit?

The coordinator should become familiar with such travel aspects as cancellation fees, refunds, and travel insurance, or should obtain the services of a travel expert. For example, if an individual participant becomes ill or cannot participate in the group travel for some other reason, what are the financial obligations of the participant and/or the coordinator?

Will the Airline Provide a Special-Rate Ticket for the Leader?

If the group leader is a travel agent employee, this question need not be explored, but if the group leader is a participant or a conference staff member, the airline might approve a special-rate ticket or even a complimentary ticket, depending on the number of travelers and the cost of travel.

When Will the Group Leader Meet the Airline and/or Airport Personnel?

The group leader should meet the airline or airport personnel before the first participants arrive at the airport, possibly several weeks before the participants' anticipated arrival. One result of such a meeting could be the development of specific information for the participants that is sent out to them before they depart from their home cities.

If possible, the group leader should walk through the path and procedures that participants will follow, from arriving at the airport until boarding time. In some cities, the participants might meet at a designated location and be transported as a group to the airport; in other cities, each participant arrives individually.

What happens when the participants reach the airport? Where should they go? What should they do with their luggage? Where should they check in? All these questions need to be answered so that instructions can be sent to the participants.

How Will the Tickets Be Handled?

Tickets can be sent to each participant individually, or the group leader can distribute them as participants arrive at the airport or another designated meeting location.

Who Assigns Seats?

Sometimes, planning airplane seating can be almost as difficult as planning banquet seating. Factors that must be considered include smoking and nonsmoking sections, aisle or window seats, size of the person, the front of the airplane or the rear, and whom to seat (or not to seat) with whom. If possible, the participants should make their own seating arrangements, but for an employer sponsor or a small conference, the coordinator may have to make these arrangements.

Who Selects the Routing?

Even when participants travel as a group, some participants will still have preferences. The participants may have no options if the flight is nonstop, from the point of departure to the destination city, but some cities have more than one airport. When a choice is available, someone must decide which airport to use.

The airport choice can make a significant difference in routing and sometimes in cost. A layover, for example, might be attractive to the participants as a form of a preconference tour. With the variations in airline price structure, the layover may not add to the cost of the air travel. If the layover does entail an additional cost, the participants should be consulted as to whether they want to make that layover.

Alternate routes may allow for some sightseeing from the air, such as viewing the Grand Canyon. When the arrival city is different than the venue, ground transportation might be provided to take the participants through an interesting area on the way to the conference city.

The coordinator should explore all the possibilities of group travel. The risk of not doing so is the probability of being criticized at a later date for not making full use of the travel opportunities.

Do the Participants Know the Baggage Allowances and Limitations?

Baggage allowances and limitations are constantly changing, particularly for international travel. If the participants are frequent air travelers, they will probably know the current regulations, but it is risky to make that assumption.

For domestic travel, the major problem concerns carry-on luggage. The general rule has been that each passenger is limited to one bag that can be placed under the seat or in the overhead rack. Each airplane, however, has a different configuration. Some airplanes, for example, have compartments for hanging garment bags, while others do not.

International travel is even more complicated. In addition to airline regulations, each airport can have its own baggage regulations that are enforced at the generally hectic check-in time. Most airports have moved away from weighing luggage but rather count pieces so that each traveler can check up to two bags. For group travel, some airports allow bags to be averaged: When a traveler has one only bag, for example, another is allowed three. Other airports, even with group check-in, treat each traveler separately and try to assess an additional baggage charge against the traveler with three bags. Local airline personnel should be able to advise on the current practice in specific airports (though an international airport can change its regulations at any time).

The previous discussion assumes that the group travel will be via economy or tourist class. Business or first-class travel may afford more latitude for baggage allowances, in addition to other amenities.

Do All Participants Have Required Passports and Visas?

If the participants are not experienced international travelers, the coordinator must make sure that they have obtained passports and visas early enough to allow for meeting all requirements. To obtain visas for group travel, the passports for all the participants must be presented at the same time; participants living in different cities must send their passports to one location for proper handling of visas. Usually, this location is a city where the foreign countries to be visited have a consulate or Washington, D.C., where they all have embassies. Even in Washington, variations are possible. The Venezuelan Embassy, for example, issues visas through its commercial office in Baltimore.

Will There Be Group Check-In?

Airlines welcome group check-in because it simplifies their work. In exchange, they may be willing to provide some special amenities, such as welcoming signs at the airport, special waiting rooms, and baggage handling. The airline, or travel agent, may provide special tags or markings for the group's baggage so that it is readily retrievable. Some tags are made of leather and could display the name of the airline, travel agent, or, if possible, the conference—good publicity for the sponsor's next offering.

Are Any Special Meals Required?

For participants traveling as a group, the conference has already started, so climate setting is important. Consideration should be given to special in-flight diet or meal requirements. Airlines usually do a good job of providing special meals if given sufficient notice.

Can the Airline Make an On-Board Welcoming Announcement?

The conference climate can be enhanced by a simple announcement over the airplane's intercom, welcoming the participants. To avoid confusion, the conference staff should submit a written announcement to an airline representative, and arrangements should be made to give it to the flight attendant in charge.

Do Any of the Participants Have Medical Problems?

All information on medical problems should be provided to the airline prior to departure, in case the need for in-flight medical assistance should arise. Participants who need prescription drugs should be advised to make sure they have an ample supply packed in their carry-on baggage. For international travel, those drugs should be kept in their original packing with the contents clearly marked by the manufacturer or the pharmacist.

How Does the Airline Provide for the Handicapped?

Airlines have been among the leaders in providing for handicapped passengers. As long as the airline is contacted in advance, various arrangements are possible, such as wheelchairs, special seating on the airplane, and electric carts to take the physically handicapped from the door of the airport to the door of the plane.

On Arrival, Who Will Collect the Baggage?

Either the participants can be responsible for their own baggage, or the group leader can claim the baggage with the assistance of skycaps. Whatever system is used, the participants should know exactly what it is, so they can plan accordingly.

Will the Group Be Returning Together?

Group travel arrangements sometimes allow participants to depart from the conference individually, but usually travel must be on the original carrier. By clarifying this with both the carrier and the participants, the coordinator can avoid confusion and negative feelings. If the participants are not aware of ticket restrictions, they may make plans that ultimately result in much higher fares. Early negotiation can lead to postconference travel, which is an added benefit for the participants and another reason for attending the conference.

The confirmation procedure should be clearly understood by all participants. The group leader usually handles confirmations for participants returning as a group; participants returning individually are responsible for themselves. Since confirmation procedures vary, each participant should know what must be done. In addition, confirmation requirements are different for international travel than for domestic travel, and the participants should be informed of the appropriate procedure.

Airport Transfer

A coordinator need not always provide for the movement of participants from the airport to hotels or to the conference site. At times, airport transfer should be provided in the interest of the conference as well as of the participants.

Where Is the Airport Located in Relation to the Hotels?

In the United States, airports are generally located a considerable distance from the hotels that are used for conferences. Some coordinators, however, prefer to use a hotel in or near the airport (if such a facility is suitable) because it eliminates the necessity for airport transfer.

Employer sponsor conferences of under 100 participants might use an airport facility; if not, the sponsor might provide for airport transfer. The same would apply to a public seminar sponsor. When airport transfer is used, provision should be made for late arrival of aircraft because the ground transportation supplier might assess a waiting time charge.

Does the Site Provide Courtesy Transportation from the Airport?

Many sites provide courtesy vehicles for airport transfer. Because transportation can be expensive, the site that provides this service gains quite a competitive edge with coordinators. When the site does provide courtesy vehicles, the participants need to be notified of what kind of vehicles are available and how to obtain them. Since the vehicles may only be available at certain times, it may be necessary to notify the facility of anticipated times of arrival. Vehicles must be provided that accommodate the participants' baggage.

Do Participants Need Information on Traveling from the Airport to the Hotels or Site?

Experienced travelers are used to finding their way from an airport to a hotel or site, but less experienced travelers need help. Participants can be left to fend for themselves, but that can have a negative impact on how they feel about the conference. A coordinator can at least provide such information as the types of transportation available, comparative costs, approximate travel time (rush hour and other times), where transportation is boarded, and starting and closing times of operation.

Participants can be shocked when they think a site is located close to a major airport but learn that it is miles away when they arrive. Many good conferences have started on a negative note when participants find out they must make a long unplanned trip at an additional expense. It may be impractical to provide shuttle service to a distant site, but it is relatively easy to provide information about available buses, such as the name or number of the bus, where it leaves from, and the cost.

This foresight is even more critical for international conferences because participants may not be familiar with the country's language or travel customs.

Where Is the Closest Public Transportation?

Public transportation is available at or near many airports. Some participants prefer to use mass transportation from an airport since it is usually less expensive. Maps can be provided as part of preregistration material, so participants have the option of using mass transportation.

Should Airport Transfer/Shuttle Service Be Provided?

A coordinator can provide shuttle service from the airport to the conference hotels. A small membership sponsor conference might provide shuttle service by using a bus that holds fifty passengers. An employer sponsor might use a van that holds ten passengers.

The decision to provide shuttle service must be carefully considered. For a membership sponsor or public seminar sponsor it can be expensive. As an employer sponsor usually pays all the costs for participants, the service could prove less expensive and more comfortable than public transportation. Other considerations about shuttle service are discussed below.

Field Trips, Tours, and Sightseeing

A wise coordinator generally contracts for the ground transportation required for field trips, tours, and sightseeing. To do that, a coordinator must be able to get satisfactory responses to the checklist items in this section.

Who Will Negotiate for Ground Transportation?

The coordinator or a qualified person in the secretariat usually handles these negotiations, which can be time-consuming and involve significant sums of money. In addition, a well-planned and important event can be ruined by poor ground transportation.

Is the Company Bonded?

The coordinator should verify that the ground transportation company is bonded and that the bond protects the cordinator. Bank references should be checked; if the contractor is having cash flow problems, contract performance may be jeopardized.

What Is the Track Record of the Company?

Contractors should be able to provide a list of conferences and groups that they have served in the past. These references should be checked. Site personnel can sometimes be helpful in selecting a contractor because they may have past experience with many of the contractors. The LCVB can also help by providing lists of contractors and an analysis of past performance.

What Is the Safety Record of the Carrier?

Because the safety of the participants is of prime importance, the local police or motor vehicle office should be consulted about the carrier's safety record. For example, it would be important to learn if any of their drivers have ever been cited for speeding. Local authorities are concerned and will appreciate the coordinator's interest in this factor.

Does the Carrier Have All the Appropriate Licenses?

Again, the local authorities can be helpful in clarifying this point, which becomes very important if the ground transportation will cross state lines. If the carrier is to provide airport transfer or shuttle service, special licenses or permits may be required, since each airport has its own provisions regarding common carriers.

How Are Costs Calculated?

Costs for ground transportation can get very complicated, including such items as minimum charges, different rates for daytime and nighttime usage, and other factors. The cost can be based on mileage, and, if so, the method of calculating mileage—whether by odometer reading, a map, or a pre-determined figure—should be stated because the differences can be significant when translated into dollars. Other questions are relevant: What is the cost of an out-of-town trip? What if the vehicle has to deadhead, that is, transport passengers one way but return empty? What is the cost for waiting time when, for example, the participants are taken on a field trip? If billing is on an hourly basis, does the time start at the garage or at the participants' point of departure? Does the carrier charge for tolls and parking?

What Is the Cancellation Fee?

When the coordinator must cancel an event for which transportation has been contracted, is the deposit refundable under some conditions, such as weather? What if the event must be rescheduled after a contract has been drawn up— is there still a cancellation fee? A minimum number of participants may be needed in order to make a tour or sightseeing trip economical. If a tour company is being used, the contract should account for the possibility of cancellation because of inadequate registration.

Does the Ground Transportation Contract Have a Nonperformance Stipulation?

The other side of the previous question is the possibility of the contractor canceling at the last minute. The agreement must state what constitutes nonperformance, which is a legal question that a lawyer should review.

Legal recourse may eventually recover expenses, but meanwhile the participants are waiting and a coordinator must have some back-up position. The last resort, of course, is to cancel the event, but the coordinator should have other options. Another contractor might be obtained at the last minute, and though this can prove costly it may be necessary. Alternative forms of transportation might be used, including public transportation.

Does the Carrier Have Appropriate and Adequate Insurance Coverage?

Insurance rates, particularly liability, are skyrocketing. If the carrier does not have adequate insurance, it may be necessary to supplement that with insurance purchased for the particular conference. An employer sponsor might have a policy on employees that could cover this contingency.

What Is the Anticipated Load?

How many participants will be involved in the particular event? If pre-registration or previously purchased tickets are required, the coordinator can be specific. On certain types of trips, limitations may be imposed by external factors. On a field trip, the number might be limited by the host. The same might apply to tours and sightseeing, though these situations usually have more flexibility. It may be possible to produce a range, say, of at least twenty-five participants but no more than seventy-five or that a particular event will accommodate no more than 100 participants. If several hotels are being used, the original negotiations would be conducted using an estimate of how many participants would be in each hotel. Just prior to the opening of the conference, it may be possible to refine this number based on actual hotel registrations, which could require changes in routing or number of buses required.

How Many Vehicles Will Be Needed?

The number of participants, the contractor's equipment, and the destination are all factors to be considered. An exotic or historic site might be on the itinerary, but the roads may not permit large buses; several smaller vehicles (possibly at a higher cost) might be more suitable. The need for back-up equipment is also a factor. Only very large contractors are able to replace vehicles immediately or have the flexibility to provide a large vehicle rather than a small one, or vice versa.

What Is the Legal Capacity of Each Vehicle?

Each vehicle has a legal capacity, usually announced in a framed notice in the vehicle. It is less commonly found in vans and minivans, but the legal capacity should be spelled out, including the rules regarding standing room.

Who Will Inspect the Vehicles?

Before a contract is signed, the vehicles should be inspected, including the vehicles' mechanical condition, cleanliness, and exterior appearance. Ripped seat cushions or floor pads communicate a good deal about the reliability of the contractor. As conditions may change between the inspection and the time the vehicles are used, another inspection may be required just prior to utilization.

Should Buses Be Air-Conditioned?

When the vehicle is used in parts of the United States with a hot and humid climate, the participants will expect air conditioning. Air conditioning can also contribute to participant comfort in dusty or noisy areas.

Do the Buses Have Facilities for Handicapped Participants?

The major concern of the physically handicapped is getting on and off buses, because they usually have very high steps. Many buses have features that deal with this problem; the most common is a lift at the front door that allows wheelchairs to be hoisted up to the passenger level. That lift can also be used for participants who use crutches or canes and for older participants with arthritis or similar ailments.

Blind people can enjoy a tour through the use of earphones and a commentator. Deaf people should be seated so that they can see a person signing, if that is necessary for the trip.

Should Each Bus Have Sanitary Facilities?

For short trips, toilet facilities are unnecessary, but on longer trips or tours, they can contribute to a comfortable trip. Of course, those buses with toilets will be more expensive than buses without them. In most cases, with well-planned rest stops, regular buses usually suffice.

If the Drivers Are Unionized, What Is the Status of the Contract?

Negotiations for the use of the vehicles are usually conducted many months before the conference starts. In the interim, is a contract due to expire or to come up for renegotiation? It is not suggested that each negotiation will produce a strike or disruption of service, yet, as with site selection, the coordinator does not want to get involved in a union dispute.

Are the Drivers Uniformed?

It is not essential that the drivers be uniformed, but it certainly instills confidence in the carrier's continuity and safety.

Does the Carrier Provide an Attendant?

For some long trips, it is helpful to have an attendant on the bus who looks after the needs and comfort of the participants. An attendant is essential for international tours, where the participants and the driver do not speak the same language.

How Long Is the Journey and Will There Be Rest Stops?

The length of the journey should be clearly understood by all concerned, especially by the participants who may have other commitments after the trip is over and assume that they will return to the conference at a given time.

Participants who take medication must know when the bus will take rest stops for water or other liquid. If the bus does not have sanitary facilities, then participants should have some idea of when there will be rest stops.

What Time Must Participants Be Ready to Board?

Field trips can be scheduled as the first event of the day, as in Example C, Event 20B (see Chapter Three), or starting at some other time. The boarding time must be coordinated with other conference events; otherwise, the participants may have to leave other events early or miss them altogether in order to go on a field trip.

Will Boarding Be at One Site or Several?

When the participants are lodged in many hotels, a decision must be made whether to have all the participants board at one hotel or to have the bus stop at several hotels. The latter procedure adds to the time required to get the field trip on the road. If enough participants are staying at different hotels, several buses can leave from these hotels and rendezvous at the destination or at a rest stop along the way. If a separate conference site is being used, the transportation can leave from there, with each participant being responsible for getting to the site as they would for any session.

Will Smoking Be Allowed?

Airplanes have a fairly sophisticated ventilation system and are usually much larger than buses, so smoking and nonsmoking sections can be segregated fairly easily. On a bus, no matter where the smokers are located, the smoke circulates throughout the entire bus.

If smoking is permitted, the participants should know about that, as some of them may choose not to go on the trip, particularly those with allergies that are triggered by the smoke. Others may also avoid the trip due to their feelings about the results of passive smoking (inhaling the smoke produced by smokers). If more than one bus is being used, it is a good idea to designate some as smoking and some as nonsmoking.

Is It Necessary to Provide Food and Beverages?

The provision of food will depend on the length of the journey and the availability of food at rest stops. In the United States, rest stops inevitably have some kinds of refreshments, so food or snacks might be provided as an amenity rather than a necessity. The same holds true for beverages, except alcoholic beverages. Should drinking be permitted on the bus? On a long trip, some participants may imbibe to the point where they lose self-control and ruin a well-planned trip or arrive at a destination inebriated and are then refused permission to enter the plant, office, or site. Coordinators generally prefer to avoid making any decision regarding alcohol and just hope nothing will happen.

Are There Any Interesting Sights Along the Route?

The bus can pass points of interest even during a short trip, and some bus drivers will point them out to the participants, even though this function may not be part of their job. In reviewing the route, the coordinator should ask about the interesting sights along the way and if they will be described. A slight change in the route may even be planned in order to pass interesting points. Whether the bus should stop is a matter of negotiation related to the purpose of the trip and the time available.

Will Guides Be Needed?

Guides may not be necessary for a field trip, but for tours and sightseeing they are essential. Though not required in the United States, in many other countries guides are tested and licensed. Multilingual guides may be necessary, depending on the country and the participants. Even in the United States, multilingual guides may be needed if the foreign participants are not completely fluent in English. In this case, interpreters at the conference might be able to interpret the guide's words on the tour.

Do the Buses Have Working Microphones?

A working microphone is usually essential on a tour bus. Such buses generally have a microphone, and it may only be necessary to check the condition of the equipment. Although local commuter buses can be used for trips, they usually do not have microphones and that limitation should be considered.

Shuttle Service

Shuttle service, as discussed in this section, refers to transportation provided among facilities, excluding the airport. If all the participants stay—and events are held—in one facility, there is obviously no need for shuttle service, but if more than one hotel or site is used, shuttle service may be required, depending on the distance involved and perhaps the weather. Some of the items relating to the contractor and equipment that should be checked (track record, insurance, provision for handicapped, and safety record) have been discussed in the previous section and will not be repeated here.

Will a Contractor Be Needed to Provide Shuttle Service?

Some municipalities provide buses at no charge to the conference when the hotels and site are on regular routes, so the bus company needs only to add additional vehicles. In some situations, it may mean only a slight detour from regular routes or providing participants with information on the nearest regular stops for buses that will take them to the conference site.

Coordinators who are considering local public transportation should examine routes and schedules and how they relate to the hotels and conference site. Most local public transportation companies provide maps that can be given to participants, including information on rates, schedules, and whether exact change or tokens are required.

What Transportation Is Available in and Around the Site?

Some newer conference sites are located adjacent to or near public transportation. In Stockholm, for example, the International Conference and Trade Center is located right next to a commuter train station, and participants who are staying in downtown Stockholm are given passes for the train. Before pursuing a contract for shuttle service, a coordinator should explore available public transportation. Even if a coordinator has previously used a site, public transportation changes constantly and a new exploration is in order.

Is On-Site Parking Available?

Most sites provide some kind of parking at little or no cost to those registered for the conference. (Downtown [in-city] hotels, however, frequently do not reduce parking charges.) For some conferences, suitable parking facilities may preclude the need for shuttle service.

What Are the Commuting Patterns Around the Site?

When shuttle service is required, a coordinator should check the commuting patterns in the site area and around the pickup points. The design of the conference may have to be changed, perhaps starting or ending a half-hour earlier or a half-hour later than originally planned, so the shuttles can avoid traffic jams. The days of the conference should also be taken into account, as traffic patterns vary on Mondays and Fridays in some cities. The time of year is also a factor. Traffic information is generally available from the contractor and the LCVB.

How Will Shuttle Pickup and Drop-Off Points and Routes Be Determined?

The coordinator and the contractor need to review the pickup and drop-off points and be prepared to negotiate. Numerous pickup points, for example, may be too expensive for the budget, and compromises should be negotiated.

The route should also be negotiated, since it concerns, in part, those hotels or areas where there will be a concentration of participants. Alternate routes, the length of the trip, and cost are all factors that have to be weighed to arrive at the best answer to this question.

Will a Dispatcher Be Provided?

Problems may arise at the site where many buses arrive and depart at the same time. An on-site dispatcher can make any adjustments that may be necessary. The dispatcher should be an employee of the contractor and have the authority to make changes, such as calling for additional equipment or replacing equipment that is not functioning properly.

Can the Buses Have Special Signs?

The buses should at least have a clear sign that indicates the route number or, better still, the hotels served. Participants should not have to search for the right bus. In addition, a coordinator should explore the possibility of displaying other signs that draw attention to the conference and the sponsor. This matter should be explored with the bus company and municipality far in advance of the conference, as special governmental approvals may be required. The cost of such signs may not have to be charged to the conference budget. The LCVB might be encouraged to pay all or part of the cost, as the signs also show how active the bureau is in bringing business to the local community. A private contractor might also absorb part of the expense as advertising that the company provides this kind of shuttle service.

Can Participants Leave an Event Early?

Sometimes, shuttle service is only provided at the start and end of the day. What if some participants must leave the conference earlier or later than the hours of shuttle service? Such travel might be considered the responsibility of individual participants, and for small conferences, this decision would probably not cause any negative feelings.

The same vehicles used for shuttle service can sometimes transport participants to and from off-site conference events. Conferences in Dallas, for example, might use a special ranch outside the city. For events like these, all pickups are usually made at one time, and the buses remain at the site until everybody is ready to return—the simplest and most economical method. The shuttle service might return on an "as needed" basis, that is, the buses start returning at a stated hour and continue to leave as they fill up until all the participants are transported back to their hotels or a specific drop-off point.

Will Special Vehicles Be Required?

If many VIPs are attending the conference, limousines or executive coaches may be required in addition to the usual buses.

Horse-drawn vehicles are an attractive alternative in such cities as Williamsburg, Virginia or Atlanta, Georgia. Of course, they are much slower than other conveyances and do not take as many participants, but for some small conferences they can provide an exciting alternative.

Participants may find double-decker buses interesting; they certainly enhance the dull routine of moving back and forth between the hotels and the conference site.

Different cities have other forms of shuttle service available. Stockholm is built on many islands, and on one of these is the Sveriges Lararforbund, a conference center maintained by the teacher's union. The island can be reached from downtown Stockholm by regular ferry service—and is free of charge!

Leaving the Conference

How Does the Conclusion of the Conference Relate to Traffic Patterns Around the Conference Site and Hotels?

Adequate planning can prevent conflict between the conclusion of the conference and local traffic. Hotel check-out time usually does not conflict with traffic, since most hotels require check-out between 12:00 and 3:00 P.M. At that time, getting to the airport does not present any problems in most cities, with some exceptions.

The city's traffic patterns must be carefully explored; successful conferences can be spoiled by departure problems. Unfortunately, many participants will have long memories concerning that final activity. Careful planning and coordination between the conclusion of the conference and transportation from the site can leave them feeling very good about the conference.

Is It Necessary to Arrange for Group Transportation to the Airport?

In large conferences, participants are usually left on their own to make whatever arrangements they wish, and when sufficient transportation is available, this does not present a problem. When many participants are departing all at once, however, the result can be unnecessary chaos. Hotel concierges or doorpersons can usually make arrangements for taxis or other transportation, and participants should be alerted to that resource.

Should Car Pools Be Arranged?

A one-day conference, such as Example A (see Chapter Three), can be expected to draw many participants who drive to the conference, so it may be possible to help them arrange car pools. Although arranging car pools may seem like an unnecessary burden for the coordinator, it can establish a psychological contract among all concerned and result in a higher number of participants. Car pooling can reduce the participants' transportation expense, make effective use of limited parking facilities, and decrease traffic problems around the site.

A possible problem may occur at the end of the day. In Example A (see Chapter Three), Event 14—reception is provided for several reasons. One is to allow the participants to avoid the traffic jams that occur in many of our major cities from 4:00 to 6:00 P.M. If participants are car pooling, it may be possible to arrange some attractions that would keep them at the conference until the end of the reception. There could be an inducement to stay in the form of a reduced parking rate. However, if liquor is served during the reception, the participant who is driving should be encouraged to limit intake or be provided with some other alternatives.

Chapter 15

Entertainment Possibilities

CHECKLIST FOR ENTERTAINMENT

Selection

_____ Will we have entertainment?

_____ Has a budget been provided for entertainment?

_____ What type of entertainment relates best to the theme of the conference?

_____ What type of entertainment relates best to the participants?

_____ What type of entertainment might be offensive to the participants, sponsor, or companions?

_____ How much lead time is necessary to prepare entertainment?

_____ Will the entertainment be provided through a professional agency?

_____ Has anyone seen the entertainment prior to selection?

_____ Will prior users of the entertainment be contacted?

_____ How many times, and when, will entertainment be used?

_____ Should the coordinator have a formal contract for entertainment?

_____ What entertainment equipment does the site have?

_____ What are the union requirements?

Local Resources

_____ Does the site have any entertainment that would be appropriate for the participants?

_____ Are there any nearby attractions for entertainment?

_____ Is local talent available for entertainment?

_____ Does the site or surrounding area offer any unique entertainment opportunities?

At the Conference

_____ Who has responsibility for coordinating the entertainment?

_____ What is the back-up position if the entertainment is a no-show?

_____ Will the entertainers require rehearsal space and time?

_____ Is a special setup required?

_____ Will the entertainers require dressing rooms?

_____ Will the entertainers require refreshments, food, or other amenities?

SOURCE: _The Comprehensive Guide to Successful Conferences and Meetings_ by Leonard Nadler and Zeace Nadler. San Francisco: Jossey-Bass. Copyright © 1987. Permission to reproduce hereby granted.

T he coordinator should carefully consider whether entertainment can contribute to the success of the conference. In most cases, well-planned entertainment can make a significant contribution.

Entertainment covers a wide range of activities, from a stand-up comedian to a full orchestra to a complete stage show. As used in this chapter, entertainment means a live presentation, performed for and sometimes with the participants. In some countries, entertainment is similar to what are called party games in the United States, including charades (where the participants themselves take turns entertaining) or even the long-time favorite bingo. The purpose is purely entertainment, and this point is stressed because it is also possible to use some of those activities for other purposes. Sports, recreation, and cultural events are covered in Chapter Four.

Reasons for Entertainment

The specific reasons for providing entertainment at a conference must be examined in relation to the purpose of the conference, the design, the participants, and the budget. Though a one-day conference rarely needs entertainment for a welcome change of pace, a five-day conference design usually needs entertainment to supplement other related events. Entertainment may be designed as its own event or integrated into a banquet or similar event. At some conferences, entertainment is provided just before the general session, as part of climate setting for that event.

Make or Buy?

The decision must be made whether to use internal or external resources for entertainment, or a combination of both.

The Checklist

Selection

Will We Have Entertainment?

This question must be answered separately for each conference. For example, if the conference is the first of a series to be offered by a membership sponsor, it should be recognized that using entertainment might establish a precedent for the rest of the series. If the conference is already part of a series, what kind of entertainment was provided in previous conferences and how was it received? Should entertainment be offered again, and if so, how might it be improved?

An employer sponsor must carefully consider how entertainment relates to the purpose of the conference and the image of the sponsor. Poorly planned entertainment can be viewed as frivolous and a poor use of the sponsor's resources, but entertainment can also be seen as one of the fringe benefits accruing to those who are invited to employer sponsor conferences.

A for-profit public seminar sponsor might offer entertainment to attract participants. In this case, the quality of entertainment must be high enough to communicate that message. A nonprofit public seminar sponsor must consider the advisability of entertainment in light of the purpose, the sponsor, and the source of funds.

Has a Budget Been Provided for Entertainment?

Entertainment costs must be included in the conference budget. As negotiations proceed, it will probably be necessary to modify the budget item. No problem arises if less money is required, of course, but if negotiations indicate the need for more money, the coordinator must be informed immediately and a decision made about the budget. The budget must cover not only entertainer fees, but such associated costs as travel, accommodations, rehearsal expense, back-up musicians, and any other costs that might be associated with the entertainment.

What Type of Entertainment Relates Best to the Theme of the Conference?

The conference theme may automatically indicate the appropriate type of entertainment. A theme such as "Working Together" suggests entertainment emphasizing how people (actors and actresses) cooperate and work together rather than as singles. The "working" suggests that the entertainment could be related to that term rather than recreation. The relationship between the theme and the entertainment should be immediately recognizable to everybody. If explanations are necessary, it is probably not the best choice of entertainment. The entertainment may have no relation to the theme, but what must be avoided is entertainment that is in conflict with the theme. A conference on "Dealing with the Budget Crisis," for example, should avoid an expensive extravaganza.

What Type of Entertainment Relates Best to the Participants?

The range of participants is so broad for some conferences that is is almost impossible to select entertainment that pleases everyone. In some conferences, however, the mix of participants is more homogeneous, and the entertainment should be planned to appeal to as many participants as possible. If the age range of the participants is fifty to sixty-five, for example, a rock group would probably hold little appeal; they might be more enthusiastic about "Music from the Big Band Era." A sophisticated group of participants may find the off-color humor of a cocktail lounge comedian very amusing, but the same act would hardly be the right selection for a religiously oriented conference.

What Type of Entertainment Might Be Offensive to the Participants, Sponsor, or Companions?

It is not easy to know beforehand how an entertainer will be received, but some obvious situations can be avoided. If the conference is in Las Vegas, Atlantic City, or another gambling venue, the participants will probably be very receptive to entertainment that contains elements of gambling in its many forms. The entertainment at these resort areas commonly includes scantily clad females and other sexually suggestive stage elements; participants who attend a conference in those venues are unlikely to have negative feelings about that kind of entertainment at their conference.

In other venues, however, those forms of entertainment may be completely inappropriate. Participants who attend with their spouses may feel uncomfortable, and those who would not normally attend the strip shows in some resort areas would walk out in protest when that type of entertainment is foisted on them.

How Much Lead Time Is Necessary to Prepare Entertainment?

The amount of lead time depends on the type of entertainment and its relation to the theme. Usually, the coordinator first develops the theme and the core design of the conference, providing time and space in the program design for some kind of entertainment. If only one entertainer is needed, agencies can be contacted and lists of possible acts developed. Big-name entertainment, however, may require up to six months' lead time, and even then many of these entertainers do not commit too far in advance, except for large and lucrative attractions.

The general rule is to start with as much lead time as possible, which means beginning the selection process as soon as the design is firm enough to specify the date and time of the entertainment. Then, the type of entertainment should be determined, a sometimes time-consuming decision if the design committee and the sponsor must be involved.

Will the Entertainment Be Provided Through a Professional Agency?

Almost all good entertainers are represented by professional agencies. Working with an agency or an agent may be costly, but the additional cost is more than warranted given the agency's services. As agencies usually represent more than one entertainer, they can provide the coordinator with choices; of course, a coordinator can deal with more than one agency at a time, but that is time-consuming and may not be necessary.

Some agencies offer substitutes that are acceptable. There is a significant market in look-alikes, minor entertainers who look like and imitate some major entertainers, both living and dead (such as Elvis Presley look-alikes). This is not intended to be deception, and, at the right moment, participants are informed that the performer is a look-alike. The participants usually enjoy the joke on themselves and do not resent having been fooled, and the cost is much less than when hiring the original entertainer.

Has Anyone Seen the Entertainment Prior to Selection?

Selecting unpreviewed entertainment is risky; even if the entertainer is a big name, the coordinator should have some kind of advance look at the program that particular entertainer would provide for the conference. Most entertainers have a wide range of acts and may be able to tailor the act to the specific conference participants and theme.

It is even more essential to preview lesser-known entertainers. Agencies are known to extol the accomplishments of their clients, but their opinions are obviously biased. As coordinators are not often expected to be adept at selecting performers through auditions, they might find someone with reliable judgment who has seen the act.

Will Prior Users of the Entertainment Be Contacted?

Another alternative is to contact coordinators who have used that entertainer for their conferences. Contacting previous users not only serves to check on the entertainer but also provides an opportunity to check out the agent's reliability and cooperation. Some disreputable agents are known to people in the field, and the coordinator should try to contact people who have had experience with agents and entertainers.

How Many Times, and When, Will Entertainment Be Used?

Although most conferences use entertainment only once during the program, it may be used more frequently. A conference on a ship or similar isolated venue may provide entertainment each night, as the participants do not have many other alternatives. If the conference group is only one of many on a ship, the cost of regular entertainment is built into the cost of the ship. If the entire ship is being booked for one conference, special arrangements for entertainment must be made. A band might be scheduled to perform several times, once for dancing, once to provide music before the general session opens, and perhaps another time in connection with the exhibition, dressing differently and performing a different musical program for each event.

Should the Coordinator Have a Formal Contract for Entertainment?

Having a formal contract with the entertainer or agent is important. Legal advice may be needed, though in some situations a simple letter of agreement is enough. The intent, as with most contracts, is not only to develop an ironclad document that will hold up in court (it is more important to avoid lawsuits) but rather to put into writing the agreement of the coordinator and the entertainer/agent on such items as dates, fees, travel, accommodations, commissions, substitutions, staff costs, equipment costs, and cancellation.

What Entertainment Equipment Does the Site Have?

Some entertainment equipment may already be available at the site. For example, the site may provide a stage, which may merely consist of a raised platform or may actually include a full theater with hangings, curtains, catwalks, and sophisticated lighting equipment. The public address system (speakers), spotlights, and other equipment may be permanently built into the facility. The site may have some standard scenery or backdrops. Almost all acts require a piano; if one is available at the site, the coordinator should make sure it is tuned.

On the other hand, the site may have no equipment and may have limitations that make the procurement of that equipment economically unfeasible. The ceiling in the room planned for the entertainment may not be high enough to mount lights or loudspeakers, or the room may not have sufficient space to erect backdrops or any kind of scenery.

What Are the Union Requirements?

In the United States, the entertainment industry has many well-established unions, and in most situations union performers will not play on the same program with nonunion performers. Unions have rules on the minimum pieces for a band or orchestra, hours, and overtime. Performers may bring their own back-ups, but the union may still insist on standby performers who must be paid by the user, the coordinator. In each case, the coordinator must investigate the entertainment union regulations for the particular site.

Local Resources

Does the Site Have Any Entertainment That Would Be Appropriate for the Participants?

Some sites, particularly hotels, provide entertainment for their guests, which include the conference participants. Hotel entertainment usually has a bar or cabaret setting but might be in a dinner theater format. The range of entertainment is great, and the coordinator might find it expeditious to utilize what is available, if appropriate. A special block of tickets for participants or a special show exclusively for participants might be arranged. The coordinator should also explore the attractions scheduled immediately before the opening

316 Successful Conferences and Meetings

and just after the closing of the conference. The entertainers might agree to arrive one day early or leave one day late in order to provide entertainment for the participants at only a slightly extra charge.

Are There Any Nearby Attractions for Entertainment?

Even if the site does not provide entertainment, nearby facilities might. Arrangements may require ground transportation but can simplify the search for entertainment as part of the conference.

Is Local Talent Available for Entertainment?

Some areas have high-quality local entertainment. These local groups are probably amateurs or semiprofessionals, however, so caution must be exercised. Rather than rely on a local recommendation, the coordinator should audition the group or assign a qualified person in the secretariat to do it. Despite possible limitations, local groups are generally less expensive than professionals brought from a distance and may be equally as entertaining. Different parts of the United States offer different music, dance, and customs, which could prove entertaining for participants from other parts of the country. The LCVB and local members of a membership sponsor are helpful sources for this search. Employer sponsors and public seminar sponsors are less likely to opt for local entertainment, but even they might be interested in something unique.

Does the Site or Surrounding Area Offer
Any Unique Entertainment Opportunities?

The conference locale can offer unique entertainment possibilities. A conference held in a city on the Mississippi River can rent one of the famed riverboats for a ride on the river and entertainment with a local focus. The Potomac River also provides an opportunity in the Washington, D.C., area, where a boat holding up to 200 people can be rented for a cruise and dinner on the river with optional entertainment. Theme parks have proliferated since Disneyland opened many years ago. Some are general; others focus on a local event or piece of history. Most of these parks make special arrangements for groups and provide an entertaining experience for the participants.

At the Conference

Who Has Responsibility for Coordinating the Entertainment?

If entertainment is a minor factor in the overall conference design and does not involve extended auditions and negotiations, the coordinator should have no difficulty with this task. For a large conference, however, coordinating entertainment can become a time-consuming operation, and the coordinator should designate someone else to handle the responsibility.

Figure 43. Site Entertainment Rehearsal Factors.

_____ Rehearsal date and time confirmed

_____ Rehearsal room assigned

_____ Room availability confirmed

_____ Other personnel needed

     _____ Electrician

     _____ Musicians

     _____ Sound Engineer

     _____ Stage crew

     _____ Supporting cast

SOURCE: _The Comprehensive Guide to Successful Conferences and Meetings_ by Leonard Nadler and Zeace Nadler. San Francisco: Jossey-Bass. Copyright © 1987. Permission to reproduce hereby granted.

What Is the Back-Up Position If the Entertainment Is a No-Show?

In the event of a no-show, whether due to natural disaster or double-booking, all that matters is that the participants expect entertainment and it is not available. If possible, the coordinator should have a back-up position. The back-up plan depends on the amount of notice the coordinator receives and the opportunities that are available. The coordinator should identify nearby entertainment that could serve as an acceptable substitute. The replacement act may require a premium payment, but that may be necessary under these conditions.

Will the Entertainers Require Rehearsal Space and Time?

Most entertainers require at least one rehearsal at the site, and the coordinator should consider the site factors shown in Figure 43.

The coordinator should confirm the place, date, and time of the rehearsal. Has a rehearsal room been assigned? In some situations, this may have to be the actual room where the entertainment will take place; in other instances it may only be necessary to have a room where the entertainers can practice together. The time of the rehearsal is particularly important if that room (or nearby rooms) is being used for other events. A band rehearsal, for example, can be very disruptive for a session in an adjacent room. Finally, other personnel may be required for rehearsals, including electricians, musicians, sound engineer, stage crew, and the supporting cast.

Is a Special Setup Required?

The entertainers may require special setups, such as scenery, props, or the placement of the piano. An extensive setup may mean that some rooms or space will not be available for other conference activities, and that must be considered when integrating entertainment into the conference design.

Will the Entertainers Require Dressing Rooms?

Although many entertainers can use a sleeping room or suite, some require special dressing rooms. If dressing rooms are required, they may have to be located close to the entertainment room. Dressing rooms may only be required for a brief period, just before or after the performance, or may be needed for longer periods of time.

Will the Entertainers Require Refreshments, Food, or Other Amenities?

Besides monetary payment, food and beverages are usually given to entertainers as part of their compensation. As some entertainers do not eat until after their show, which could be long after the kitchen has closed, special food arrangements may be necessary. Some horror stories that have been attached to this item can be avoided. One top-level entertainer and his large entourage held a dinner party after the show—and charged it to the sponsor! The coordinator had agreed to provide dinner after the show—but did not realize it would be for more than fifty people! Fortunately, most entertainers are more considerate, though their food and drink needs will probably be different from those of the participants.

Chapter 16

Developing a Budget

CHECKLIST FOR BUDGETING

Income

Fees (from Figure 44)	$ _____
Grants	_____
Advertising	_____
Exhibitors	_____
Company allotment	_____
Cosponsors	_____
Other (from Figure 45)	_____
Total Income	$ _____

Fixed Expenses

Coordinator

Fee/salary	_____
Expenses	_____
Total coordinator expenses	_____

Design Committee

Travel	_____
Meeting expense	_____
Total design committee	_____

Marketing

Brochures	_____
Advertising	_____
Mailing lists	_____
Postage	_____
Total marketing	_____

Office Supplies and Expense

Stationery	_____
Telephone, telex	_____
Postage, shipping	_____
Total office supplies	_____

Prepaid expenses

Deposits	_____
Honoraria	_____
Insurance	_____
Total prepaid expenses	_____
Preregistration materials	_____

Staff (Secretariat)

    Salaries (permanent staff) _____

    Salaries (temporary staff) _____

    Payroll taxes _____

    Fringe benefits _____

    Expenses _____

        Total staff expense _____

            Total fixed expenses $ _____

Variable Expenses

Audiovisual equipment _____

Companion program _____

Computer services _____

Contract services _____

Entertainment _____

Exhibition _____

Equipment _____

Field trips _____

Gratuities _____

Ground transportation _____

Hospitality suite _____

Interpreters, translators _____

On-site personnel _____

Participant supplies

    Participant book _____

    Badges _____

    Amenities _____

        Total participant supplies _____

Presenters

    Accommodations _____

    Travel _____

    Honoraria and fees _____

    Participant packets _____

        Total presenters expenses _____

Printing and reproduction _____

Prizes, awards, and mementos _____

Public relations _____

Secretariat _____

Security   _____

Shipping   _____

Sightseeing   _____

Signs   _____

Site

   Sleeping rooms   _____

   Meeting rooms   _____

   Food and beverage (from Figure 46)   _____

   Functions   _____

     Total site   _____

Steering Committee   _____

Evaluation   _____

Follow-up   _____

     Total Variable Expenses $ _____

Budget Summary

Gross income $ _____

Less:

   Total fixed expenses   _____

   Total variable expenses   _____

     Total expenses   _____

   Income after expenses   _____

   Less: Miscellaneous   _____

     NET INCOME $ _____

SOURCE: *The Comprehensive Guide to Successful Conferences and Meetings* by Leonard Nadler and Zeace Nadler. San Francisco: Jossey-Bass. Copyright © 1987. Permission to reproduce hereby granted.

Many conference planners dislike working with the budgetary aspects of a conference, but as with many other activities in our lives, the budget is a controlling factor. Indeed, whoever controls the budget controls the conference!

Which comes first—the budget or the design? As with many such questions, the answer is, "It depends." An employer sponsor or a nonprofit public seminar sponsor may stipulate a budget figure, and the coordinator must work within that figure. The budget for a for-profit public seminar sponsor is usually based on a certain dollar amount, or percentage of profit. A membership sponsor seeks to make a profit, though the exact amount may be unstated, but usually a membership sponsor cannot afford to conduct a conference at a loss.

The term *profit* must be used cautiously. Nonprofit public seminar sponsors and membership sponsors, for example, usually use the word *surplus* or a similar term instead. However, because this terminology has more to do with IRS regulations than with budgeting, we will use the word *profit* in this chapter.

Developing the Budget

A budget of some kind must be developed before the conference is held, since it must be considered in planning. Because the budget changes as different sites are considered, negotiations are held, and other factors in the design begin to coalesce, constant budget review is a necessity. The budget should not be considered as final until late in the planning process, and even then, some flexibility must be retained. The first budget estimates are based on general calculations that include some of the main items on the checklist.

We are not suggesting any specific accounting system for the budget process, as it must be part of the regular accounting system the sponsor uses, which may change some of the categories and nomenclature on the checklist.

Control of the Budget

If possible, the coordinator should control the budget, that is, all changes in the budget should either be initiated by, or at least developed in conjunction with, the coordinator. The paid staff of one membership sponsor retained control of the budget and only allowed the coordinator, a volunteer, to see bits and pieces of it; as a result, the coordinator worked half blind. Ultimately, all budget decisions were made by the staff, and the coordinator was powerless.

Recognize that the budget does not give the coordinator or anybody else any funds; it is only a planning document that provides information about the financial opportunities and constraints. At the same time, it reflects decisions about the conference.

The design committee must also be involved in the budget process, particularly when it is empowered to make decisions. Even when this committee can only recommend, it must know the budget implications of its recommendations.

At some point in the planning process, the budget must be officially approved, and everyone concerned should have a clear understanding of who has the power to approve the final budget. In most cases, the sponsor has this power, but the specific person within the sponsoring organization who can give final approval should be identified.

Control of Expenditures

A budget essentially communicates income and expense estimates though nothing on the expense side can actually be spent without somebody's approval. We strongly urge that that person be the coordinator; otherwise, the coordinator cannot be expected to have any responsibility for the expenditures.

The coordinator is, of course, bound by the budget, though budgets have some degree of flexibility. To the extent possible, the items and amounts that are flexible should be stated in writing as part of the budget process. For example, can the coordinator switch amounts from one item in the budget to another? A common practice is to allow about 10 percent (or some other percentage or amount) increase or decrease on a switch, without going back for new approval.

The following checklist is intended to be comprehensive, so not all of the items apply to every conference. The terms used are generally accepted, though some items may vary among organizations. The sponsor's accounting system may also use terms that are different than those on the checklist.

It is obvious that the checklist in this chapter is different from those in the other chapters. In other chapters, the checklists are composed of a series of questions. In this chapter, the checklist is the pro forma budget, and each item will be discussed.

The Checklist

Income

Fees

The major source of conference income is usually the fees paid by the participants, and fee structures vary widely (see Figure 44). For example, a membership sponsor can offer its members reduced fees to encourage them to preregister. The first "early bird" registrations can occur about a year before the event. Several months later, another slightly higher fee is announced. Usually the fee is only increased twice, as it can become very confusing to the prospective participants and greatly complicate the bookkeeping. Late (or full-fee) registration is that which occurs after the last reduced fee. The same approach, economic incentive, can be used to encourage nonmembers to register early. Obviously, that fee will be higher than the fee for members.

Another approach ties in the conference fee with the membership fee, that is, a nonmember participant can register for the conference at a rate that includes membership for the following year. This strategy takes careful calculating but can be effective. A danger is not in the conference aspect but in the membership area, for this inflates the number of memberships and can produce misleading data.

An employer sponsor usually does not charge fees, so this item is not likely to be a source of income for that type of sponsor. The for-profit public seminar sponsor can use the reduced-rate approach by offering discounts to alumni who have been participants at a previous conference of the sponsor.

Reduced fees may also apply to companions when they are included in the design (see Chapter Eleven), and these fees should parallel those for regular participants. Companion fees can be a significant source of income for membership and public seminar sponsors, which use this technique to increase attendance of regular participants.

Scholarships (sometimes called papering the house, Annie Oakleys, courtesy registrations, and freebees) present another means of offering reduced rates or waiving fees entirely. A sponsor may have many good reasons for offering scholarships. A professional membership sponsor may offer scholarships to students who are entering the field and cannot afford the full registration. Scholarships may also be used to draw participants from countries whose exchange rates make it prohibitive for potential participants to pay the full amount. A for-profit public seminar sponsor sometimes offers reduced fees or scholarships to participants who represent a large market, such as a major corporation. This form of scholarship allows selected people to attend and thus to preview seminars that the sponsor may market to their corporations in the future. When a public seminar sponsor conference has an embarrassingly low registration, scholarships or reduced-fee registrations will fill the hall and avoid cancellation of the conference. Of course, this must be done very cautiously since in no way should this information be conveyed to other participants, who have paid the full fee. A nonprofit public seminar

Figure 44. Participant Fee Structure.

Regular Participants (Members)

Regular conference fee

Number of participants expected × fee = $ ______________

Reduced fees

First early registration

Number of participants expected × fee = ______________

Second early registration

Number of participants expected × fee = ______________

Late (full-fee) registration

Number of participants expected × fee = ______________

Regular Participants (Nonmembers)

Regular conference fee

Number of participants expected × fee = ______________

Reduced fees

First early registration

Number of participants expected × fee = ______________

Second early registration

Number of participants expected × fee = ______________

Late registration

Number of participants expected × fee = ______________

Companions

Regular conference fee

Number of companions expected × fee = ______________

Reduced fees

First early registration

Number of companions expected × fee = ______________

Second early registration

Number of companions expected × fee = ______________

Scholarships

Number of participants expected × fee = ______________

Dailies

Number of participants expected × fee = ______________

TOTAL $ ______________

SOURCE: *The Comprehensive Guide to Successful Conferences and Meetings* by Leonard Nadler and Zeace Nadler. San Francisco: Jossey-Bass. Copyright © 1987. Permission to reproduce hereby granted.

sponsor might have a mixture of full-fee and scholarship participants, depending on its sources of funds.

For a conference of three days or more, some participants will be dailies or walk-ins (participants who sign up for only one day of the conference), though some sponsors prefer not to have dailies. On the other hand, a for-profit public seminar sponsor sometimes organizes a conference so that it consists only of dailies, encouraging participants to attend only those days or those sessions that are of interest to them. This is high-risk strategy, of course, but it has worked well for some sponsors.

Grants

A grant is given to a sponsor to conduct a conference on a specific topic or for a particular group of participants. The grant can be in the form of money or in-kind reimbursement; the grantor provides services to the sponsor or pays suppliers directly on behalf of the conference.

An employer sponsor might get a grant from a foundation or a government agency, as was done during the War on Poverty program of the 1960s. Membership sponsors and public seminar sponsors receive grants from many sources, including foundations, government agencies, corporations, and even individuals. Generally, a grant is for a well-defined purpose and, in most cases, can be combined with other income to provide sufficient budget for the conference. The terms of a grant should clearly state whether the grantee (the sponsor) is permitted to supplement the budget from other sources.

Advertising

A souvenir program can be printed, accepting paid ads from members and others related to the organization. When an exhibition is held in conjunction with a conference, exhibitors can be given the benefit of placing an ad at a lower rate than nonexhibitors.

Exhibitors

Exhibitors are a significant source of income for a membership sponsor (see Chapter Ten). The same holds true for a for-profit public seminar sponsor, depending on the purpose of the conference and the kinds of participants who attend. A nonprofit public seminar sponsor can also hold an exhibition but must be careful not to endanger its nonprofit status. Exhibits at an employer sponsor conference are usually placed by the sponsor itself and therefore are not income-producing.

Booth rentals are the major source of revenue from exhibitors. Exhibitor registrations are not usually a significant source of income; exhibitors are typically given a certain number of complimentary registrations as part of the booth fee. Additional exhibitor registrations are charged the regular fee.

Company Allotment

This item, applying only to the employer sponsor, is the in-house budget to fund a conference. The amount of the allotment may be determined first, which means the budget cannot exceed that amount, or the expenses may first be approved, and then the necessary amount allotted to the conference budget.

Cosponsors

Some conferences have a major sponsor and one or more cosponsors, that is, other organizations with a common interest. Although all sponsors sometimes function as equals, this arrangement usually leads to problems; having one major sponsor usually works better. The relationships among cosponsors must be developed very carefully so that the original sponsor's objectives are not lost.

Cosponsors are common in membership conferences. Two organizations may have similar interests, and rather than split into two conferences with the possibility that both will fail, the two join forces. A cosponsor in an employer sponsor conference would probably be another department or division of the major sponsor.

Other

Conferences have many other potential sources of income, as shown in Figure 45.

Tape. At membership sponsor conferences, presentations are commonly audiotaped or videotaped and sold to participants and the general public. Frequently, the keynoter or general session speaker will be taped, as well as other selected sessions. Written permission must be obtained from the presenter—some presenters agree only if they receive a royalty or some form of remuneration.

Contributions. Nonprofit public seminar sponsors and membership sponsors can obtain contributions from a variety of sources. Although some contributors do not desire recognition, most expect some kind of announcement or printed notice. Contributions are frequently in the form of participant packets (folders, envelopes), souvenirs, pads, writing implements, films, AV equipment, or other materials for the use of the participants, or services before or during the conference. From an accounting viewpoint, contributions may be handled either as a deduction from the relevant expenses or as income.

Interest. Preregistration fees, if not expended immediately, can earn interest. In times of high interest rates, this can be a significant source of income for some conferences; when interest rates are low, this source may not be significant.

Publications. Conference publications can produce sales revenues, but publication expenses (such as editing, printing, advertising, warehousing, mailing, and absorbing returns and bad debts) must also be accounted for. (Expenses can be deducted and the net income listed here, or the gross can be estimated here with the expenses listed elsewhere in the budget.) Some sponsors need to be made aware of these publication costs. For-profit public seminar sponsors with publishing units are probably familiar with the expense side, but many membership sponsors are not. For a membership sponsor, the publication of conference proceedings might be acceptable as

Figure 45. Other Possibilities for Conference Income.

Tapes	$ _____
Contributions	_____
Interest	_____
Publications	_____
Novelties and mementos	_____
Tours	_____
Food and beverage functions	_____
Exhibition-only admissions	_____
TOTAL OTHER INCOME	$ _____

SOURCE: *The Comprehensive Guide to Successful Conferences and Meetings* by Leonard Nadler and Zeace Nadler. San Francisco: Jossey-Bass. Copyright © 1987. Permission to reproduce hereby granted.

a loss, since it could be considered as a service to the members or as marketing for the sponsor.

Conference sponsors can also sell the publications of others. Books and other materials can be obtained on a consignment basis with the unsold items to be returned. This arrangement lowers the sponsor's risk but requires appropriate personnel to staff the selling area, as well as to arrange for control and security of the materials and funds.

Novelties, Mementos, and Souvenirs. Novelty companies produce a wide variety of special souvenir items, such as mugs, hats, writing implements, and paperweights, which can display the name of the sponsor, the theme of the conference, the logo, or any other pertinent information. Like publications, novelties can also be a loss item, so the coordinator should consider an outside contractor, since these mementos cannot be considered a service to the members. The contractor usually provides the necessary items; the conference provides the space and receives a percentage of sales. The return is much less than if the items are sold directly by conference personnel, but using a contractor requires no direct budget expense.

Tours. Coordinators should usually stay out of the tour business, a specialized area that should be left to the experts. If the coordinator is a member of a large conference management organization, a special unit within that organization may handle tours. Otherwise, a coordinator may find that tours are much more complicated and produce less revenue than might be expected.

Many conferences provide various kinds of tours for the participants before, during, and after the conference. If a tour is part of the conference package, it will not produce any special income, except for the sale of additional tickets to spouses or companions. In return for space at the conference, the tour operator may share a percentage or make a fixed payment into the conference account. Some tour operators work on the premise that they are doing the coordinator a favor by providing this service to the participants and will not share income with the conference.

Food and Beverage Functions. In general, a coordinator should not seek to turn these functions into sources of income; on the other hand, it is not advisable to give these activities away, for they are expense items to the conference. Certain meals should be included as part of the conference fee; others (special luncheons or dinners) may have an extra fee.

Generally, extra income from meals comes from dailies or participants' friends or spouses, who are not registered for the companion program but are joining them for a special meal. When included in the regular participant fee, food is readily handled, but when considered as an income possibility, extreme care must be exercised. Meals should be priced so that it is more advantageous to register as a regular participant than to pay for functions separately. If space is limited, priority must be given to regular participants.

Exhibition Only. The coordinator should establish a price for those who want only to visit the exhibits as opposed to the conference activities.

Fixed Expenses

Coordinator

The coordinator usually earns a fee or salary. When the coordinator is an internal employee of the sponsor organization, the sponsor can decide that there will not be any charge. When the coordinator is external, some kind of expense must be listed here unless the coordinator is functioning strictly as an unpaid volunteer.

An employer sponsor with a regular coordinator position can charge the coordinator's salary off to individual conferences or allocate the salary by means of an overhead formula or some other cost accounting method. The cost of an external coordinator is usually a direct charge to the particular conference.

A membership sponsor may have two charges under this item. A membership sponsor that conducts many conferences during the year or one large annual conference usually has full-time conference staff and allocates their salaries to the particular conference. In addition, a membership sponsor might also pay an external coordinator (usually a member) a small fee, which should be charged to the particular conference; at other times this external coordinator may agree to serve as a volunteer for no fee.

A for-profit public seminar sponsor always has a coordinator for each conference, so it needs to know exactly what each conference costs. When a coordinator works on more than one conference at a time, which is a strong possibility, an appropriate charge is made to each conference account.

The coordinator for a nonprofit public seminar sponsor may be any of the possibilities discussed above, so how the expense is handled depends on the funding base. If the conference is being externally funded, the grantor or contributor may want an exact accounting of funds.

Fringe benefits for salaried coordinators should also be included as an expense to the conference budget, as well as any reimbursement for a coordinator's travel, meal, and lodging expenses.

Design Committee

The design committee usually does not receive any fee or salary (see Chapter Two). The design committee of an employer sponsor is usually drawn from different parts of the organization. Depending on the customary practice of the sponsor, the expenses of design committee members may be charged to the conference account. It is also possible (but unusual) to charge "lost" time to the conference account, that is, the time the design committee members are away from their jobs on conference business.

If the design committee is expected to visit the conference site some distance from the usual workplace, travel expenses are usually provided. This practice is customary for an employer sponsor, but for a membership sponsor or a nonprofit public seminar sponsor, it depends on whether the design committee has agreed to volunteer and pay some, or all, of their own expenses. The for-profit public seminar sponsor usually does not use an external design committee, but if it did, it would probably pay the committee's expenses.

Funds may also be provided for meeting expenses, including rent for a meeting room, meal functions, breaks, and possibly some equipment and material expense, particularly when the design committee is meeting at a location away from the sponsor's facilities.

Marketing

Costs for brochures must be estimated and then verified. Even the cost of producing brochures in-house should still be charged to the particular conference.

The cost for print and electronic advertising can be specifically determined once the extent of the advertising has been agreed on. If more than one conference is to be promoted in the same advertisement, the costs can be allocated among the different conferences.

The process of estimating costs for mailing lists usually starts by testing a few lists or by buying a limited number of them and then purchasing additional lists if more are needed. For budget purposes, the costs for mailing lists should be overestimated rather than underestimated; it is more desirable to go under budget on actual costs than to have a budget overrun. When mailing lists are used, postage can be expected to be a significant expense.

Office Supplies and Expense

Some sponsors do not want to get involved with extensive cost accounting on this item, so they merely charge a percentage or fixed amount to the conference budget. This practice is certainly acceptable in some cases, but in others it can produce a distorted financial picture. A coordinator has little choice but to follow the practice established by the sponsor.

An employer sponsor can use its regular stationery for conference purposes, but other sponsors may prefer stationery that is printed especially for a particular conference.

Telephone and telex can be a significant expense, particularly for an international conference. Budget estimates depend on how the sponsor charges internally for these services. If the coordinator is external, the sponsor may require that all telexes be sent through the sponsor's own telex system; though this can be very time-consuming, the coordinator must comply. If the coordinator does not have installed telex service, it is possible to get one on an as-used basis, that is, no ongoing fee, just a charge for every telex sent and received. (One such service, for example, can be reached by telephoning 1-800-628-9030.) If the coordinator has a computer with a modem, other direct telex services are available.

Postage and shipping costs also depend on how the sponsor wants this function to be handled physically and financially. For many conferences this expense can constitute a significant budget item.

Prepaid Expenses

Prepaid expenses must be paid before the conference begins and, in some cases, are not refundable. Various kinds of deposits may be required. The site may require a deposit, particularly when exhibit and session room space are under contract. Nonrefundable deposits may be necessary for audiovisual equipment, ground transportation, entertainment, and other services. In each case, some form of contract or documentation should be written on what the deposit covers, how much of it is refundable, and under what conditions.

Some presenters, particularly keynote speakers and other VIPs, are paid honoraria or fees. Those presenters who are in demand usually require a nonrefundable down payment, which covers the presenters in case the conference no longer requires their presentation or is canceled.

Insurance has become an increasingly expensive item. Cancellation insurance reimburses the sponsor for specifically agreed-on expenses, at least the unrecoverable deposits, in the event the conference is canceled. Some conferences may need insurance for storms, inclement weather, and similar natural disasters, particularly when the site is a ship or located in an area that could be isolated by snows or floods.

At some sites, liability insurance is the responsibility of the sponsor; with the increasing number of claims in this area, such insurance should receive careful consideration. Some form of health insurance might be advisable when the conference is attended by a substantial number of elderly or international participants who might have some special but unforeseen medical needs.

Preregistration Materials

Some preregistration materials, such as brochures, should be charged to other items, such as marketing, but other preregistration materials like registration forms and information should be accounted for here. An important piece is a preliminary program, typically a brief sheet or pamphlet listing some or all of the presenters and possibly containing information about housing and transportation.

Materials might be made available at the end of an annual conference to advertise the next one. Examples are printed materials, souvenirs (miniature cowboy hats that announce the dates of the next conference in Dallas), or pens printed with the dates and venue of the next conference. These items should be billed to that future conference rather than entered here.

Staff (Secretariat)

Although the secretariat works during and after the conference, the budget item is listed here because some commitment must be made to the size and extent of the budget for the secretariat. Actual expenditures for the secretariat might be less than budgeted, but, unfortunately, coordinators tend to underestimate the cost of the secretariat.

Employer sponsor secretariats are usually composed of employees of the sponsor. Depending on the organization's accounting system, the secretariat costs may be allocated directly to the conference, or a general overhead percentage can be applied. Membership sponsor and nonprofit public employer sponsor secretariats can be regular employees of the sponsor, volunteers or a combination of both. Although volunteers are unpaid, the budget can list an amount that the secretariat would have cost if volunteers were not available and a corresponding income item for volunteer services. A for-profit public seminar sponsor normally has permanent staff who serve as a secretariat unless the sponsor conducts an unusually large number of conferences at the same time, which requires supplementing the regular staff with outside help.

Salaries appear on the budget. To get a good financial picture, the budget might separate permanent employees from other classifications. In this budget, temporary includes part-time as well as full-time employees.

Payroll taxes and fringe benefits for regular employees and direct hires must be entered. For temporary personnel, the coordinator might use an agency that supplies temporary help. The general practice is that the coordinator pays an hourly or daily wage, and the agency pays the necessary payroll taxes and any fringe benefits.

Expenses for the secretariat may include some meals or other amenities. If a member of the secretariat is expected to travel with the design committee or to accompany the coordinator on site selection tours, provision should be made in the budget for the appropriate travel and accommodation expenses.

Variable Expenses

These expenses vary according to the number of participants and whether the conference is actually held. In most cases, an increase in the number of participants will be accompanied by a corresponding increase in income. Computer spreadsheet programs can be extremely useful in figuring these kinds of "what if" calculations and in updating such interrelated items as number of participants, supplies, and food functions throughout the planning process.

The variable expenses are described below.

Audiovisual Equipment

During site negotiation for a small conference, the coordinator may be able to get some AV equipment from the site at no additional charge. Some coordinators provide minimal AV equipment for presenters but assess a charge to the presenter for anything above a certain amount. This practice may help the budget, but it will certainly discourage some presenters from using AV equipment. Exhibitors sometimes provide equipment at no charge—just for the publicity.

Most conferences use some AV equipment, and sponsors have to consider factors that affect this budget item. A sponsor that offers numerous conferences might find it more economical to purchase some frequently used AV equipment, such as overhead projectors (though an amount would still be budgeted in order to amortize the equipment over several conferences). A sponsor can easily use its own AV equipment when a conference is held in the sponsor's home city. When the conference is located in a different city, it may be more economical and safer to rent the equipment in the site city rather than paying for shipping and possibly for damage or loss.

Companion Program

All costs of the companion program should be entered here as an expense. See Chapter Eleven for a detailed discussion of companions.

Computer Services

If the sponsor has a computer within the organization, the computer cost may be absorbed as general overhead. Many organizations charge out computer use to those who actually use it; since the computer can keep an accurate time record of users, it is very easy to assess those charges. If outside computer service is needed, it can be listed under this heading or under "Contract Services" below. The Resources section at the end of this book lists some software packages available for conference planning applications.

Contract Services

This is a broad category, but the items listed under it must be specific. If AV or computer equipment is rented, it could appear under this item or under the specific type of equipment. Whatever the decision, the designation of expenses must be consistent.

Entertainment

The possibilities for entertainment are numerous and are discussed in Chapter Fifteen. Once the entertainment is determined, its cost should be entered here. See Chapter Fifteen for thorough coverage of conference entertainment.

Exhibition

This item should reflect the direct expenses attributable to the exhibits. The site may charge for the exhibit space, but the conference budget may have to absorb the cost for some of the draping, drayage, signs, and similar expenses. Of course, the intent is to recover that cost, and more, through charges to the exhibitors.

Frequently, a special book listing all the exhibitors, their personnel, and their products is developed and is distributed during the conference. The cost may be offset by ads or may be included as part of the booth cost. The expense of producing the publication should be listed in this part of the budget.

Equipment

Like contract services, this is a broad category, but the items, such as AV, computer, and exhibit-related equipment, must be very specific and be listed in only one place in the budget.

Field Trips

If the design calls for a field trip, not sightseeing, but an organized trip to visit a conference-related place, the transportation part of the expense will probably be reflected under that item in the budget, but such field-trip expenses as fees and meals should be included here.

Gratuities

Gratuities are difficult to budget because policies vary so much among nations, sites, and people. The word *tip* is considered the acronym for "to ensure performance" or "to ensure promptness." The term *gratuity* means the same but connotes that it is given afterward to reward performance. A good source on tipping is Schein, Jablonski, and Wohlfahrt (1984).

Outside the United States, tipping seems easier but really is not. The International Federation of Women's Travel Organizations has produced a valuable little pocket guide on the subject (available through Carolyn J. Yarborough, 7432 Caminito Carlotta, San Diego, CA 92120). In many countries, about 15 percent is included in restaurant and hotel bills; the customer has no decision on whether to tip, regardless of the quality of the service. In some countries, however, the gratuity does not even go to those who provided the service, and it is customary, on receiving change after paying a bill to leave coins or small paper money on the tray. How much to tip, even in the United States, always presents a quandary. For conference purposes, sometimes it is a percentage of the total bill, while at other times it may be on a per capita basis. The tip may be related to the time required for the performance or just related to local custom, although there may be the need for a gratuity if extra or complex service is required.

Tipping in the United States conforms to some general guidelines, but these are only guidelines; the coordinator should explore the situation to determine a budget amount. For hotel rooms, 15 percent of the total bill is the guiding factor, but some prefer to use the room cost before taxes are added as the basis for the 15 percent. It is advisable to clarify the amount of gratuities during negotiations. The questions to ask are: Is a charge added to the bill for service, or are gratuities voluntary? Are additional gifts or gratuities expected?

The gratuity can be given to a variety of individuals (as shown in Figure 46) and others who might be included in a particular situation. Some gratuities might appear under this item of the budget or added to another element (for example, gratuities for chambermaids might be included in the site budget).

When and to whom to give gratuities can also be a delicate issue. If the gratuity is not added to the bill, should it be given to each individual or to one individual for distribution to the others? Some contend that the tip should be given before the conference starts to *ensure* performance; others take the stance that it should be given after the conference ends to *reward* performance. Still others opt for giving part of the gratuity before and part after, if performance warrants. The frequency of contact between the coordinator or sponsor and the particular individuals who might receive gratuities is an important factor to consider. At a one-time affair, there is certainly less pressure regarding gratuities than if there are to be repeat conferences, where the same people on the list in Figure 46 will again be asked to provide service.

Ground Transportation

This can be a major budget item, particularly if several hotels are being used in conjunction with a convention site (see Chapter Fourteen).

Hospitality Suite

Hospitality suites are usually located in a hotel, but they may also be set up in a conference site. Negotiations for a hospitality suite should be conducted at the same time as site negotiations. The purpose of a hospitality suite is to extend special hospitality to selected participants, presenters, local dignitaries, and the press. As food and drinks are usually provided, funds for this should be included in this item. The coordinator and the site must also agree on those authorized to order amenities for this suite.

For a membership sponsor conference, it is usually expected that the president of the organization will have a special suite. If it is large enough,

Figure 46. Possible Recipients of Gratuities.

Airport luggage handlers	Guides
Bartenders	Maitre d'
Captain—food and beverage service	Porters
Catering manager	Room service
Chambermaids	Sommeliers (wine stewards)
Checkroom	Sports pros
Chef	Telephone operators
Chief housekeeper	Transportation
Clerical workers	Drivers—bus, taxi, limousine
Door people and bell people	Starters—dispatchers
Front desk	Waiters and waitresses at meal functions
Food and beverage manager	

SOURCE: *The Comprehensive Guide to Successful Conferences and Meetings* by Leonard Nadler and Zeace Nadler. San Francisco: Jossey-Bass. Copyright © 1987. Permission to reproduce hereby granted.

this can become the official hospitality suite. (Scheduling for this suite should be controlled by the secretariat in order to avoid double bookings or other embarrassments.) The employer sponsor hospitality suite is usually under the auspices of the highest ranking officer present. Public seminar sponsors may make similar arrangements, but they will generally be more restrictive.

Interpreters and Translators

These two terms are sometimes used interchangeably and therefore incorrectly. Interpreters provide oral meaning; translators deal with the written word. Either talent may be required for a conference, but note that an individual may be an excellent translator and yet not be able to function as an interpreter. Generally, most interpreters can also do translation. For an international conference, this expense is almost mandatory. In Example B (see Chapter Three) the general sessions were provided in English but were simultaneously translated into Spanish, even though the conference was held in the United States. Interpreters work very hard under constant pressure and can be very expensive. Generally, at least two interpreters are required each time the service is necessary. They work twenty minutes on and twenty minutes off. Unless the site has appropriate physical facilities, interpreting equipment must be budgeted, particularly when simultaneous interpreting is used.

On-Site Personnel

Local personnel are sometimes used at the site for registration, the exhibition, or special functions. As indicated earlier, it is probably best to contract for these people rather than to employ them directly. The site personnel or the LCVB should be able to advise on local contractors who can provide such personnel.

Participant Supplies

Many kinds of supplies can be provided for participants, ranging from small manila folders to elaborate attache cases. The expense for some of the items may be offset by contributions of money, products, or services from exhibitors or from other interested parties.

The most important item is the participant book (see Chapter Eighteen), which can be part of the participant's packet or distributed separately.

Badges, a necessity for almost any conference, can be very inexpensive or a significant budget item (see Chapter Seventeen).

Participant packets can also include amenities, such as writing implements and paper imprinted with the conference's message. Evaluation forms might also be included in the packet, though opinions differ on the effectiveness of this practice (see Chapter Nineteen).

The LCVB can usually provide maps and other material about the local area, such as lists of restaurants, recreational areas, and historical sites. The coordinator may also wish to include headache tablets, a sewing kit, and similar amenities.

Presenters

Each conference usually establishes policies on the expenses to be absorbed by the sponsor and by the presenters. Generally, keynote speakers receive full reimbursement of all expenses in addition to the honorarium. Resource people may receive only air fare, accommodations, or just a free registration. (Some membership sponsors require presenters to register and pay the regular fee!)

Accommodation expenses must be carefully defined for the particular conference and each presenter. The item can include room, meals, liquor, laundry, telephone, and other related charges.

Travel expenses must also be made explicit, including such items as class of travel, layovers, and the type of ground transportation at both ends of the flight.

The down payments of presenter honoraria and fees are listed under fixed expenses; the remainder should appear here.

Participant packets are commonly given to presenters. If only a few are involved, the cost can be absorbed under Participant Supplies above. If many presenters need packets, the cost can be significant and should be charged under this heading.

Printing and Reproduction

This expense appears under Fixed Expenses above, but some additional items, such as a daily conference newsletter, may be required after the conference starts. Many copiers are adequate for these purposes, but if more than 1,000 participants attend, alternative means of reproduction might be required.

Prizes, Awards, and Mementos

At many conferences, participants receive some kind of recognition (as has been discussed earlier). An employer sponsor may award prizes for outstanding sales or performance. A membership sponsor might present the outgoing officers with such awards as gavels, certificates, plaques, and gift coupons. Participants at a for-profit public seminar sponsor conference expect to receive certificates.

Sponsors frequently give all participants mementos of the conference. The host facility sometimes provides these items at no cost, depending on the size of the conference and the income that can accrue to the host facility.

Public Relations

Costs must be estimated here for this extremely important activity. For a thorough discussion, see Chapter Thirteen.

Secretariat

Costs related to the on-site functioning of the secretariat include various supply items (as discussed in previous chapters). In addition, members of the secretariat can be expected to be present at some meal functions and at other events. These event expenses can be charged to the specific event (such as a banquet) or under this heading.

Security

The cost for this item can vary greatly. If VIPs are involved, the cost of security can be quite high, though the site may have sufficient security personnel and include this expense as part of the total site cost.

Shipping

This item includes shipping materials and equipment to the site before the conference and back to the sponsor or coordinator at the end of the conference.

Sightseeing

Recreational sightseeing should not be confused with the Field Trip item above, which is part of the purpose of the conference. Sightseeing is considered an expense only if it is included in the fee. If the participants are free to make their own sightseeing arrangements, this item need not be considered.

Signs

Signs and banners are important for conducting an effective conference. Some sites provide a minimal number of conference signs at no cost, while others charge for any conference signs provided. (Signs within the exhibition hall are usually charged as an exhibition expense.) Examples of signs for which expenses should be listed include banners displaying the name of the conference; signs outside presentation rooms; directional signs to indicate the location of special rooms (such as the common room or presenters' ready room), the registration area, or other significant locations; and table signs for luncheons and other meal functions.

Site

If the participants make their own arrangements for accommodations, the sleeping room item may not be a large amount, though it will have been a factor in negotiations. The amount entered here should represent only what the coordinator is responsible for paying through the master account. An employer sponsor budget might show the charge for all the participants here, and likewise with a public seminar sponsor, if the conference price includes accommodations. The cost for the coordinator, secretariat, and presenters could appear here or under other relevant items in the budget.

There may not be any cost for meeting rooms, depending on negotiations. If there is a cost, it would appear under this item of the budget.

Food and beverage can be a very difficult item to negotiate; some of the considerations are found in Chapter Nine. A worksheet for these expenses is presented in Figure 47. The entries here are the results of negotiations. Note the guarantee item: Although this item is usually negotiated at an early stage, it might have to be changed as the conference date approaches. Indeed, in some situations it may have to be changed as late as twenty-four hours before the event.

The cost of any special functions, particularly a banquet, should also be listed here. In addition to food, it would include such items as decorations and other special requirements for that particular function. Chapter Three describes some examples of special functions: Example A, Event 16 (reception); Example B, Event 19 (reception); Example C, Event 5 (regional socials); and Example D, Event 12 (beer and conversation).

Steering Committee

The cost of refreshments for steering committee meetings (see Chapter Twenty) should be listed here. Depending on when and where they meet, this item could be included as part of the hospitality suite.

Evaluation

Evaluation costs money, and the exact amount can only be determined after the evaluation has been designed as discussed in Chapter Nineteen. The coordinator may choose to have the evaluation designed by external resources, and the charge would be negotiated. In addition, there may be the cost for printing instruments, training interviewers, or other factors as determined by the evaluation design.

It is important that provision be made for funds for the necessary meetings, reproduction, or any other items concerned with using the evaluation results.

Figure 47. Food and Beverage Expenses.

Day 1

Breakfast (Event _____)

    Type: _____

    Guarantee × cost = $ _____

Morning break (Event _____)

    Type: _____

    Guarantee × cost =   _____

Lunch (Event _____)

    Type: _____

    Guarantee × cost =   _____

Afternoon break (Event _____)

    Type: _____

    Guarantee × cost =   _____

Dinner (Event _____)

    Type: _____

    Guarantee × cost =   _____

Reception (Event _____)

    Type: _____

    Guarantee × cost =   _____

        Total for Day 1 $ _____

Day 2

Repeat above for each day of the conference.

    TOTAL FOOD AND BEVERAGE $ _____

SOURCE: *The Comprehensive Guide to Successful Conferences and Meetings* by Leonard Nadler and Zeace Nadler. San Francisco: Jossey-Bass. Copyright © 1987. Permission to reproduce hereby granted.

Follow-Up

There is always some kind of follow-up after a conference, as discussed in Chapter Nineteen. It may only be a meeting of the design committee or it could be something more elaborate. Some funds will be necessary for this activity.

The follow-up of one conference may also be the first planning meeting for the next conference. It becomes important, therefore, for a decision to be made as to which conference budget will be charged for the expense.

Budget Summary

The last variable item is miscellaneous or what is sometimes called the fudge factor—an important item whenever high inflation causes costs to soar significantly from the time the budget is approved until the conference is held. A certain percentage of total expenses, usually from 3 to 10 percent, should be added here.

The bottom line (net income) can be stated in many ways. An employer sponsor or a nonprofit public seminar sponsor might wish that figure to be $0.00. A membership sponsor generally views conferences as a source of income (though, for tax purposes, profit may be termed "surplus" or "excess of income over expense"). A for-profit public seminar sponsor would expect the bottom line to show a profit; sometimes such a sponsor will state the necessary percentage of net income based on either gross income or expenses. The coordinator must be aware of what is required by the sponsor.

Chapter 17

———◆·◆·◆———

The Registration Process

CHECKLIST FOR REGISTRATION

The Form

_____ Who has responsibility for developing the registration form?

_____ What information will be requested on the form?

Preregistration

_____ Have the dates for the various stages of preregistration been firmly established?

_____ Will confirmations be sent to preregistered participants?

_____ If a computer was used for preregistration, will the data be available at the conference?

_____ Will exhibitors be provided with a preregistration mailing list?

Registration Procedures

_____ Have the location and availability of the registration area been determined?

_____ Will signs indicate the location of the registration area?

_____ Has traffic flow in the registration area been checked?

_____ Will separate lines be provided for preregistered participants?

_____ Can adequate writing space be provided?

_____ Will writing implements be available?

_____ Is the registration area sufficiently ventilated?

_____ Will the lighting be adequate for staff and participants?

_____ Will there be other traffic in the area?

_____ Does the secretariat have a sufficient supply of all registration forms?

_____ Will a computer be used during registration?

_____ Where will registration materials and equipment be stored when not in use?

_____ Will registration personnel need to communicate rapidly with other conference personnel?

Registration Desk

_____ Who will be in charge of the registration desk?

_____ Have participant packets been prepared?

_____ What kind of badges will be provided?

_____ What will be on the badges?

_____ When will badges be made available?

_____ Have special provisions been made for group registrations?

_____ Where will the bulletin board be placed?

_____ Will tickets be sold for special events?

Service and Information Desk

_____ Is a service desk needed?

_____ How will preregistrants' problems be handled?

_____ What action should be taken when the secretariat has no record of advance registration?

_____ Will preregistrants whose checks have not yet cleared be admitted to the conference?

_____ Will service desk personnel be able to provide information about the conference?

_____ Will desk personnel be able to provide information about the sponsor?

_____ Can membership status be verified?

_____ Can dues be collected at this conference?

_____ Are publications available for sale?

_____ Will lost badges or function tickets be replaced?

_____ What is the policy about on-site requests for press and other special-privilege passes?

_____ How should unauthorized people be handled?

Personal Needs of Participants

_____ Will lodging information be available?

_____ Will the conference offer special hospitality?

_____ Can tours and sightseeing be arranged?

_____ Will the conference provide shopping services?

_____ Will interpreters be needed?

Financial Aspects

_____ Who will be in charge of financial activities?

_____ Who will be responsible for the cash count?

_____ What kinds of checks will be accepted?

_____ Which credit cards will be accepted?

_____ Will purchase orders be accepted?

_____ Is it acceptable to bill a company or an organization?

_____ Have a refund policy and procedure been established?

_____ Can participants pay for individual events?

Staffing

_____ Will volunteers, paid help, or a combination of both be used?

_____ Which types of personnel are needed?

_____ Who will supervise the registration staff?

_____ Has a staffing schedule been developed?

_____ Will the registration staff be trained?

_____ Will the staff engage in an operational dry run?

_____ Will the staff have a policy manual?

Supplies and Services

_____ What is the condition of the site telephone equipment?

_____ What supplies and equipment will be needed?

SOURCE: *The Comprehensive Guide to Successful Conferences and Meetings* by Leonard Nadler and Zeace Nadler. San Francisco: Jossey-Bass. Copyright © 1987. Permission to reproduce hereby granted.

Registration is frequently the first person-to-person contact between the participant and one of the conference personnel. The way registration is handled sets the climate for the conference. It communicates the concern, or lack of it, by the sponsor and conference staff for the participants. If handled well, it becomes a signal to the participants that the conference has been well designed and implemented.

Registration Forms

The forms used for registration should be carefully developed. The composition of the forms depends on the participants and the amount of data needed.

The major purpose of the form should be conference registration. This may seem obvious, but too many forms are used to obtain other information. The attitude of some sponsors and coordinators seems to be that "As long as we are paying for this mailing, let us see what other information we can get." The essentials should be agreed on, and the form designed to gather only that information.

The registration form must also serve participants' needs by providing such information as dates, costs, and related activities. Many participants need this information to obtain approval for funds and time to attend the conference, so the form must be clear on these data. Questions to elicit other information should be kept to a minimum; no one likes to answer unnecessary questions.

The material aspects of the form must be carefully considered. Although expensive, a form with carbonized paper provides the participant with an exact copy of the registration form. The spaces for participants' responses are typically in the form of boxes, which are helpful when the information is to be transcribed onto a computer or used for compiling mailing lists and making name badges.

The Checklist

The Form

Who Has Responsibility for Developing the Registration Form?

Although final responsibility rests with the coordinator, form development can be assigned to the secretariat for that unit must process the forms. An experienced secretariat knows what worked and what did not work in the past.

What Information Will Be Requested on the Form?

A new form should be developed for each conference. Forms from the sponsor's previous conferences can be used as a basis for the current form, but each conference has unique elements that must be reflected on the form. The heading should provide the basic information: name of the conference or sponsor, dates, theme, and venue. The logo of the particular conference should be prominently displayed. A typical registration form is presented in Figure 48.

The space requesting the registrant's name can be complicated. The last name is usually requested first. This usually does not present any problems, but even in the United States we now have so many different minority groups, that the words *last* and *first* may not adequately cover the situation. Some married women prefer to use a hyphenated name that includes their unmarried name and the husband's family name, though there is a lack of agreement as to the order. If Mary Smith marries James Jones, is she Mary Smith-Jones or Mary Jones-Smith?

International participants attending a conference held in the United States can complicate things further. "Last name" in the United States usually means family name, but in many nations "family name" has a different meaning. Take the name "Rahim bin Hassan," a typical name in Moslem countries. The "bin" means "son of," so Rahim is the participant's name but Hassan is his father's first name, not the family name. To accommodate U.S. procedures, the individual might enter "Hassan, Rahim," which may satisfy the form requirements but can be a problem in receiving mail in his home country. In addition, some participants in international meetings resent the imposition of U.S. or Western culture onto their own.

Another example is from some Spanish speaking countries. Take the case of Isabel Arape who is married to Julio Cuevas. Her married name can be either Isabel Arape Cuevas or Isabel Arape de Cuevas. The "de" is the old traditional form, still used by some, that says that she belongs to Cuevas. Feminists might object to this, but that is the custom in most Spanish-speaking countries. How should she complete the name block?

An employer sponsor might like to know the position of a registrant, but since this information is readily available from company files, why ask it?

Figure 48. Information Requested in a Typical Registration Form.

Name: _____
                    (last)   (first)

Title: _____

Address: _____
                    (department, division, or unit)

         _____
                    (organization)

         _____
                    (street or P.O. box)

         _____
                    (city)   (state)   (zip code)

Telephone (home): _____

Telephone (business): _____ (ext) _____

Name (for name badge): _____

Fees

Advance Registration (must be postmarked by [date]):

    Member (rate): Membership No. _____ $ _____

    Nonmember (rate):   _____

    Companion (rate):   _____

    Special events (with rates):

        Preconference workshops   _____

        Tours, sightseeing   _____

        Banquet   _____

        Total Advance Registration $ _____

(Cancellation Policy)

On-Site Registration:

    Member (rate): Membership No. _____ $ _____

    Nonmember (rate):   _____

    Companion (rate):   _____

Figure 48. Information Requested in a Typical Registration Form, Cont'd.

Daily (rate):   _____

Special events (with rates):

    Preconference workshops   _____

    Tours, sightseeing   _____

    Banquet   _____

    Total On-Site Registration $ _____

Method of Payment:

_____ Check (personal or company)

_____ Purchase order (government or company)

_____ Credit card

Checks and purchase orders should be drawn to: _____

_____

Please answer the following:

1. Have you previously attended one of our conferences?   Yes _____   No _____

2. How did you learn of this conference?

    mailing _____   colleague _____

    advertisement _____

       (which publication? _____)

    other (please describe): _____

3. Are you volunteering to attend this conference, or are you being sent by your organization?

    Volunteer _____   Sent _____

    If you checked "sent," who sent you?

4. Which sessions do you plan to attend?

    (provide list of concurrent and breakout sessions, also any other events for which this information would be helpful)

SOURCE: *The Comprehensive Guide to Successful Conferences and Meetings* by Leonard Nadler and Zeace Nadler. San Francisco: Jossey-Bass. Copyright © 1987. Permission to reproduce hereby granted.

A membership sponsor, particularly a social or civic organization, would probably not need this information.

The level of detail needed for the address response—business, home, mailing address—should be determined. A mailing address is essential to acknowledge preregistrations. For on-site registration, the address may be needed to produce a participant roster or mailing labels for the exhibitors. A membership sponsor may want to use the registration form to up-date its records; if so, the address request should conform to previous forms.

The detail required, such as department, division, and organization, should also relate to purpose. Figure 48 makes provision for a five-digit zip code, but the new nine-digit codes might reduce the cost of some mailings. A public seminar sponsor might want very specific and correct address information in order to build a mailing list for future conferences or for other marketing activities.

Telephone numbers can be helpful to contact a participant if the registration form is incorrectly or incompletely filled out or if a problem arises with the participant's payment.

Name badges are extremely important. Some participants do not want their first name on their badges for various personal or organizational reasons. Rather than guess, ask the question. Space might be left for people to hand print what they wish above the printed material on the badge, and in this case, the item would not appear on the registration form.

The fees section is very important for it not only specifies how much must be paid but also provides some idea of the various events at the conference. Wherever "rate" is noted, the specific amount for that item should be stated. Note that the form provides for both preregistration and on-site registration, though it is possible to use two separate forms.

For a membership sponsor, member number is important. Note that the membership sponsor usually has a separate nonmember rate; some sponsors set the rate so that it is financially beneficial to become a member at the time of the national conference. A special companion rate may also be offered (see Chapter Eleven).

All special events should be included in the regular conference fee, but when that is not possible, the events should be listed with the rates. The description of those events should appear in the marketing material that accompanies the preregistration forms. If tours and sightseeing are being handled by an outside contractor, they are not included on the form if payment goes directly to that contractor rather than through the secretariat.

Preregistration forms should always state the sponsor's cancellation policy. It can range from no refund to total refund, and the amounts, conditions, and dates should be clearly stated on the form.

It is important to mention acceptable methods of payment for both preregistration and on-site registration. If the sponsor does not accept purchase orders or credit cards, that policy should appear on the form.

In Figure 48, the second part of the form contains some questions that the coordinator should consider carefully before using. Some might provoke negative feelings or slow down on-site registration. If the information is necessary, an alternative is to place a questionnaire in participant packets, to be returned at a later time, with the expectation of receiving less than total response.

Question 4, "Which sessions do you plan to attend?" might be asked, particularly in preregistration, to get some feel for which sessions might be more popular than others. That information can be useful in making room assignments and provides some feedback on how participants view the relevancy and importance of some of the sessions.

Preregistration

Have the Dates for the Various Stages of Preregistration Been Firmly Established?

A preregistration cutoff date needs to be established. (Two dates may be established, but more than two would probably not be advantageous.) Preregistration has several purposes, one of which is to encourage participants to register early. This is done through a two-tier fee schedule, with financial benefits available to those who register early. Preregistration also provides some indication of the number of participants to be expected at the conference.

A membership sponsor conference coordinator can check the current preregistration count against a similar count for a previous conference and make some predictions about registration figures. That information allows for some fine-tuning of plans for hotel rooms, function rooms, and probable attendance at events.

An employer sponsor may use preregistration so that participants do not have to take time to register when arriving at the site. Generally, all of the participants of an employer sponsor can be preregistered, and the secretariat can make arrangements for transportation and lodging and prepare the materials necessary for the conference. A public seminar sponsor usually prefers preregistration in order to know what other arrangements might be required, such as scholarships. For a for-profit public seminar sponsor, preregistration provides data on the probable financial effects.

The opening date for preregistration is the date the preregistration forms are available. The other important date is, when does it close? When there is a two-tier registration fee, the first tier must close on a specific date. The usual terminology is "preregistration forms must be postmarked no later than _____ ." When international participants are expected, the date should be realistic and based on actual receipt by the secretariat rather than a postmark.

Will Confirmations Be Sent to Preregistered Participants?

Every preregistration should be acknowledged with a letter. Receipt of the preregistration sometimes triggers other activities, such as sending preconference materials for participants to read before coming to the conference. If the request for hotel reservations was not included in the preregistration material, it should be sent with the acknowledgment.

Participants should be urged to verify the acknowledgment and to notify the secretariat immediately if it contains any error. If they have signed up for a special event, such as a reception, the confirmation should verify that information. Despite such an admonition, some participants will wait until they arrive at the conference to contend that the acknowledgment was incorrect.

If a Computer Was Used for Preregistration, Will the Data Be Available at the Conference?

There are computer programs, and more are emerging, that can be very helpful in processing preregistrations. This computer data will be needed during on-site registration.

Will Exhibitors Be Provided with a Preregistration Mailing List?

The sponsor frequently offers exhibitors a list of preregistered participants (see Chapter Ten). If that is the case, the secretariat must follow through to be sure that such a list is available and sent to the exhibitors.

As preregistration usually takes place over a long period of time, a date should be established when the secretariat will send that list to exhibitors. It must be close enough to the opening of the conference to include all preregistered participants, but far enough away that exhibitors' mailings arrive before participants leave for the conference.

Registration Procedures

Have the Location and Availability of the Registration Area Been Determined?

The location of the registration area should be determined during site negotiations but the coordinator should recheck those arrangements at least a week before the conference is to open. The original agreement may have been altered by a change in site personnel, construction changes, or another conference occupying the same site either just prior to or during the conference. These problems arise infrequently, but when they do arise they must be dealt with immediately; the day of registration or one day before registration may be too late to deal with the problem. In a hotel, the registration area is often a public area that must be blocked off and appropriately set up. All areas near the registration area should be checked; a change in the traffic pattern on another part of the floor can still affect the registration area.

Will Signs Indicate the Location of the Registration Area?

For most participants, this is their first physical contact with the conference. Signs that make it easy for participants to find and reach the registration area help set a positive climate for the conference. A hotel usually has a main entrance, and it is fairly easy to place signs there. If most of the participants are staying in the same hotel, signs for the registration area can be placed at the hotel registration desk. Hotel personnel sometimes prefer to place the sign on the signboard that lists the functions in the hotel for that day. That is good, but not enough. Many participants do not search for the hotel signboard; they look for a sign that tells them where to register for their conference. Most hotels are very cooperative on this point. Convention centers with many entrances should have signs at each entrance to direct the participants to the registration area.

Has Traffic Flow in the Registration Area Been Checked?

The registration area should be marked with clear directions and clearly identified registration lines. Participants should not have to wander around trying to find the correct line. Several members of the secretariat, clearly identified by large badges (or buttons with the words "Ask me" or "Can I help you?") might monitor the registration area, providing participants with forms, answering questions, and generally making the participants as comfortable as possible through a necessary, but sometimes tedious activity.

Registration at a small conference may not be a problem. For some employer sponsor conferences, conference registration and hotel registration can be combined so that participants receive their room key, hotel material, and participant packet in one place. A large conference, however, must consider traffic flow. If many participants are expected to register at the same time, separate stations and lines can be set up, according to the last name of the participant. Preregistration can help determine how to divide the alphabetical lines, and stations can be assigned accordingly. For a large on-site registration, the coordinator can only guess.

With the familiar bull pen technique used in banks and airports, all participants enter a single line and then go to a registration station as it becomes available. In this way, participants are not penalized just because the last names of many other participants happen to start with the same letter.

The registration procedure is easiest when all participants receive the same participant packets. Personalized packets can be filed behind the registration desk in alphabetical order, or just the personalized material, such as badges and function tickets, can be placed in envelopes and filed in alphabetical order. When the participant registers, the secretariat person combines the personal envelope with the "generic" packet.

Will Separate Lines Be Provided for Preregistered Participants?

Although it is possible to use the same lines for both preregistered participants and on-site registrants for some small conferences, separate lines generally work better. Separate lines communicate that preregistrants are handled more rapidly than the others and so encourage more participants to preregister the next time. Preregistered participants can be handled very quickly. The name badges have already been prepared; the participant merely has to present the preregistration acknowledgment, receive the appropriate packet, and is free to leave the registration area.

Can Adequate Writing Space Be Provided?

On-site registration usually requires the participant to fill out a form. This should be done not at the registration desk but at another place in the area where stand-up tables are available. (Stand-up tables avoid the need for chairs, which clutter the area.) The tables should be placed in the general registration area but far enough away from the lines so they do not interfere with the registration operation.

Will Writing Implements Be Available?

Carbonized on-site registration forms should be filled out with ballpoint pens, which should be kept attached by a chain or cord to the writing table. Secretariat staff should monitor the area frequently to ensure that the pens are still there and are working.

Is the Registration Area Sufficiently Ventilated?

Adequate ventilation ensures the comfort of the participants, who are in the area only a short time, and members of the secretariat, who are working in the area the entire registration time. Insufficient ventilation can lower secretariat efficiency and result in costly errors or less than courteous service to participants. If the building's ventilation system is not adequate, strategically placed fans can help to circulate the air. In addition, a break schedule can be planned so that no member of the secretariat is confined to poorly ventilated areas for more than a reasonable amount of time (probably thirty minutes).

Ventilation is particularly important in winter in the northern United States, when registering participants wear heavy clothing and might have to wait on registration lines. During the registration procedure, participants generally wear their outer garments and get increasingly uncomfortable. If this is a problem, a temporary checkroom can be established in the area.

Will the Lighting Be Adequate for Staff and Participants?

Sufficient illumination is important for participants to fill out the registration forms and for the secretariat to read the forms, handle cash, and read any other documents the participants may present at registration.

Some conference centers have specific registration areas that have sufficient lighting. Other conference centers merely provide space that has some form of fixed lighting, which may have to be supplemented. Even though the coordinator should have checked this out during negotiations, the registration location may have been changed, so lighting should be checked again prior to setting up the registration area.

Few hotels have regular registration areas for conferences, which means that lighting can be a significant factor and should be examined thoroughly.

Will There Be Other Traffic in the Area?

For a small conference held in a hotel, with the registration area off to one side of the main lobby, the traffic created by other hotel guests is of little or no consequence. If the registration area has been set up in or near a restaurant, lounge, or similar public area, the traffic can be a problem. For a large conference held in a conference center, traffic only presents a problem if other activities are going on in the center at the same time.

Does the Secretariat Have a Sufficient Supply of All Registration Forms?

When all the participants are preregistered, forms are not a problem, but if any participants are registering on-site, careful attention must be paid to this question. Even when on-site registration forms are sent out with mailings, the secretariat should operate on the premise that no participants will bring those forms with them.

In addition, the participants might also need forms for special events, questionnaires, or other printed information. The forms and materials not placed in the participants' packets should be readily available at the registration area.

Will a Computer Be Used During Registration?

A computer is useful for storing and retrieving preregistration and on-site registration data for many such purposes as name badges, participant lists, and anticipated session attendance figures. On-site, at least two members of the secretariat should be completely familiar with both the hardware and the software. In addition, many computer consultants advise having a back-up system, an option that the coordinator should investigate.

A computer may need a dedicated electrical line, that is, nothing else on that line but the computer. When a nondedicated line is used, it should be checked to determine the other equipment served by that line. Other electrical equipment on the same line can cause temporary surges that may damage a computer or cause a loss of data. The on-site computer may be stand alone or be connected to a mainframe at the sponsor's site through a modem and dedicated phone line.

Badges, lists of participants, and other computer outputs require printers, which should be checked and backed-up at the site as early as possible.

Where Will Registration Materials and Equipment Be Stored When Not in Use?

Storage is a minimal problem for one-day registration periods, but when registration continues over many days, materials and equipment must be stored. Arrangements must be made for a locked storage room near the registration area and for transporting equipment (by bell people, dollies, or carts, as necessary).

*Will Registration Personnel Need to Communicate
Rapidly with Other Conference Personnel?*

Although the secretariat members at the registration area should be able to
handle almost all situations, they might need the assistance of the coordinator
or a specific member of the secretariat who is not in the area. They must have
a way to communicate rapidly by telephone, paging system, or walkie-talkie.

Registration Desk

Although the word *desk* is used, it might in fact be an entire area composed
of many desks.

Who Will Be in Charge of the Registration Desk?

One person should be in charge of the registration desk. It may not always be
the same person because of the need for breaks and meals, unless registration
is limited to a short period of time, say two hours. When the registration period
is longer, at least one substitute is required. The important point is that one
person who can make decisions should be at the desk at all times.

Have Participant Packets Been Prepared?

The participant packets should be prepared before registration opens
regardless of the number of participants and the size of the packets. Assembling
the packets after registration opens puts a great deal of pressure on the
secretariat and increases the possibility of errors.

Some of the items to insert in the packet include a welcoming note from
the sponsor, the participant book, exhibition book, pad, writing implement,
evaluation forms, area maps, badge, and function tickets.

What Kind of Badges Will Be Provided?

Several options are available, depending on the needs and budget of the
conference. The stick-on badge has an adhesive backing that can be affixed to
almost anything. The badges can be blank or printed with the conference or
sponsor logo or another message, such as "Hello" or "I am _____ ." These
badges are relatively inexpensive, but they can damage ultrasuede, leather, and
some other fabrics. The badges generally do not adhere for more than part of
a day and so are not suitable for a multiday conference.

The pin-on badge has a clear plastic holder into which a paper card can
be inserted. The cards can be preprinted or filled out by the participants at
registration time. When purchasing pin-on badges, it is important to check on
the plastic holders, some of which tend to separate, causing the participant to
lose the card, and the size and quality of the pin and how it is attached to the
plastic. Some pins separate easily from the plastic and result in lost badges;
other pins are so small that they cannot penetrate some fabrics, such as wool
suits.

An alternative are badges with neck cords attached to the plastic holders. The cord can be made of a variety of materials, including twine, plastic, and metal.

Clip-on badges use bulldog clips that are permanently affixed to the plastic holder with a rivet. The clips should be able to rotate so that the badge can be clipped from the top or side.

Badges can be encased in slip-in plastic folders that are designed to slide into the breast pocket, held in place by a plastic lip that prevents the plastic from slipping down into the pocket. The folder can also contain a pouch or pocket for a daily program, a useful feature for a program of several days' duration.

Permanent badges are seldom used for conferences, but they are available in laminated or heat-sealed plastic and can be used with all of the attaching devices described above.

What Will Be on the Badges?

At most conferences, badges are an extremely important item: They help participants identify each other and help the conference staff with security. Badges may not be necessary for a small employer sponsor conference, however, where participants can be expected to know each other. At an employer sponsor conference, where the participants come from different parts of the organization, the coordinator should verify that the participants do indeed know each other. It is not unusual in large organizations to find that people have passed each other in the hall, sat at meetings together, and seen each other in the snack bar or cafeteria without really knowing even the exact name and title of the other person.

For most conferences, printed badges are essential and the print on the badge should be clear and readable from a reasonable distance (at least eighteen inches). The type on the badge should be large and stand out clearly from the background color of the label. In general, large bulletin typewriters can meet most of this problem but not all. Well-done, hand-lettered badges can alleviate this problem when there are not too many badges to be prepared.

Badges vary in size, and the amount of print on the badge must fit the available space. The participant's name, correctly spelled, is the most crucial information. To ensure correct spelling, the sample registration form shown in Figure 48 requests the participants to print or type the letters and also asks them if they want a different name on the badge.

The badge might also display a company name. When all participants are employed by the same company, this would be redundant and the same might apply to the participant's title, though the company location, division, or unit might be clearly noted on the badge. A membership sponsor might include this information or give the home state of the participant or the unit of the sponsor to which the participant belongs.

Badges can be color coded in many ways to show the different categories of participants. Some possibilities are shown below.

- White—regular participant (no distinction between preregistered and on-site)
- Red—officer or official of the sponsor
- Blue—companion
- Green—one-day participant (with a different color for each day). A newly developed badge slowly changes color through the day, so that by the end of the day it has faded or changed to another color that is considered ineligible for other days' conference activities.
- Yellow—presenter
- Orange—exhibitor
- Purple—award winner
- Colored border—secretariat, coordinator, staff

    To reduce the number of colors needed and the cost of printing many different colors, white badges can be used with different-colored ribbons, patches, or stripes that denote the categories.

    Colored badges can also be used for other purposes. In Example A—One-Day Conference (Chapter Three), the badges might indicate the particular workshops to which participants have been assigned. This might also be accomplished by using the same colored badge for all but putting a workshop group number on badges.

When Will Badges Be Made Available?

Generally, badges should be given to participants on-site at registration rather than sent to participants with the preregistration acknowledgment, mainly because some of the preregistered participants may forget to bring them to the conference. Badges for preregistered participants should be prepared before registration opens and should be filed alphabetically, or placed in participant packets that are filed alphabetically. Badges for on-site and daily registration, of course, must be prepared at registration time.

Have Special Provisions Been Made for Group Registrations?

Group registrations occur when a conference establishes a special rate for two or more participants from the same organization or when international participants travel to the conference as a group with an interpreter. In these situations, one person may be allowed to register for the group and a special station provided.

Where Will the Bulletin Board Be Placed?

The central conference bulletin board containing announcements about registration or changes in the conference schedule (not a message board for individual messages) should be located in the registration area. Since the participant book was printed before registration began, many changes are possible, such as sessions added or dropped, room changes, time changes, and information on special events. The secretariat should carefully prepare the bulletin board to provide that information and should monitor the board frequently to remove any unauthorized announcements and to be sure that the announcements on the board are up-to-date and correct.

Will Tickets Be Sold for Special Events?

Special events (banquets, field trips, tours) may require special tickets and additional payment. If these events were announced in the marketing material and participants were able to sign up and pay for them when preregistering, the tickets should be placed in their packets and given to them at registration time.

   If the tickets are to be sold on-site, they should not be sold in the registration area but away from the lines of registering participants. Selling tickets can be a slow process, involving a variety of questions and cash transactions. At most conferences, tickets should be sold at a separate station, such as the service desk.

Service and Information Desk

Is a Service Desk Needed?

One major purpose of a service desk is to reduce or eliminate delays in the regular registration lines caused by problems that require special handling and additional time. A member of the secretariat should be at the desk at all times, handling each problem as it develops. The service desk should be located in the same general area as the main registration desk, with clear signs indicating its purpose. Instead of a separate desk, a small conference may only need a separate station at the regular registration desk.

How Will Preregistrants' Problems Be Handled?

Participants preregister for many reasons, and one is to reduce the time and energy required for conference registration on-site. Despite this, problems arise and the preregistrants should be able to receive prompt assistance.

What Action Should Be Taken When the Secretariat Has No Record of Advance Registration?

What happens when a participant claims to have preregistered but does not have an acknowledgment form and the secretariat has no record of the preregistration? The situation has to be investigated, and the secretariat member who is on duty should be completely familiar with the procedure.

   The problem is frequently one of timing: The participant may have preregistered but too close to the opening of the conference to have received an acknowledgment. In this case, the information should be in the secretariat files. In another common case, a participant may have delegated the registration procedure to a coworker or subordinate, who forgot to send in the preregistration forms. The participant could be registered on-site without paying, subject to later payment if the preregistrant's money has not been received. It is a financial gamble, but one that must sometimes be taken.

Will Preregistrants Whose Checks Have Not Yet Cleared Be Admitted to the Conference?

Although most checks accompanying preregistration have probably cleared before the start of the conference, some international participants' payments may not. For some countries with foreign exchange problems, checks may take a month or more to clear, so international participants often arrive at the conference before their checks have cleared. Generally, these international participants should be admitted, unless an unusual prior incident suggests otherwise.

Will Service Desk Personnel Be Able to Provide Information About the Conference?

The service desk personnel should be selected and trained so that they can answer any questions the participants might ask. A record should be kept of any questions that were not handled satisfactorily as a help in planning future conferences.

Will Desk Personnel Be Able to Provide Information About the Sponsor?

Desk personnel should be knowledgeable about the sponsor, particularly at a membership sponsor conference where nonmember participants may be stimulated to join. Some coordinators even staff the desk with an officer or member of the organization, so a prospective member can have direct contact with a member rather than the secretariat. (In this case, officers and members should only staff the desk for short periods on a rotation schedule.) Although the sponsor often has a booth in the exhibition area to which interested participants can be referred, prospective members should be given immediate attention when they come to the service desk.

Can Membership Status Be Verified?

For a membership sponsor, membership status can be important during registration when the fee depends on that status. Not all members carry appropriate membership identification such as a card or number, but the registration desk, if it uses a computer, should be able to quickly verify membership status from a membership list. If the registration desk has any doubts, the participant should immediately be referred to the service desk. The most common problem found at the service desk is that the participant's membership has lapsed and all that is required is a renewal.

Can Dues Be Collected at This Conference?

Participants should be able to pay dues at a membership sponsor conference. If dues are included in the conference fee, then the matter could be handled at the registration desk, but if dues are separate from registration, participants should be able to pay dues rapidly and get a receipt. The secretariat should plan for dues transactions by having a supply of membership forms and receipts and a means of controlling incoming cash.

Are Publications Available for Sale?

Membership sponsors and public seminar sponsors can sell publications at a conference by setting up a "store" in the exhibition area or in a common room. As all participants must pass through the registration area, that becomes a desirable place to sell publications.

Selling can take several forms. Outright purchase means that the secretariat must provide for a cash box, receipts, and inventory control. Another way is to take orders for future delivery; though this eliminates the need for inventory control, it adds a mailing cost. Sponsors that only want to display material for information purposes should indicate this with a sign that tells participants how to purchase any of the publications.

Will Lost Badges or Function Tickets Be Replaced?

Participants can be expected to lose badges, particularly at multiday conferences. An employer sponsor may not find lost badges to be particularly important, as the badges are mainly for initial introductions. Badges may be crucial for a public seminar sponsor or a membership sponsor, however, as they permit entry into sessions and the exhibition area. If the secretariat can determine a legitimate loss, it is judicious to replace the badge. A participant rarely attempts to obtain a second badge for a friend, colleague, or companion illicitly.

Function tickets are another matter. They represent a direct outlay of funds, and replacing them in any number means a loss of revenue to the conference. Participants should be advised to sign their names on each function ticket in case they are lost. Notice should be given that lost function tickets will not be replaced. Despite this notice, the secretariat can agree to replace some function tickets, particularly for a large banquet, where not all participants are expected to attend.

What Is the Policy About On-Site Requests for Press and Other Special-Privilege Passes?

Press passes and other materials are usually provided to a specific list of people in the press room (see Chapter Thirteen). Some legitimate press people, however, may not be on the list. Rather than antagonize these people and lose press coverage, the secretariat could provide for press registration on-site, either in the press room or at the service desk.

Requests for special-privilege passes may come from an exhibitor who asks for a pass to the exhibition for a potential customer or from a resource person who asks for passes for nonparticipants whom they have invited to their sessions. Before the conference, a written policy should be developed that addresses these kinds of requests. The secretariat should be able to point to that written policy for most situations. Despite a written policy, the secretariat will probably have to make immediate decisions on a few unusual requests.

How Should Unauthorized People Be Handled?

People sometimes request a pass for a particular event in order to see a friend or business acquaintance. A written policy should disallow these requests; instead the secretariat should be prepared to relay or post messages to participants and exhibitors and assume the responsibility to make sure those messages are delivered.

Personal Needs of Participants

Will Lodging Information Be Available?

Preregistered participants should have no lodging problems, but on-site registrants may have housing needs. These last-minute needs can be an effective way to use all the space that the coordinator has requested in the headquarters hotel and other hotels. If housing is tight, as is frequently the case for a large membership sponsor conference, the secretariat should arrange to have someone at the registration area who can assist. This person can be a representative of the LCVB or another local person who knows the facilities and has direct contact with the responsible individual in each facility.

Will the Conference Offer Special Hospitality?

In this context, hospitality means some personal, social events outside of the conference, although it may start with the conference. For a membership sponsor, the participants who live near the conference venue might agree to open their homes to other participants, a frequent form of hospitality at international conferences that is also appropriate for some domestic conferences.

An employer sponsor's hospitality events should be part of the conference design, and preparations should be completed prior to registration. A public seminar sponsor rarely provides special hospitality, though there is nothing to prevent them from doing so if it is appropriate. In many cities in the United States, friendship societies, sister city arrangements, international fraternal orders (Lions), and local universities are interested in participating in hospitality arrangements.

Can Tours and Sightseeing Be Arranged?

Participants will have been informed about tours and sightseeing possibilities through the conference marketing material. Preregistration probably provided for signing up for those activities, though many participants tend to wait until the start of the conference before making those arrangements. Although tours and sightseeing should be handled by professionals (see Chapter Fifteen), the coordinator can contract with them or merely allow them space in the registration area so that interested participants can sign up.

Will the Conference Provide Shopping Services?

Some people think that shopping is only appropriate for companions. Quite the contrary, participants are also interested in shopping. If participants are from a different part of the United States or from a foreign country, they will probably want to take home gifts for family and friends, mementos and souvenirs for themselves, and special items from the geographical area. Sometimes, the participants only need information about local items and where they can be purchased. For some conferences, a tour to local factories or outlets should be planned as a conference event option. If not, some of the participants may intentionally miss sessions in order to shop.

Many international participants are expected to bring back gifts. For example, one of the authors received a telex asking him to fly to India immediately to serve as a consultant to a conference in progress and in trouble. On his arrival, the consultant met with representative participants from seven countries, and, strange as it may seem, the overriding problem was that the conference design did not allow time for participants to shop before returning home. The design was changed to allow that time, and the conference continued to a successful conclusion.

Will Interpreters Be Needed?

Interpreters may be needed for an international conference. (Interpreters provide oral communication between languages; translators provide written communication.) For some international conferences, the coordinator provides interpreters because they are essential for total participation in the conference. The interpreters should be briefed about the registration procedures and be able to assist the international participants in preparing the registration forms. It is also possible for a group to bring their own interpreters, but in addition, participants may need language help outside of sessions, for personal visits, shopping, or sightseeing. Depending on the nature of the conference, the participants may make their own arrangements, or the conference may provide bilingual people, such as university students or friendship society members, to handle minimal social conversation.

Financial Aspects

Who Will Be in Charge of Financial Activities?

Conferences include two major financial activities: receiving money and paying bills. For a limited number of financial transactions, one person may suffice, but frequently two people are more effective.

When money is to be received in the registration area, the person with that responsibility should be stationed in that area since that is where financial problems will arise, usually concerning acceptance of checks, credit cards, and purchase orders.

Payments will be made at various times and places: Cash payments may have to be made at the exhibition; petty cash disbursements can be expected many times during a conference; and hotel and catering bills may have to be paid at the completion of the conference. All of these payments should be coordinated through one individual.

Who Will Be Responsible for the Cash Count?

Each day, any cash received for registration, dues, function tickets, publications, and tours should be accounted for in the secretariat office. The cash count should be verified independently by two or more individuals at the close of each conference day and itemized on a special form. When large sums of money are involved, the person receiving cash should be bonded. Most registration areas are not very secure, and it may be advisable to hire a security guard just to protect the cash.

What Kinds of Checks Will Be Accepted?

A policy should be established and distributed before the conference on the type of acceptable checks—individual, company, out-of-state, foreign, and so on.

Which Credit Cards Will Be Accepted?

American Express, VISA, Master Card, and Diners Club are commonly accepted credit cards, though others could be equally acceptable. Before developing a policy about accepting any cards at all, verify the amount that will have to be paid to the credit card companies from the conference budget. If the policy is to accept credit cards, there must be a procedure for handling potential registrants who present outdated or voided credit cards.

Will Purchase Orders Be Accepted?

Purchase orders are sometimes issued by companies to pay for goods and services. The U.S. government, for example, generally insists that employees use purchase orders for conferences rather than paying individually and then seeking reimbursement. A member of the secretariat should understand how to read purchase orders. Lack of signatures in certain places or missing vouchers and other attachments can delay or even preclude payment. Unfortunately, some companies (and the U.S. government) do not honor all the purchase orders they issue for several reasons, but the net result is the same—the conference loses those fees.

Is It Acceptable to Bill a Company or an Organization?

Some participants come to a conference and say, "Bill my organization." If that is acceptable, a policy should be established and then followed. (For an employer sponsor, it is not necessary.) A public seminar sponsor might adopt this policy with certain companies, and a membership sponsor might allow this payment procedure (even if it loses some money) rather than antagonize members.

Have a Refund Policy and Procedure Been Established?

Cancellation and refunds are different. The conference marketing material should give a final date for cancellation until which date some percentage of the registration fee will be returned. Refunds come into play after that date and a policy should be established. For example, will a refund be given if a participant is hospitalized or dies just before the conference? Or during the conference, if a participant gets notice of the severe illness or death of a spouse, parent, or other close family member? Are participants eligible for any refund and, if so, for what reasons and how much?

Can Participants Pay for Individual Events?

The simplest and soundest financial approach is to institute one blanket fee to cover all conference events. Most employer sponsors and some public seminar sponsors will find that this approach simplifies payment, but the situation of a membership sponsor is more complex. Some participants prefer a package deal, particularly if they are to be reimbursed by an employer or other entity. Others, particularly those on their own or on a limited budget, may prefer to wait until the conference starts to select particular events to attend, depending on how much additional money will be required.

Staffing

Will Volunteers, Paid Help, or a Combination of Both Be Used?

Registration is an extremely important part of the conference, and it is much more than just a clerical operation. Because registration personnel represent the sponsor, coordinators generally prefer to use regular, experienced staff. Volunteers may be motivated, but some of them are less committed—so less effective—than regular employees.

Additional personnel are needed for many conferences. A membership sponsor or a nonprofit public seminar sponsor might seek volunteers to work in the registration area. (As used here, "volunteers" signify people who are not paid for the hours they work, but who might be reimbursed for travel and meals.) Many volunteers are retired people who seek the challenge and stimulation of working with others. They have excellent work records and approach volunteerism with the same degree of responsibility they exhibited for paid work in previous years.

Another alternative is to hire paid temporary workers who can be obtained from the LCVB or local firms that supply temporary workers. These workers might not have any more experience than the volunteers, but being paid, they can be expected to be on time and to work the required hours without any deviations. When registration requires a large staff, a coordinator can utilize a combination of volunteers and temporary help, but the coordinator should make sure that the unpaid volunteers do not feel that they are being treated unfairly.

Which Types of Personnel Are Needed?

The decision on whether to use regular staff, volunteers, or temporary employees must be considered in light of the kinds of competencies needed in the registration area. Registrars work directly with the participants; they need skill and experience in working with various kinds of people, in solving problems, and in remaining unruffled after several hours of pressure. Registrars are supplemented by clerks, who arrange materials, file, and do many "go-fer" tasks. Typists are necessary, particularly if badges are prepared at the registration area. If money is collected at registration time, a qualified cashier is required.

The numbers of personnel depend on the ratio of preregistered participants to predicted on-site registrants. For example, several cashiers may be necessary if the registration area is open at all times for several hours or days. All registration personnel need breaks. It is not a good idea to ask a participant to "Please wait, the cashier is on a break and will be back in fifteen minutes."

Who Will Supervise the Registration Staff?

One member of the secretariat should be in charge of the registration area at all times, and that person should be responsible for supervising staff. All registration personnel should know exactly who that person is—ambiguity leads to confusion for the participants as well as the staff. The member of the secretariat who is given that responsibility should have supervisory training and experience. Although it may be an assignment for just the duration of the conference, it is extremely crucial: Poor supervision of the registration area can have a negative effect on the conference, despite all the excellent design work.

Has a Staffing Schedule Been Developed?

Regardless of size, the registration staff requires a schedule to know each person's starting and quitting time, break time, and meal breaks. Clerks are not usually interchangeable with cashiers, nor registrars with typists, so careful scheduling, agreed to by all, is essential. If possible, the entire registration staff (permanent employees, temporary employees, and volunteers) should be involved in developing the schedule. Because the staff often consists of different kinds of personnel, conflicts may arise, necessitating the need for conflict resolution. One person from the secretariat should have the authority to make the final scheduling decisions.

Will the Registration Staff Be Trained?

If all staff are experienced, training may not be necessary, but such a staff is unusual. Therefore, consideration should be given to training and provided for in the budget. Depending on the size and experience of the staff, the training might range from one hour to several days and cover customer relations, handling the registration flow, emergency procedures, decision making, processing of the various papers associated with registration, and briefing the staff about the sponsor and the type of participants anticipated.

Will the Staff Engage in an Operational Dry Run?

The larger the staff, the more crucial the need for a dry run of registration procedures conducted in the registration area. This simulation may be difficult, for the site may not be able to make the area available prior to setting up the registration area for the conference. If this restriction becomes evident during negotiations, the dry run should be conducted just before the actual registration, if possible.

Will the Staff Have a Policy Manual?

Some kind of policy or information manual intended for the staff is desirable even for a small conference. For a small one-time conference, a coordinator might decide that it would be too time-consuming. It may be difficult to develop a manual for a first-time conference, but it can be expanded and improved after each subsequent conference; for a conference using many staff, such a manual can be extremely useful and well worth the effort.

Supplies and Services

What Is the Condition of the Site Telephone Equipment?

Registration activities require telephones, from one phone to numerous phones in or near the registration area. These phones should be used only by the secretariat for registration activities.

Some hotels can provide direct-dial phones in the registration area that go through the regular hotel switchboard and that are billed to the conference budget. A convention center usually cannot provide this kind of service, so the secretariat must make arrangements directly with the local phone company.

The phones should only be used for certain purposes by designated personnel. For example, a participant might claim that registration was mailed, and to confirm this, the participant who wants to call the home office about his lost preregistration should do it on a public phone, not on one in the registration area. In other cases, volunteers have tied up phones, calling home or making other personal calls. Incoming calls will probably be few and far between, but they should be directed to the individuals who have been trained and assigned to that function.

Figure 49. Typical List of Supplies for the Registration Area.

_____ Registration forms	_____ Strong box
_____ Writing implements	_____ Typewriters
_____ Receipt forms	_____ Calculators or adding machines
_____ Wastebaskets	_____ Badges
_____ Paper	_____ Badge holders
_____ Staplers	_____ Furniture
_____ Staple removers	_____ Bulletin board
_____ Paper clips	_____ Thumb tacks or stick pins
_____ Tape	_____ Scissors

SOURCE: *The Comprehensive Guide to Successful Conferences and Meetings* by Leonard Nadler and Zeace Nadler. San Francisco: Jossey-Bass. Copyright © 1987. Permission to reproduce hereby granted.

What Supplies and Equipment Will Be Needed?

Figure 49 lists some common items needed for almost any registration area. A coordinator who plans many conferences should maintain a checklist (similar to the one shown in the figure) to which items can be added and removed. Without such a list, a coordinator can expect to incur additional time and expense for on-site purchases. The list should also be checked against a list of supplies available from the site at no charge or at a minimal cost.

A large supply of registration forms should be kept on hand. Generally, there should be many more forms available than can be used. If the registration requires more than one form, adequate supplies of each form should be kept on hand.

The secretariat and the participants need writing implements. As part of the marketing effort, ballpoint pens or pencils carrying the name and date of the conference can be produced, and the available supply should be used, for they have no real value after the conference. Some sites, particularly hotels, have pencils and pens imprinted with the site name and may be willing to provide these in quantity at no charge.

Receipt forms may be needed by participants for reimbursement or tax purposes. International participants usually need receipts for reimbursement or currency exchange purposes. If cash is involved, numbered receipt forms are essential for cash control.

Enough wastebaskets should be on hand so that paper can be discarded rapidly and easily. Each registration table should have a wastebasket, if possible.

Registration procedures require typing paper, note pads, staplers, staple removers, paper clips, cellophane tape, and masking tape.

When cash transactions are involved, a strong box is essential. The size, configuration, and safety features should fit the amount of cash expected and the level of security required.

Typewriters are a necessity, but the kind and quantity must be planned carefully. Unless the conference is in the same city as the sponsor or coordinator, rental should be considered. If badges are to be produced at registration, a bulletin (large type) typewriter should be available. Regular typewriters may also be needed for filling out registration forms or other tasks; calculators and adding machines are handy for figuring out fees and payments.

A good supply of blank badges and badge holders should be on hand for on-site registration. The secretariat should have a sufficient supply of each color badge, as described earlier in this chapter.

The registration desk needs furniture, including desks, tables, and chairs. A large conference may also need a counter or some other divider between the secretariat and the participants. The coordinator and secretariat should always keep in mind that the registration area is the first point of contact for the participants, so it should be comfortably furnished and carry the theme of the conference.

Refreshments for the staff should be set up away from the registration desk. The participants should not be able to see the refreshments, and the secretariat should not partake of the refreshments while on duty. Refreshments can range from water and paper cups to fresh coffee and china cups, or whatever is deemed appropriate by a coordinator.

The bulletin board, whether provided by the site or the secretariat, should be large enough for the expected number of notices and contain thumb tacks or stick pins to hang the notices on the board.

Such items as scissors may seem minor until the need for them arises. Before setting up the registration area, the secretariat should walk through all the procedures and add items to this list as needed.

Chapter 18

Preparing a
Participant Program Book

CHECKLIST FOR PARTICIPANT BOOK

Form

_____ Who will select the form of the participant book?

_____ Will the conference provide a separate companions book?

_____ What type of cover would be most appropriate?

_____ How will the book be distributed?

_____ Will the book be distributed prior to the conference?

_____ How should requests for additional books be handled?

_____ Will two books be produced—one for use during the conference and another to take home?

_____ Will the book have removable daily session sheets?

_____ Would a pocket schedule be helpful?

_____ What is the budget for the participant book?

Contents

_____ Who will make decisions about the content of the participant book?

_____ Will the book provide a place for the participant's name?

_____ What should be included in the table of contents?

_____ Who is responsible for writing and editing the session descriptions?

_____ Are the session numbers in the book correct?

_____ Does the book contain a personal planning page?

_____ Does the book contain a personal goal-planning sheet?

SOURCE: *The Comprehensive Guide to Successful Conferences and Meetings* by Leonard Nadler and Zeace Nadler. San Francisco: Jossey-Bass. Copyright © 1987. Permission to reproduce hereby granted.

The participant book (also known as the conference book and program book) enables participants to understand the design of the conference and how they can participate. A simple design for a one-day conference may require only a single page; more complex designs might require a participant book of several pages—or even a carton of reading materials for preconference preparation. The most common forms of this book are looseleaf binders or large plastic envelopes, commonly called portfolios. The book is essential for participant use during the conference; after the conference it serves as a reminder, as well as a resource book.

The Checklist

Form

Who Will Select the Form of the Participant Book?

The coordinator should make the final decision on the form of the book, usually with the advice and assistance of professionals in the graphic design field. In the case of an annual membership sponsor conference, the coordinator should examine books of previous conferences to explore changes that could improve the book.

Will the Conference Provide a Separate Companions Book?

The companions program may be included in the participant book or produce a separate book if several pages are needed to cover all the activities. This decision also means that the companions must receive a different packet than that distributed to the participants. Chapter Eleven discusses companions in detail.

What Type of Cover Would Be Most Appropriate?

The cover should clearly indicate the name of the conference, the logo, the date(s), and the theme. The cover should be attractive, but the choice of paper stock and use of color must be within the available budget. Too often, covers for participant books use four-color printing and expensive artwork just because the money is available. Under those conditions, the cover may communicate the wrong message to the participants—that more effort has been put into the book than into the conference.

How Will the Book Be Distributed?

The book can be distributed in many ways, and the method chosen must be congruent with the purpose. To enhance the sponsor's image, the book may be sent out as part of the marketing effort, recognizing that not everyone who receives it will attend the conference. Or the book can be sent only to preregistrants, as part of the acknowledgment as well as to provide participants with information before the conference opens. Although this method of distribution can be very helpful when participants must choose among numerous concurrent sessions, a heavy book can be a very significant mailing expense. The most frequent time of distribution is at registration when the book is included in the participant packet or is distributed along with it.

Will the Book Be Distributed Prior to the Conference?

If the book contains preconference material, such as readings, questionnaires, or surveys to be done in the local community or job situations, it must be sent out before the conference opens. The preconference material can form a book insert, which the participant completes and returns before the conference or during registration. If the participant is supposed to use the material during the conference, it should be bound into the book.

Sending the book to participants always incurs the risk that they will not bring the books to the conference—unless they see a good reason for using the book before and during the conference. Worksheets are a good example. The authors sent out participant books before a public seminar conference. They were looseleaf books, and the program for each day was carefully noted. Each session had different reading materials. The participants were urged to (1) review the program for each segment (morning, afternoon, evening) and decide which session would be of most interest to them, (2) complete the form in the book that focused on their objectives for that session, (3) read the materials for the sessions that they selected, and (4) jot down questions they planned to ask during these sessions.

How Should Requests for Additional Books Be Handled?

This is another one of those political questions that arise during a conference, usually of a membership sponsor or public seminar sponsor. Let us assume that it is a legitimate loss. The policy could be that the book is replaced for a nominal fee, perhaps $2.00. The intent is not so much to recover the cost as to encourage participants to exercise care in how they protect their books.

Participants sometimes request extra books to submit to employers as justification for attending the conference. Members of the design committee may desire an extra copy to show an employer, to legitimize the fact that they devoted extra time and effort to the sponsoring organization. As the result ultimately benefits the sponsor, the request might be honored.

Some books are excellent resources, so participants may want extra copies for others who did not attend. Again, extra copies can be beneficial to the sponsor, even though they cost money.

Though very few books are actually sold to nonparticipants, some coordinators put a price on the participant book just to communicate that it has value. Whatever the policy adopted for extra copies, the coordinator should implement it as consistently as possible, so that no participant feels treated unfairly.

Will Two Books Be Produced—One for Use During the Conference and Another to Take Home?

The participant book is an excellent item to take home or back to the job, since it contains useful information on presenters and exhibitors. However, participants may resist carrying thick, heavy books around during the conference. One option is to prepare a brief version for the use during the conference, one that contains only the information needed for the sessions. Such material as the welcoming letter, list of the design committee, and some of the other items listed later in this chapter need not be included.

Will the Book Have Removable Daily Session Sheets?

Another way to solve the heavy book problem is to use looseleaf or perforated binding so that the pages for each day's sessions can be removed. Each day's sessions should be printed on different color paper, and the participants should be provided with a folder or portfolio to hold the sheets when they are removed from the book. This encourages them to at least take the pages for each day if they prefer not to carry the whole book.

Would a Pocket Schedule Be Helpful?

A pocket schedule, which contains the relevant room and session information for the entire day, or sometimes the entire conference program in a very abbreviated form, can work well particularly if the badge being used has a pocket (see Chapter Seventeen).

What Is the Budget for the Participant Book?

The budget for the book is usually a controlling factor. If the book is to be used only during the conference, it should cost less than a book designed to have additional uses after the conference.

The participant book may be turned into a source of income by selling advertising space to exhibitors, nonexhibiting suppliers, "sponsors," and other interested parties. Publishing an exhibitors book, however, may preclude this option. See Chapter Ten for discussion of the exhibitors book.

Contents

Who Will Make Decisions About the Content of the Participant Book?

Since many subjects and items can be covered in a participant book, one person must have the authority to make decisions about the contents. That person should be the coordinator, because it is the coordinator who will have to answer questions as to why some material was included or omitted after the book is printed. A coordinator for a membership sponsor may want the design committee to review the proposed table of contents, but a coordinator for an employer sponsor would not find this necessary. A public seminar sponsor might want others to be involved, since the participant book can also be a marketing piece for the sponsor's other conferences or activities.

Will the Book Provide a Place for the Participant's Name?

A place for the participant's name should be included on the first page, and each participant should be encouraged to write in his or her name immediately upon receiving the book. There are two reasons: It personalizes the book, reinforcing the participant's commitment to the conference, and on a more mundane level, it allows for recovery of lost books. A sign should be posted in the registration area suggesting this.

The initial page could include the following:

Name _____
Conference registration number (if available) _____
If found, please return this book to the secretariat in room _____ .

Note that this item does not ask the participant for such information as hotel name, room number, or home address. This is a safeguard; if the book falls into the wrong hands, people might use it for illegal or unscrupulous ends.

What Should Be Included in the Table of Contents?

The participant book must be designed for the specific upcoming conference. Even when the sponsor conducts annual conferences, the table of contents should be carefully reviewed each time to ensure that it is pertinent. A sample table of contents is presented in Figure 50, though, of course, not every participant book will contain all the items listed. The book should start with a note of welcome from a high-ranking official in the sponsoring organization. A membership sponsor might also attempt to acquire a brief letter from a high-level government official, such as the mayor of the venue city, the governor

Figure 50. Sample Table of Contents for a Participant Book.

Welcome to participants
Registration information
Design committee
Officers
Award winners
Sponsor
Site map
Exhibit information
Blank pages
Matrix
Track information
Individual sessions
Related events
Hosts, introducers, and monitors

Badges
Transportation
Receptions
Meals
Message center
Common room
Lost and found
Post office
Smoking policy
Presenter listing
Daily listing
Emergencies
Embassies and consulates
Religious services

SOURCE: *The Comprehensive Guide to Successful Conferences and Meetings* by Leonard Nadler and Zeace Nadler. San Francisco: Jossey-Bass. Copyright © 1987. Permission to reproduce hereby granted.

of the state, or even the President of the United States. The LCVB, congressional representative, or lobbyist might be very helpful in obtaining these letters.

The participant needs registration information, even though it may already have been provided in preconference material. This information, particularly the hours of registration, may help participants in case they need to return to the registration area for any reason.

A membership sponsor design committee does not often receive sufficient recognition, and the book is one place to recognize the work they have done as volunteers. Employer sponsors generally do not recognize a design or advisory committee, though sometimes it is in everyone's best interest to mention the committee members. A public seminar sponsor may list the members of the design committee in certain situations.

A membership sponsor can recognize its officers in the book with text and photographs. The same can be done for award winners, including in the text clear descriptions of the awards and why each individual received one. The sponsor must be identified in the book: A membership sponsor participant book might include information about membership, activities, and a membership application; an employer sponsor might include the annual report or sections of it.

If the site is large, as many conference centers are, a site map should be included that indicates the rooms by name or number, entrances and exits, rest rooms, elevators or escalators, staircases, public telephones, food service areas, and any unusual features of the site. (The location of the secretariat room should not be noted, but the location of the service desk should be indicated.) If the site is a hotel, the same information should be provided, as well as phone numbers for the duty manager, front desk, concierge, and others who might be needed by a participant. When the participant book is enclosed in a large plastic envelope, a diagram of the site can be printed on the outside of the envelope for ready reference.

The decision about exhibit information should be made in conjunction with the exhibit manager (see Chapter Ten). Even if the sponsor plans an exhibitors book, some information should be included in the participant book, such as hours of operation and location. If no separate exhibitors book is planned, the participant book should contain a map of the exhibition area, list of exhibitors and their personnel, and any special features of the exhibit or the exhibit area.

Blank pages for the participant's notes are important. A pad or separate blank sheets could be included in the participant packet, but participants tend to lose these items, particularly after the conference, making recall difficult if not impossible. Blank pages can be placed at the end of the book or at the end of each day's session material, depending on the design.

The matrix (entire program) of the conference should be included in the book on one page, if possible. A one-day conference matrix would list only the main events of the day. A conference of more than one day would use matrices similar to the examples presented in Chapter Three.

When a track design is used, the book should note the name or number of the track in the session descriptions. The tracks should be explained in a separate section of the book, and the specific track sessions should be listed with time, title, presenter, location, and possibly session descriptions.

The most important part of the book consists of the descriptions of individual sessions, listed in numerical and chronological order. Each day should be clearly identified, perhaps with color-coded pages, though that may add to the cost of the book. For a large conference, with numerous concurrent sessions, it may even be necessary to distinguish the morning sessions from the afternoon sessions.

Although the exact layout of this section differs from one participant book to another, a typical example is shown below.

Thursday—December 11, 1986
4:00–5:30 P.M.
Event: 10
Session: 15   Location: California Room
                                                 Hotel Bristol

                 The Effective Use of Audiovisual Equipment

Presenter: Thomas Jones   ┌─────────────────┐
                                          │ Photo of   │
            AV Coordinator   │ presenter   │
            ABC Company, San Diego, CA   └─────────────────┘

Description of session:

Objectives:

            Experience   *Involvement*

       |_____| |_____|

The day and time should be prominently displayed in the upper left-hand corner. The session room is noted on the top; listing the name of the hotel indicates that several sites are being used.

The event number and the specific session number should be clearly shown. The title of the session should be prominent, specific, and direct—too often participants sense that an advertising copy writer has written the titles, and stylish titles can interfere with effective communication. The presenter's name, title, and organization are noted, and a photo can be included. The description should be precise and concise, followed by a clear statement of the session's objectives. The presenters should write the descriptions and objectives, but the secretariat should edit them to ensure clarity and compatibility with corresponding statements for the other sessions.

Two other factors—experience and involvement—may also be extremely useful for some designs. The presenter should estimate the level of experience (usually stated in years) that the participant should have in order to benefit from the session. The kind of involvement expected of the participant, ranging from lecture to workshop, is also noted. When numerous concurrent sessions are scheduled, this information can assist participants in making their choices.

After the general and regular sessions, information about the related events, such as recognition, mixers, lounge areas, common rooms, cultural activities, home hospitality, job exchange, and resource centers, should be included in the participant book.

A membership sponsor that depends on member volunteers should provide recognition for hosts, introducers, and monitors. They could be listed in the section on individual sessions under the appropriate session, or in a special part of the book.

Badges are an important part of any conference, and the participant book should note the meaning of the different color badges and streamers and the procedure to replace lost badges. If apropos, this section should include specific information on how badges are used to gain admission to sessions, food and beverage functions, and the exhibition.

Participants usually need various kinds of transportation-related information. When shuttle service is provided, the schedule, routes, and pickup/drop-off points should be listed. Participants may want to know about transportation to and from the airport. In a large city, they may wish to have information about the local urban mass transit system. Regulations concerning taxis vary from one city to another, so participants should have information on the taxis in the venue city.

Receptions should be carefully described in the book, so that participants know what to anticipate and what to wear. The times should be clearly stated, particularly the closing time. The location should be described as specifically as possible, particularly if it is different than the building where sessions are held. For some unfathomable reason, some coordinators insist on keeping some of the details about a reception a secret. Will the bar be cash, hosted, or a combination? Will any food be served? Participants like to know those things so they can plan their own meals and activities. For an international conference, if there is to be a receiving line, participants can be asked to bring name cards.

Meals are usually an essential part of a conference. For a small conference of under fifty participants, it may not be necessary to have meal tickets, as name badges usually suffice. When the groups get larger, tickets are a good way to exercise control. The description of the meal functions should note that tickets will be required as well as the time and place of the meal.

For every conference, there should be some kind of message center, the scope and extent depending on the size and type of conference. The details about the message center are contained in another chapter, but mention is made here since the information about the center should be included in the participant book.

Not every conference has a common room, but if there is one, the location should be clearly specified and should list the services that are available in that room. The common room is a room that is open to all the participants at any time. There are no sessions in that room, and tables and chairs should be provided so that participants can just sit and talk to each other. The room can contain the message center, an information desk, and other services for the participants. If there are any limitations on hours when the room is open, these should be noted.

The location and hours of operation of the lost and found office should be mentioned. If the room is difficult to find, instructions or a map should be included in the book.

Participants frequently seek post office services, including stamps, cards, and mailing packages. A conference post office usually has services only for outgoing mail but may also provide stamps and covers for international participants who collect those items or want to use them as souvenirs. In the United States, the postal service usually does not have a station or substation in a conference site, so the location of the nearest post office should be noted in the book.

The book should state the conference's policy on smoking, indicating how seating will be arranged in rooms, or any other factors of which participants should be aware.

Participants can benefit from an alphabetical list of presenters. A sample listing is shown below.

Jones, Thomas. The Effective Use of Audiovisual Equipment.
Monday, #10–15. 4:00–5:30 P.M. Hotel Bristol,
California Room. (Page X.)

The last reference is the page number in the participant book that provides other information on the session, such as its objectives and description.

For a multiday conference, the book might include daily listings—just the major activities of the day with no details. For Example C—Five-Day Conference (see Chapter Three), the listing might be as follows:

Tuesday
General Session
Concurrent and Breakout Sessions
Lunch
Concurrent Sessions
Special Interest Groups and Film Festival
Cracker Barrel Sessions

The participant book should provide information on emergencies. Telephone numbers for medical assistance are important, and for an international conference they are a necessity and should also mention what languages are spoken by the medical personnel. Participants at an international conference may also need the phone numbers of their embassies or consulates for passport or visa assistance.

Some participants will be interested in religious services, particularly if the conference overlaps any special religious holidays. Hotels frequently list houses of worship in the area but only for the major faiths, and even these lists may be incomplete. The LCVB can provide lists of houses of worship and their proximity to the site, and the listing can be included in the book.

Who Is Responsible for Writing and Editing the Session Descriptions?

Too often, a coordinator relies solely on the presenters to write their own session descriptions. This produces a contest among presenters as to who can write the most attention-getting copy, which is not necessarily the copy that best describes the session. Presenters should submit the original copy, bound by the word limit set by the coordinator, and then someone should edit the content. One person should have overall responsibility for editing this section to ensure comparability among the descriptions. That person should be completely familiar with the participants and what they need to know in order to make decisions about sessions and presenters. The final copy should be sent to the presenters for their review, but the final decision must be in the hands of the person designated by the coordinator to produce the copy.

Are the Session Numbers in the Book Correct?

Before the book is sent to the printer, the session numbers on the design should be checked one last time against those in the book. In numerous cases this comparatively simple step was not done, resulting in errata sheets, special notices, and confusion.

Does the Book Contain a Personal Planning Page?

When the conference design includes concurrent sessions, participants can be provided with a page, either in the book or as a separate sheet, on which they can list the sessions they want to attend on a particular day. A separate sheet is preferable to marking up the book and continually searching for the pages that contain the next series of sessions.

Does the Book Contain a Personal Goal-Planning Sheet?

At some conferences, participants can be helped by a sheet that focuses on their goals for the entire conference and their goals for each particular day. That sheet can pose questions such as: Why am I here? What do I expect to get out of this conference? What exhibits do I want to see? What questions do I want answered? and Whom do I want to meet? Space should, of course, be provided for responses.

Chapter 19

Evaluation and Follow-Up

CHECKLIST FOR EVALUATION AND FOLLOW-UP

Planning for Evaluation

_____ Have evaluations been used in past conferences?

_____ Will this conference be evaluated?

_____ What will be evaluated?

_____ Who will be involved in the evaluation?

_____ Who is responsible for designing the overall evaluation?

_____ What budget is required for evaluation and follow-up?

_____ Who will be responsible for distributing the evaluation forms?

Conducting the Evaluation

_____ When will evaluation take place?

_____ What evaluation methods will be used?

_____ What methods will be used to encourage participants to evaluate during the conference?

Using the Evaluation

_____ Who is responsible for seeing that the evaluation data are analyzed?

_____ Who will receive the results of the evaluation?

_____ What form should the analysis take?

_____ Who will be responsible for seeing that the results of the evaluation are utilized?

Follow-Up

_____ Will any additional materials be sent to the participants after the conference?

_____ What efforts will be made to record good ideas for future conferences?

_____ Will linkage be provided to the next conference?

_____ Should copies of the participant book, handouts, and other materials be retained?

SOURCE: *The Comprehensive Guide to Successful Conferences and Meetings* by Leonard Nadler and Zeace Nadler. San Francisco: Jossey-Bass. Copyright © 1987. Permission to reproduce hereby granted.

Although evaluation and follow-up cannot be completed until after the conference, planning for both activities actually starts when the conference is being planned.

What Is Evaluation?

Evaluation is the activity concerned with gathering specific information related to objectives or goals. Evaluation is sometimes confused with research, but the two tasks differ significantly (Nadler, 1979). The major conceptual difference is that in evaluation the object is to find out *what* happened, while in research the focus is on *why* it happened. Every conference requires some kind of evaluation, but very few conferences need research; when research is required, it is best to contract with outside professionals in the field.

Through evaluation, the coordinator wants to find out what happened at the conference in relation to the planning. Generally, how did things go, and what did the participants get out of the conference? If it is a training conference, there will be specific behavioral objectives of some kind, but the emphasis in this book is on those conferences that do not have such objectives. This does not mean that evaluation cannot take place, rather that it can be more difficult than when specific behavioral objectives are used.

Quantitative and Qualitative Evaluations

For many years the emphasis of most evaluations was the quantitative side or "number crunching." The quantitative evaluation is designed to produce numbers that can be added, manipulated, and statistically analyzed to produce various kinds of measures (mean, median, mode, chi square) that allow for comparison and in-depth analysis. Undoubtedly, part of any evaluation should rely on quantitative approaches, and the availability of computers enhances the use of the quantitative approach.

More recently, increased attention has been given to the qualitative approach (Patton, 1980), or what is referred to as "soft" data. The increased attention has produced new techniques for data gathering and treatment, but it is still difficult to do qualitative evaluation. The quantitative method is easier to design, administer, and analyze than the qualitative method. Yet, each method has its advantages and limitations and each must be considered when planning conference evaluations.

Who Does Evaluation?

Sponsors that offer many conferences usually have an internal person or unit who has responsibility for evaluation. An employer sponsor might rely on its human resource development unit to do the evaluation task. It is also possible to contract out for these activities, but it can be expensive. To do the job effectively, the external resource must be involved from the very beginning of the conference design process and must stay with it until the end. The job may also require on-site work during the conference.

Why Follow Up?

There are various reasons to follow up a conference and different ways to do it. One aspect of follow-up concerns what will be done with the evaluation, for the use of those results constitutes one form of follow-up. For example, the evaluation results of one conference concerning the site can be very useful when planning another conference even though the topic or design will be different.

Effective follow-up can stimulate the participants, for although the formal conference ends at a particular time, the participants can be encouraged to take some actions in the future related to what happened at the conference. Follow-up will be useful for a future conference, not the present one, so why should the coordinator include that expense in the current budget? These are policy matters that should be explored with the sponsor when the budget is being discussed.

The Checklist

Planning for Evaluation

Have Evaluations Been Used in Past Conferences?

If the sponsor has conducted past conferences and has evaluated them, the coordinator and design committee should obtain the evaluation methodology and data from the earlier conference(s) (1) to determine whether the present conference should be evaluated, and (2) if so, to assist in planning the evaluation of the current conference. Data from previous evaluations should help them avoid the same mistakes and plan a better conference and evaluation.

Will This Conference Be Evaluated?

Evaluation should not be taken for granted; the coordinator should always check that the sponsor wants one. Why should a conference be evaluated? Among the reasons for evaluation are to determine if (1) objectives were met, (2) the conference was cost-effective (within budget or profit-making), (3) participants were satisfied, and (4) planning needs to be altered for future conferences. A sponsor sometimes does not want an evaluation, and the coordinator should accept that decision. The most frequent reasons for *not* wanting an evaluation are that it is too costly and that the sponsor does not intend to do anything with the results.

What Will Be Evaluated?

Evaluating every element of the conference may require extensive resources, and the data may not be worth the effort. Figure 51 presents a list of the various factors that can be evaluated. The coordinator should check the ones to be evaluated for this particular conference.

In general, the evaluation of any part of the conference should be geared to focus on what worked, what did not work, what should be changed for the future (if there is one), and what were some new ideas that came out of the conference.

Both the coordinator and the sponsor should consider evaluating the coordinator to gain valuable feedback on the coordinator's performance. Coordinator performance is not always synonymous with the success of the conference. The coordinator may have produced a successful conference but at a tremendous cost in expense and relationships. On the other hand, the coordinator might have done a perfect job, but the conference was a disaster due to factors outside the coordinator's control, such as an airline strike, or a change of personnel at the conference site. Coordinator evaluation should answer such questions as: Was the coordinator available when needed? How well did the coordinator work with others? Did the coordinator meet deadlines? Did the coordinator provide leadership?

The design committee should be asked to produce a report on how they functioned, including suggestions for the next design committee, if one is to be used. In addition, as a form of qualitative evaluation, it might be very effective to ask others to evaluate the work of the design committee, answering such questons as: Did the committee function effectively? Did the committee understand its functions and responsibilities? How satisfactory was committee planning?

Although the steering committee has a very short life, existing only during the conference, it too should be evaluated to determine its effectiveness as a technique. Data gathered from others about the steering committee can be helpful in activating a steering committee for future conferences. Some questions to be answered by the evaluation are: Were the steering committee members prepared for their assignment? What were some of their decisions during the conference? Did they receive recommendations from participants? Did they relate well with the coordinator?

Figure 51. Conference Factors That Can Be Evaluated.

_____ Coordinator

_____ Design committee

_____ Steering committee

_____ Secretariat

_____ Relevancy of the theme

_____ Clarity of purpose

_____ Total design

_____ Related events

_____ Site

_____ Marketing

_____ Public relations

_____ Budget

_____ Resource people
         (speakers and presenters)

_____ Transportation

_____ Exhibition

_____ Registration

_____ Participant book

_____ Entertainment

_____ Breaks

_____ Receptions

_____ Companions

SOURCE: *The Comprehensive Guide to Successful Conferences and Meetings* by Leonard Nadler and Zeace Nadler. San Francisco: Jossey-Bass. Copyright © 1987. Permission to reproduce hereby granted.

Because the secretariat does a good deal of its work behind the scenes, not everyone is able to evaluate that group. Certainly, considering the importance of the secretariat to the effective planning and implementation of the conference, this body should be evaluated. The focus should be on how the group functioned, not on the individuals, unless the same people might be used in future secretariats. Some questions to be answered by the evaluation are: Was staffing adequate? What services were requested but not provided? What are some of the problems that were not resolved? How could the function of the secretariat be improved?

Even though the evaluation will be done after the conference is over, the relevancy of the theme should still be evaluated. Participants sometimes complain that the theme, as conveyed to them, did not accurately represent the thrust of the conference, and the participants' feedback on the theme can be helpful in developing themes for future conferences. Some questions to be answered by the evaluation are: Was the theme relevant to the participants? How was the theme communicated during preconference activities? How was the theme reflected in the design?

The conference's clarity of purpose might be evaluated, unless the conference is held for stated behavioral objectives or is an annual event. In the former case, those who have written the objectives should also plan for evaluation, though it may be limited only to this aspect of the conference. In the latter case, the purpose is self-evident and clarity need not be evaluated. In all other cases, evaluation can be helpful in forming the objectives for future conferences. Some questions to be answered by the evaluation are: How well did the participants understand the purpose of the conference? How was the purpose communicated to them?

The total design should be evaluated, and some questions to be answered by the evaluation are: Was the conference held at the right time of year? Was the length of the conference appropriate? Were sessions too long or too short? Was the flow appropriate?

The related events cover a wide variety of activities (see Chapter Four). The coordinator should identify those events actually used in the specific conference and plan for their evaluation.

Evaluation of the site is important for many reasons; if it does nothing else, it at least provides an opportunity for the participants to vent their anger and frustration about site factors that are essentially outside the purview of the coordinator and the conference. The data might provide important insights for the site personnel, and the comments of the participants can be helpful when selecting the next site for the same group or type of participants. Not every item of feedback will be negative, and the positive factors regarding the site are also helpful. Some factors to be evaluated are: What was the condition of the sleeping rooms? Was food service satisfactory? How helpful were site personnel? Was this site appropriate for the conference?

It might be said that the evaluation of the marketing effort can be measured by the number of participants who attended. Although there is some truth in this statement, evaluation should also uncover which marketing strategies worked and which did not, determine the effectiveness of direct mail pieces or print advertising, and obtain suggestions from the participants and suppliers for future marketing efforts. Some questions to be answered by the evaluation are: What was the quality and appropriateness of the marketing pieces? Were mailings helpful and timely? Was the advertising useful?

Assessing the public relations effort in terms of the number of interviews or lines in the print media is helpful, but the evaluation should also analyze the total PR effort and ways to improve it in the future. Some factors to be evaluated are: Did public relations people participate? How receptive were the media? Were resource people and participants utilized for public relations?

An evaluation of the budget should not be limited to calculating the bottom line. A budget is an important tool for viewing the conference from many angles. Differences between the anticipated budget and actual expenses can be explored, analyzed, and explained. Some factors to be evaluated are: How did anticipated and actual expenditures compare? Were all expenditures represented by budget items?

The most frequently evaluated elements of a conference are the resource people, perhaps because they are so visible. Resource people should be evaluated in terms of their specific sessions rather than broad generalizations. An example of a typical evaluation form, to be filled out by participants immediately after a session, is shown in Figure 52. Evaluation forms typically try to obtain too much information from the participants on a single form at the end of the session. One result is that fewer forms are completed and turned in. The forms should be short, specific, and easy to complete.

Two elements are involved in the evaluation of transportation. The first element is transportation to and from the conference, if part of the conference package. The second element is ground transportation, if provided. When the conference furnishes transportation of any kind, some questions to be answered by the evaluation are: How was transportation arranged? When were tickets sent? What was the quality of carrier service? Did they adhere to posted

Figure 52. Example of a Session Evaluation Form.

Session Number _____   Resource Person _____

1. Resource person's presentation: (please check one)

    excellent _____   very good _____   fair _____   poor _____

2. Was the purpose of the session clear?   Yes _____   No _____

3. Were the purposes of the session met?   Yes _____   No _____

4. Would you recommend this session be offered again?

    Resource Person: Yes _____   No _____

    Topic: Yes _____   No _____

5. Comments:

    (Please make any comments you wish to expand your answers to the questions. Using the number, note which questions you are commenting on.)

SOURCE: *The Comprehensive Guide to Successful Conferences and Meetings* by Leonard Nadler and Zeace Nadler. San Francisco: Jossey-Bass. Copyright © 1987. Permission to reproduce hereby granted.

schedules? Was ground transportation satisfactory? What transportation was needed but not provided?

An exhibition is sometimes a crucial part of the conference, and evaluation is essential. The participants can provide data concerning the relevance of the exhibition to the conference and to their own needs and expectations. The exhibitors should also be given the opportunity for feedback to the coordinator, particularly if they will be contacted again for a future conference. Some of the factors to be evaluated are: What was the location of the exhibition? What was the freedom of access? Was the exhibit utilized by the participants? What was its relation to the total conference design? What time was the exhibit available?

All participants go through some form of registration, and that activity is essential in establishing the climate of the conference. Some questions to be answered by the evaluation are: Was registration handled in a rapid and efficient manner? Was the process simple? Was help available when needed? Were the hours and place of registration suitable?

Evaluation of the participant book depends on its complexity. If the book consists of one page, evaluation may not be needed, but a book that contains many pages should be evaluated. Some questions to be answered by the evaluation are: Was all the necessary information provided? Was the book well organized? What other information would have been helpful? Could the form of the book be improved?

Entertainment should be evaluated more in terms of its relevance and appropriateness to the particular conference than its quality. Some questions to be answered by the evaluation are: Was the entertainment suitable for the conference? Should there have been more or less entertainment? What kind of entertainment should be sought for the next conference?

Breaks can be an important part of the conference, and some questions to be answered by the evaluation are: Were enough breaks provided? Were the breaks too long or too short? Were refreshments satisfactory? What other kinds of breaks would be useful for the next conference?

The need to evaluate receptions depends on how important they were to the conference design. Some questions to be answered by the evaluation are: Were the times and places of the receptions adequately announced? How did the receptions contribute to the total conference? Were food and beverage sufficient?

If the conference allowed companions, this aspect of the conference should be evaluated. The evaluation of the individual sessions for companions can utilize a form similar to that shown in Figure 52. In addition, the evaluation procedure can provide an opportunity to rethink the whole issue of companions. Some questions to be answered by the evaluation are: Was the companion program a success? Should a companion program be offered again? Should anything be done differently? Should companions be encouraged to attend?

Who Will Be Involved in the Evaluation?

The matrix shown in Figure 53 identifies the factors to be evaluated and the people who should be involved in providing evaluation data. Each respondent should evaluate from a particular vantage point. For example, even if members of the design committee participate in the conference, they should be asked to respond as committee members, not as participants. This evaluation procedure requires different data-gathering instruments (questionnaires, interviews) for each respondent group, depending on the need for detail.

Not every respondent needs to be asked about each item, as shown in the matrix. The design committee, for example, need not be asked about the steering committee, as the latter committee does not begin to function until the work of the former committee is completed. The participants generally cannot evaluate the coordinator unless they come in frequent contact with that person during the conference.

Who Is Responsible for Designing the Overall Evaluation?

The question of who relates directly to how, since the competencies of the individual selected to design the evaluation will be reflected in how it is designed. A coordinator might assume responsibility for designing the evaluation or external professional specialists can be obtained. The person responsible must identify what is to be evaluated, develop the appropriate data-gathering instruments, arrange for administration and data retrieval, analyze the data, and prepare a report. Whoever designs the evaluation might—or might not—conduct the evaluation.

Figure 53. Evaluation Matrix.

Factors \ Respondents	Design Committee	Steering Committee	Participants	Presenters	Exhibitors	Secretariat	Coordinator	Site Personnel	Suppliers
Coordinator	X	X		X	X	X	X	X	X
Design committee		X	X	X	X	X	X		
Steering committee			X	X	X	X	X	X	
Secretariat	X	X	X	X	X		X	X	X
Theme			X						
Clarity of purpose			X						
Total design		X	X	X	X				
Related events		X	X	X					
Site	X	X	X	X	X	X	X		
Marketing	X		X	X	X	X	X		
Public relations	X	X	X	X	X		X		
Budget	X	X				X	X		
Resource people	X	X	X			X	X		X
Transportation	X	X	X	X		X	X		
Exhibition	X	X	X		X	X	X	X	X
Registration	X	X	X	X	X	X	X	X	
Participant book	X	X	X	X	X	X	X	X	X
Entertainment	X	X	X			X	X	X	
Breaks	X	X	X	X		X	X	X	
Receptions	X	X	X			X	X	X	
Companions	X	X	X	X		X	X	X	

SOURCE: *The Comprehensive Guide to Successful Conferences and Meetings* by Leonard Nadler and Zeace Nadler. San Francisco: Jossey-Bass. Copyright © 1987. Permission to reproduce hereby granted.

What Budget Is Required for Evaluation and Follow-Up?

Any form of evaluation requires a budget, but the amount can only be determined after an evaluation plan has been developed and approved. General budget guidelines are needed before the plan is developed so that opportunities and limitations can be identified. Computers can be helpful in the evaluation process, and it may be possible to use the sponsor's computer. If not, it means purchasing computer time from some external source.

The budget may mitigate against doing evaluation, since the evaluation results are available only after the conference is completed. Because the evaluation cannot enhance the recently completed conference, the coordinator may be reluctant to budget it adequately.

Who Will Be Responsible for Distributing the Evaluation Forms?

The data-gathering forms must be completed, reproduced, stored, and delivered to the site before the conference opens. The evaluation forms can be included in participant packets, distributed at sessions, or distributed at the close of the conference. The person in charge of these tasks should also distribute the forms, collect them when completed, and deliver them to whoever will do the analysis.

Conducting the Evaluation

When Will Evaluation Take Place?

The timing of the evaluation affects the responses. For example, an evaluation done immediately after the close of a session, even before the participants leave the room, tends to be influenced by the "halo effect," reflecting how the participants feel about the session rather than how beneficial it was for them. During the session the presenter may have told funny stories or used dramatic audiovisual equipment, leaving participants in a warm glow about the session. Although the evaluation forms can control a bit for this effect with carefully worded questions, their responses can be expected to reflect their immediate subjective feelings. An evaluation obtained one day or several weeks later can be expected to produce different results. Feelings will be replaced to some degree by a more detached, objective reaction to the substance of the session; the responses may still be positive, but for different reasons.

Collecting evaluation forms at the end of sessions has a significant drawback: Dissatisfied participants may have already left the session without evaluating it. Therefore, their discontent is not counted in the evaluation, producing skewed results. Room monitors can encourage early-departing participants to fill out a card, but those participants are usually concerned with leaving quietly and getting rapidly to another session. Similarly, some participants enter a session in the middle, so their evaluations may not be as valuable as those who were in the room the entire time. To separate those cards would require more effort than is available. The caution is that the person analyzing the forms must recognize that they may not be a precise evaluation of the event.

The timing of the evaluation, therefore, should be related to its purpose. If the intent is to determine how the participants benefited from the sessions and how they are using that experience, the evaluation must be delayed until the participants are able to use the results of the sessions. If the intent is to find out if the participants enjoyed the conference, evaluation right after the sessions is more likely to produce that information.

Asking for participants' responses days or weeks later introduces the factor of participant recall. Other activities will have intervened since the end of the conference, and the participant may have difficulty recalling a specific session in order to evaluate it. In addition, the respondent will tend to compare sessions on a subjective scale that cannot be ascertained by the evaluators. These "contamination" factors suggest that it might be best to obtain evaluation of specific sessions immediately after the sessions, despite any prejudice to the data produced by the halo effect.

What Evaluation Methods Will Be Used?

The most common evaluation method is a questionnaire that can range from a single page to several pages. Designing a questionnaire requires skill, for it is much more than just phrasing a couple of questions (Sudman and Bradburn, 1982). A typical short questionnaire is shown in Figure 52. The questionnaire must be piloted or tested to be sure that the questions are clear and that the respondents will be able to answer them easily.

With a closed questionnaire, the choices of the respondent are limited usually to either a "yes" or "no." (Though such other responses as "Does not apply," "Do not know," or "Doubtful" can be added, it is generally better to avoid the alternatives unless it is clear that the yes-no choice is too restrictive for some respondents.) A closed questionnaire can also use a scale, such as "excellent" to "poor," employing discrete responses that have no overlap. The scale can use numbers, but the questionnaire instructions should be absolutely clear as to which end of the scale is "high" and which is "low," and the scale should have an even number of choices (usually four or six) to eliminate the possibility of respondents automatically taking a middle-ground position.

An open-end questionnaire requires that the respondents write out replies. This takes time and some respondents may not wish to devote that much time to evaluation or may have difficulty expressing themselves. As shown in Figure 52, both types of questionnaires can be combined by providing a space for comments.

Interviews can be used, either a scheduled interview (formal questions) or an open-end or in-depth interview (general questions). This method requires skilled interviewers and is time-consuming but produces different data than a questionnaire. Some participants prefer the interview, so they can express themselves more fully. It is not necessary to interview all the participants, and certain techniques can ensure an acceptable sample.

The interview need not be in a one-on-one format or even use an interviewer. For example, participants can be asked to come to a designated room for the evaluation interview. On arriving at the room, the participant finds a list of interview questions and responds into a tape recorder. The same method can use a videotape recorder, but that usually requires a technician to operate the equipment.

Data gathering must relate to how the data will be handled or analyzed. The computer is an exceptional tool for handling quantified questionnaire data but is much less useful for data gathered by in-depth interviews. If a great deal of any type of data is to be gathered, however, consideration must be given to using a computer.

A small conference can use either the questionnaire or interview method and gather data from all the respondents; an evaluation of a large conference could not possibly interview all the participants, so a sampling technique must be used. The questionnaire can be used for a large conference, but the analysis should show how many responses were received compared to the total population.

What Methods Will Be Used to Encourage Participants to Evaluate During the Conference?

For an employer sponsor conference, participation in the evaluation can be made mandatory, but for membership sponsor and public seminar sponsor conferences, participants must be encouraged to take part in the evaluation. There are several ways to encourage participants to provide evaluation data. Introducers or monitors can make frequent announcements reminding participants to fill out evaluation forms; these announcements should be made at the end of each session, and, if possible, they should allow a few minutes for participants to complete the evaluation forms at that time, before they leave the room.

The procedure for collecting the evaluation forms should be made as simple as possible. For small sessions, one or more monitors or other volunteers should be stationed at the door(s) to collect the evaluations as the participants leave the session. An alternative is to provide boxes, either in the rooms or in the halls, but that technique will not produce as many evaluation forms as when people do the collecting.

Participants can be given incentives to encourage them to complete and turn in the evaluation forms. For example, participants can be given the opportunity to exchange evaluation forms for lottery tickets, to be submitted for a drawing to be held at the end of the conference. Care must be exercised when using this kind of incentive, as it may encourage some participants to produce more forms than are legitimate or may encourage only a certain type of participant to turn in the form and thereby skew the data.

Using the Evaluation

Who Is Responsible for Seeing That the Evaluation Data Are Analyzed?

Analysis of the evaluation data is an extremely important activity, much more than merely adding up columns of figures or typing up a report. The coordinator or other responsible person must read and interpret all the data to see what they tell about the conference, the participants, marketing, and the various other elements about which data were gathered.

The coordinator might not be the appropriate person to do the analysis, as the coordinator is part of what is being evaluated. This does not signify a low level of trust, but any person can be expected to be influenced by being evaluated, and the coordinator is also being evaluated in this process. Conference evaluation, however, is seldom rigorous or threatening enough to make it impossible for the coordinator to do the analysis.

Who Will Receive the Results of the Evaluation?

Before the analysis, all parties should agree about who will receive the results. When the results are to be seen only by the coordinator and sponsor on a very informal basis, they should meet to discuss the results. However, the results— or some of the results—are frequently shared with other people: The design committee, resource people, conference site personnel, exhibitors, and others often receive an analysis of that part of the data that applies to their specific activities.

What Form Should the Analysis Take?

The coordinator should consider the recipients' level of interest and their need for detail. An informal analysis may not even require a written report, though some form of written document is generally helpful. At the very least, the coordinator should write a basic narrative report of the data. If a quantitative approach was used, the data can be presented effectively through tables and charts. The temptation is to use statistical analysis when quantifiable data are available, but caution should be exercised: Not all the recipients of the analysis can be expected to be familiar with statistics, and using complex statistical measures may inhibit the usefulness of the report.

An essentially narrative report can be used for qualitative data. Some recipients will only be interested in the highlights, while others will want detail, so the report should be organized with this in mind, perhaps by placing a summary in the opening of the report followed by details in the remainder of the document.

Producing a good report requires resources, so money should be budgeted for this project (unless it is subsumed under the expense for the coordinator). The report can be kept simple, as it is not generally an item that requires an elaborate cover or a multicolor presentation. A nonprofit public seminar sponsor may have to devote more time and energy to the evaluation report than other types of sponsors, particularly when the conference has been funded by several sources and each wants to know what they received for their contribution.

Who Will Be Responsible for Seeing
That the Results of the Evaluation Are Utilized?

The planners of the evaluation should consider how the results will be used. All too often an evaluation is produced, and little or nothing is done with it.

The two main uses of the results are for feedback on the conference just concluded and for planning future conferences. The results can be shared and utilized by many of the respondents listed in Figure 53, though that does not mean that each of them should receive a copy of the final evaluation report or any part of it. For example, if the data regarding the site did not produce any significant results, the site need not receive a detailed report. The most important use of the results is for planning future conferences, and the person responsible should make sure that the evaluation results are available to those who will have this function.

Follow-Up

Will Any Additional Materials Be Sent to the Participants After the Conference?

The rate of return of evaluation questionnaires sent to participants at some time after the conference will vary. To stimulate response, some conferences also include with the questionnaire copies of the papers presented, a packet of conference handouts, or the reports of work groups. Some conferences publish and sell this material, although they usually send a free copy to each participant.

What Efforts Will Be Made to Record Good Ideas for Future Conferences?

When planning a conference, the coordinator and the design committee frequently have good ideas that are discarded as inappropriate for the present design. A system should be developed to retain these ideas in some readily retrievable form.

During the conference, the ideas that worked well should receive special notice and be retained for use in future conferences. The evaluation can also produce good suggestions from the participants and others—suggestions and ideas that should be retained for designing future conferences.

Will Linkage Be Provided to the Next Conference?

Assuming that the sponsor conducts another conference, the coordinator and design committee of the next conference—even if different that the current personnel—should not have to start from scratch. Many participants will be well aware of the conference's history and will have certain expectations of which the coordinator and design committee should be aware. When a sponsor has held previous conferences, a review of the material from those conferences should be the first step in conference planning.

Should Copies of the Participant Book, Handouts, and Other Materials Be Retained?

Saving conference materials requires space and control, both of which incur expense. The general rule is to save all documents from a conference, but this desire must be weighed against the probable need for those materials in the future.

Many coordinators retain materials from their conferences to avoid reinventing the wheel for each new conference. Similar steps can be followed, some of the same suppliers can be used, and many checklists are interchangeable. Although the coordinator will have to do more than merely change the headings, these materials can provide a solid base for planning the next conference.

Chapter 20

Conducting the Conference

CHECKLIST FOR CONDUCTING THE CONFERENCE

Staging Book

_____ Will a staging book be prepared?

_____ Who will have copies of the staging book?

_____ Who is authorized to make changes?

Opening the Sessions

_____ Will each session have an introducer?

_____ Will each session have a monitor?

Message Center

_____ Should a message center be provided?

_____ What form should the message center take?

_____ Who should staff the message center?

_____ How will emergency messages be handled?

_____ Should telephone service be provided for outgoing calls?

Steering Committee

_____ Has the purpose of a steering committee been clarified?

_____ Are the differences between the steering committee and the design committee clear?

_____ Will a steering committee be formed?

_____ How will the members of the steering committee be selected?

_____ How will the members of the steering committee be identified by the participants?

_____ When will the steering committee meet?

_____ Will anyone else attend the steering committee meetings?

_____ Will refreshments be provided for the steering committee meetings?

_____ How will the steering committee members receive recognition?

Daily Communications

_____ Will the conference produce a newsletter?

_____ How will the newsletter be distributed?

_____ Will a bulletin board be used for daily announcements?

_____ Will announcements be made at any events?

General

_____ Will trained personnel be available to direct participants?

_____ Will a "town crier" be used for sessions?

_____ Will copies of transparencies and slides be provided in handouts?

_____ How will participants know which sessions will be taped?

_____ What supplies will the secretariat need?

This is the payoff! If all the planning and preparation discussed in previous chapters have been done well, the conference will probably go smoothly. In this chapter, you will find references to material that has appeared in other chapters—here it all comes together.

The Checklist

Staging Book

Will a Staging Book Be Prepared?

Usually produced by the secretariat, the staging book (also called the staging guide, coordinator's book, secretariat book, planning book, and instructions) is a page-by-page set of directions for the staff for conducting the conference. Each event has at least one page, though some events require additional pages for special instructions. The book should be loose leaf or a similar format that provides for easy removal for making copies of pages for various conference and site personnel. A page from a typical staging guide is presented in Figure 54.

Each page starts with the conference name, since the site may host several conferences at the same time. The dates and venue of the conference should also be prominent, as that information is helpful for retrieval when preparing the conference report.

To illustrate how the staging guide is used, let's complete a sample page using Example A—One-Day Conference, Event 3, described in Chapter Three. Figure 55 shows a page from a staging guide filled in with the information from this example. The event number in this example is 3. Because this event is composed of several concurrent sessions, they are labeled alphabetically beginning with 3-A. For each event/session, one person has responsibility for all the necessary planning and coordination. For a small conference, the coordinator may have this reponsibility for all events; a large conference may require as many as ten different people, each with responsibility for specific events.

The event name (or session title) is then entered, followed by the date and day of the session. The reason for both is to ensure accuracy. The date uses numbers, and some people may not write clearly, so also entering the day serves as a double check. The time is the hour that appears on the program, in this case 9:45 A.M.

The location is the room where the session will be held, and the secretariat should make sure that the site has not renumbered or renamed the room. Although the session is scheduled to start at 9:45 A.M., setup must begin earlier. This relatively simple setup starts at 9:00 A.M. As several rooms are being used for other concurrent sessions, the times could be staggered, or it can be agreed that the time stated is when the setup begins for all the rooms. The secretariat should not enter this time until it has been agreed to by housekeeping, or whoever is responsible for room setup.

The doors open time indicates when the session participants can enter, and it is also the latest time that the session monitor should arrive at the room to check on setup and related matters.

The name of the presenter(s) should be listed, as well as the name of the introducer and the monitor.

Any handouts should be listed here by title. Handout control numbers can also be used, so the handouts are tied to the session by the specific event number (in this case the first handout might be labeled "3-A-1"). If there are only two or three handouts, they can be controlled in this fashion, but if a large number of handouts or other materials will be used, a control sheet should be established for them and attached to this page of the staging guide. The monitor needs this list to verify that the correct handouts are in the room.

The same applies to AV equipment: All equipment should be listed and checked by the monitor. Presenters usually bring their own slides or transparencies, but the secretariat can request that these be deposited in the secretariat or AV room before the session to make sure that they are compatible with the AV equipment and that they are delivered to the room.

Signs are needed in several places. There should be one at the door to the room specifically stating the number of the session, title, and name of the presenter. On the podium there should be a sign giving the name of the conference, the logo, or whatever the sponsor agrees would be helpful. It may be necessary to have other signs (as discussed in Chapter Six).

The specifics on room setup have been discussed in another chapter, and in the staging book they are reduced to writing and obviously should be set up for the number of anticipated participants. It is also possible to just enter the maximum number of people the room will hold. Whichever system is used, it should be used consistently on all the pages of the staging guide.

The style possibilities were shown in Figures 15 through 30, and a setup diagram should be drawn in the space provided. It need not be to scale, but should clearly show what is expected. When water is provided, that

Figure 54. Blank Pages from a Staging Guide.

Conference Name
Dates
Venue

Staging Guide

Event No. _____   Responsibility _____

Event name: _____

Date: _____ Day: _____ Time: _____

Location: _____

Setup begins: _____ Doors open: _____

Presenter(s):   _____

_____

_____

Introducer: _____

Monitor: _____

Handouts: _____

_____

AV equipment: _____

_____

Signs: door   _____

        podium _____

        other   _____

Figure 54. Blank Pages from a Staging Guide, Cont'd.

Conference Name
Dates
Venue

Staging Guide (Page 2)

Event No. _____   Responsibility _____

Event name: _____

Date: _____ Time: _____

Room Setup

Occupancy: For _____ participants

Style: Name _____

(diagram)

Water: _____

Ashtrays: _____

Podium: Water _____   Ashtray _____   Lectern _____

Microphones: Type _____ Number _____

Special instructions: _____

_____

_____

Introducer's closing announcements:

_____

_____

_____

SOURCE: *The Comprehensive Guide to Successful Conferences and Meetings* by Leonard Nadler and Zeace Nadler. San Francisco: Jossey-Bass. Copyright © 1987. Permission to reproduce hereby granted.

Figure 55. Sample Pages from a Staging Guide.

The World of Tomorrow
February 18, 1987
San Antonio, Texas

Staging Guide

Event No. ___3-A___   Responsibility ___*Larry*___

Event name: ___*New Modes of Transportation*___

Date: ___*Feb. 18*___   Day: ___*Wednesday*___   Time: ___*9:45–10:30 A.M.*___

Location: ___*Room 345*___

Setup begins: ___*9:00 A.M.*___   Doors open: ___*9:15 A.M.*___

Presenter(s): ___*William Archer*___

Introducer: ___*Harry Gross*___

Monitor: ___*none*___

Handouts: ___*Listing of modes*___

AV equipment: ___*overhead projector*___

Signs: door ___*3-A—New Modes of Transportation*___

podium ___*sponsor's banner*___

other ___*none*___

Figure 55. Sample Pages from a Staging Guide, Cont'd.

The World of Tomorrow
February 18, 1987
San Antonio, Texas

Staging Guide (Page 2)

Event No. _____3-A_____   Responsibility _____Larry_____

Event name: _____New Modes of Transportation_____

Date: _____Feb. 18_____   Time: _____9:45–10:30 A.M._____

Room Setup

Occupancy: For _____20_____ participants

Style: Name _____classroom_____

S   P
            O

S = screen   P = presenter   O = overhead projector

Water: _____on each table_____

Ashtrays: _____back row of tables only_____

Podium: Water _yes_   Ashtray _no_   Lectern _no_

Microphones: Type _____lavaliere_____   Number _____1_____

Special instructions: _____none_____

Introducer's closing announcements:

_____Break will be held in Room 350._____

_____There are two people at the door to collect your evaluations._____

SOURCE: *The Comprehensive Guide to Successful Conferences and Meetings* by Leonard Nadler and Zeace Nadler. San Francisco: Jossey-Bass. Copyright © 1987. Permission to reproduce hereby granted.

should be noted on this page. The placement of the ashtrays should reflect the smoking/no-smoking policy that has been established.

The podium is the generic term for where the presenter will be. This could be on a platform in front of the room, off to the side of the room, or near the AV equipment. It is the place the presenter works from, and there should be provision for water and perhaps an ashtray. If a lectern is provided, its position should be noted. The type and number of microphones should be stipulated, as well as their location.

Any special instructions should be noted, but kept to a minimum. These might be items such as a session that will occupy two blocks of time, or the need for complimentary badges. (If the coordinator finds that the same special instruction is repeated for several sessions, this form should be changed so that item is a regular listing.) Special instructions can be easily overlooked or misunderstood, so they should be reviewed by two or three people in the secretariat to assure effective communication.

The entry for the introducer's closing announcements should be specific, frequently actually scripted.

Who Will Have Copies of the Staging Book?

The secretariat should keep the master copy of the staging book. Copies of individual pages should be made and distributed as needed.

Who Is Authorized to Make Changes?

Even with careful planning, the staging book may have to be changed during a conference. A new room assignment, a different starting time for a reception, or a change in AV needs should all be reflected in the staging book, and all changes should be made by only one person, usually the head of the secretariat. Some coordinators prefer to be the only individual authorized to make changes, but this policy is usually not necessary or practical for a large conference.

Opening the Sessions

Will Each Session Have an Introducer?

Sessions should be started on time and on a positive note by a person who was prepared to serve as an introducer and who performs the functions shown in Figure 56. The introducer for each session should be carefully selected during the planning stage, not at the last minute. The introducer has very specific duties and should be chosen in relation to the presenter to be introduced.

The introducer should accept responsibility for these duties, part of which is exercising constraint and recognizing that the invitation is to introduce, not to present. That means to refrain from telling jokes and stories as part of the introduction!

Figure 56. Introducer's Duties.

_____ Accept responsibility	_____ Arrange to meet the presenter
_____ Contact the presenter	_____ Verify the introduction
_____ Check in at secretariat	_____ Attend the session
_____ Wear a special badge	_____ Thank the presenter

SOURCE: _The Comprehensive Guide to Successful Conferences and Meetings_ by Leonard Nadler and Zeace Nadler. San Francisco: Jossey-Bass. Copyright © 1987. Permission to reproduce hereby granted.

The introducer should contact the presenter before the conference opens. Some of the details concerning the introduction can be discussed at that time and arrangements made for a personal meeting early in the conference.

The introducer should check in with the secretariat on arrival at the conference. This serves as a checkpoint for the secretariat and provides them with an opportunity to give the introducer any new or additional instructions, as needed.

Although a special badge is not required, it is one way of saying thank you to the introducer. Sometimes, a streamer attached to the regular badge is used instead.

The introducer should have arranged, at an earlier time, to meet the presenter. If there are many presenters, the coordinator should have set aside a special room where the introducers and the presenters can meet. If there are only a few presenters, arrangements can be made to meet at the secretariat or some other well-defined location.

When the introducer and presenter meet, the introducer should verify the details of the introduction, including pronunciation of the presenter's name, the presenter's title, and a very brief bio if one is not contained in the participant book. The title of the session should be given exactly as listed to help the participants confirm that they are at the right session. Above all, the introducer should be brief, for the participants have come to hear the presenter, not the introducer.

The introducer must remain for the entire session. Apologies are woefully inadequate when an introducer concludes his remarks and leaves. Usually, the introducer sits in the audience with the participants, though in a large session or a general session the introducer might sit on the platform.

The introducer's thank you to the presenter at the conclusion should be very short. The introducer should not summarize or draw any conclusions from what has been said, as that is not the role of an introducer.

Will Each Session Have a Monitor?

Where several rooms are in use at the same time, room monitors are desirable. Figure 57 lists a wide range of monitor duties, but not all monitors perform all the tasks on the list. For example, if introducers are used, some of the duties on this list would be performed by them rather than by monitors. When

Figure 57. Room Monitor's Duties.

_____ Check in at secretariat

_____ Special badge

_____ Check on room setup

_____ Check on AV requirements

_____ Greet presenter

_____ Check on handouts

_____ Handle distribution of handouts or other materials

_____ Check name badges

_____ Enforce smoking regulations

_____ Encourage appropriate seating

_____ Close door at start of session

_____ Count participants

_____ Help seat latecomers

_____ Enforce fire laws on total occupancy

_____ Distribute evaluation forms

_____ Collect evaluation forms

_____ Function as introducer (if no introducer)

_____ Thank presenter (if no introducer)

_____ Make announcements (if no introducer)

_____ Collect undistributed materials

_____ Check out at secretariat

SOURCE: *The Comprehensive Guide to Successful Conferences and Meetings* by Leonard Nadler and Zeace Nadler. San Francisco: Jossey-Bass. Copyright © 1987. Permission to reproduce hereby granted.

introducers do not show up as planned, however, monitors provide a back-up position.

Monitors may be part of the secretariat or, as frequently the case with membership sponsors, volunteers from among the participants. A public for-profit seminar sponsor may use regular staff, while a public nonprofit seminar sponsor could use either regular staff or volunteers, depending on the sponsor and the type of participants at the conference. An employer sponsor will generally use the secretariat.

If monitors are not members of the secretariat, they should check in at the secretariat. This practice serves several purposes. It provides the secretariat with specific knowledge of which sessions are covered and which are not. When a monitor does not check in, the secretariat must utilize a back-up monitor; usually a monitor who has already handled a session or is at least familiar with the monitor's duties. The monitor sometimes carries handouts or other materials to the session. If they are too heavy or bulky, the secretariat should make other provisions, but the monitor should verify them. When checking in, the monitor can receive information on the latest announcements or any changes that should be communicated to the participants at the session.

Monitors should have a special badge, since they are performing special tasks before, during, and after the session. Presenters and participants can become confused by the behavior of this individual if they do not recognize that person as a monitor. The special badge also provides some recognition for the monitor, when that person is also a participant.

The monitor should check on the room setup, based on information provided by the secretariat during check-in. If the room is arranged incorrectly, the monitor should immediately communicate with the secretariat. The secretariat should make the necessary adjustments with the site personnel, not the monitor. The same applies when the monitor checks on AV requirements. Any discrepancies should be discussed with the presenter, who might be willing to accept minor differences, such as a change in the position of an overhead projector. The monitor, if competent in this area, should also check to see that the AV equipment is working.

The monitor should greet the presenter and check on handouts, particularly if they are to be delivered from a central source. The handouts should arrive at least fifteen minutes before the start of the session. If they do not arrive, the monitor should communicate this information to the secretariat.

The monitor should work with the presenter on how to handle distribution of handouts or other materials. The monitor is supposed to assist the presenter; overeager monitors might rush in and distribute the materials without taking the time to find out that they are take-home pieces to be distributed at the end of the session.

The monitor may not relish acting in a police capacity, but sometimes it is necessary to check name badges to ensure that only registered participants gain admittance to the room. In an unusual situation, such as when a big-name presenter is scheduled for a small room, the secretariat should provide additional support for the monitor.

The monitor should enforce the smoking regulations, which have been published in the participants book; if any participants object, the monitor need only refer to the book.

Although free seating is the general rule at most sessions, the monitor must sometimes encourage appropriate seating, such as urging participants to move to the front of the room, to sit in a special configuration, or to leave certain seats open. In a general session, the monitor should be sure that any reserved seats are utilized only by the appropriate people.

The monitor should close the door at the start of the session and open it if the room gets stuffy. Participants usually respect the role of the monitor, particularly if the monitor has been identified by a badge.

The monitor can be asked to count the participants. In a large session, all the monitors should count at the same time (say fifteen minutes after the session begins) so that there is no double-counting of those participants who go from one room to another. The participant count is frequently needed by the coordinator to assess participation at the conference and the drawing potential of presenters.

If there is sufficient room, the monitor can help to seat latecomers by pointing out vacant seats or by asking latecomers to wait in the back of the room until an appropriate time in order to not interrupt or disturb the presenters.

Sometimes monitors must enforce fire laws on total occupancy for a given room. If participants have any objections, the monitor should be able to call security to get the necessary help. The monitor should not become involved in a shoving or shouting match with any participant.

If a session is to be evaluated, the monitor should distribute evaluation forms unless they are included in the participants' packets. The monitor, or preferably the introducer, should refer to those forms and encourage participants to fill them out. The monitor can be asked to collect the evaluation forms, or the introducer can remind the participants to drop them in the appropriate place when they leave.

If the session has no introducer, the monitor should assume some of the introducer's functions (see Figure 56), such as thanking the presenter and making announcements authorized by the secretariat.

The monitor should collect undistributed handouts or materials and return them to the presenter or the secretariat. In most sites, materials left in the room at the end of the day are collected and thrown away by housekeeping or clean-up personnel, even though some of those materials could be used again in other situations during or after the conference.

Finally, the monitor should check out at the secretariat and turn in evaluations and materials. Also, the monitor should report any unusual occurrences to the secretariat, such as a presenter not showing up and sending a substitute, or a strong negative reaction by participants, such as walking out en masse before the end of the session. If there have been any special positive factors, these too should be reported.

Message Center

Should a Message Center Be Provided?

If there is going to be a message center, it must be organized carefully. An employer sponsor might want to have a message center, so that employees can be easily reached. On the other hand, the employer sponsor can decide that the conference takes precedence over any business messages, except for dire emergencies. The public seminar sponsor might have a message center as one way of providing for the needs and concerns of the participants. A membership sponsor must almost always have a message center, to facilitate contacts among the participants and to take messages from back home.

What Form Should the Message Center Take?

In a conference of fifty or fewer participants, the message center can be rather informal, and the secretariat could handle it with no difficulty. As the number of participants increases, however, the task becomes more complicated. The coordinator should consider the number and type of participants and the anticipated kinds of messages that may have to be handled. Telephones must be covered by people who can take messages and condense them into the limited space available on printed message forms.

When the conference has fewer than 100 participants, a bulletin board can be used to post messages. One person should post the messages on the board in alphabetical order. For more than 100 participants, it may be necessary to use pigeon holes or some other device that enables participants to rapidly access messages placed in alphabetical order. Using the electronic mail capability of computers is an excellent way to handle this, with provision for printing out messages (hard copy) as needed.

The message center is usually limited to handling messages, but it could be expanded to include packages and mail. This requires additional space and security.

Who Should Staff the Message Center?

The secretariat can usually handle the message center, though the LCVBs can also be a source of experienced personnel. They are usually paid, though some volunteers might be available.

How Will Emergency Messages Be Handled?

The person in charge of the message center must make the determination of what is an emergency. The usual practice is not to interrupt a session but to relay an emergency message to the appropriate participant immediately after the session. If only one or two rooms are being used, a notice can be placed on the door or given to the room monitor. When several rooms are being used, the message can be given to the introducer with instructions to announce the name of the participant and the fact that the introducer or the message center has an urgent message for the participant.

Should Telephone Service Be Provided for Outgoing Calls?

Most sites have banks of public telephones, so it may not be necessary to make any special provisions, and given the state of technology, it is usually fairly simple to make long-distance calls to remote places. Problems arise when direct dialing is not available at the site or in the site city. Operators must be used, and they may have difficulty with foreign names and geography. Some participants may need assistance in placing calls, and they should be directed to the conference service desk. When a large number of international calls are expected, the local phone company can sometimes provide a qualified employee to be at the service desk.

Steering Committee

Has the Purpose of a Steering Committee Been Clarified?

A steering committee is a group that is not used often enough. This is not the design committee under another name, though some members of the design committee may also serve on the steering committee. The purpose of the steering committee is to provide the coordinator with a feedback mechanism during the conference, as well as a group of participants to work with should design changes be required. A steering committee is useful only for a multiday conference, where changes can be made and integrated into the design while the conference is in progress.

The membership of the steering committee should be identified before the conference begins and be composed of participants who are in prestigious positions in the sponsoring organization. An employer sponsor might choose high-level company officials; a membership sponsor might pick officers of the organization or other leaders; a public seminar sponsor tends to rely on its own employees but might include some participants.

While the conference is in session, the coordinator is usually "listening with a third ear," trying to keep in touch with how the participants are responding to the design and to the resource people. Despite this sensitivity, the coordinator can easily miss some important signals that need immediate attention. Once the conference is over, it is too late to make changes and worthless to offer apologies for what could have been readily changed. The members of the steering committee should be briefed on their role and encouraged to listen to what the participants are saying, particularly any complaints they might have.

As a result of the feedback from the steering committee, the secretariat and the coordinator may find that some elements of the conference need to be changed. The coordinator can do that without asking anybody but often finds it helpful to relate the problem to a group of participants who can offer some recommendations or reactions.

In one three-day employer sponsor conference, the participants came from different parts of the same organization. When the design was reviewed in the opening session of the conference, participants complained that they needed more time for lunch, since they had to go back to their offices. They asked for two hours for lunch even though the design called for only one hour. The coordinator (who was external) said that the request would be taken under consideration.

As the day progressed, the attitude of the participants changed drastically. The coordinator was aware of some of this attitude change but did not get all the signals that were being sent by the participants. At the end of the day, he met with the steering committee and asked what should be done about lunch for the next two days. The steering committee members gave their perceptions of the participants' desires. In essence, the participants now wanted to retain the two-hour lunch, but turn it into a working session related to the purpose of the conference! It was even suggested that the company should pay for lunch to be brought into the site. The coordinator was stunned and wondered aloud if the participants were really asking for a fancy catered lunch at company expense. He was told that all the participants asked for were sandwiches, fruit, and a soft drink.

With that information, the coordinator immediately contacted the appropriate person in the sponsoring organization and asked if a working lunch could be provided. His request was met with some amazement, but the sponsor agreed to provide such a lunch for the next two days. The following morning, the coordinator presented the plan to the participants and received a resounding round of applause. The working lunches proved to be extremely beneficial. Later, some of the participants congratulated the coordinator on listening to their needs, as expressed through the steering committee, and responding to them.

Are the Differences Between the Steering Committee and the Design Committee Clear?

The design committee can easily turn into the steering committee, but the differences between the two groups are considerable (see Chapter Two). The design committee concludes its work before the conference begins, but the work of the steering committee does not start until the conference does and ends with the conclusion of the conference. A member or two of the design committee can be on the steering committee, however, and a member or two of the steering committee can (and probably should) be on the next design committee, if one is organized.

Will a Steering Committee Be Formed?

A decision must be made as to whether or not there will be a steering committee. If the decision is made not have to one, then the coordinator must find other ways to gather feedback during the conference. If the decision is to form a steering committee, specific actions must be taken before the conference begins, so the steering committee can start functioning immediately at the opening of the conference.

How Will the Members of the Steering Committee Be Selected?

The coordinator can select the members of the steering committee, but this is the least desirable method. An external coordinator may not know enough about individual participants to make effective selections; an internal coordinator might be inclined to choose less critical or less sensitive members. A better way is to ask the design committee to designate one or two members of its group to serve on the steering committee or to identify a future design committee and ask them to serve. Influential, well-known and respected participants make good steering committee members. Not everybody wants to serve on a steering committee, once they know the task, since it takes time and means attending the conference with a slightly different agenda than the other participants.

How Will the Members of the Steering Committee Be Identified by the Participants?

Members of the steering committee should be identified by badges or streamers. This is important for participants should know that they have a channel for direct input to the coordinator or others conducting the conference. The

steering committee for a conference of fifty participants may not need identification, but the committee must be identifiable in larger conferences.

When Will the Steering Committee Meet?

The steering committee should agree to meet at a specific time at the end of
each day. Holding the meeting at the end of the day allows the coordinator
and secretariat to take appropriate action before the next day's events. A
breakfast meeting does not allow sufficient time to make any changes
recommended by the steering committee.

Will Anyone Else Attend the Steering Committee Meetings?

For the most part, meetings of the steering committee should be limited to
committee members, the coordinator, and the supervisor of the secretariat,
though others may be invited as needed. If the committee has questions
concerning the site, a decision maker from the site personnel should be invited.
If the committee has complaints about AV equipment, a representative of the
suppliers should be invited.

Will Refreshments Be Provided for the Steering Committee Meetings?

Providing refreshments shows appreciation for the steering committee,
particularly as their meetings are usually held late in the day. Finger food is
probably most appropriate, as well as alcoholic and nonalcoholic beverages,
and provision should be made in the budget for these refreshments.

How Will the Steering Committee Members Receive Recognition?

Large conferences can list and thank the members in the participant book; a
small conference can ask members to stand or come to the platform so that
everyone can thank them for their efforts.

Daily Communications

Will the Conference Produce a Newsletter?

When a conference extends beyond one day, a daily newsletter can be very
helpful. Its main purpose is to provide the participants with up-to-date
information about any changes in the printed program, but it can also be used
to highlight some elements of the program. A specific concurrent session,
however, should not receive more publicity than is provided to competing
concurrent sessions.

A newsletter should be issued daily for the duration of the conference,
and each day's paper should be a different color. It should be published by the
secretariat with a designated editor who has responsibility for making the
quick decisions that are required to publish a daily newsletter.

How Will the Newsletter Be Distributed?

Once the decision is made to publish a newsletter, special provisions should be made for distribution. Generally, the participants should receive this newsletter very early in the day so they can note any changes and react to new information. If all participants are in the same hotel, the newsletter can be slipped under their doors very early in the morning, perhaps inside the free daily newspaper provided by some sites. Copies can also be posted on bulletin boards, but they should be removed at the end of each day. When all participants have breakfast together, the daily newsletter can be distributed as they enter or leave the area. Of course, not everyone eats breakfast so other forms of distribution should accompany this method.

Will a Bulletin Board Be Used for Daily Announcements?

For a conference of fifty or fewer participants, the daily newsletter can be produced on a bulletin board rather than making copies. The bulletin board can be designed to look like a page from a newsletter with a banner headline and columns. It can be changed daily and also use different colors to highlight the daily change.

Will Announcements Be Made at Any Events?

Daily announcements can be made at sessions and at other events, but it is not desirable to rely on this form of communication because not all participants attend each event. The announcements should be used to reinforce those that have appeared in the daily newsletter or on the bulletin board.

General

Will Trained Personnel Be Available to Direct Participants?

In addition to signs, trained personnel should be stationed at strategic points to assist participants. The personnel assigned to this function should know not only the physical layout of the site, but also how to cope with participants who are lost or frustrated. These personnel should be trained to give brief, accurate, and polite responses.

The strategic points chosen depend on the facility. The usual ones are at entrances to the site, elevators, escalators, open staircases, and junctions of important corridors.

The personnel could be those who were used during registration but are no longer needed for that function as most registration is completed before the sessions start. They could be members of the secretariat who are not needed for other duties at that time. A membership sponsor might use volunteers, but since this assignment means that they will not be able to get to sessions on time, they will only be available at certain times.

The people providing this service should be clearly designated. A common method is to provide them with a badge or sash that says "Ask me!"

"Can I help you?" or something similar. They might also be provided with large, distinctive headgear that can be seen above the crowd.

Will a "Town Crier" Be Used for Sessions?

An old-fashioned town crier, bell and all, can be used to get people to sessions. One or more criers can walk through the halls before sessions are to begin, ringing a bell and announcing "Sessions are about to start. Please proceed to your selected rooms. Sessions are about to start." For a general session or an exhibition opening, the town crier can lead people through the corridors to the doors of the general session room.

Will Copies of Transparencies and Slides Be Provided in Handouts?

All too often, a presenter is halfway through a presentation before announcing to the participants, "You do not have to copy the material on the slides. The handouts you receive will include this material." If the participants know this beforehand, through either the participant book or an announcement at the start of the session, they can devote more of their energy to following the presentation.

Some presenters bring their own handouts, others submit them to be reproduced by the secretariat. In either case, the presenter should indicate when they are to be distributed. The handouts might be given to each participant as they enter the room, if they are to read them before the session or use them during the session. Some presenters prefer to have the handouts distributed during the session at the point of need. Handouts can also be prepared as take-home pieces that are given to participants as they leave the room.

If handouts are to be picked up by participants, adequate table space and location must be provided. If they are to be distributed, the presenter should notify the secretariat (1) if additional help will be needed for distribution or (2) if there are any special instructions, such as a situation where a presenter wants to provide form A for one part of the room and form B for another part.

How Will Participants Know Which Sessions Will Be Taped?

If some sessions are to be taped, this information should appear in the participant book, again on the sign outside the sessions that will be taped, and finally announced by the introducer. This gives participants options when choosing which sessions they will attend and how they will participate.

What Supplies Will the Secretariat Need?

Many of the supplies have been discussed earlier in Chapters Eight and Seventeen. They may need to be supplemented, in quantity, for the use of the secretariat—for example, additional paper, wastebaskets, and so on.

Chapter 21

Resources for Conference and Meeting Planners

This chapter presents a variety of resources for coordinators and others involved in various aspects of conference and meeting planning. Although every effort has been made to provide up-to-date information, the reader should recognize that organizations, suppliers, and their addresses change constantly. The reader should be cautioned that a listing does not indicate an endorsement, just as omission does not indicate an assessment of the value of a resource.

Organizations

Air Transport Association of America
   1709 New York Avenue, N.W.
   Washington, DC 20006
American Association for Adult and Continuing Education
   1601 Sixteenth Street, N.W.
   Washington, DC 20036
American Hotel and Motel Association
   888 Seventh Avenue
   New York, NY 10019
American Society for Training and Development
   1630 Duke Street
   Box 1443
   Alexandria, VA 22313
American Society of Association Executives
   1575 I Street, N.W.
   Washington, DC 20005
American Society of Travel Agents
   4400 MacArthur Boulevard, N.W.
   Washington, DC 20007

Association of Group Travel Executives, Inc.
   320 East 58th Street
   New York, NY 10022
Association of National Tourist Office Representatives
   Barbados Board of Tourism
   800 Second Avenue
   New York, NY 10017
Convention Liaison Council
   1575 I Street, N.W.
   Suite 1200
   Washington, DC 20005
Council of Engineering and Scientific Society Executives
   2000 Florida Avenue, N.W.
   Washington, DC 20009
Cruise Lines International Association
   17 Battery Place
   Suite 631
   New York, NY 10004
Exhibit Designers and Producers Association
   60 East 42nd Street
   New York, NY 10017
Exposition Service Contractors Association
   1516 South Pontius Avenue
   Los Angeles, CA 90025
Foundation for International Meetings
   1400 K Street, N.W., Number 750
   Washington, DC 20005
Health Care Exhibitors Association
   5775 Peachtree-Dunwoody Road, Suite 500-D
   Atlanta, GA 30342
Hotel Sales and Marketing Association International
   1400 K Street, N.W., Suite 810
   Washington, DC 20005
Institute of Association Management Companies
   5820 Wilshire Boulevard, Suite 500
   Los Angeles, CA 90036
Insurance Conference Planners Association
   c/o Equitable
   1285 Avenue of the Americas
   New York, NY 10019
International Association of Auditorium Managers
   500 North Michigan Avenue, Suite 1400
   Chicago, IL 60611
International Association of Conference Centers
   362 Parsippany Road
   Parsippany, NJ 07054

International Association of Convention and Visitors Bureaus
    1809 Woodfield Drive
    Savoy, IL 61874
International Association of Fairs and Expositions
    P.O. Box 985
    Springfield, MO 65801
International Communications Industries Association
    3150 Spring Street
    Fairfax, VA 22031
International Conference Industry Associations
    1400 K Street, N.W., Suite 750
    Washington, DC 20005
International Congress and Convention Association
    J. W. Brouswerplein 27
    P.O. Box 5343
    Amsterdam, The Netherlands
International Exhibitors Association
    5103-B Backlick Road
    Annandale, VA 22003
International Hotel Association
    110 East 59th Street, Suite 900
    New York, NY 10022
Meeting Planners International
    1950 Stemmons Freeway
    Dallas, TX 75207
National Association of Exposition Managers
    P.O. Box 377
    Aurora, OH 44202
National Passenger Traffic Association
    310 Madison Avenue
    Room 420
    New York, NY 10017
National University Continuing Education Association
    Conferences and Institutes Division
    One Dupont Circle, N.W., Suite 420
    Washington, DC 20036-1168
Professional Convention Management Association
    2027 First Avenue North
    Suite 1007, Commerce Center
    Birmingham, AL 35203
Religion Convention Managers Association
    205 Enid Lane
    Northfield, IL 60093
Religious Conference Management Association
    One Hoosier Dome, Suite 120
    Indianapolis, IN 46225

Sales and Marketing Executives International
    6151 Wilson Mills Road
    Suite 200
    Cleveland, OH 44143
Society for the Advancement of Travel for the Handicapped
    5014 42nd Street, N.W.
    Washington, DC 20016
Society of Company Meeting Planners
    2600 Garden Road, Suite 208
    Monterey, CA 93940
Society of Government Meeting Planners
    1133 15th Street, N.W.
    Washington, DC 20005
Society of Incentive Travel Executives
    271 Madison Avenue
    New York, NY 10016
Travel Industry Association of America
    1899 L Street, N.W., Suite 600
    Washington, DC 20036

Sites

The publications listed below are generally available for purchase. Besides these, many national and international hotel chains issue annual publications, available at no cost, which provide listings of their facilities.

Arena Stadium Guide
    Amusement Business
    Box 24970
    Nashville, TN 37202
        Lists auditoriums, exhibition halls, and convention sites.
Conference Services Directory
    Association of College and University Housing Officers
    Central Support Services Office
    101 Curl Drive
    Columbus, OH 43210–1195
Directory of University Conference Facilities and Services
    Kansas State University
    1623 Anderson Avenue
    Manhattan, KS 66502
        Lists college and university meeting facilities, including meeting room capacities, food service, housing, and support services.
Gavel—Meetings and Conventions
    Murdoch Magazines
    News Group Publications
    One Park Avenue
    New York, NY 10016

Lists hotels, resorts, conference centers, convention halls, convention bureaus, hotel chains, theme parks, and other information. Published annually.

Hotel and Motel Red Book
American Hotel Association Directory Corporation
888 Seventh Avenue
New York, NY 10019
Lists sites with information on capacity of meeting rooms and availability of equipment.

Meeting News
Gralla Publications
1515 Broadway
New York, NY 10036
Guide to sites, suppliers, and services. Published annually.

National Hotel Information Center
155 East 55th Street
New York, NY 10039
Offers a resource library of videotapes and other materials related to sites.

Official Hotel and Resort Guide
P.O. Box 5800
Cherry Hill, NJ 08034
Describes over 25,000 hotels worldwide, city maps with convention centers, and other features. Published annually.

Successful Meetings—Facilities Directory
Bill Communications, Inc.
633 Third Avenue
New York, NY 10017
Lists hotels, convention centers, airlines, cruise lines, and hotel chains. Published annually.

Presenters and Entertainment

This section lists agents or suppliers of presenters and entertainers. In addition, numerous nonprofit organizations, universities, and government agencies also provide presenters for conferences at little or no cost.

Allied Booking Company
2321 Morena Boulevard, Suite J
San Diego, CA 92110
American Lecturers Association
150 Marine Avenue
Brooklyn, NY 11209
American Program Bureau
850 Boylston Street, Suite 420
Chestnut Hill, MA 02167
American Society of Association Executives
"Finding the Right Speaker"
1575 I Street, N.W.
Washington, DC 20005

The Associated Clubs, Inc.
   One Townsite Plaza, Number 315
   Topeka, KS 66603
Bolton/Fusco Associates
   240 South Feldner Road
   Orange, CA 92668
Brian Winthrop International, Ltd.
   2109 Broadway
   New York, NY 10023
Business Owner Consulting Group
   P.O. Box 09326
   Columbus, OH 43209
Cass Harrison Productions, Inc.
   1140 Avenue of the Americas
   New York, NY 10036
Celebrity Speakers Bureau
   50 Music Square West, Suite 405
   Nashville, TN 37203
Center for Contemporary Management and Education
   3215-H Calumet Drive
   Raleigh, NC 27610
Conference Speakers International, Inc.
   1055 Thomas Jefferson Street, N.W., Suite 300
   Washington, DC 20007
The Contemporary Forum
   2528a West Jerome Street
   Chicago, IL 60645
Contemporary Speakers Bureau
   3511 Davenport Street, N.W., Suite 411
   Washington, DC 20008
David Belenzon Management, Inc.
   P.O. Box 15428
   San Diego, CA 92115
Entertainment Coordinators, Inc.
   585 West End Avenue
   New York, NY 10024
The Entertainment Designers
   3460 Crews Lake Drive
   Lakeland, FL 33803
Entertainment Etc.
   1450 Madruga Avenue, Suite 301
   Miami, FL 33146
Entertainment Themes, Inc.
   1212 Commerce Building
   St. Paul, MN 55101
Evans Entertainment Design, Inc.
   555 North Avenue, Suite 3K
   Fort Lee, NJ 07024

The Fazio-Keel Group, Ltd.
    1230 Seventeenth Street, N.W.
    Washington, DC 20036
Florida Speakers Bureau, Inc.
    75 Meadow Lane
    Zephyrhills—Tampa Bay Area, FL 34249
Gene Mayl Productions
    Box 366
    Dayton, OH 45401
George Carlson and Associates
    113 Battery Street
    Seattle, WA 98121
The Gilbert Miller Agency, Inc.
    21243 Ventura Boulevard, Suite 241
    Woodland Hills, CA 91364
Harrison-Berkall Productions, Inc.
    527 Madison Avenue
    New York, NY 10022
Henry Walker, Inc.
    3616 Empire State Building
    350 Fifth Avenue
    New York, NY 10018
Holly Mitchell Presents
    1616 Glendon Avenue
    Los Angeles, CA 90024
Howard Lanin Productions, Inc.
    59 East 54th Street
    New York, NY 10022
International Entertainment Bureau
    3612 North Washington Boulevard
    Indianapolis, IN 46205
International Speakers Bureau
    100 Everett Street
    Lakewood, CO 80226
Jack Blue Agency
    1554 Fairfax Street
    Denver, CO 80220
Jimmy Duffy Music
    5421 East Harmon, Suite D-15
    Las Vegas, NV 89122
Joan Frank Productions
    9550 Forest Lane, Suite 101
    Dallas, TX 75243
Jordan Enterprises
    Lenox Square Box 18737
    Atlanta, GA 30326
Joseph D. McCaffrey, Agency
    1218 Chestnut Street, Room 809
    Philadelphia, PA 19107

Keedick Lecture Bureau, Inc.
  850 Boylston Street
  Chestnut Hill, MA 02167
Key Seminars Speakers Bureau
  5912 Newton Avenue
  Minneapolis, MN 55419
Kim Dawson Agency, Inc.
  1643 Apparel Mart
  P.O. Box 585060
  Dallas, TX 75258
Kreer and Associates
  111 East Wacker Drive, Suite 1212
  Chicago, IL 60601
The Leigh Bureau
  49-51 State Road
  Princeton, NJ 08540
Lenz Talent Agency
  1630 Aztec
  Las Vegas, NV 89109
Lordly and Dame
  51 Church Street
  Boston, MA 02116
M.E.W. Agency
  370 Lexington Avenue
  New York, NY 10017
Multi Entertainment, Inc.
  20229 Northeast 15 Court
  Miami, FL 33179
National Speakers Association
  4747 North 7th Street, Suite 310
  Phoenix, AZ 85014
National Speakers Bureau
  222 Wisconsin Avenue
  Lake Forest, IL 60045
National Speakers Forum
  1629 K Street, N.W., Suite 500
  Washington, DC 20006
Opryland Talent Agency
  2802 Opryland Drive
  Nashville, TN 37214
Partners in Excellence
  2696 North University Avenue, Suite 210
  Provo, UT 84604
Plaza 3 Talent Agency
  3242 North 16th Street
  Phoenix, AZ 85016
Podium Management Associates, Inc.
  434 East 52nd Street
  New York, NY 10022

Podium Professionals
   3440 Brentwood Court
   Ann Arbor, MI 48104
Professional Speakers Bureau
   Box 2007
   Buellton, CA 93427
The Program People
   P.O. Box 1426
   Oak Brook, IL 60521
Richard Fulton, Inc.
   101 West 57th Street
   New York, NY 10019
Ross Associates Speakers Bureau, Inc.
   515 Madison Avenue, Suite 900
   New York, NY 10022
Royce Carlton, Inc.
   866 United Nations Plaza, Suite 4030
   New York, NY 10017
Showcase Associates, Inc.
   911 Cypress Avenue, Elkins Park
   Philadelphia, PA 19117
Show Talent International Agency
   831 North Fairfax Avenue
   Los Angeles, CA 90046
Speakers Bureau International
   P.O. Box 19442
   Las Vegas, NV 89132
Speakers International, Inc.
   1015 West Woodland, Suite 1A
   Lake Bluff, IL 50044
Speakers Unlimited
   Box 27225
   Columbus, OH 43227
Speak Up for America
   6819 Elm Street, Suite 3
   McLean, VA 22101
Success Leaders Speakers Service
   Lenox Square Box 18737
   Atlanta, GA 30326
Talent Network, Inc.
   5200 Main Street, Suite 210
   Skokie, IL 60077
Universal Speakers and Entertainment
   235 Bear Hill Road, Suite 203
   Waltham, MA 02154
Washington Speakers Bureau
   123 North Henry Street
   Alexandria, VA 22314

Media

These directories can be valuable resources for marketing and public relations purposes.

Ayer Directory of Publications
  N. W. Ayer, Inc.
  1345 6th Avenue
  New York, NY 10105
    Listings of most daily and weekly newspapers and magazines.
National Directory of Newsletters and Reporting Services
  Gale Research Company
  Book Tower
  Detroit, MI 48226
    Lists nationally circulated newsletters.
Radio Contacts and Television Contacts
  Larimi Communications
  246 West 38th Street
  New York, NY 10018
    Lists radio and television stations with addresses, phone numbers, reporters' names and specialties, bookers for talk and interview shows, and program and news directors.
Syndicated Columnists Directory
  Public Relations Publishing Company
  888 Seventh Avenue
  New York, NY 10106
    List columnists, with home addresses.
TV News
  Larimi Communications
  246 West 38th Street
  New York, NY 10018
    Lists key TV staffers.

Periodicals

Many magazines and newspapers carry information about conferences. The publications listed below devote many pages to items of direct interest to coordinators and suppliers on a continual basis.

The Meeting Manager
  Meeting Planners International
  3719 Roosevelt Boulevard
  Middletown, OH 45044–6593
Meeting News
  Gralla Publications
  1515 Broadway
  New York, NY 10036

Meetings and Conventions
   Murdoch Magazines
   News Group Publications
   One Park Avenue
   New York, NY 10016
Successful Meetings
   Bill Communications, Inc.
   633 Third Avenue
   New York, NY 10017
Telecom: Teleconferencing Newsletter
   Center for Interactive Programs
   Lowel Hall
   610 Langdon Street
   Madison, WI 53703
Training and Development Journal
   1630 Duke Street
   Box 1443
   Alexandria, VA 22313
Training: Magazine of HRD
   731 Hennepin Avenue
   Minneapolis, MN 55403

Lists and Listings

Some of the companies listed below supply mailing lists for marketing the
conference; others publish directories or provide lists of various conferences
and meetings. Such lists are particularly valuable for an open membership
sponsor conference or a public seminar conference.

American Business Lists, Inc.
   5707 South 86th Circle
   P.O. Box 27347
   Omaha, NE 68127
Edith Roman Associates, Inc.
   875 Avenue of the Americas
   New York, NY 10001
The 1st Seminar Service
   86 Middle Street
   Lowell, MA 01852
Hugo Dunhill Mailing Lists, Inc.
   630 Third Avenue
   New York, NY 10017
Seminar Clearing House International, Inc.
   630 Bremer Tower
   St. Paul, MN 55101
Seminars—List Services
   1402 East Skyline Drive
   Madison, WI 53705

Trainet
American Society for Training and Development
1630 Duke Street, Box 1443
Alexandria, VA 22313

Bibliography

The books and articles referred to in this book, as well as additional resources, are listed below.

Adam, H. *Meetings, Conventions, and Incentive Travel: 4349 Ideas and Money Saving Tips.* Jenkintown, Pa.: Helen Adam & Associates, 1985.

Alles, A. *Exhibitions: Universal Marketing Tools.* New York: Wiley, 1974.

American Society of Association Executives. *Making Your Convention More Effective.* Washington, D.C.: American Society of Association Executives, 1972.

American Society of Association Executives. *Guidelines for Effective Association Conventions and Meetings.* Washington, D.C.: American Society of Association Executives, 1978.

Auger, B. Y. *How to Run Better Business Meetings: An Executive's Guide to Meetings That Get Things Done.* St. Paul, Minn.: 3M Company, 1979.

Bradford, L. P. *Making Meetings Work: A Guide for Leaders and Group Members.* San Diego, Calif.: University Associates, 1976.

Burke, W. W., and Beckhard, R. (eds.). *Conference Planning.* (2nd ed.) Alexandria, Va.: NTL Institute, 1970.

Caddylake Systems. *You Can Organize a Successful Meeting—Large or Small.* Westbury, N.Y.: Caddylake Systems, 1985.

Cavalier, R. *Achieving Objectives in Meetings.* Chicago: Program Counsel, 1973.

Coates, J. *Enrollment Analysis.* Manhattan, Kans.: LERN, 1985.

Cooper, S., and Heenan, C. *Preparing, Designing and Leading Workshops.* New York: CBI Publishing, 1979.

Davis, L. N., and McCallon, E. *Planning and Evaluating Workshops.* Austin, Tex.: Learning Concepts, 1975.

Dieffenderfer, R. A., Kopp, L., and Cap, O. *Workshops.* Columbus, Ohio: The National Center for Research in Vocational Education, 1977.

Drain, R. *Successful Conferences Convention Planning.* New York: McGraw-Hill, 1978.

Draves, W. A. *Marketing Techniques for Office Staff.* Manhattan, Kans.: LERN, 1986.

Dubey, R. E., and others. *A Practical Guide for Dynamic Conferences.* Lanham, Md.: University Press of America, 1982.

Eitington, J. E. *The Winning Trainer.* Houston, Tex.: Gulf, 1984.

Elliott, R. D. *Mailing Lists: How to Build and Maintain a High Quality Mailing List.* Manhattan, Kans.: LERN, 1982.

The Executive's Guide to Meetings, Conferences, and Audiovisual Presentations. New York: McGraw-Hill, 1983.

Falk, C. F., and Miller, P. *Market Research in Adult Learning.* Manhattan, Kans.: LERN, 1986.

Ferrel, R. *Field Manager's Guide to Successful Meetings.* New York: Successful Meetings, Book Division, 1977.

Finkel, C. *Professional Guide to Successful Meetings.* New York: Successful Meetings, 1976.

Fletcher, L. *How to Design and Deliver a Speech.* New York: Harper & Row, 1984.

Hon, D. C. *Meetings That Matter.* Austin, Tex.: Learning Concepts, 1980.

How to Make Your Sales Meetings Come Alive. Rochester, N.Y.: Dartnell, n.d.

How to Participate Profitably in Trade Shows. Rochester, N.Y.: Dartnell, n.d.

Ilsley, P. J. (ed.), *Improving Conference Design and Outcomes.* New Directions for Continuing Education, no. 28. San Francisco: Jossey-Bass, 1985.

Jeffries, J. R., and Bates, J. D. *The Executive's Guide to Meetings, Conferences, and Audio Visual Presentations.* New York: McGraw-Hill, 1982.

Jones, J. E. *Meeting Management: A Professional Approach.* (Rev. ed.) Stamford, Conn.: Bayard Publications, 1984.

Jones, M. *How to Organize Meetings: A Handook for Better Workshop, Seminar and Conference Management.* New York: Kampmann, 1981.

Helen Adam and Associates. *Meetings, Conventions, and Incentive Travel.* Jenkintown, Pa.: Helen Adam and Associates, 1985.

Kirkpatrick, D. L. *How to Plan and Conduct Productive Business Meetings.* Rochester, N.Y.: Dartnell, 1976.

Leffel, G. *Designing Brochures for Results.* Manhattan, Kans.: LERN, 1983.

Leroux, P. *Selling to a Group: Presentation Strategies.* New York: Harper & Row, 1984.

Library of Sales Conference Ideas. Monterey Park, Calif.: Sales Communication, 1977.

Matkokwski, B. S. *Steps to Effective Business Graphics.* San Diego, Calif.: Hewlett-Packard, 1983.

Meeting Planners International. *Meeting Professionals Handbook.* Middletown, Ohio: Meeting Planners International, 1985.

Meeting Planning Institute. *The Meeting and Convention Publicity Kit.* Ft. Washington, Pa.: Meeting Planning Institute, 1985.

Munson, L. *How to Conduct Training Seminars.* New York: McGraw-Hill, 1983.

Murray, S. L. *How to Organize and Manage a Seminar.* Englewood Cliffs, N.J.: Prentice-Hall, 1983.

Nadler, L. "Designing and Implementing a Facilitating Conference: A Case Study." *Training and Development Journal,* 1977, *31,* 54–60.

Nadler, L. "Research: An HRD Activity Area." *Training and Development Journal,* May 1979, *33,* 60–66.

Nadler, L. *Designing Training Programs: The Critical Events Model.* Reading, Mass.: Addison-Wesley, 1982.

Nadler, L., and Edelman, L. "Training Leaders for Living Room Learning." *Adult Leadership,* 1967, *16* (3), 81–83, 119.

Nadler, L., and Nadler, Z. *The Conference Book.* Houston, Tex.: Gulf, 1977.

Newman, P., and Lynch, A. E. *How to Run an Effective Meeting.* New York: McGraw-Hill, 1979.

Ostrand, K. *Trips and Tours Manual.* Manhattan, Kans.: LERN, 1985.

Parker, L. A. (ed.). *Teleconferencing Resource Book.* New York: Elsevier Science, 1984.

Patton, M. Q. *Qualitative Evaluation.* Newbury Park, Calif.: Sage, 1980.

Professional Convention Management Association. *Professional Meeting Management: The Complete Guide to Convention and Meeting Planning.* Birmingham, Ala.: Professional Convention Management Association, 1985.

Redden, M. R., and others. *Barrier Free Meetings: A Guide for Professional Associations.* Washington, D.C.: American Association for the Advancement of Science, 1976.

Rindt, K. E. *Handbook for Coordinators of Management and Other Education Programs.* Madison: University of Wisconsin, 1968.

Schein, J., Jablonski, E., and Wohlfahrt, B. *The Art of Tipping: Customs and Controversies.* Wausau, Wis.: Tippers International, 1984.

Schindler-Raiman, E., and Lippitt, R. *Taking Your Meetings Out of the Doldrums.* San Diego, Calif.: University Associates/Learning Resources, 1975.

Schrello Direct Marketing. *Marketing In-House Programs.* Long Beach, Calif.: Schrello Direct Marketing, n.d.

Seekings, D. *How to Organize Effective Conferences and Meetings.* (2nd ed.) New York: Nichols, 1984.

Shea, G. *Managing a Difficult or Hostile Audience.* Englewood Cliffs, N.J.: Prentice-Hall, 1984.

Shenson, H. L. *Strategic Seminar and Workshop Marketing.* Manhattan, Kans.: LERN, 1985.

Simerly, R. *Successful Budgeting for Conferences and Seminars.* Manhattan, Kans.: LERN, 1984.

Sork, T. J. (ed.). *Designing and Implementing Effective Workshops.* New Directions for Continuing Education, no. 22. San Francisco: Jossey-Bass, 1984.

Sparks, S. *One Day Outings.* Manhattan, Kans.: LERN, 1985.

Sudman, S., and Bradburn, N. M. *Asking Questions: A Practical Guide to Questionnaire Design.* San Francisco: Jossey-Bass, 1982.

Suleiman, A. S. *Developing and Marketing Successful Seminars and Conferences.* Miami, Fla.: The Marketing Federation, 1982.

Techniques for Business Meetings and Presentations. Rochester, N.Y.: Dartnell, 1976.

This, L. *The Small Meeting Planner.* (2nd ed.) Houston, Tex.: Gulf, 1976.

Walker, S. B. *Conference Planning.* Washington, D.C.: National Training and Development Service, 1975.

Wolfson, S. M. *The Meeting Planners' Complete Guide to Negotiating.* Washington, D.C.: Institute for Meeting and Conference Management, 1984.

Computer Software

Computer software is now produced for planning conferences and related applications. The market keeps changing—old software products are disappearing and new ones are emerging all the time. Thus, the reader is advised to investigate the product and the manufacturer thoroughly before purchasing. We have avoided giving specifications as to cost, computer compatibility, functions, and other items, since these tend to change.

ACEware Systems
  1818 Erickson
  Manhattan, KS 66502
    Program: The Conference Coordinator
    Applications: cost accounting, participant registration, income reports, enrollment, letter-writing, rosters, name tags, and labels.
Advanced Solutions, Inc.
  1332 Walnut Street
  Philadelphia, PA 19107
    Program: MAC and TINY MAC
    Applications: help in planning conferences, travel.
Aztech Corporation
  1621 Connecticut Avenue, N.W.
  Washington, DC 20009
    Program: Conference Ware
    Applications: name badges, labels, billing, meeting event structure, management and statistical reports.
Capricho Software
  600 Esplanade Avenue
  New Orleans, LA 70116
    Program: CPS
    Applications: name badges, form letters, information on suppliers in selected cities, cost breakdowns, proposals, registration.
Conference Auto Ministrator
  Information Breakthroughs
  445 West Main Street
  Wyckoff, NJ 07481
    Applications: accountings, track expenses, issue checks.
Congrex USA
  c/o DLB Associates, Inc.
  P.O. Box 19172
  Washington, DC 20036
    Program: Conference Management
    Applications: name badges, form letters, signs, event file.
Delta Software Systems
  28 East Rahn Road, Suite 114
  Dayton, OH 45429
    Program: MARS
    Applications: name badges, tracks information, sends out preconference materials, cross-references lists of resource people.
Information Breakthroughs
  445 West Main Street
  Wyckoff, NJ 07481

Program: Conference Auto Ministrator

Applications: accounting, tracks expenses, issues checks, name badges and labels, access to participants by number codes, assigns hotels, automatic cut-off on events to avoid overbooking, prepares questionnaires and forms, sends materials to speakers, integrates changes.

K/M Data Systems
P.O. Box 10844
Greensboro, NC 27404

Program: REGISTRAR

Applications: registers participants, confirmations, logistics, income reporting, CEU reporting, name badges, rosters, and mailing labels.

Meeting Systems, Inc.
777 Canterbury Road
Westlake, OH 44145

Program: Meeting Management System

Applications: Generates reports and letters related to meetings and registration forms.

Noesis Computing
615 Third Avenue
San Francisco, CA 94107

Program: MEETINGTRAK

Applications: accounting, name badges, tracks participants, sorts participants, sorts exhibitor information, tracks speakers.

Paradigm Networks
3323 North Campbell Avenue, Suite 4
Tucson, AZ 85719

Program: Destination (Around Town, Flight Time, Show Time)

Applications: coordinates staff, vehicles, supplies, and facilities.

Peopleware
1300 114th Street, S.E., Number 112
Bellevue, WA 98004

Program: REX

Applications: accounting, name badges, mailing lists, confirmations and receipts, attendance income report, session selection at time of registration.

Silton-Bookman Systems
4966 El Camino Real, Suite 222
Los Altos, CA 94022

Program: Registrar

Applications: registers participants, plans logistics, prints letters, tracks costs, prints rosters.

System Dynamics
P.O. Box 4031
Santa Barbara, CA 93140

Program: CRIS

Applications: name badges, labels, tracks participants, meals, and member records.

Topitzes and Associates
  6401 Odana Road
  Madison, WI 53719
      Program: PC/Name tag
      Applications: name badges, rosters, prints CEU certificates, and stores
      information.

Index